Sally Rochester Ford

Raids and Romance of Morgan and his Men

Sally Rochester Ford

Raids and Romance of Morgan and his Men

ISBN/EAN: 9783337064907

Printed in Europe, USA, Canada, Australia, Japan

Cover: Foto ©ninafisch / pixelio.de

More available books at **www.hansebooks.com**

RAIDS AND ROMANCE

OF

MORGAN AND HIS MEN.

BY

SALLY ROCHESTER FORD,

AUTHOR OF "GRACE TRUMAN," "MARY BUNYAN," ETC.

Reprinted from the Mobile Edition.

NEW YORK:
CHARLES B. RICHARDSON,
596 BROADWAY.
1864.

Entered according to Act of Congress, in the year 1864,
BY CHARLES B. RICHARDSON,
In the Clerk's Office of the District Court of the United States for the Southern District of New York.

RAIDS AND ROMANCE

OF

MORGAN AND HIS MEN.

CHAPTER I.

THE DETERMINATION.

"The cause is a noble and a just one, my son, and if you have decided you must go, I will no longer oppose you."

Thus spoke Mr. R. to his eldest son Charles, a youth of nineteen years of age, as the two stood in consultation beneath a large elm-tree in front of their dwelling, in Jefferson county, Kentucky, near the city of Louisville.

Charles R. was the eldest of a family of six children—four boys and two girls. Charles, or "Charley," as he was familiarly called by his family and friends, was a fine exponent of true Kentucky character;—noble, impulsive, brave; quick to perceive the right, ready to defend it.

When, on the 15th of April, 1861, the dread voice of war echoed and re-echoed throughout the land, rousing the millions from their peaceful pursuits into the wildest fury, fired with patriotic ardor, Charley besought his father to allow him to seize his gun and rush to the defence of the South. The father objected. His child was young, he was his eldest boy and greatly beloved; and, moreover, amid the rapid rush of dread events, which had so convulsed the nation, Mr. R., influenced by his life-long love for the old Union, had not been able to decide satisfactorily to his own mind where the right rested.

But the fearful unfoldings of the war policy of the administration which took place between the date of Lincoln's "War Proclamation" and the time of which we write, had fully decided him in favor of the South; and although a man distinguished for his reticence and aversion to all unnecessary political discussions, he boldly avowed his position, and defended it by clear and logical argument, whenever it was attacked. And his opposition to his son's enlisting under the Southern banner was dictated by his attachment to him, and not indifference to the cause.

On the morning of the day of which we speak, Charley (as we shall continue to call him throughout this narrative) had gone into the city, as was his daily custom, to learn the news and procure the morning paper for the family. Passing along Green-street, in the vicinity of the Custom-house, he met young Fox, an old friend of his, whom he had known for years.

"Why, I thought you were in Dixie Land, Amos," exclaimed Charley, in surprise, as the two encountered each other.

"Silence, Charley, do not betray me," whispered the young man, as he slipped his young friend's arm through his and turned into Third-street towards Broadway. The two walked quickly along, avoiding observation, until they reached the Commons outside the city. Then seating themselves on the grass at the root of an old beech-tree, which stood removed some paces from the public road, the two engaged in conversation.

"Charley," said his friend to him, "I know you have from the beginning of this war been anxious to go South. Buckner is now in Kentucky, as you know, and every Southern man who can bear arms ought to join him. I have spoken to a great many of our acquaintances, and there is a number of young men now ready and only waiting for an opportunity to get through."

"And this is all that deters me," responded Charley, his whole countenance expressive of the strong emotion that fired his breast. "I have been thinking over the matter for days, and once or twice I have spoken to father about it. You know he has always objected to my going, because he thinks I am too young; but his opposition seems to be yielding. And I know, when he sees I am determined to go, he will consent. I shall make every thing ready, and the first opening that presents itself, I will go. But tell me, Amos, how did you get back, and what are they doing down at Bowling Green? We have had so many rumors here, no one knows what to believe."

"I came on the cars to Elizabethtown. Being detained there

a few days, I was caught by the blockade of the railroad, and had to take a buggy to come to the city."

"But tell me, Amos, why did not General Buckner and his troops come to Louisville? Last week everybody expected him. Ladies kept themselves and children dressed and in readiness to leave at a moment's notice. Union men sent their money and silver-ware to Jeffersonville. Old Prentice, it is said, had all the valuables of his printing-office moved over the river, and he himself went over every night that **he might** be safe from Buckner and his men. The whole place **was** one scene of wild excitement, everybody appearing to have taken leave of their **wits.**"

"General Buckner would have taken possession of Muldrough's Hill, most assuredly, had it not been for an untoward accident on the railroad. **I do not know whether he ever designed moving** on Louisville."

"And what was this accident? **Do tell** me all you know, Amos, with regard to the Confederates **coming** into Kentucky. We know nothing here."

"You must promise me secrecy, Charley. I do not know how long I may have to stay here. And should my name be known **as connected** with their movements, I would certainly be arrested."

"Trust me, Amos, I will keep every thing most masonically," **responded Charley,** drawing closer to the side of his friend.

"I must begin back, in order fully to explain the whole matter to you satisfactorily."

"**Do so.** I wish to know every incident."

"But wait a moment. Yonder is John Lawrence crossing the Common. Our old friend John, you remember him. He has just returned from Yale, completely disgusted with the **Yankees** and every thing pertaining to them, and is longing to get South. Let me call him."

"We can trust him?"

"**Oh, yes,** thoroughly with us, and as true as steel."

Charley rose, and advancing a few paces from the tree, beckoned **to the young man who was** leisurely pursuing his way from the high-road across the open grass-plot that intervened between it and the woodland to the left. His attention was arrested, and with quick step he advanced to the spot where Charley stood. The two approached the tree. Young Fox stepped forward and grasped the hand of his old friend, shaking it most cordially.

"I have not seen you for a long time, John," said he, as he continued to hold his hand. "You have been living with the Yankees for the last two or three years. How do you like them?"

"Plague take them. Don't talk to me about liking Yankees, Amos; I detest the whole narrow-minded, nigger-loving, thieving race. And if I could have my wish, I would send a bullet through the last one of them before sundown."

"You are ready to shoulder your gun against them then, are you?"

"Yes, at any moment. But tell me, how is it you are here? I made inquiry for you only a few days back, and your brother told me you were South. How did you get through, and what are they all doing down there? General Buckner is at Bowling Green we know, and the boys are having a glorious time, we hear, but further than this we can learn nothing."

"Amos will tell us all about it, John. He was just about to begin, when I discovered you passing across the common, and I begged of him to allow me to call you. I knew you would be so gratified to hear of Buckner's move into Kentucky, and his occupation of Bowling Green."

The three seated themselves. Removed as they were from the road, there was no probability of intrusion or interruption.

"All I tell you, boys, is to be kept secret. Our enemies must not be made aware of our most trivial movements. It is necessary to deceive them, for I tell you, boys, we have a great deal to do before we are ready to give them fight."

The two readily acceded to his proposition, and the young man commenced his narrative.

"On the 17th of this month, General Buckner, then at Camp Boone, dispatched Dick Wintersmith to Elizabethtown to seize all the cars and locomotives that were concentrated at that point. He had previously written in cipher to Colonels Hardin Helm and Reed, who resided in that town, to hold themselves in readiness to assist in such a movement, which would take place in a few days, as it was necessary they should have rolling-stock to transport their troops rapidly into the State. Wintersmith proceeded in haste to Russellville, from which point he telegraphed Helm, 'All right. I will be up on next train.'

"From Russellville he went to Bowling Green, where he made known the secret of his expedition to Dr. ——, a true Southern man, with whom he left the business of guarding the bridge over Barren river, which was to be done in such a manner as to avoid all suspicion. It was necessary to use every precaution, for had the Home Guard or Union men for a moment supposed what was on hand, they would have torn up the tracks, or destroyed bridges, thereby frustrating the whole project.

"Having made every arrangement for safety and success at this point that his limited time would permit, Wintersmith came on to Cave City.

"Here, as you are aware, the trains pass each other. As the train bound for Bowling Green came up beside the up-train, Blanton Duncan, who you know is an excitable man, rushed to the platform and called out to **know if** Mitchell La Beet was on board, stating in a hurried nervous manner that twenty policemen from Louisville were in waiting at Elizabethtown to **arrest him** as soon as he should reach there. This, of course, was alarming intelligence to Major Wintersmith, who felt **for a moment** foiled in his undertaking. But being self-possessed, and of a brave, daring nature, and fully realizing the importance of the work intrusted to him, he in a moment decided to call in the counsel and aid of several gentlemen on board the **cars, who** he well knew were Southern, and would dare any thing to serve their cause. The few minutes allowed him to execute his purpose were actively employed in providing for guarding the road at all points where it was feared rails might be removed or bridges burned.

"**With two** or three friends on whom he could depend in any exigency, he pursued his way to Elizabethtown, not knowing but **that he would be seized** as soon as he should reach the depot, yet **determined to risk his** life in the accomplishment of his trust. **Reaching** Elizabethtown, and ascertaining that there was no such police force there, as Colonel Duncan had mentioned, his first inquiry was for Colonel Helm. To his bitter disappointment and deep chagrin he learned that that personage had left the town and set out with his family on the morning train for Nashville.

"At the depot he met **Colonel Reed,** who, **with others, had** come down to meet him.

"'And Helm is gone!' was **his exclamation, as he** seized Reed's hand.

"'Yes,' was the response.

"'And what is our prospect? No Union force here, I suppose?' he asked, hurriedly, of his friend.

"'None.'

"'Well, then,' added Wintersmith, 'we shall accomplish the work. Are you armed, Reed? What we do must be done quickly. Not a moment to lose. And we must proceed quietly, also. Any alarm will ruin us.'

1*

"Major Wintersmith, accompanied by his telegraph operator, whom he had brought with him from Nashville, and followed by young La Rue, a nephew of John L. Helm, rushed, without a moment's delay, up stairs into the telegraph office, which was situated at the depot. The operator, scared out of his propriety by this sudden appearance in his room of two armed men, and awed by their stern words and determined manner, made but little opposition, and with a few remonstrative remarks yielded up his position to the young man who came with Major Wintersmith.

"'Dispatch to Louisville,' commanded the major, 'that the cars are off the track. Nobody hurt. Will be in late this afternoon.'

"The order was obeyed. The Yankee operator placed under guard, and the major, with the assistance of Colonel Reed, young La Rue, and others who readily joined his standard as soon as his object was known, proceeded, with all possible energy, to seize all the locomotives and cars found in the place. One engineer positively refused to yield.

"'We do not wish to hurt you, sir,' said Major Wintersmith to him in a tone which bespoke the decision of his heart, 'but we must have your locomotive and train, and it is useless for you to resist. We are armed, and determined to perform the work assigned us by our authorities.'

"'Well, gentlemen,' replied the engineer, who was convinced of the propriety of acquiescence, 'I yield only to force, and I wish this distinctly understood.'

"'Oh, certainly, sir,' replied the major, 'we compel you.'

"'Will you give me a certificate to this effect?'

'Assuredly, sir.'

"The certificate was written, and the engineer withdrew, leaving Major Wintersmith and his friends in possession of the train.

"This was a most valuable acquisition—the locomotive being the finest on the road; and moreover the cars were laden with such provisions as the Confederate troops most needed."

"Bravo, bravo!" shouted the two listeners, wild with the enthusiasm with which the major's success had inspired them. "Three cheers for Wintersmith and Reed!"

"And I do hope," added young Lawrence, "that the Confederates may get every pound of the vast stores that for weeks have been accumulating at Elizabethtown. Father has a large quantity of bacon and flour there, and, in his name, I bid Buckner and his brave followers a hearty welcome to it all. Three times three for the South!" he vociferated, as he took off his cap and waived it energetically in the air. "May she triumph on every battle-field, and whip the Yankees to death in every engagement. But resume your narrative, Fox."

"As soon as Major Wintersmith had obtained full possession of all the rolling-stock, and so guarded it as to secure it against any attempt at recapture, he sent a locomotive and tender, with about twenty armed men, led by Colonel Reed and La Rue, towards the Junction, for the purpose of capturing the train from Lebanon to Louisville, and also the evening train from Louisville to Bowling Green. This undertaking was eminently successful in getting possession of both trains, but, unfortunately for the sortie, some wretch escaped from the train while it stood at the Junction, and ran about half a mile in advance, and tore up the rails; and when the train came dashing along at full speed, a few minutes afterwards, the front passenger car was thrown off the track, and precipitated some thirty or forty feet down a precipice. The next car, strange to say, was detached and fell directly across the road.

"This, as you may well imagine, was a fearful situation for the expeditionists. Some two or three locomotives, together with a freight and construction train were behind the fallen car. This must be removed and the road repaired before there was any possibility of advancing towards their destination. They were momentarily expecting an attack from the Home Guard of that region, who, they had been informed, were assembling to capture them. And, to add to their troubles, night was rapidly approaching and the rain began to fall heavily.

"But nothing daunted, the boys, led by Colonel Reed, threw off their coats and set about removing the car that blocked up the road. It was an arduous undertaking. They worked with right good-will, using fence-rails and whatever they could make available to expedite their work. The passengers, of whom none were killed, and only one man severely bruised, lent their assistance. They were mostly Southern men, and those who professed Unionism were not so tenacious of their avowed principles as to prevent their participating in the novel and exciting work. But the task was a gigantic one, and it was near the morning before the car was hurled over the precipice to take position with its predecessor. This being at last done, it was the work of but a few minutes to replace the rails, bring back the locomotive, which had strangely leaped the gap and landed safely on the other side, attach it to the train, and drive at full speed to Elizabethtown.

"Meanwhile Major Wintersmith had placed the town under martial law, sent out pickets and videttes, dispatched messengers to Bardstown and other points to collect together some companies which were in a state of partial organization, and bring them in, and made all necessary preparation to return to Bowling Green, where he was to meet General Buckner and the troops from Camps Boone and Trousdale."

"And what was the sum total of the expedition, Fox?" asked Charley. "The major and his friends must have gotten a rich booty."

"They took eight good locomotives; among the number that superior one I mentioned, which is by far the best in the West, about two hundred cars, fifty of these being construction cars, which are so much needed at Bowling Green, an immense amount of provisions of all kinds, which will be most acceptable to Buckner's army, and all this without the loss of one life."

"Capital!" exclaimed young Lawrence, springing to his feet, and again tossing up his cap with cheers for Wintersmith and the Confederacy. "I heartily wish, boys, that they would come and take Louisville as easily."

"But tell us, Fox, why did not General Buckner come to Louisville?"

"I am not sure that he designed the occupation of our city. He wished, however, to possess Muldrough's Hill, and the day after he reached Bowling Green, he sent forward the Second Kentucky, Hanson's regiment, for this purpose. But, unfortunately, some vile Unionists had torn up the road, and the cars containing the men were precipitated from the track."

"Anybody hurt?" interrupted Charley.

"Not a man. It was really providential that no life was lost. Before the road could be prepared, Rousseau had advanced, and thus General Buckner's designs were wholly frustrated."

"How unfortunate!" exclaimed Charley. "This city would have been an easy prey, and General Buckner and his men would have been hailed as deliverers, benefactors, by a large portion of the citizens. Now, I fear, it is too late—too late. These hordes of blue-coated Abolitionists that daily pass through the streets, must necessarily impede his progress: I fear may prevent it altogether."

"And this is why General Buckner did not come to Louisville," remarked Lawrence. "We could not tell why it was, but this explains it all. Rumor gave a thousand reasons, but you know nothing can be credited in these days of falsehood and exaggeration."

"Do you think, Fox, that Buckner will come soon?" asked Charley thoughtfully.

"Not soon."

"And why?"

"Because of his want of men. He has but a small force, much less than persons suppose; but he is determined to remain in his present position. As to whether he will advance, that will depend entirely upon the reinforcements he shall receive and the force sent against him."

"If he cannot come to us, John, we will go to him. We should not remain idle here while our cause is suffering for men to defend it. What say you, John, shall we not hazard every thing to reach Buckner?"

"Yes, Charley, I shall go home and make arrangements to leave at the very earliest opportunity. When do you go back, Fox?"

"I leave to-night."

"Could you not delay a few days in order to give Charley and me time to get ready?"

"I am under promise, and have made all my arrangements to set out at ten to-night, otherwise I would wait for you with pleasure. But you will find opportunities for getting through. Young men are constantly leaving this portion of the State to join Buckner. There is a camp near Bloomfield, where whole companies have several times rendezvoused and gone through. Your safest way would be to go there. But list, what does that music mean?"

"Another abolition regiment wending its way to the Nashville depot, no doubt," replied young Lawrence. "My blood grows hot as I think of their polluted feet desecrating the streets of our city. It is hard to bear the sight, boys. And yet, where is the remedy?"

"It can be found only in throwing ourselves against them, John, and driving them back to their own homes. We are subjugated unless we can conquer."

"True, true; there is no other hope. And I for one will risk my life for freedom."

The three arose and walked towards the city. At the corner of Broadway and Third-street they separated, each to enter upon active preparations for joining the army at Bowling Green.

An hour afterwards, Charley and John encountered each other in front of the Galt House.

"I shall leave to-morrow night, Lawrence. I have just seen young Ashmore, who tells me that my only hope is to go through Bloomfield, as suggested by Fox. He sets out to-night."

"I will go with you, Charley."

"Meet me, then, to-morrow night, at the first toll-gate on the Bardstown pike. I shall be in the city again to-morrow, but for fear I may not see you, I now will make this agreement."

"Very well."

Charley made some necessary purchases, and without delay drove homeward.

CHAPTER II.

THE PARTING.

As Charley reached the stile, he saw his father approaching the house through the lawn. Securing the horse, he hastened to meet him and unfold to him his purpose. The father was not surprised. For weeks he had observed the restless, thoughtful manner of his son, and had divined the cause. It had given him much anxious thought and many a heart-pang, for he was conscious the time was fast approaching when a final decision must be had. He could not forbid his son's going, yet he felt very averse at his immature age to yield him to the chances of a war which he already foresaw must be sanguinary and protracted.

Therefore, when Charley broke his intentions to him, he endeavored with all a father's yearning tenderness to dissuade him from his purpose.

Charley listened to his father's arguments, but remained unconvinced.

"I must go, father, and go now. It will not do for me to delay longer," he replied, with fixed determination, to his father's objections. "To remain at home while the Southern cause is calling aloud for aid, would be disgrace, infamy. You yourself, father, could not respect me, if I should hesitate, now that our own Kentucky is invaded by the dastard abolition foe."

His face was flushed—his voice trembled with the depth of his emotion—his dark hazel eye glowed with patriotic fire.

The father gazed upon his son—the opposition yielded. The noble ardor of his boy had conquered him.

The two passed into the house. The family were made acquainted with the young man's resolve. Witheringly the intelligence fell on the fond mother's heart. Like the fiery shaft that suddenly darts from the surcharged cloud, spreading death and desolation over the beautiful and glowing landscape, so came this terrible blow to sweep away in darkness and sadness every hope, every joy. She bowed her head in silence. No word escaped her lips, as she sat gazing on the smouldering embers in the grate.

How could she give her boy, her eldest-born, her well-beloved son to the horrid fate of war? Her heart stood still before the appalling picture.

"Oh, my son!" she exclaimed, after a few minutes' thought, "I cannot let you go. It is more than I can bear. You are so young, so inexperienced. You cannot conceive of all you will have to undergo, even if you could get through safely. But this is impossible. Danger is on every side. The enemy is scattered on every hand, and the Home Guard, an undisciplined mob, are well armed and infest every town and cross-road. There is no way open for you."

"I know it all, mother, and have fully considered all I shall have to undergo, but I would brave all this and tenfold more to strike for the right. I must go, and that immediately. These dangers that you speak of increase every hour."

"But *how can you go*, my son? You cannot make your way through the Federal lines. *There is no way.* We are hemmed in on all sides."

"There is a camp, mother, near Bloomfield, in Nelson county. I will make my way to it and get out with others. Men are constantly going to Buckner from this point."

The mother could not give her consent. Neither could she further oppose the unalterable purpose of her son. With that sadness which only a mother's heart can feel under a similar trial, she busied herself with the necessary preparation to secure a comfortable outfit. Every thing was conducted quietly. Neighbors might betray, servants might tell tales.

"Lu," said Charley to his sister, who sat beside him sewing away as fast as she could on some flannel under-garments for her brother, "you must go into the city to-morrow and bring out Mary Lawrence."

"But she will not come, Charley. You know John is going to the army, too."

"I will see John, and get him to come here with me. We will leave together."

"Oh, well, that will answer finely. I should like to see John once more before he turns soldier. He used to be one of my great friends. But I have not met him since his stay among the Yankees. I might not admire him so much now."

"He is not changed, Lu, only improved. You would be charmed with him. He is so agreeable, so noble, and so handsome."

"Ah, don't speak his praises too rapturously. It might revive the old flame. You know we used to play sweetheart when we were children."

"Oh, yes, so you did, and who knows what may result from your meeting to-morrow? But you will bring Mary out, won't you? And get her, Lu, to go to Elrod's and have her ambrotype taken for me. She will not refuse."

"Very well. I shall do all I can to meet your requests."

"Dear, kind sister you are," said Charley, throwing his arms around her neck and kissing her soft, white cheek.

"I cannot go with you to-night, Charley," said his friend to him as they met the next day at Manderville's clothing-store.

"And why not, John?" asked Charley, surprised.

"Mother is quite sick to-day. As soon as I told her last night of my arrangement to go out with you, she was seized with one of her old attacks, and Dr. Hardin told pa this morning that if I should persevere in my intention, it might cost her her life. You know she has a disease of the heart, and is likely to die at any moment. I feel that I can scarcely relinquish my undertaking. I have made every preparation. See that large package of goods there. Pa got me a complete outfit, and, moreover, has bought me a splendid horse from Bacon's. But my duty to my mother, Charley, is beyond my duty to my country. And I feel that I must delay until I can gain her consent."

"I regret this, John, deeply regret it. But you have decided rightly. Good-by, my friend, time presses me. I hope we shall soon meet again, where, with the brave hearts of the South, we can shoulder our arms in freedom's cause."

They grasped each other's hands firmly, and with a hearty shake and a word of adieu the two friends parted.

It was the sunset hour. Charley and Mary sat beside the open window, looking out upon the still, quiet scene beyond. The lawn with its carpet of green, and shaded here and there by clumps of grand old forest trees, spread out before them. Beyond it, in the distant horizon, was the dim hazy outline of the city. The rich mellow rays of the autumnal sun were flooding the western sky with radiant glory, such as we dream lights up the far away abode of the angels. It was a soft, sweet moment for love.

The two young hearts sat there in silence, each pulsating with that fervent emotion. "What an age of anxious bliss we often live in a few moments!" The hand of the dial has scarcely moved over the horoscope of time, but we have, in these few fleeting moments, added to our experience either of pleasure or pain, years of thought and feeling. Oh, these dashes of joy or of grief, how far adown our life-path they throw their gladness and their gloom! Charley was first to break the silence.

"You will not forget me, Mary, when I am gone? Years may pass before we meet again. Others will gather round you, and perhaps will strive to win your love. Will they succeed? The thought is madness to me. You know I loved you, Mary, when in our earliest years we used to go with the Sabbath-school to our holiday pic-nics, or in winter-time meet with our schoolmates in our childish parties. I have loved you always, ever. My affection for you has never known change. And could I feel now that you could love another; that while I am away, an exile from my home and friends, you should cease to think of me, forget to love me—Oh, the thought is anguish—but I will not doubt you, Mary. You have ever been true, even when far away. Shall I not rely on your constancy in the future as I have found it in the past?"

Great tears stood in Mary's large blue eyes, as Charley's words of doubt fell on her ear. She felt that her heart was wronged even by a suspicion of her faithfulness. The pearly drops gathered and chased each other down her flushing cheeks. In a voice broken with emotion, she said:

"How can you doubt me thus, Charley? You do me wrong to dream that I could ever forget you. I have always been true. When we were separated for months, you had never a reason to suppose for a moment that I ceased to remember you. Why should you feel so now that I am older, and have loved you longer?"

"Oh, I do not doubt you, Mary," he answered, clasping the soft, dimpled hand in his, and pressing it to his lips. "Pardon me if my language seemed to betray a thought of change in your affection. You know love is jealous, apprehensive."

"Oh, do not say so, Charley; you pain my heart. Love should be without suspicion, trusting, confiding. I do not doubt you. I do not feel that any dark-eyed daughter of Dixie could ever supplant me in your love."

"Never, never, Mary. In life and in death I shall prove faithful to you. And should I never return, should I fall unnoted, and no friend be near to bear my dying words to you, rest assured that as now your image shall dwell in my heart, and naught but the dread hand of death shall ever wrest it from its shrine."

Mary looked upon him in her artless beauty. Tears were streaming from her eyes, and her color came and went with the varying emotions of her heart. Never had she appeared to Charley half so lovely. Her dark auburn curls were thrown back from the full smooth brow, whose whiteness was that of the Parian marble. And from the liquid depths of those large beautiful eyes, fringed with their long silken lashes, and now suffused with tears, spoke out the true loving soul of woman in all its ingenuous tenderness and trust. She was about to break the silence that had succeeded Charley's impassioned avowal, when a buggy drove to the stile, and a gentleman sprang hastily from it, and throwing wide the gate entered the yard with a rapid step.

"Oh, it is John! My mother! my mother!" exclaimed Mary, hastening to meet her brother.

Her conjecture was but too true. Mrs. Lawrence had grown suddenly much worse, and Dr. Hardin had requested that Mary, who was her mother's nurse in her attacks, should be sent for.

In a few moments Mary was bonneted, ready to accompany her brother to the city. Charley waited for her in the hall.

"The ambrotype, Mary. Did you not have it taken for me?"

She drew the picture from her pocket, and handed it to him. As he received it he detained her hand a moment, and placed on it a beautiful diamond ring.

"And yours, Charley—am I not to have it?"

"Lu will give it you, Mary. I left it at the gallery to be finished. Write me, Mary, when I am gone."

She sweetly smiled assent, as she turned those soft speaking eyes up to his. He led her to the stile, and kissing her burning cheek, assisted her into the buggy. The brother seated himself beside her. A look of love through the fast-falling tear-drops, answered by one which spoke far more eloquently than language could have done the deep passionate idolatry of Charley's soul, and the lovers parted to meet—when? Ah, when?

Night drew on. The busy preparations were completed. The best horse was saddled, and brought to the door. The mother's burdened heart was well-nigh breaking. The father passed through the house with a bewildered, distracted air, like one seeking some object which his mind does not fully comprehend. Lu was grave to sadness. Tenderly she loved her brother, and sadly her heart was grieved at the thought of his leaving home. But her youthful imagination clothed even her sorrows with the bright-hued tints of hope. And in the future she already saw her brother receiving the honors and fame which the brave patriot merits.

"God be with you, and shield you, my son, in the dread day of battle," sobbed the weeping mother, as she pressed her son to her bosom in the parting embrace. She could add no more. **Her** heart was too full **for words. She could only weep** as she held him in her arms. **The father gave his blessing—**

"God be with you, Charley. Remember **the cause for** which you **go forth to fight,** my son, and may you **be spared to** return to us."

Lu kissed him, weeping bitterly, as she threw her arms about his neck, while Lilly and Willie, the youngest-born, clung to him as if they would not let him go. It was a sad, solemn moment— one when the heart forgets the past sorrows for the present, and beats with fearful forebodings of the years to come. Charley alone, of all the group, looked out with hopeful eye on the path before him. Bidding them good-by, he mounted his horse, and turned from his home to seek **his way to the Confederate army.**

CHAPTER III.

FINDING THE CAMP.

The soft stars of September studded the heavens, shedding a pale dreamy light over the still earth. The night air was chill. The evening breeze, which had now increased to a stiff north wind, swept southward from the river. But neither the chastened beauty of the one, nor the discomfort of the other, could serve to distract the thoughts of our young hero from the glowing visions that filled his mind. He was taking a look-out into the future, and with that hopefulness peculiar to the young, which all the accumulated experience of the world, taught in history, biography, homily, didactics, and the every-day life of all who are growing old, cannot school, warn, or overcome, his earnest soul was crowning that future with fame, honor, and enjoyment. All the wild and brilliant excitement of a soldier's life was before him, and his young heart bounded with rapturous exultation as in imagination he dashed on through victorious conflict towards the goal of his hopes.

Alas! poor, inexperienced boy! He was revelling amid the rainbow tints of fancy. He saw not the labored march, the tentless bivouac, the gore of the battle-field, the loathsome prison-house. He thought not of the home he had left; not of the kind mother who was even then offering up a prayer for her boy's safety; not of the indulgent father, to whom the long night-watches were hours of restless, anxious fear; not of the loving sister whose tears of affection were then bedewing her sleepless pillow; aye, even the image of the dark-haired, gentle Mary was momentarily obscured by these dazzling phantoms of war.

On and on he rode, busy with his own inspiring thoughts. He met only a passing traveller on the journey. As day broke over the earth, weary and chilled he neared Bloomfield, where he expected to find Captain Jack Allen, with his men. He entered the town as the gray mists of morning were lifting themselves from the humid earth. As he approached the inn he saw crossing the highway two men, like himself, equipped for travel. He glanced at their horses. They were jaded, evidencing a long and rapid ride.

Without hesitation, he spurred his horse to their side.

"For Captain Allen's camp?"

Startled, they looked at him—it was but for a moment, they seemed to understand his mission as if by intuition—and bowed assent.

"Where is it situated?"

"We do not know," answered the elder of the two travellers, a man of forty years of age, and whom we shall call Mr. Bryant, "nor have we dared to ask any one we have met."

"You do not live in the vicinity, then, gentlemen?"

"We have come from Franklin county since yesterday evening, avoiding, as far as we could, all public roads, lest we might perchance fall into the hands of the Home Guard. These are dangerous times for Southern men to be travelling in the direction of Bowling Green. Have you no idea where the camp is?"

"None."

Just then the travellers passed a house by the road-side. The farmer was on the front porch. He looked for a moment at the strangers, stepped out and bowed, with a pleasant smile. Mr. Roberts had seen many such travellers in the last two weeks, and he full well understood their business.

"He looks like a friend, gentlemen. I'll trust him," and Charley reined up in front of the stile.

"We are seeking for Captain Jack Allen's camp, sir. Can you direct us to it?"

"Captain Allen and his men have gone to Dixie, my friend—left night before last."

"Is it possible for us to overtake them, sir?" interposed Mr. Bryant. "We wish to go through, but fear to set out alone."

"Have you no guide, gentlemen?"

"None, sir."

"And do not know the country?"

"Never have passed over a foot of the way."

"Then, sir, it would be attended with great danger to go alone There is a regiment of Lincolnites at Lebanon, another at New Haven, and I am told the Home Guard beyond are constantly seizing every one whom they suspect of attempting to make their way to Buckner."

"What shall we do?" asked Charley, starting from his seat. "I must get through if it cost me my life."

"You must all remain with me, gentlemen, for the present," responded Mr. Roberts. "There will be some recruits here in a few days, I am told, a company of men from one of the adjoining counties. You can go through with them."

"Is there no danger in doing this?" asked Mr. Bryant, hurriedly.

"None in the world, sir. We are all right in this region. You may go where you please, and say and do what you please. No spies here in Dixie. Not a Lincoln man in the neighborhood."

The men alighted, and at the kind invitation of their host seated themselves before a good smoking breakfast.

Our young hero began to realize that there were *difficulties* in the path to glory. But he was not a whit daunted. Naturally brave and enduring, with a love for the novel and exciting, the new-found trouble but heightened his zest and increased the interest of the undertaking. He chatted pleasantly of the risks that must everywhere beset their way, and reiterated his purpose to achieve his object or perish in the attempt. It was soon ascertained he was from Louisville, and many were the questions asked by his new friends relative to the state of affairs in that noted city.

"How many troops have passed through Louisville, Mr. R., since Rousseau brought his 'Kentucky' regiment over from Jeffersonville?" asked the host, as with his guests he assembled around the bright wood fire in the best room of the house. "I happened to be in the city at the time this quasi-Kentucky regiment marched through on their way to Elizabethtown, and, really, if all of Lincoln's defenders are like that squad of jail-birds and wharf-rats, I think General Buckner can come to Louisville whenever he gets ready. They can offer but poor opposition. Why, I tell you, gentlemen, there was scarcely a man in the regiment that could hold up his head."

"Several regiments of Indianians have been sent forward since then to join Rousseau, and many of them were fine-looking men. They had the air of men who can and will fight. I fear, sir, General Buckner will have hard work to get to our city. Troops are now being sent forward daily."

"Who is this Colonel Rousseau?" asked the younger of the two men, who had hitherto taken but little part in the conversation. "He has been figuring in Frankfort for the past few months, as a member of the legislature. I have met him there frequently, and have several times heard him speak. He seems to me to be a coarse, vulgar man, devoid of honesty and of patriotism; destitute, indeed, of every thing but bombast and selfishness."

"Why, sir," interposed Mr. Roberts, "he was one of the captains in that distinguished Indiana regiment that ran so gloriously at Buena Vista. You remember Jeff. Davis called out to his men to open their ranks and let the flying Hoosiers pass, and then huzzaed, 'Come on, my brave boys, let us retrieve the day.' The cowardly Hoosiers then vowed vengeance against Colonel Davis, and I suppose Rousseau thinks now is a fine time to pay off the old score; but, I trow, he will have hard work to wipe out the disgrace of that day."

"Do you know his standing in Louisville, Mr. R.?" interrogated the young man.

"He commands but little respect, I believe, sir. I have no personal acquaintance with him. Indeed, I did not know of his presence in our city until his name was offered for the State senate. I have heard, since then, from those who knew his status at that time, that he was a pettifogger, noted for his impudence and coarseness; a hanger-on at the Police Court and around the Jail, making a penny wherever he could. If a low case was to be tried, Rousseau was sure to be connected with it; and would often, when engaged in a suit, delay trial from time to time, in order to extract money from his unfortunate opponent by way of compromise. I have heard it said he would suborn witnesses—creatures from the most wretched classes, whom he appeared to know well—and with these as his tools, together with his bluster and audacity, would often succeed where a more honest and honorable man would have entirely failed."

"But how was he elected to the State senate?—a man of such a character. Was it not a disgrace to his constituents?" inquired the young man, who appeared from some unknown reason to feel either a deep interest in Rousseau, or an eager curiosity to ascertain his past history.

"There was a vacancy in the State senate, caused by the death of one of its members, and it became necessary to elect a man to fill the unexpired term. Rousseau offered himself; there was no opponent. He was successful, and thus, for the first time in Kentucky, he found himself in position. This occurred before the presidential election. The frequent called sessions of the legislature, which became necessary from the distracted state of the country, and in which he has ever striven to make himself conspicuous for 'loyalty,' have given him some notoriety. A few months ago, he solicited a commission to raise a regiment. Of course he had no difficulty in obtaining it, as he was introduced to Lincoln as 'Captain Rousseau,' who had fought gallantly in the Mexican war, and who was now a State senator from Kentucky. He bore, in addition to this, a letter of recommendation from old Prentice, with whom he is bosom friend at drinking saloons and wine parties. His zealous advocacy of 'The Government,' as the measures of the administration are now denominated, introduced him to the president as a fitting instrument to carry out his purposes in our State.

With a colonel's commission in his pocket he returned to Louisville, and by ridding the cities of New Albany and Jeffersonville of the outcast and outlawed population, he has secured a force with which he hopes to add fresh laurels to his wreath in his patriotic endeavors to 'crush out this wicked rebellion.'"

"And this is '*Colonel*' Rousseau's history, is it!" exclaimed Mr. Roberts; "and it is just as I expected, gentlemen. I have always understood his character was doubtful, but I had not known how mere *circumstances* had made him a hero. I tell you, sirs, that nine-tenths of these Kentucky Federal officers are of the same stamp with Rousseau—little men without one whit of merit—made great by the events of the hour, and—"

A loud knock was heard at the door. Mr. Roberts arose to open it. As he did so, he encountered a man of medium height, dressed in a suit of dark jeans. Beside him was a youth of about twenty years of age. The strangers bowed, bidding him "Good-morning."

"Walk in, gentlemen, walk in," said Mr. Roberts, throwing open the door and motioning them to the fire. They stepped forward, descried the three guests, and hesitated. Mr. R., divining their reason, whispered to them, "All right, no danger; these are friends."

"I call, Mr. Roberts," said the elder of the two, before taking the proffered chair, "to ascertain where the rendezvous is in this neighborhood for Southern men, and whether there is any probability of getting through to General Buckner from this point. I learned in Bloomfield that Captain Allen had left a few days since, but apprehensive that some difficulty might arise from further questioning on this subject, I did not make known to my informant the object of my inquiry."

Mr. Roberts, in a few words, gave the desired information to the gentleman, and again requested them to be seated. They were in the act of accepting his invitation, when another rap was heard at the door. The guests cast meaning glances at each other: several of them betrayed evident emotion.

"Do not be alarmed, sirs," said Mr. Roberts, pleasantly, observing the trepidation of some of his guests. "Friends, no doubt," and he opened the door and ushered in the three newly arrived strangers.

"Good-morning, Captain Utterback!" exclaimed the eldest of the three, a man of about forty years of age, with a very pleasant countenance, a noble form, and a slight sprinkle of gray mid his black hair, as he approached the fireside, and grasped the hand of one of the men who rose to welcome him. "We have overtaken you at last, after a weary ride over a dreadful road."

Captain Utterback, after greeting his friends, and introducing them to the gentlemen present, called Mr. Roberts aside. After a few moments' conversation with the host, he returned to the room, and announced to his men his readiness to leave.

Charley and his two friends understanding that the captain was going out in search of Camp Secret, decided to accompany him and his men.

"Any danger of betrayal from our numbers, Mr. Roberts?" inquired the captain.

"None, sir, none. You have no enemies in this region."

The men mounted their horses and turned into the road. As they did so, they saw approaching them from the direction of the town a group of four horsemen, followed by a buggy containing an elderly gentleman and a servant; and yet a few paces in the rear, two others, whose horses looked jaded from travel. The party halted.

Captain Utterback looked steadfastly at them for a moment. "For camp, gentlemen?"

They answered in the affirmative.

"We are just setting out for that point," pleasantly remarked the captain, "and if you will receive our escort we shall be most happy to give it you."

The offered favor was most gladly accepted, and the men wheeled into line.

Our young hero was excited and cheered with the animated prospect. Already had he taken position beside the young friend of the captain.

The party proceeded on the public road about two miles further west of Bloomfield, then suddenly turning to the right of the highway, they passed through a narrow lane, succeeded by an open field, then across a small stream, into a dense forest. As they were about to enter, they were accosted by armed men.

"Who goes there?"

"Friends of the South," answered Captain Utterback.

"**Pass in,** and follow the road, it will lead you to camp," was the response of the guard.

The horsemen entered. Proceeding a few hundred yards, they came suddenly upon a large hollow, studded with small rail-pens, which were covered with straw.

"This is 'Camp Secret,' boys," said the captain, lifting his hat, and giving three cheers for the South.

His example was lustily followed by the men, who made the old woods ring again with their shouts. A few moments more, and Charley and his friends found themselves "in camp," for the first time. They saw there a few armed men, whose business it was to guard the place.

There were new arrivals throughout the day, of groups of two and three, sometimes more. Some were on horseback, some on foot, others in buggies. By evening, the camp presented a very animated scene; new acquaintances were made, adventures related, jokes passed—vengeance against the Lincolnites sworn by all.

Baskets of nice, warm dinner mysteriously appeared in their midst. No one asked whence they came. It was enough to find them there, with their inviting contents, ready to appease the quickened appetites. The viands were spread and partaken of with right good zest; toasts were drank to the downfall of the Yankees and the success of the South. "Sleeping apartments" were selected for the night, straw couches arranged, with their covering of blankets and overcoats, and pillows of saddle-bags and carpet-sacks.

"Why, how do you do, Mr. Simrall?" said Charley, as a solo horseman rode through the guard, and approached where he was standing beside young Wickliffe, of Bardstown, the two engaged in earnest conversation.

"Why, how do you do, Charley? I did not expect to find you here. On your way to Dixie, I suppose."

"Yes, sir; going out to fight for the South. Will you not join our company, Mr. Simrall?"

"Oh, yes, Charley. I have set my face towards the Sunny South, to link my destiny with hers, whether it be for weal or for woe."

Mr. Simrall dismounted, and leading his horse some paces from where the two young men were resting, secured him to a small ash-tree, then approaching a group of men who were standing in the inclosure formed by rail-pens, he made some inquiries relative to the preparations necessary for the night, and the probable stay of the men at "Camp Secret."

An hour afterwards, as Charley and young Wickliffe, who already found each other agreeable companions, were seated on an old log talking over the prospects before them, which spread out in fair enchanting colors to their youthful and now highly excited imagination, they observed four horsemen dash into camp.

One was slightly in advance of the others. He was about medium height, well-formed, and sat his horse with an elegance not often equalled even by the best riders. Every feature of his face bespoke daring and determination. His mustache was trimmed with exquisite precision. The suit of dark jeans was fitted to his handsome form, and the immaculate shirt collar, turned over the narrow black neck-tie, contrasted well with the bosom of dark flannel.

As he rode forward to the group he lifted his hat, and spoke. There was manly dignity, combined with graceful ease, in the movement. His manner fixed the attention of our young hero, who felt, he scarce knew why, an irresistible impulse to move forward towards the stranger. He did so, followed by Mr. Simrall and young Wickliffe.

On approaching nearer, Mr. Wickliffe recognized the stranger—it was JOHN H. MORGAN, OF LEXINGTON.

CHAPTER IV.

FIRST CAPTURES.

Very soon after the arrival of Captain Morgan and his men in camp, young Wickliffe took him aside, and the two engaged for some minutes in earnest conversation.

"An excellent idea, Mr. Wickliffe. The men will then all be well armed, and we will be more likely to cut our way through if attacked. You are familiar with the cross route, and will lead the expedition?"

"Know every foot of the road, Captain Morgan. Have travelled it many a time when I was a boy, after rabbits and squirrels, and nothing would please me better than to capture the Home Guard, dastardly wretches! and give them safe lodgment in 'Camp Secret' for a few days. It would dissipate their patriotism, I tell you, sir."

Several others, among them Captain Utterback, Basil Duke and Curd, who had accompanied Morgan from Lexington, and Captain Miner, were called, and the matter laid before them. The plan was highly approved by them all; and another expedition, for a similar purpose, was set on foot, to be carried out by the Anderson county boys, headed by Duke and Curd. Twenty-five men were chosen for the dash upon Lawrenceburg, and thirty-five to accompany Crisp Wickliffe, the latter undertaking being regarded as far more hazardous. Among this number was Charley, who was eager for an adventure.

Every thing was as speedily and quietly arranged as it was possible. A strong spring wagon, which Captain Morgan's men had brought through from Lexington, was detailed for the enterprise to Bardstown to bring into camp the captured guns. The expedition to Lawrenceburg was to go unarmed, with the exception of a few good marksmen, and the men were to bring their trophies with them.

Duke and his men set out as soon as the darkness of the night veiled their movements. About an hour and a half later, young

Wickliffe, with his thirty-five followers, armed to the teeth, left the camp and struck out into the country. On and on they went, through farms and lanes, as fast as the rough nature of the road would allow, until they reached the turnpike leading into the town, a quarter of a mile from the place. It was midnight, and as dark as Erebus. No moon gave her light, and the stars were shut in by heavy black clouds. Not a sound was heard save that made by the tramping horsemen.

"We must be as noiseless as the tomb," said young Wickliffe to Charley, who rode beside him. Every thing must be done with the utmost quiet, for if we are betrayed in this matter we shall be captured after we set out from Camp Secret."

They proceeded in groups of four or five on the grass-grown paths by the roadside—the wagon keeping a respectful distance in the rear—until they reached the edge of the town.

The men were then halted, and Crisp Wickliffe, with two others, dismounted and set out to reconnoitre. They proceeded very cautiously to the guard-house, where were deposited about one hundred Lincoln guns, which had been clandestinely introduced into the State.

"Who goes there?" called out the drowsy watchman, as the sound of approaching footsteps roused him from his unquiet slumbers.

No answer was made. The men advanced.

"Halt! Who are you?" cried the alarmed sentinel, as he seized his gun and presented it.

"A friend," answered Wickliffe, disguising his voice. "I come with a command."

The sentinel lowered his gun. Its clash on the pavement defined its position. Quick as thought young Wickliffe seized it, while his companions took the man in charge.

"Not a word, or your life pays the forfeit." The fellow hushed his breathing as he felt the muzzle of the pistol at his head.

"Now tell me," demanded Wickliffe of his quaking prisoner, "how many guns are here, and how I can get them."

The information was readily given, the man feeling that thereby he might purchase his life.

The three, with their prisoner, returned to the men. Ten of the company, headed by Wickliffe and Charley, and followed by the wagon, returned to the guard-house, effected an entrance, secured the hundred guns, loaded the wagon, and in triumph rejoined their companions.

It was daylight when the victorious party returned to camp, bearing with them their poor affrighted prisoner. A loud huzza went up as they rode in with their trophies.

Young Wickliffe and his men were all heroes, and many a mess was enlivened that morning with a recital of their adventures.

The expedition to Lawrenceburg was equally successful, and in a little while the whole camp rang out in loud welcome as Duke's party entered, laden with their spoils. Each man had two, and some as many as three guns, the result of their daring. They had captured sixty-five pieces, and the little camp found itself in possession of arms enough for all its unarmed men, and some to spare.

Thus handsomely equipped, and each fearing that every moment's delay added to the hazard of the task before them, it was decided to make immediate arrangements for setting out to join Buckner. After a few minutes' consultation, it was unanimously agreed, by both soldiers and civilians, that John H. Morgan should lead the expedition. The position was accorded, as if by intuition, to the young and gallant captain, and, the promptness of his acceptance, and the ease with which he at once assumed the responsible position, gave evidence that he was "born to command." Throughout the day recruits were constantly coming in, until the number in camp was augmented to four hundred. Captain Morgan decided to set out that evening, about sundown, travel all night, and rest in some secluded spot through the next day, if it should be found impracticable to proceed on their journey.

During the day, a Louisville journal was brought into camp by a friend from Bloomfield. The men gathered round to hear it read. They had been for two days shut in from the stirring events of the seething world without.

"List, boys," called out Mr. Leach, as his eye ran down the news column. "Here is a striking morsel of intelligence for us."

Pausing a moment for the noise of merriment to subside, he elevated his voice to its highest tone, and with great gravity read the following announcement in Prentice's own words:

"CAPTURE OF JOHN MORGAN.—John Morgan, captain of a little secession company at Lexington, Ky., with his men, was captured by the Home Guard, on their way to Dixie, in search of their rights. They are now on their route to Frankfort, where we hope they will find their rights and enjoy them to the fullest extent."

"Well, John, your *ruse* has succeeded admirably," said Duke to the captain, slapping him on the shoulder, and breaking out into a hearty laugh, in which he was joined by all present. "Prentice is deceived this time, and we are safe. You could not have made a more capital hit."

CHAPTER V.

SETTING OUT FROM CAMP SECRET.

It was four o'clock in the **evening of the 28th of** September, 1861. The busy preparations **for the march, which** throughout the day had occupied the camp, were **over.** And the force which for four days had been quietly assembling at "Camp Secret," **were** in line, ready to move. They were about **four** hundred strong. Two-thirds of the number **were mounted, the remainder on foot.** But all were well armed.

And there they stood, a band of noble patriots, headed by their brave and daring captain. They were leaving home and friends— **all that made** life dear to them—to espouse a cause which the popular voice pronounced infamous and hopeless. Branded as traitors **by the** Legislature of their own State, frowned upon by public sentiment—doomed, in the event of failure, to the felon's cell—no **roll of drum or stirring fife to** nerve their hearts to martial deeds— **no waving** flag presented amid the cheers and loud acclaim of an excited **multitude, to** lead them on to glorious victory—no "God speeds" rung out on the tumultuous air from friends and fellow-countrymen—naught, naught, save the blessing and tears of kindly sympathy of the few females of the neighborhood, **who had gathered** to witness their departure.

Their pathway was **beset with direst danger. An armed foe** before and around them, **vigilant for their capture—a country to pass through almost impracticable to travel—no prospect of pay,** rations, or clothing—the cause **they sought** feeble, struggling apparently **hopeless—what had** these **men to** nerve them to the undertaking? Simply this **heaven-**bestowed motive: they believed *they were right—their cause just;* and thus believing, they could do and dare, **suffer** and die, rather than be crushed beneath the fragments of a broken Constitution, rent by the hand of a vulgar despot.

Say you such men can be conquered? It is impossible. Fanaticism and fiendishness may hurl their wild and lawless hordes of armed minions against them, but they will be scattered, blasted; and, like the mighty hosts of Egypt's proud monarch, perish in their heaven-doomed undertaking.

The word of command was given, "Forward, march!" A general movement followed the command, and from the infantry a voice rang out in notes sweet and clear,

"Cheer, boys, cheer; we march away to battle."

Voice after voice caught up the measure, until throughout the ranks there pealed one loud, harmonious strain. Handkerchiefs were waved in response from the group of weeping females, and silent prayers offered there for their success have found answer in a hundred victorious conflicts since.

Slowly they crossed the silvery stream that bounded their camp in front. Casting one look of parting on this rendezvous of patriotism, they defiled into the narrow lane that led into the main road.

As the strains of the chorus died out, a voice caught up the words,

"Though to our homes we never may return,
 Ne'er clasp again our loved ones to our arms,
 O'er our lone grave some faithful heart will mourn:
 Then cheer, boys, cheer; such death hath no alarms."

In buggies and on horseback, in the rear of this band of true-hearted men, followed a number of citizens. Doomed for opinion's sake, by the tyrant at Washington, seconded by the treacherous sycophants of their own State, they were going out in sadness from the bosom of their families, preferring the sorrows of exile to the horrors of imprisonment, or the ignominy of a base oath extorted from them by cruel violence.

Many a manly heart heaved with deep emotion, and many an eye all unused to weep was bedewed with tears as the thoughts of home, with its helpless inmates, soon to be the prey of a base foe, rose up before the mind of the father and brother. Did not the pitying eye of the Lord Jehovah look down upon this brave band of patriots, and have not the wrongs these freemen then endured come up before Him in remembrance, when defeat and panic and route have overtaken the insolent oppressor?

Pickets had been thrown out on the Bardstown pike six miles ahead. The intervening country was friendly, and as the column moved on by the few farm-houses that stood on their route, sunny-faced children, with smiling matrons, waved them a blessing, and loudly cheered for "Jeff. Davis and Buckner."

The column neared the Bardstown turnpike. It was expected that an encounter would take place with the Home Guard at this point. But when Captain Morgan reached the road, he found it in possession of his pickets, who reported the way entirely clear. Falling into this road, they proceeded about a quarter of a mile, then suddenly debouched to the right, and entered upon what is known as the New Hope road. The folds of night gathered over them as they took up their line of march along this rough, broken route; and, enveloped in the darkness of a starless night, they felt secure from all danger of the enemy.

CHAPTER VI.

THE FIRST NIGHT'S TRAVEL.

As we have said, it was rayless darkness. Thick clouds covered the face of the heavens. The country was hilly, and, at every step of advance, the road grew more difficult. It was hard, rough work for these men, all unused to midnight marching. But their guide—"Kit Carson," as he had dubbed himself—knew every step of the way, was fully acquainted with every turn, hill, and stream, and every point likely to be occupied by the Home Guard, and under his direction the column moved safely on. Captain Morgan was untiring in his endeavors to avoid difficulties and cheer the men, frequently passing along the entire lines to see that all was right.

Charley had found a very agreeable companion in Wood, of Nelson county, and the two youthful heroes whiled away the dark and chill night hours in hopeful lookouts into their future, and scathing comments on a perjured administration, which, under the name of "the best government in the world," was rapidly sweeping away every bulwark of liberty.

The road, which was scarcely more than a bridle-path, lined on either side by thick underbrush, interspersed with gigantic trees, was, in many parts, almost impassable. It was difficult for the mounted men. Those on foot often lost their way and straggled into the brush, while a buggy unfortunately veering to the right or left found itself suddenly brought to a stand-still by a tree or a clump of scraggy black-jacks, and the only alternative was for the footmen to lift the vehicle back into the narrow road. Then the way to the main road had to be felt, and there was no range in which to turn.

There was a man of the party endeavoring to take through a lot of twenty-five mules. When day dawned, he found himself with only three of the pesky creatures left.

There was an old man in company, Mr. Johnson, of Arkansas, who afforded great amusement to those in his immediate vicinity. He had been spending the summer in Kentucky, and delaying too long, had been caught by the blockade of the railroad, and was driven to seek his home by this dreadful route. **The** old gentleman was out of health, impatient, and wicked.

He **was** driven by his servant-man, Bob, a boy the old man prized highly. Bob knew his master's peculiarities, and how to humor his fits of passion.

As the difficulties increased, the old man grew more and **more** excited, then petulant, and then, unable to restrain his wrath longer, he burst **forth** into a most furious invective against all living flesh. **Just at this juncture the horse made** a misstep, the buggy struck a tremendous **rock, the old man** was unseated, and had not Bob caught him, **he would have been dashed headlong** from the vehicle.

"I wish to God Jeff. Davis, Abe Lincoln, all the **cussed politicians**—yes, and the **whole** world, was miles **deep in hell**," he exclaimed in the very fulness of his phrensy.

"Oh, my dear sir, don't, I beseech you, place us in that horrid region," called out his fellow-traveller, in advance, highly amused at the fidgety old Southerner. "I have left a wife and children in Louisville, **sir,** and I do hope they will be spared this dreadful **fate.**"

The old man could **not be appeased.** He continued to pour anathema-maranathas on all creation.

About midnight, Captain Morgan rode along the lines, announcing the approach to the Rolling Fork, a deep, and rocky stream, **the passage of which** would be attended with delay, perhaps with **difficulty** and danger. When old Mr. Johnson heard this, he seized the reins, drew himself up to the fullest height, and "swore he would never die content until every man who **had brought about** this cussed state of affairs had had his head taken off smack and smooth."

"Now, Bob, **I tell you, boy,**" he said most emphatically, as he handed Bob the **lines,** "if you do drown me, Bob, I'll shoot you— Do you hear me, Bob? Hold your reins tight, and follow close to that buggy."

"**Yes, sar—yes, sar, master:** I'll take you through safe, sar. If **anybody can git** you through, Bob can. Don't be skeered, master; I'll git you through, sar."

The Rolling Fork is a branch of "old Salt River"—as it is generally called—that stream so famed in Kentucky's annals, of which poets have sung and politicians jested.

The "Fork" is a deep and fearful current, and at the point

where the column had to cross it, a high hill rises abruptly on the southern bank. Lights had been placed by friendly hands on each side of the stream to guide the men in their passage. The blazing pine-knots threw a vivid glare over the dark and sullen waters, and gave the outline of the frowning hill in front.

"'Halt!' rang out through the lines. Footmen were ordered to mount behind the men on horseback, that there might be no unnecessary delay. Captain Morgan rode to the rear to see that all was in readiness. Gaining the front, he ordered the guide to advance. Kit Carson plunged into the stream and reached the opposite bank. Captain Morgan and Lieutenant Duke followed. "Advance!" and horseman following horseman dashed in and crossed over. Now came the buggies. Captain Morgan returned to the middle of the stream and remained there to direct their movements.

At last old Mr. Johnson's time came. With fierce and loud imprecations he essayed to follow. Midway the stream, his horse losing his footing, plunged furiously.

"Oh! my God! I'm gone! I'm gone! Bob, if I am drowned I'll have you hung. Do you hear that, boy? Hold that horse, or we'll be at the bottom of this cussed creek in a minute.

A loud peal of laughter rang from the shore as the old man, with these last words on his lips, emerged weezing and puffing from the "cussed creek."

The road was so steep and rocky that horses had to be taken from the provision-wagons, and the wagons lifted by the men to the brow of the hill.

Bob, with the assistance of others, succeeded in getting his master over all immediate difficulties, the old man screaming out all the time, "Now, Bob, if you do kill me, I'll have you hung, boy. Do you hear that, Bob?"

The road was worse now than ever. They had struck a spur of the ridge, of which Muldrough's Hill is the most noted. On they went as fast as the nature of the route would admit, nothing of interest occurring until about three o'clock in the morning, when Captain Morgan dashed along the lines bidding the men to be silent—not to speak above a whisper, as it was feared they were in the neighborhood of some Home Guard pickets.

The column was halted, scouts were thrown in advance, headed by Captain Morgan and led by Kit Carson.

After a hasty reconnoissance, they returned and reported "No danger." The way was now supposed clear of all obstacles, and, as the road improved, they quickened their pace.

At daylight they crossed the Lebanon branch of the railroad. It was expected to have a skirmish here with the Guard, who had captured six of Captain Jack Allen's company at this point a few days before. But not a soul was seen up and down the road as far as the eye could reach.

In three hours more they were in the neighborhood of friends, where they halted to refresh themselves and feed their horses. It was found that three men were missing from their number. What befell them could never be ascertained. The party was now beyond the enemy's lines.

That night they encamped near Hodgenville, in La Rue County. As this was a hostile section, they found great difficulty in procuring food for themselves and horses. They succeeded in purchasing some corn-bread and meat, which, added to their stock on hand, served to stay their appetite for the night.

Early the next morning (Monday) they set out for the Confederate encampment on Green river, opposite Mumfordsville. And as they felt themselves freed from all apprehensions of attack, each one breathed more freely, and joke and laugh resounded along those ranks of weary yet determined men.

Not knowing but that a force of the enemy might endeavor to capture him in the vicinity of Green river, Captain Morgan very wisely sent forward videttes to see that the route was clear. It had become known in the encampment that Morgan and his men would reach the river that evening, and it had been decided to send out an escort to conduct them in. Accordingly, Major Wintersmith, with two others, crossed the river and proceeded a few miles in the direction of the expected advance. They had rode but a short distance, before they perceived two men approaching them. They were well mounted, and their guns were carelessly depending from their shoulder.

"Halt!" cried out the major, as soon as he was sufficiently near to make himself heard.

The men thus accosted reined in their horses, dropped their bridles, seized their guns, and in the twinkling of an eye were ready to fire upon their supposed enemy.

"Friends!" cried out the major, just in time to save himself and companion from the unerring bullet of the riflemen. "We come to meet Captain Morgan."

Instantly the guns were lowered, and the two rode forward. A moment more and the parties had alighted, hands were grasped in friendly greeting, and welcomes extended in the name of the

Second Kentucky—Colonel Hanson's noted regiment—to Captain Morgan and his brave followers.

An hour more and the whole force had crossed the river, and in a style at once dashing and impressive, rode into camp.

Loud and long and pealing were the shouts of welcome sent up by the Kentucky boys, as they beheld this large reinforcement to their numbers. Hats were flung high in the air, and their cheers for old Kentucky echoed and re-echoed along those grand old hills, while "Cheer, boys, cheer"—their battle-song—burst in joyous notes from groups gathered around the newly arrived friends.

There were stationed at this point, in addition to Colonel Hanson's regiment, Captain Jack Allen and his men, besides hundreds of others who had found their way thither from different parts of the State.

Charléy recognized in Colonel Hanson's regiment many of his old friends who had left Louisville some months before, for Camp Boone, among them Adjutant Frank Tryon, young Benedict and Delph, who hailed his arrival with open arms.

Our young hero, eager for an opportunity to serve his country's cause, soon enlisted in Company C, of the Second Kentucky, and entered immediately upon the duties of a soldier. Others joined the Second Kentucky, while most of the men found their way into the regiments of Colonels Hunt and Lewis.

Captain Morgan and his company of forty men did not unite themselves to any command. Morgan wished to act as a partisan ranger, and addressed General Buckner a note, asking to be allowed to serve in this capacity. But it not being deemed prudent to grant the request, and Morgan not wishing to be a burden to the cause, moved his men to the north bank of the river, rented a vacant house for them, and provided for all their wants. With this as his headquarters, he made the country between Green river and Bacon creek the scene of many a daring exploit, which history will yet record to the honor of John Morgan, Kentucky's noblest chieftain.

CHAPTER VII.

THE ESCAPE OF MORGAN AND HIS MEN FROM LEXINGTON, AS GIVEN BY ONE OF THE PARTY.

CAMP FIRES were blazing brightly. The cold and silent stars looked out from their far-off blue home in heaven upon the quiet scene. The soft moonlight kissed the cold earth and lay in silvery sheets of beauty on the bosom of the gently stealing river. Silence had thrown its deep spell on every object, only broken at long intervals by the low monotone of the watch-dog.

Two men threw themselves beneath a large tree in front of a tent door, near one of the camp-fires.

"I will tell you, Will, the whole story," was the reply of the younger to the question of his friend. "We have had a hard time getting through to join this Southern cause, and I think with Morgan that we have a right to serve it as we think best. We had a company of sixty men, well drilled and well armed. John Morgan was our captain, and Basil Duke whom you have seen with us here, was first-lieutenant. Our intention was to serve our State,—to drive from her borders any foe that dared invade her soil. An order came to disarm the State Guard. We had long been objects of suspicion by blinded Union men, who had, in various epithets conferred upon us, spoken out their disapprobation of our course. The Home Guard, under a Captain Woodson Price, who was more distinguished for his artistic taste than good sense, had uttered base threats against us. This, of course, we did not heed. But when that infamous craven legislature at Frankfort invited Anderson into Kentucky, and placed Crittenden in command of the militia of the State, we saw what awaited all Southern men. Our company, of course, disbanded to avoid suspicion. As soon as General Buckner reached Bowling Green, Captain Morgan decided to join him. He made his purpose known to as many as he could meet, and they to others. It was assented to by a large majority. Preparations for leaving were secretly made. Each man had secured his gun and determined never to yield it, though he should die for refusing to do so.

"We met at our secret rendezvous from night to night, and reported progress. It was deemed most prudent to leave the city in companies of two or three, at different hours and by different routes, thus avoiding suspicion. We assembled at Lawrenceburg. Our arrangements for provisions were intrusted to one of the company whom we knew to possess remarkable spirit and tact. As we passed along the streets we could hear threats pronounced against John Morgan and his men, and it was said currently and believed, that the most prominent of us were to be arrested. This we determined to avoid. The day appointed for setting out at length came round. Captain Morgan found himself narrowly watched, and was compelled to leave Lexington on foot, and meet a friend with his horse beyond the city limits. Others of us had to pretend we were going to Paris and Georgetown on business.

"On departing, we could bring nothing with us that would jeopardize us, so we had to leave our baggage and guns to our friends who were less suspected, and who were to come out at night. Some were to leave Wednesday, some that night, and others less noted not until Thursday. Our plan succeeded admirably. I believe not one, who set out for Camp Secret, has been arrested yet.

"In the course of twenty-four hours after Morgan entered Lawrenceburg, he found himself at the head of fifty men. We remained there a few hours awaiting others whom he hoped would join us. Some of our bravest men are behind. But they had large families, and I suppose felt they could not leave them. At Lawrenceburg, Morgan hired a man he could rely upon, and sent him to Louisville to inform old Prentice that he and his men had been captured."

"That was a happy *ruse*, indeed," interrupted the eager listener. "I am convinced, after hearing your story, that Captain Morgan should be left to pursue his own course. He can aid the cause in Kentucky, perhaps, better than any other man. His family influence is extensive. He can command money, is acquainted with the State, and, above all, is a man of decision, energy, and daring."

Weeks passed by. Charley had become measurably inured to the duties of a soldier's life. He could stand on picket or guard, go scouting or foraging, make coffee or corn-bread. Prompt, obedient, kind, he won the respect of his officers, and the esteem of his fellow-soldiers, and his faithfulness and daring had obtained the favorable notice of his colonel.

His letters to his friends at home were characterized by a spirit of cheerful endurance of present discipline, and heroic determination to make good his cause in the field of conflict. Hopeful, buoyant, he gilded the future with the bright hues of joyous expectancy, yet he realized that the life he had chosen was one of labor and hardship. "We shall have to endure many trials, mother, suffer many privations, make many sacrifices, but we shall conquer, shall surely triumph; the justice of our cause insures success. There is not a man in our regiment that would not prefer death to submission." His letters to Mary breathed the same spirit of hope and confidence, tempered, however, by a feeling of sadness at their separation, and an earnest desire that their meeting might not be far distant.

Poor Mary! Over her young loving heart there had crept a shadow. And she who through life had ever been so joyous, so happy, was now sad and thoughtful. Most of her time was passed with her mother, whose health grew daily more feeble, and who clung to her child with that feeling of dependence which the weak manifest towards the strong.

Meanwhile the Lincoln hordes were pouring into Kentucky, possessing themselves of every point deemed important to their purpose of subjugation. The great heart of the State stood still before the unfoldings of the dread panorama. And those whose voice had been for "Union" at the polls and in private, now began, with fearful forebodings, to ask themselves if the bayonet would accomplish the desired end. But what could be done? They had courted the oppression of the tyrant; had forged the fetters that enchained them. And now they stood helpless, hopeless, the victims of their own pusillanimity and avarice. While those who had ever opposed the coercion of free and sovereign States as the overthrow of civil liberty and constitutional right. robbed of their arms and of every privilege of freemen, denounced as traitors, watched in every word and act, realizing that any show of resistance would be sheer folly, suffered themselves to be borne along by the current, and even swept into the fearful vortex. Better far had they resisted in the outset, and driven the invader back from the banks of the Ohio.

Poor degraded, subjugated Kentucky! Thine is a sad story of vacillation and fear; of wrong and oppression. The faithful chronicler of this wicked war must pen with shame and regret thy irresolution, and its ruinous results. While I write, as one of thy children, I weep as my thoughts go back to thee in thy deep humiliation, and linger amid thy once lovely scenes—thy once free and happy sons and daughters, now so oppressed, so downtrodden. But thou wilt arise from thy fallen position. Even while I weep, the glad tidings comes sweeping in the breeze, "Kentucky determines to be free!" And now, at the last hour, thou wilt break the chains that bind thee, and wilt stand ranged with thy Southern sisters, proudly free, determinedly defiant.

A vote of a party legislature had invited Anderson, of Sumter notoriety, into the State to take charge of the troops within her borders. This was a cunning pretext to open the way for the formidable army that was soon to be thrown against Buckner at Bowling Green. The purpose of the Lincolnite dynasty had been served, and Anderson, the man of an hour, the fool of an unprincipled party, had been superseded by Buell, who was concentrating his force as rapidly as possible, in front of Bowling Green. His advance, under Rousseau, already extended beyond Elizabethtown, and between that point and Louisville troops were being massed in numbers. Paducah, Smithland, and several interior towns were already in their possession.

Major Breckinridge, having made his escape through the Federal lines, had reached Bowling Green, and there, in an address to the people of Kentucky, resigned his seat in the Federal congress, and announced himself ready to serve the Southern cause in whatever position might be assigned him. He received the commission of brigadier-general, and the Kentucky regiments were formed into a brigade, of which he was given the command. Hanson's force was recalled to Bowling Green, and General Hindman thrown into position at Green river.

It was proposed to establish a Provisional Government for Kentucky, that she might be represented in the Confederate congress. It was decided the Convention for that purpose should meet at Russellville. The Federal authorities heard of the movement, and declared the Convention should never assemble, and it was determined to throw Crittenden's force so as to menace Russellville, and prevent the proposed meeting. General Buckner, learning the Federal programme, ordered Breckinridge to move from Bowling Green to Russellville.

It was the middle of November when Breckinridge and his command set out for Russellville. The weather was cold and damp, and the roads muddy. It was the first marching his troops had done; but his men bore it like veterans, and not a word of complaint was heard throughout the lines.

Charley now began to experience something of the hardships of the campaign before him. As he threw himself on his blanket, weary with the fatigue of the day's march, and looked up into the face of the bending heavens above him, thoughts of home and its comforts, of its loved ones whom he might never again behold, stirred the deep depths of his soul. Tears sprung to his eyes, and he wept like a child. It was not sorrow nor apprehension, but tender remembrances of the past that caused him thus to grieve. There he lay thinking, his bosom heaving with varied emotions, his wearied frame stretched out on the hard ground, with no cover from the cold night air but his blanket wrapped around him, his knapsack for a pillow. As he dwelt on the wrongs inflicted on his State, the insolence of the oppressor, the sufferings that must necessarily follow in the train of horrid war, then turned to the insulted South, noble in her determination, heroic in her struggle, his heart grew strong within him, his physical sufferings were forgotten, he heeded not his cold, hard bed, thought not of his empty haversack, dreaded not the bloody battle-field.

The Convention assembled, protected by those gallant men who fully thwarted the plans of the Federals, keeping them at bay. About seventy counties were represented in the body. Resolutions were adopted, declaring that in view of the unconstitutional acts of the administration at Washington, and the belief that the war was one of usurpation and subjugation, Kentucky, as a sovereign State, had a right to withdraw herself from the Federal compact, and choose her own position.

On the 19th of November, the Ordinance of Secession was passed. George W. Johnson was made Provisional Governor, and members to the Confederate congress were appointed from every district in the State represented in the Convention.

The Assembly having adjourned, Breckinridge, with his forces, was ordered back to Bowling Green. After remaining there for some days, the order was given that they should go back to Rochester, a point on Green river, in Butler county, in order to prevent a supposed flank movement of the Federals.

From Rochester they returned to Bowling Green, and proceeded to Cave City, where, after remaining for several weeks, they were dispatched to Glasgow, to intercept an anticipated movement of the enemy in that direction. The rain poured in torrents, freezing as it fell. The men were drenched through and through, as they ploughed through the dreadful roads, knee-deep in mud. On and on they trudged, over many a weary mile, dripping with wet, shivering with cold, ready to sink with fatigue.

The alarm was false, and after they had proceeded one-third of the way, a courier came to countermand the order. Back the whole force was turned, to retrace the miserable road. The men were sorely tried under this unnecessary experience, and their displeasure found vent in bitter murmurings.

Many a "narrow house" at Bowling Green, all unmarked by love's kind hand, tells the sad tale of this dreadful march. And in many a quiet churchyard and family burying-ground throughout Kentucky, the stricken mourner bends over the quiet dust of the loved one lost, whose life was there sacrificed.

Our young hero had a fine constitution, which had been well preserved and developed. But those drenching marches had sorely tried it, and its vigor and power had finally to succumb before the insidious advance of disease, which first manifested itself in a slight cold, and then rapidly developed itself into a severe attack of pneumonia. Now rose up before his fevered imagination all the horrors of the hospital, with its tearful sufferings, its almost certain death.

"Oh, do not take me there!" he said, pointing to the gloomy building that stood before him. "Leave me here to die."

Through the exertions of Lieutenant Tryon, a bed was procured for him in a private house, to which he was borne, and where he was as carefully attended as circumstances would admit. There was a great deal of sickness in the army at Bowling Green, and every house was filled with the sufferers. Measles, fever, and pneumonia prevailed most fearfully.

Charley grew rapidly worse. His symptoms were of the most alarming nature. His physician, Dr. Lindley, pronounced the case as one of a malignant character, and gave but little encouragement to hope for his recovery. A friend of Charley's, from Louisville, being informed of his situation, sought him out, that he might minister to his sufferings. This gentleman found him in a small unventilated room, where lay three other sick soldiers, two on the floor, one in the bed beside Charley.

The air was foul with the fumes of tobacco, while the greatest untidiness and neglect were everywhere visible. Charley was wild with fever. He, of course, required the most profound quiet, and yet a band of musicians was quartered in the building, and ever at their pleasure they made the air resonant with their martial rehearsals. The kind friend found he must certainly die if left to remain in that dreadful condition, and determined to hazard his removal, despite the assertion of the physician, who declared imperatively that such an act would be followed by certain death.

An apartment was secured away from the noise and confusion of the town, and thither Charley was taken. A skilful nurse was procured, and after weeks of pain and feebleness, he so far recovered as to be pronounced beyond danger.

It was a cold, bleak morning in December. The snow, which had fallen the previous night, covered the earth with its white mantle of purity. The sun shone brilliantly out from the cloudless heavens, and as his golden beams fell over the earth, they awoke to life a flood of glorious radiance most beautiful to behold. The majestic trees, draped in their robes immaculate, caught up the dazzling effulgence, and sent it back in prismal loveliness over hill and plain and ice-clad brook.

Charley sat, a convalescent, beside the hugely blazing log-fire, which, sparkling and crackling as if in merriment, sent its dancing flames, of fiery hue, here and there, up, across, athwart, as if in merry mimic of carnival holiday. His chair was so situated as to give him a full view of the scene without, through the window at his left, from which the red curtain had been lifted. There he sat, thinking, thinking. And of what could he be thinking but of home and Mary? He sighed most deeply, and passed his hand slowly over his pale brow, as there came up before him the long, long, weary days since he had heard from the loved one whose image lived in his heart, whose soft sweet look was ever with him, whether in the weary march, or in the still deep hours of midnight he lay dreaming of the bliss to come.

"To see her once again," he said to himself, as he leaned his head on his hand, "would be more to me than the elixir of life to Oriental magician. I should be well again, could I but look on her faultless form, gaze into the pure living depths of those soft blue eyes, and clasp that gentle hand in mine. But, ah me, many a day shall come and go before we meet. And it may be—yes, it may be—" He dared not complete the dread sentence. He shuddered with fear like one seized with a sudden chill—tears came to his eyes, and he bowed his head yet lower on his hand.

Thus he sat for several minutes, thinking, fearing, feeling. Then rising, he walked feebly to a little dressing-stand on the other side of the fireplace, and took from its drawer a picture. Reseating himself, he opened it, and gazed intently on the face before him.

His countenance wore the look of saddened love—his cheek was flushed, his hand trembled.

A rap was heard at the door. Supposing it was his physician, whose hour it was to make his morning call, he hastily thrust the picture into his bosom (its usual resting-place), and wiping the tears from his eyes with his hand, he assumed, as far as he could, his wonted look of cheerfulness. The door opened. Charley turned to bid the physician good-morning. His eye rested on a strange form, muffled in overcoat and comforter to shut out the bleak winter air.

Charley bade the visitor "Good-morning," and requested him to walk to the fire, pointing him to a chair which stood near the dressing-case.

The stranger did not obey the invitation, but stood eyeing the invalid with a quizzical look. Charley's face colored deeply, and strange fancies began to fill his bewildered brain. The visitor threw off his cap, and hastily drew the comforter from his face.

"John!" ejaculated Charley, as he stretched out his thin, pale hand towards him. It was all he could say, for a moment. John Lawrence (for it was he), the brother of Mary, and Charley's life-long friend, grasped the feeble hand and shook it most heartily. Then drawing the chair to Charley's side, he recounted to him all the incidents of his escape from Louisville, and the various adventures that had befallen him by the way.

"And I have two letters for you, Charley." And the young man turned up the left leg of his pantaloons, and with his knife making an opening in the lining, drew forth two sheets of tissue paper, closely written, and tossed them into the invalid's lap. "I tell you, my friend, they have had many a hair-breadth escape, and could they tell their own story, it would prove no uninteresting history, I assure you."

Charley tore off the gauzy envelopes, and looked for the signatures. One was from his sister Lu, the other from Mary. What a smile of happiness overspread his wan face, giving to it an expression peculiarly interesting, as eagerly his eye glanced over the contents of these dear missives. Like the breathings of the Angel of Life, stole the eloquent words of love into the innermost recesses of his soul, arousing to renewed vigor every animal function.

The letters were read and laid aside for a reperusal, and conversation resumed, when the physician, pausing a moment after knocking, entered the door and approached his patient.

"Ah, better to-day, Charley," said Dr. Lindley, pleasantly, as he turned from shaking young Lawrence's hand, and took the arm of his patient. "I think you will no longer need my care."

After a few minutes' conversation, the physician rose to leave, telling Charley he would not call again, unless sent for, as he was now entirely free from danger, and only needed care to restore him to health.

Young Lawrence, or John, as we shall most frequently style him in our future narrative, remained with his friend for several hours, and when he left to report himself, and obtain a position in Colonel Hanson's regiment, if possible, it was under promise to return as soon as this business could be arranged. John was not only placed in the desired regiment, but also in Company C, a vacancy having been made by the death of one of the members.

Charley, as Dr. Lindley had said, grew rapidly well, and in the lapse of two weeks from the physician's last call, he was ready to join his regiment, and resume his duties as a soldier.

Many a familiar face was absent. Some lay on beds of lingering languor in the dreary hospitals. Others were quietly resting beneath the new-made earth in the soldiers' burying-ground.

CHAPTER VIII.

GENERAL BUCKNER ORDERED TO REINFORCE FORT DONELSON.

CHRISTMAS came and passed. But little of a striking character connected with the Confederate army in Kentucky had yet transpired. They had served for months to hold in check the immense Federal force that had been thrown into the State, and thus had rendered to the Confederacy most valuable service, by giving it time to expand and strengthen its resources.

It was the last days of January, 1861. The army had remained at Bowling Green since the 18th of September previous. Each day intelligence was received that the Yankees would very soon make an attack. Already had the gallant Terry fallen at Green river. Already had all the troops been withdrawn from along the line of the Louisville and Nashville railroad, and concentrated behind the fortifications at Bowling Green, and their old encampments were occupied by the advancing foe, who warily yet steadfastly moved on towards the accomplishment of his purpose.

It became evident to General A. S. Johnston that Bowling Green must be evacuated, particularly as the enemy was now making extensive preparations to attack Forts Henry and Donelson by water; but his determination was to hold out at the above mentioned place as long as possible, in order that the fortifications at Donelson might be made as strong as practicable.

General Buckner had received orders from General Johnston to move with his division against the Federal General Crittenden, who with a considerable force was posted at Rochester, a small town in Butler county, of which mention has hitherto been made. In obedience to the command, General Buckner took with him eight regiments, numbering in all about seven thousand men, among them the Second Kentucky, Colonel Hanson, the Fourteenth Mississippi, Colonel Harper, and the Third Tennessee, Colonel Brown. General Floyd accompanied him with his Virginia troops,—the whole force amounting to about nine thousand. The command left Bowling Green for Rochester via Russellville. The rain commenced to pour in torrents on the first day of the march.

Reaching Russellville, it was found impossible to proceed further, owing to the impassable state of the roads. While thus detained, orders came to General Buckner to hasten to Donelson, for the purpose of reinforcing the garrison there.

Charley, seated on a camp-stool at the door of his tent, his paper resting on his knee, was busily writing a letter to Mary. The rain fell unceasing from the thick black clouds above. The winter wind blew fiercely through the leafless branches of the old forest-trees, which stood like the grim sentinels of some enchanted land. Its voice sounded mournfully solemn as it swept onward by the tent door, over the dreary meadow-land, and lost itself amid the thick undergrowth of the dark gloom of the dense forest beyond. To the ear of Charley, it seemed like the low plaintive dirge of a lost spirit. The scene was dreary and cheerless enough to oppress the stoutest heart with loathing disgust for the present, and dread apprehensions for the future, and, despite of all his endeavors to the contrary, Charley's words would breathe a true spirit of subdued thought very near akin to sadness. The dark trials which were so soon to be realized by many a bold defiant heart, seemed to throw their shadows over the present, and to forewarn of coming defeat and humiliation.

"I know not why I thus feel, my dear Mary," wrote Charley, after speaking his fears and apprehensions. "It is so unusual for me to be overcome by gloomy presentiments. But I cannot rid myself of the feeling. Indeed, it reaches conviction, that there is sorrow in store for us. I have never been so impressed before since I parted with you, and my dear, dear friends. It must be this miserable weather—this ever-continued dropping of the cold chill rain, and mournful sighing of the bleak wind. I must not yield to such impressions; they unfit me for duty, life, every thing. They will pass away, no doubt, with the sunshine, should that ever again return; and then I shall be myself again."

"Orders are to move immediately to Fort Donelson. Quick, boys, be ready as soon as possible. Cars are in waiting to carry us to Clarksville. Not a moment must be lost." And the speaker left the door of the tent to deliver his commands elsewhere.

Charley hastily added an explanation, enveloped and directed his letter, and requesting his friend John to attend to all preparations, hastened to the post-office. All was energy and bustle throughout the encampment. In thirty minutes after the issuance of the order, the Second Kentucky was marched on board the cars, which immediately conveyed them to Clarksville, *en route* to Fort

Donelson. This was on Tuesday, February 11th. On Wednesday they reached Donelson by boat. Thursday the attack was made on the fort by the land forces of the Federals, under General Grant.

It was now evident to the men that some fighting must be done; they were now, for the first time, to meet the foe. Victory or death was their watch word, and nobly did they make it good throughout those memorable three days, when, from early morning until night, they repulsed, with superhuman energy, the hosts of the beleaguerers.

CHAPTER IX.

DONELSON—FIRST DAY'S ATTACK.

What varied emotions are called into life at the mention of that name—Fort Donelson! Emotions of sadness, as the mind recalls the sufferings, privations, and defeat of those gallant men —those more than Spartan defenders—who, for three long weary days of carnage, maintained the unequal contest against such fearful odds; and who at last yielded because nature, exhausted, could no longer obey the biddings of their unconquerable courage: emotions of unbounded admiration, as we think of the daring, endurance, patriotism, and nerve manifested by that devoted band, who, under circumstances the most trying, without food or adequate clothing, meeting and driving back through the day the countless hordes of the assailants, and at night, hungry and worn from the conflict, sleeping in trenches filled with mud and ice, till many were frozen, while the pitiless sleet beat furiously over them, yet, like veterans, like brave, patriotic men as they were, meeting all these horrors, enduring all this unparalleled hardship unmurmuringly, and with firm, undaunted soul, rising with each rising morn to strike for freedom and for right.

This dreadful war hath many a page all bright and glorious with the heroic daring, the patriotic fortitude, the brilliant victory of Southern freemen, but none can ever be more lustrous, can ever speak in words of more thrilling eloquence to the generations of all coming years, than that of Donelson, the synonym of all that is sublime in suffering, heroic in daring, and nobly triumphant in patriotism.

On the 10th of February, General Pillow reached Donelson, and took command. Immediately every thing was in busy activity, to place the fort in a defensive condition against the expected attack by land and river.

"The space to be defended by the army was quadrangular in shape, being limited on the north by the Cumberland river, and on the east and west by small streams, now converted into deep sloughs by the high water, and on the south by our line of defence.

The river-line exceeded a mile in length. The line of defence was about one mile and a half long, and its distance from the river varied from one-fourth to three-fourths of a mile."

The line of intrenchments, of a few logs rolled together, and but slightly covered with earth, formed an insufficient protection even against field artillery.. Not more than a third of the line was completed on the morning of the 12th. It had been located near the crest of a series of ridges, which sloped backwards to the river, and which were again commanded in several places by the ridges at a still greater distance from the river. This chain of heights was intersected by deep valleys and ravines, which materially interfered with communications between different parts of the line. Between the village of Dover and the water batteries a broad and deep valley, extending back from the river, and flooded by the high water, intersected the quadrangular area occupied by the army, and almost completely isolated the right wing.

There were but thirteen guns, and, on trial, it was found that only three of this number were effective against the gunboats. The garrison numbered only "13,000 troops, all told." These consisted of Tennessee and Mississippi regiments, under General Pillow, General Floyd's brigade, and a portion of General Buckner's command from Bowling Green, which did not reach the fort until the 12th, only the day before the attack, while General Floyd did not arrive until the morning of the 13th.

The morning of the 13th of February rose bright and beautiful. Just as the first rays of the dawning sun, bursting through the fleecy clouds of the morning, fell over the earth, the loud booming of the cannon aroused the expectant garrison, and announced the beginning of that fierce conflict which was to last throughout three fearful days.

The men sprang to arms, eager for the contest. Soon, under the direction of their officers, they were formed into line of battle, and in a few brief moments the strife commenced on the right wing, commanded by Buckner, and raged in wildest fury.

On and on came the moving lines of the foemen, encountering the well-directed fire of infantry and artillery. The massed columns wavered and fell back with fearful slaughter. Not a Southerner faltered. Officers displayed the most daring courage, riding up and down the ranks cheering their men, and inciting them to deeds of valor, while the men, fighting for homes and liberty, rivalled each other in death-defying heroism.

At 10 o'clock, the extreme right of General Buckner's line, under Colonel Hanson, was desperately attacked, the enemy advancing in column, manifesting a determination to take the position at all hazards. On came the serried hosts.

"Wait, boys, until they come within range of your guns," was the command.

The gallant 2d Kentucky, fired with a desire to repulse the dark foe, could scarcely restrain their ardor. "Fire!" The order ran swift along the line, and volley after volley of musketry, mingling with the roar and bursting of shells and the crashing of artillery, poured into the ranks of the assailants. Ah, it was a fearful sight to witness the carnage and death that swept along that close, dense line. Like grain before the reaper's sickle, they fell, mowed down by bullet, shell, and shot. Affrighted, they paused—'twas but for a moment: rallying, they pressed forward. Again sped the horrid missiles of death from the intrenchments, and down went scores of the rash besiegers, mangled, torn, bleeding, writhing in the tortures of agony and death. Discomfited, the decimated regiments retire, to make room for others, who dash on to the same dreadful fate. Thrice is the attack made on this point by fresh and heavy forces—thrice is the foe repulsed with dreadful slaughter. The batteries of the Confederates, managed with precision and skill—each man performing his part with the greatest enthusiasm—at every discharge, cut long lanes through the serried columns of the assailants.

Repulsed, defeated at this point, the enemy, with fresh troops, turned his assault on the position beyond General Buckner's left, held by Colonel Heiman, and flanked by Grave's battery, which, from its location, swept with its deadly fire the valley through which the Federals had to advance.

On they came, with firm, undaunted step, knowing not that they were marching to the death. With banners proudly waving, and officers splendidly uniformed, cheering their men to victory, they dash on—on—on! All is silent on the part of the besieged. With a shout of triumph the armed forces press forward. Loud, as if a thousand thunders had leaped from their wild storm-cloud—reverberating through the valleys, and bounding against the hills, to be re-echoed in tenfold fury—burst upon the air the hideous bellowing of the wide-mouth cannon; while the crash and hiss of shredding bullets which fell like the thick hail on the close lines, sweeping down in one wide welter, hundreds of stricken men, added to the loud, wild din, until the earth shook, and the air resounded with the terrible conflict.

Louder and louder grew the mingling clash of arms: fiercer, and yet more fierce the dreadful struggle. But its fiendish fury lasted but for a few minutes. The assailants, unable to stand the leaden storm in front and the destructive flank fire from Grave's battery, like their comrades, faltered onward; then, as if broken by the hand of divine vengeance, affrighted, panic-stricken, they turned and fled in wild confusion.

Hundreds of their number lay mangled, wounded, torn, dying on the battle-field, trampled beneath the feet of their retreating comrades. Their guns had been silenced—many of their officers had fallen—yet, unwilling to yield the contest, they poured fresh troops against the intrenchments, and the deadly strife went on.

All through that long dread day, the battle raged most fearfully; and as night closed in upon the sickening carnage, the enemy, repulsed, cut to pieces, slain in hundreds, was driven to seek his position of the morning, leaving the field covered with his dead and dying. Ah, it was a sad, sad sight to see them there, cut down in their manhood's prime, in servile obedience to the behest of a tyrant.

Many who, but a few hours before, had marched forth with strong hearts, and arms well nerved, now lay stiff and cold in death. Many weltered in their gore far away from all relief, sending out on the dead, dull ear of night, piteous moans and cries for help, which, alas, would never come; for when the morning rose and woke to life their comrades, they had passed away.

On the bloody battle-field lay friend and foe in ghastly death enwrapt. Everywhere were uringled, mangled forms of men and horses, and broken remains of guns and caissons. In some places the dead bodies lay piled several feet deep. In many instances, the wounded lay pinned to the moist, cold ground by the forms of dead comrades, whose fixed and agonizing eyes looked out as if in search of the foe; while the shrieks of the suffering and dying broke in horrid cries on the ears of those who could give them no aid. Faint and low was the plaintive wail of some, as with the life-blood ebbing fast from their gaping wounds, they turned their wild, glaring eyes upward and vainly implored help.

Ah, it was a sight fearfully appalling, that battle-field of Donelson. For two miles the slain were thickly strewn, and in places where our artillery had mowed them down, they lay literally heaped, soddening in their gore.

The morning had opened beautifully bright. Towards the afternoon a fierce wind swept from the north, bringing on its careering bosom rain, and sleet, and snow. A more fearful night could not be conceived than that which rested over the blood-bathed battle-field after that first day's conflict. Those of the wounded who survived the horrors of that memorable night, had their clothes still frozen to their gaping wounds, while the sleet and snow fell pitilessly over their prostrate forms writhing in tortures of helpless, hopeless agony.

Those of the garrison who had fallen beyond the intrenchments shared the direful fate of the prostrate enemy. For so close were the two armies as they rested for the night, that neither dared to make an effort to alleviate the sufferings of their wounded.

Our men, who had fought throughout the day, weary, worn, exhausted by their superhuman efforts, threw themselves on their arms in the trenches to catch such repose as the shelling, which was kept up at intervals through the night by the enemy, would allow.

"This is terrible," said Charley to John Lawrence, who lay beside him in the pit shivering with cold, while the freezing sleet dashed into their faces and fell in icy showers over their benumbed bodies, as ever and anon the bursting shells from the enemy's batteries came whizzing through the air on their errand of death.

"Terrible! terrible!" replied his comrade. "We shall all be frozen by morning; it is impossible to live through such a night as this, lying here in the mud and snow, without any protection. But we have whipped the Lincolnites most soundly, and this is some consolation, Charley, if we do freeze to death. The poor wretches, I wonder how they feel to-night after their drubbing. I pity them, foes as they are."

At that moment a piercing moan was heard just outside the intrenchment, near where the two were lying, and a voice, in the accents of despair, gasped out, "Water! water! for God's sake, boys, give me water! I am dying!"

"That is one of our men," said Charley, rising to his knees. "Listen! don't you hear? he is near us. I must give the poor fellow water, if they kill me for it. I cannot let him lie there and die. Go with me, John, perhaps we can succeed in bringing him in!"

"They may shoot us, Charley, as they did those boys that went out just after dark to bring in our wounded. But we must risk it. I would sooner perish than listen to those pitiful groans. Have you any water in your canteen? Mine is empty."

"Enough for him."

The two rose cautiously, and, guided by the sad, low moans, proceeded warily under cover of the trees to where the sufferer lay.

"Water, boys, water," said the wounded man, as the noise of footsteps fell on his dull ear. "I am dying—will no one give me a drop of water? Oh, for God's sake, a little water, I'm dying. Just a little water, then I'll die in peace."

Bending low, and lifting the feeble head, Charley placed his canteen to the famished lips. The sufferer drank eagerly.

"God bless you, boys! I was ready to perish, but you have saved me," he said, in low, faltering tones. "Could you take me from this place? I am freezing, dying. Ah, my poor wife, my dear children! God in heaven pity them!"

"Be quiet, friend, and we will do for you what we can," whispered Charley. "If you make a noise we may all be shot. Where are you wounded?"

"There, in my ankle," and the man, with a desperate effort, struggled up and placed his hand upon the bleeding limb. As he did so, he shrieked with pain.

"Be quiet," whispered Charley, "or the Yankees will shoot us."

"The bone is shattered, and I am so faint I can't sit up," and the poor man relaxed his hold on young Lawrence's arm, and would have fallen backward to the ground had not Charley caught and supported him.

"Lean on us, and we will bear you in."

"God bless you, boys," said the wounded man, with something like animation in his voice. "I may yet live."

With great effort the two bore him within the intrenchments, and securing a place of safety and comfort for him, called a surgeon to dress his wounds.

"We shall have hot work to-morrow, Charley," said Lawrence, as they resumed their places in the trenches. "These Lincolnites have a strong force, and they will bring their gunboats into the action."

"We shall whip them for all that," was the heroic reply; "that is, if we don't all freeze to-night. But, really, I don't believe I can live till morning in this condition."

"I don't fear a thing but the boats, Charley. But I do quake a little at the thought of those monster balls whizzing round my ears."

"Soon get used to them, John. And if we die, we perish in a glorious cause. This is my doctrine, and I'm not going to let their gunboats, or any thing else, scare me. And after all, the balls from their gunboats will be directed against the water batteries, and can do us but little harm, I imagine. But their troops surprised me, John. They fought like men in earnest. I had no idea they had so much spirit. Poor fellows, they were sadly cut to pieces. Their loss must be three or four times ours."

"Oh, these Western men are brave, Charley. It's all a mistake to say they are Yankee cowards. They can fight like wild-cats. But they are pretty well used up. I think they'll need some rest before they attack us again."

"But, doubtless, they will be heavily reinforced before they renew the attack," replied Charley. "There's no end to the number of these men. This is our only danger. If they can bring fresh troops against us to-morrow, I don't see how we can hold out. But Buckner is here, and I'll trust to him."

"Yes, indeed, I'll risk my fate in his hands. He'll bring us through, my word for that."

Just then a shell came whizzing by, and exploded at no great distance from where they lay. It did no damage.

"They won't let us sleep a wink to-night, Charley. I do wish they would cease firing until daylight."

"But I must sleep, John, if they do shell us, and so must you. We won't be able to fight to-morrow if we don't. We must take our chances—no use trying to escape."

The two selected as comfortable a posture as was possible, and fell into a slumber, from which they were frequently aroused by the passage of a ball or shell, as it swept onward.

The long and dreary night passed away, and morning came all too soon for those weary men, who, worn out with the fierce contest, lay sleeping in the uncovered pits, while the sleet and snow fell thick and fast upon them.

At the tap of the drum they sprang from their fitful sleep, and seized their arms. Their hearts were brave, and they longed again to meet the baffled foe. There he lay, with his gigantic numbers, within view of the fort, but as yet manifested no signs of renewing the attack. Our men, after vainly waiting some time for his advance, snatched a hasty meal, and immediately placed themselves again in line of battle. There they stood in the trenches, through the long, dread hours, the mud and ice-water up to their knees, expecting every moment the presence of the foemen. But nothing was heard from him through the morning, save the shells which he unceasingly threw into the fort.

But he was not idle. A plan for an **attack by** the gunboats was being arranged, **and** meanwhile large reinforcements were landed from transports, which everywhere lined the river below the fort.

Their plans were fully comprehended by General Buckner, who, **in a council of** general officers called during the morning, advised **that an** immediate effort should be made by the garrison to cut its **way out,** while the enemy, prostrated by the defeat of the previous day, was comparatively helpless, **and** before the reinforcements, fifteen thousand strong, should disembark. The proposition **was** assented to by all present. General Buckner proposed to cover the retreat of the army with his division, **in** the **event** the attempt should prove a success. **The troops were drawn out,** and every preparation made, both by Generals **Buckner and Pillow,** to execute **the** movement, when, **to the surprise of the former** general, **the order was countermanded by** General Floyd, influenced to the **decision by the unwise council** of General Pillow, who alleged **the lateness of the hour as a reason** for the abandonment **of the plan.**

Early in the afternoon the gunboats were observed to be advancing to attack **the river batteries, and at** three o'clock a vigorous fire was issued from **five** boats, approaching in *echelon*, throwing shot into the fort as they moved slowly and majestically **forward.**

The gunners waited **until** the advance boats were within effective range of our guns. Then, at a signal, every gun, twelve in number, belched forth its missile of destruction and **death.**

Still, amid the dreadful storm of shot and shell the defiant fleet moves on, confident in its strength, until it approaches within a few hundred yards **of** the fort. **For a moment the** guns are silent; then, in tones louder than **Vesuvius's dread** voice, they pour forth their deafening **roar, and the fiery death-weapons speed on** their unerring course.

Higher and higher swelled the tumult—dreadful and more **dreadful grew** the fierce conflict. The ground shook as with the **throes of an earthquake.** The **air** resounded for miles with the **bellowings of the death-dealing guns. The** heavens were shut out by **the clouds of dense, black smoke.** Shells crossed and recrossed each **other at every** conceivable angle; those of the fort plunging into the **river with** fearful rapidity, sending the white spray high **in** air, or striking against the iron sides of some vessel, would make it creak and quiver through every timber.

The five boats respond with equal energy; and a sixth, somewhat modestly in the rear of the others, sends her conical shot at rapid intervals into the fort.

Now the leaden conflict rages with renewed vigor; shell and shot pour like rain over every thing. See! the Essex, mistress of the fleet, reels and plunges—she is struck, disabled. She pauses for a moment, then turning about, retires from the scene.

The gunners of the fort point their guns with precision. Then bursts forth a wild and stunning explosion. Another boat is pierced in her iron casements, and her timbers creak and crash and splinter in the air. A few moments later, and another is struck, which makes her metal sides ring. Her guns are silenced. She writhes and quivers like some dread monster in his death throes, and is withdrawn from the conflict.

The remaining boats kept up a rapid fire. The batteries fail to respond. Ah, they are at last silenced. The foe has triumphed amid his destruction. But the delusion lasts but for a moment. A fearful shock rends the air, as a broadside from the fort pours into the two remaining boats, and sends them reeling and drifting down the stream.

The foe is vanquished—his fleet crippled. Shout after shout, long, loud, victorious, rings forth on the cold winter air, as the men behold the haughty foe driven from his unholy undertaking.

Two days had passed, and yet the garrison, famished, freezing, overcome by incessant duty, held out. Yea, far more; they had repulsed the hosts of the enemy on land, and shattered his mighty fleet.

It was night, cold, freezing, rayless. The weary men again laid themselves down on their arms in the wet and muddy trenches, to snatch what sleep they could.

At headquarters, Generals Floyd, Pillow, and Buckner sat in grave consultation. The question was, "what should be done on the following day?" Should the garrison remain in the intrenchments, and attempt to vanquish the attacking foe, or should they endeavor to cut their way out, and fall back on Nashville? It was known that throughout the day heavy reinforcements had been received by the enemy, and that he had so disposed himself as even now to almost completely envelop the fort. His gunboats would command the river, thereby cutting off all reinforcements and supplies from Cumberland city. The question was a serious one, and required grave consideration. The men were greatly exhausted through fighting and loss of sleep, and it was felt that unless they could be relieved by fresh troops, it would be impossible for them to hold out more than one day longer.

The question was fully debated. Each general unreservedly expressed his opinion. At length it was determined that the garrison, if it were possible, should cut its way out, and thus attempt to gain the open country south of the fort.

It was a fearful alternative for men weary, hungry, stiff with cold, their clothes frozen to their bodies, many of them with inferior guns, to make their passage through quadruple their number of fresh troops, well-armed, and supported by heavy batteries and gunboats. Yet, desperate as it was, it was the only thing left for those brave men to do.

Well may we stand aghast, and our hearts cease their beatings, while we contemplate the dreadful picture.

It was agreed in general council that at daylight the next morning General Pillow should attack the right wing of the enemy, resting on the river, while General Buckner, with his forces, should make an effort to drive him back on the Winn's Ferry road; and, if successful in the attempt, the two forces were to unite and pursue their way through the open country southward towards Nashville.

Confident of success on the following morning, the enemy, having disposed his forces, rested quietly through the night. He felt that his victim was inmeshed, and he could, at his leisure, overcome and destroy it.

CHAPTER X.

SATURDAY'S FIGHT.

The morning came, cold and dreary. At an early hour the men were called from their sleepless night in the trenches, to prepare for the day's conflict. Ah, and such a conflict the world has rarely ever witnessed. Brave men of Donelson, honor, everlasting honor must needs be your meed from a grateful and admiring nation! And when you have passed away, and we, having conquered this bloody struggle, shall stand forth a free, happy, and prosperous people, to have fought at Donelson will be a nobler fame than to have conquered on the battle-plains of Waterloo.

At the signal the men seized their arms, fell into line, and following their leaders pressed forward to the carnage. General Pillow marched upon the right wing of the enemy, whom he found in advance of his encampment, ready to receive him. And now came one of the most sanguinary struggles recorded in the annals of any war.

The Confederates, whose watchword was victory or death, drove upon the mighty foe, sending volley after volley into his serried ranks, everywhere dealing death and ruin. But the enemy, confident in his numbers, replied with courage and determination; and as quickly as his lines were thinned they were filled up with fresh forces. On pressed the garrison, to triumph or the grave—they cared but little which, as they confronted the vile invader of their soil.

Stubbornly were their fierce onsets met, the sullen foe fighting with unwonted valor. Charge succeeded charge, as fiercer and fiercer grew the bloody strife. The thick ranks of the foe were thinned but to be supplied with fresh victims for the slaughter.

The earth shook with the fury of the battle, while the air resounded with the roar of cannon, and the loud peals of the rifle and musket. The dead and wounded fell on every side, trampled to the earth beneath the feet of the onward moving columns. At length, after the most desperate resistance, the foe wavered. Forward rushed our forces upon them with the fury of enraged madmen. But the enemy was not routed, and as the Southerners charged, they were met by a fierce and destructive fire. But the advantage gained must not be lost, and with renewed determination the Confederates dashed on. Inch by inch the foe receded, contesting every step with fearful obstinacy. But at length, after six hours' engagement, they were compelled to yield before the impetuosity of men fighting for their lives. The field was won; and shouts that made the heavens ring went up from the victorious troops as they saw the enemy were driven before them.

General Buckner, as was agreed, attacked the forces that were massed against his left. Desperate beyond conception was the engagement between this small band of heroes and the formidable hosts of the opposer. The enemy were stronger here than in front of General Pillow's position, and fought with a steady determination rarely exhibited by them. The contending columns swayed to and fro, as first one and then the other gained the advantage. The fighting on all parts of the field was of the most desperate character.

Never was there witnessed a wilder scene of combat. For, as rank after rank of the enemy fell before the furious onset, the doomed victims rushed in to fill their vacant places. On moved the garrison like an "Alpine avalanche," sweeping every thing before it. The battle-field was one of awful sublimity. The shrieks of the wounded and dying mingled with the roar of the cannon and the clash of musketry in one loud deafening din. The shells went through the air with sharp whizzing, as they sped on their mission of death.

The foe was repulsed, routed, and the conquerors mingled their shouts and cheers with those of their victorious comrades under General Pillow.

The enemy was defeated, driven back. The plan devised by the council of Confederate officers had succeeded admirably. A way of escape had been opened for the brave and gallant garrison by its own noble achievements. Quadruple its own strength of fresh troops had been driven back by men "worn with watching, with labor, with fighting."

Unfading laurels will ever wreath the brows of the heroes of that memorable 15th of February, 1861.

General Buckner's division having driven back the entire force of the enemy to the right of the Wynn's Ferry road, leaving this route and the Forge road open for the egress of the garrison, were awaiting the arrival of their artillery and the reserves that had been left to hold the trenches, when General Buckner received reiterated orders to fall back to the intrenchments on the extreme right.

Surprised, shocked, stunned at such a command at such a time, and under such circumstances, he could not believe that it had emanated from the commanding general.

To retire back **to** the intrenchments, and thus place themselves again in the power of the foe, and that, too, at the point when the object **for which the** men had fought desperately for **seven** hours was fully gained, seemed to him madness **of the wildest** nature. To fall back was the certain destruction of the entire Confederate force. **To** advance from their present safe **position** would be the salvation of the whole garrison.

Galloping back to the lines, he encountered General **Floyd, and** made known to him the orders he had received. The commanding general, surprised, astonished, pronounced it a mistake.

"**Wait, general,**" replied General Floyd to General Buckner. "**Let me look into this.** Remain in your present position until I can converse with General Pillow."

In **a very short time after this meeting,** General Buckner received **orders imperatively** to repair as rapidly as he could to his former position on **the extreme right.**

Nothing was left him but to obey, although he knew **that he** and his **men** were going back to certain death, or **inevitable surrender.**

Two miles of retreat were trod **by the weary and now disheartened** men. On nearing their intrenchments they found **the** right of their position already occupied by the enemy. A desperate fight ensued, in which the Confederates succeeded in keeping at bay about five times their number.

Night closed the **dreadful scene.** The enemy occupied the Confederate **works on General** Buckner's right, ready to resume the attack with overwhelming force as soon as the morning should dawn. The **fort** was soon reinvested by the enemy with the fresh reinforcements received, **as** was shown by a thorough reconnoissance made by Colonel Forrest. And thus, after three days' **hard** fighting, hardships, privations, and sufferings, such as soldiers have rarely ever been called on to endure, after having once extricated itself, through the want of prudence and generalship of

General Pillow, the heroic garrison was caught in the toils—doomed—sacrificed.

A sad page in our country's history. Would it had never been written.

Again the dreary night came down over the earth, wrapping in its folds of thick darkness that appalling scene of carnage.

In a tent, there sat the commanding officers of the garrison, grave, sad, thoughtful. They had essayed the daring effort of cutting their way out, but found themselves, after a successful effort, back again in their old position, and again environed by the wily foe. Their men had fought like heroes, but now they were exhausted, and could fight no longer. They could not escape secretly, for the enemy completely surrounded them, leaving no possible outlet. The command and position must be surrendered to the victorious foe—a sad, but only, alternative.

Everywhere were the horrid witnesses to that fearful struggle, which, for nine dreadful hours, had raged in wildest fury. Men—dead, dying, mangled—horses, gun-carriages, broken muskets, cartridge-boxes, knapsacks—all the paraphernalia of war—lay scattered in one wild welter. Foe grasped foe for the death-struggle, and together fell clenched in each other's gripe, while their pallid faces wore the look of deadly hate which had filled their hearts in life.

Three days of the most desperate fighting the world has ever known, had passed. The little garrison, completely overcome, lay asleep on the cold frozen earth. Men dropped from their position while standing, unable to bear up any longer under their dread exhaustion. Some of the little band had fallen on the ensanguined field, others were prostrated through fatigue and exposure. All weary and fainting, yet *they* never dreamed of yielding. They looked to the morrow for a renewal of the fight. Alas! they dreamed not of the humiliating fate that awaited them.

Again in council sat the officers, this time more grave, more thoughtful than before. Death or surrender was now the choice. There was nothing else left them.

Each of the three generals, Floyd, Pillow, and Buckner, had expressed his respective opinion. They were found to differ—General Pillow believing it yet possible to cut their way out—General Buckner demurring, regarding the project as one involving extreme hazard and a useless sacrifice of life.

Silence ensued. A scout was ushered in.

"The enemy reoccupies the lines from which we drove him during the day."

"I think the man must be mistaken," said General Pillow. "Send out another scout."

"I am confident the enemy will attack my lines by light, and, owing to the condition of my men, I cannot hold them a half hour," said General Buckner.

"Why so? Why so, **general?**" interrogated General Pillow, sharply.

"Because I can bring into action not over four thousand men, and they demoralized by **long and uninterrupted** exposure and hard fighting, while he can bring large numbers of **fresh troops to** the attack."

"I differ with you, general," responded Pillow, nervously. "I think you can hold your lines. I think you can, sir."

"I *know* my position," firmly answered General Buckner. "I know the lines *cannot be held* by my troops, in their present condition."

"Then," interposed General Floyd, "a capitulation is all that is left us."

"I do not think so," **was the quick** response of General Pillow. " **At any rate, we** can *cut* our way **out.**"

"To cut our way **out would** cost us three-fourths of our men, even if we should succeed at all; **and** I do not think any commander has **a right to sacrifice three-fourths of his command to** save one-fourth," responded the noble Buckner.

The second scout entered the room.

"The enemy completely surround us. Our works are fully **invested.**"

"Send out scouts to see if the back water can be passed by the army."

The command was immediately obeyed, two of Colonel **Forrest's** cavalry being dispatched for that purpose.

Soon they return, and report, " Cavalry can pass—infantry cannot."

"Well, gentlemen, what are we to do?" asked General Buckner, on the reception of this intelligence.

"Understand me, gentlemen," responded General Pillow, "I am for holding out at least a day longer—getting boats, and crossing the command over the river. As for myself, I will never surrender, I will die first."

"Nor will I," interposed General Floyd. "I cannot and will

not surrender; but, I must confess, personal reasons control me."

"But such considerations should never control a general's actions," responded the heroic Buckner. "I see nothing that can be done but to yield the command and the position. It is humiliating, it is true, deeply humiliating, to be driven to surrender to such a foe; but as we are, unfortunately, placed in a position where all the dictates of humanity require it, it is best, in my judgment, that it should be done."

"I shall never surrender, General Buckner," responded General Pillow, warmly. "I go out from here a free man, or die where I stand. I shall surrender to Grant neither the command nor myself."

General Buckner sat calm, grave, thoughtful. He had been overruled in his decision. Should he fall into the hands of the hated foe, he had more to meet, perhaps, than either of the other commanders. He knew the sword of vengeance had been whetted against him by his enemies at home, who stood ready, whenever he should fall into their power, to lead him to the block. He could hope for no clemency at their hands. They had denounced him as a "base traitor," a seducer of the young, a "felon, whose only doom should be the gallows." He knew that scorn and contempt would be heaped upon him; that he would be made the butt of ridicule and low jest; would be inveighed against by the press of his own city, and held up to his fellow-men as a wretch whose crime merited the most ignominious punishment. All this he knew, and as a brave, honorable man, he felt that to die would be naught compared with a fate like this. But there were his brave men around him.

They had fought with a daring never surpassed. He thought of their wives and parents, many of whom were personally known to him. Must he sacrifice them to spare himself this deep abasement? No! no!! He would save his men from death, and share their fate. Thrice noble man! Among the honorable names which shall make the page of our history illustrious, there will stand none more glorious than that of the hero of Donelson—the truly brave, the sublimely heroic Buckner.

"You have decided against me, gentlemen, and I do not wish to seem to oppose you; but my judgment is unalterably against your proposition. I cannot consent to sacrifice my men in this fearful experiment."

"Will you take command, General Buckner, and release us?"

asked General Floyd of him. "If you decide to remain, and will surrender the fort, I will pass the command to you through General Pillow. I am unyielding in my purpose to go out, let it cost what it may."

General Buckner expressed his willingness to accept the command.

General Floyd said, "I turn over the command."

"I pass it. I will not surrender," responded General Pillow, quickly.

General Buckner immediately called for pen, ink, paper, and a bugler.

"Well, general, will I be permitted to take my brigade out, if I can?" interrogated General Floyd.

"Certainly; if you can get them out before the terms of capitulation are agreed on," was the reply.

The two generals made what hurried preparations were necessary, and gathering together as many of their command as was possible, left the fort; and when daylight came they were beyond the reach of the enemy.

General Buckner immediately sent a flag of truce to General Grant, bearing the following proposition:

"HEADQUARTERS, FORT DONELSON,
Feb. 16th, 1862.

"SIR:—In consideration of all the circumstances governing the present situation of affairs at this station, I propose to the commanding officer of the Federal forces the appointment of commissioners to agree upon terms of capitulation of the forces and fort under my command, and in that view suggest an armistice until 12 o'clock to-day."

To which Grant replied in the following terms, alike unworthy of a gentleman and an officer:

"SIR:—Yours of this date, proposing an armistice and appointment of commissioners to settle terms of capitulation, is just received.

"No terms, except unconditional and immediate surrender, can be accepted. I propose to move immediately on your works."

To which General Buckner responded:

"Sir:—The distribution of the forces under my command, incident to an unexpected change of commanders, and the overwhelming force under your command, compel me, notwithstanding the brilliant success of the Confederate arms yesterday, to accept the ungenerous, unchivalrous terms which you propose."

CHAPTER XII.

THE SURRENDER.

Weary men slept on, all unconscious of the dreadful fate that awaited them. They were dreaming of the battle-field and of victory.

Morning came. The black leaden clouds of winter hung like a dark funeral pall over the doomed fort. All was still as grim death, who held his dread and silent banquet over the gory battle-field.

The reveille was sounded. Men arose from their death-like sleep and grasped their arms, to rush to the contest. But no sound of booming cannon met their ear, no warlike movements greeted their eye.

What did all this mean? Had the enemy, foiled in his attempt, withdrawn? Surely this must be so, else why this silent apathy? They look out through the gray mists, and there, waving in the morning light, is the *white flag* of surrender. Soon the dreadful intelligence runs through the ranks. They are the prisoners of the hated foe. Never, never will they submit to this ignominy. Sooner shall their own swords drink their life-blood, than they become the scoff and butt of Yankee vengeance. The whole garrison was moved as one man to oppose this shameful fate. Some cursed the treachery of their commanders. Others swore to be revenged on those who had sacrificed them. Some sat sad and dejected, stupified by the stunning blow, while many a stout man wept like an infant, when he read his humiliating doom.

Resistance was useless now. The die was cast. On came the Yankee conquerors. Strains of martial music heralded their approach.

Silent in his tent sat General Buckner. His tried and faithful staff were around him. They truly sympathized with him, but they knew the vanity of words in such a trial as this, and they attempted no consolation. Each fully approved of his course in the surrender. They knew it was all he could do, and every man expressed himself ready to share his leader's fate, let it be whatever it might.

Every thing in the fort was taken possession of by the victors, even the private baggage of the soldiers. The Yankee general, Grant, issued orders to the garrison to be ready for transportation to Northern camps.

Charley—as all of his Kentucky copatriots—had fought gallantly under the leadership of the daring Hanson. Exhausted, trembling in every nerve with fatigue and cold, he and young Lawrence sat beside each other, stupified under the consciousness of being captives in the hands of the Yankees. Silently they observed the movements of the victors, as they passed from group to group, demanding the surrender of the prisoners' arms.

"I have fought for three days, John; I have slept in those muddy trenches, exposed to driving snow and sleet; have gone without a mouthful of food for twenty-four hours; my feet are frost-bitten, and my clothes are frozen on me, but I would rather endure all this a thousand times over than to go to one of those Yankee prisons."

"And so would I, Charley. But what can we do? We cannot help ourselves. It's all that is left us now. Look at that dastardly pack of thieves. See, they are demanding Bob's money. They have taken his arms from him, and now they will rob him. But he'll not give it up. Listen, he is cursing them; and see, they cower before him—and two to one—and he a prisoner without arms."

"Let's break our guns, John. I can never yield mine to the wretches. I feel it would be an eternal disgrace."

"Agreed, Charley. But we'll have to be quick about it. They'll be upon us directly."

The two stepped behind a tent, and battering their arms as well as they could, threw them into a ditch.

"There," said John, as he dashed his into the mud with all his might, "I am saved that humiliation, anyhow. And if one of the cowardly thieves dares to insult me, I'll knock him over, if he shoots me for it the next minute."

"I could bear this thing better, John, if it were not for mother. You know how bitterly she opposed my coming to the army, and I know she will be frantic when she hears I am a prisoner. I believe I'll try to escape. It may be that I can overtake those men who went out early this morning."

"Good," answered John, "let's try it. We can get beyond the

intrenchments and secrete ourselves until the army leaves here, and maybe **we can reach some** friendly house where we can get shelter until we rest and recruit. I don't believe I **can** live twenty-four hours longer in this condition."

The two took from their haversacks the morsel **of bread they contained,** and, having carefully looked around them to **see if** danger was near, they, under cover of the tents, passed the last trench and set out on their proposed plan of escape.

CHAPTER XIII.

REMOVAL TO PRISON.

As stealthily as they could, avoiding every appearance of danger, the two young soldiers moved on until they had placed a slight elevation between their position and the fort. Just before them was some underbrush. If they could but reach it, they would be safe. They paused and looked around, to see if any one was in view. No one was near enough to watch their movements. Quickening their pace into a run, they sprang forward towards the covert. Like men running for life, they bounded onward, every muscle strained for the race.

They had almost gained it, when suddenly a coarse voice called out, "Halt, or I'll shoot you." At the same time a squad of Lincoln soldiers appeared, emerging from the bushes.

Resistance would have been folly; they were outnumbered, four to one. To attempt to elude their captors was impossible. There was nothing left them but to obey the command.

With loud oaths and fiendish imprecations they were immediately marched back to the fort; from thence to the river, where boats were in waiting to transport the prisoners to their destination.

Charley and his friend, young Lawrence, were placed on the same vessel with General Buckner, his staff, and the Kentucky officers. In this they regarded themselves most fortunate, for many of the Second Kentucky were hurried into other boats.

The prisoners were taken from the fort to Cairo. From there they were shipped by river and railway to other points. Some were sent to St. Louis, others to Alton, some to Camp Douglas, some to Camp Butler, while others were forwarded by the Ohio river to Jeffersonville, on their route to Camp Chase. Subjected to every insult, treated as if they had been brutes, rather than men, these noble patriots, who had won for themselves imperishable fame, were hurried by their vengeful captors to their various places of imprisonment. Wholly ununiformed, their clothes torn in the desperate fight, and begrimed with mud and powder; their coverings of every conceivable character—blankets of all colors, shawls of every variety, carpets of various patterns—these heroes of Donelson indeed presented a sad and touching spectacle.

And yet such was the brutality and heartlessness—such the entire destitution of every emotion of humanity in the hearts of these vulgar, sunken wretches, that they jeered and scoffed, and with low and cruel mockery taunted their helpless prisoners. But helpless as they were in the hands of a base and inhuman foe, in garb looking worse by far than their slaves at home on their plantations, they nevertheless remembered they were born freemen, and on every occasion they hurled back with defiant scorn the ruthless jests of their coarse and ill-bred assailants.

Never, perhaps, did the superior nobility of the Southern character speak out in more striking contrast to the natural coarseness and heartlessness of their vulgar foe, than on this memorable occasion.

General Buckner and staff, the officers and some of the men of the Second Kentucky, were sent from Paducah on board a steamer to Jeffersonville, Indiana.

Among the privates who were forwarded by this route were Charley, young Lawrence, and another Kentuckian named Bob Reed.

"I wonder if it is possible they will allow us to land at Louisville," said Charley to his friend, as the two stood shivering with cold on the upper deck of the boat. "I do believe they will be afraid to do so, lest there should be some demonstration in our favor."

"Why, Charley, it is a LOYAL city. There are no traitors there to make any manifestation of sympathy for *such poor, miserable wretches as we are*," replied young Lawrence, ironically.

"Could the Southern men of Louisville once catch a glimpse of General Buckner, and know for a moment what shameful humiliation he has to endure at the hands of these wretches, they would rescue him from their clutches, if it cost them their lives. I do hope they will land us there, if it be but for a few minutes. I know there will be crowds of friends to welcome and cheer us; but I fear our enemies will not be thus kind to us. It would delight them to tantalize Buckner, Cassidy, Johnson, Colonel Hanson, and all of us, by giving us only a farewell glimpse of our beloved city."

As old memories, sacred and dear, rushed to Charley's mind,

he wept. It was the first time he had shed a tear since he had fallen into the hands of the victors.

"I am unmanned," said Charley, recovering himself, after a few moments; "but I cannot help it, John. I dread the idea of imprisonment for this war. I would a thousand times **rather take** my chance on the battle-field. And to think I shall pass so near **my parents** and sisters, and yet not be permitted to see them! It **makes me a child**, John."

Ah, and there was another whose name our young hero dared not mention. What joy it would have given him could he have felt assured that even for one short moment he should behold that dear being—should catch from those cherished lips one word, or from those soft, blue eyes, so full of tender affection, one look of love.

Great was the excitement in Louisville when it was known that the boat bearing General Buckner, his staff, and the Kentucky prisoners would reach the wharf that day.

The "Daily Journal," in each issue since the fall of Donelson, **had heaped upon General Buckner every abuse that its vindictive** partisan editor could conceive. Every opprobrious epithet that the language could afford—oftentimes of the most indelicate nature—had been employed to make, if possible, his honorable name odious. Every species of torture that the fiendish brain of Prentice could **invent had** been proposed to be inflicted upon him by the citizens of his own town. He had been called "infamous wretch," "vile seducer of the young men of Kentucky," "hellish murderer of the husbands and sons of his neighbors," "double-dyed traitor to his government and State," "fiend," "assassin," "brute." This Connecticut-reared editor had said he ought to suffer, if possible, a thousand deaths on the gallows, to expiate his crime. He also proposed that "he should be shown through the city in a cage, and that loyal men and women should torture him with red-hot pincers;" that he should be doomed to a felon's cell, and there shut out from the light of day, be fed on bread and water until death should come to end his "infamous life."

As might be expected, such things had wrought **on the** fierce passions of the mob until it was wild with vengeance. Threats were everywhere uttered against the distinguished prisoner. But General Buckner had many warm friends in Louisville, men of **true** courage and high-toned honor, who would at any moment have sacrificed their lives rather than he should have been subjected to public scorn. This the cowardly editor and the hireling officials knew. And while they boasted great contempt for the prisoner and his cause, they secretly feared the influence of one and respected the other. And while through the medium of their perverted press they were deriding and abusing him, in private caucus, where the subject was seriously discussed, they decided it would not be safe to suffer the boat to land, lest there should be some overwhelming manifestation of respect and admiration for the patriot and his fellow-prisoners.

The boat was nearing the city. It was believed, by those on board, that she would touch at the wharf. Their hearts leaped with wild emotion as her turrets and spires, so familiar, shot up before their eager, longing gaze. The boat ploughed on against the current. Nearer and nearer they approached the city. With folded arms and proud and noble mien, General Buckner stood on deck, his staff around him. Never did men more bespeak the majesty of conscious right than did that silent group, as they stood there, triumphant in their defeat, sublimely strong in their apparent weakness. They were stigmatized by their deluded, vindictive countrymen as traitors; they had been the recipients of every abuse and insult, the objects of malignant hate and contemptuous scorn. They were prisoners in the hands of a cruel and unprincipled foe. Their doom they knew would be fearful—perhaps lifelong imprisonment—perhaps a violent death. Should the cause they had espoused fail to succeed, in all future history their names would be handed down to posterity covered with infamy. This was the bitterest thought of all. To an honorable man, disgrace is more dreadful far than direst pangs of death.

Motionless and pale with anxiety, Charley stood leaning on the railing. He was alone, busy with his own thoughts, which, to him, were too sacred for the intrusion of his dearest friend. Portland was passed, and the lower wharf of the city reached, yet the boat kept steadily on her course. No signs of landing were to be observed. His heart beat wildly with alternate hope and fear. He bent eagerly forward, and strained his gaze to catch a glimpse of old, familiar objects. The boat veered to the right, as if seeking the shore. Oh! how his pulses leaped! His heart quickened its throbbings; tears he could not suppress rushed to his eyes. If he could but see some dear, remembered face; grasp, even for a moment, some kindly hand; hear the tones of some familiar voice; it would sweeten the bitter cup, gild the rayless gloom. It was a moment of torturing suspense. Street after street is passed, the wharf is in sight; yet the boat moves not from its forward course. The landing is filled with spectators of all classes, from the sad, sympathizing friend, to the vicious Yankee and idly-gazing negro. His look strains itself as it wanders from group to group, searching for some one he knows.

Will not some kindly eye see him? shall he not receive some token of recognition? Surely, there must be some one in that vast assemblage who knows him—some well-remembered face that he will soon descry. But not a voice is heard, not a handkerchief waved. As fades away the brilliant mirage of the desert before the charmed gaze, and leaves behind but wild wastes and burning sands to mock the eye of the worn traveller, so died away the high and cherished hopes of the heart-sick soldier-boy, and naught remained to him but disappointment and bitter tears. The crowd stands motionless, gazing on the scene. The prisoners stand motionless, gazing on the crowd. The boat keeps on—on—the last faint hope is gone, and Charley's heart, strained with anxious desire almost to bursting, sinks, dies; and like the orphan child who sits itself down to weep under its crushing sense of loneliness, so the sad, disappointed prisoner, burying his face in his trembling hands, wept bitterly.

The boat landed on the opposite shore, at Jeffersonville. The prisoners were hurried from the boat to the depot, where the cars were under steam to carry them to Columbus, Ohio. As they were driven along, friends from Kentucky line either side of the way. Only a look of recognition, a low-spoken word of sympathy, perhaps a nervous shake of the hand, as some loving heart ejaculates a "God bless and protect you." This is all that is permitted.

As Charley was waiting his turn to ascend the steps of the car, he heard his name pronounced in a soft, low voice. He started, and looked round. There stood Lu and Mary. He sprang towards them. The guard seized and drew him back to his position, not, however, before he had received the package which his sister held out to him. A moment more, and he was rudely thrust forward, and had gained the car. Through the open window he gazed into the seething mass before him. But vainly. Lu and Mary could not be seen. They were lost in the crowd.

CHAPTER XIV.

CAMP CHASE.

What a thrill of horror seizes the soul as this dreadful name meets the ear! Synonym of injustice, cruelty, and suffering, how black will be thy calendar of crimes, when portrayed by the pen of impartial history to the gaze of an astonished world! Thy record has gone up before the tribunal of eternal, immutable justice, and fearful must be the doom that awaits the authors and abettors of thy deep, dark wrongs.

The prisoners were marched immediately from Columbus to Camp Chase, a distance of six miles, without a moment's pause for rest, which they so greatly needed. Like herded swine, they were driven into this filthy inclosure, there to remain through long months of dreary suffering, deprived of every thing like comfort or cleanliness, subjected to neglect and coarse insult, and in many instances to violent death at the hands of their brutal guard.

The members of General Buckner's staff, and all the officers of Colonel Hanson's regiment, were detained here until arrangements could be completed to transfer them to Johnson's Island, in the bay of Sandusky.

With studied cruelty the officers were prohibited from intercourse with their men, lest their influence might serve to cheer and console them under their horrible treatment. It was hoped that this measure might serve to intimidate the private soldiers, and finally force them to take the oath. But how mistaken were all such calculations! The men were actuated by the same high and patriotic principles that filled the bosoms of their leaders, and were just as determined as they, to brave death rather than submit to disgrace.

It was a loathsome, disgusting place, unfit for the abode of the most wretched criminals. Filled with every species of offensive vermin, the mud knee-deep, in which the men had to stand like beasts in the stall, with no room for exercise by day, and nothing but the bare floor of an open plank shanty, through which the bleak winds and driving snows had free access, to sleep on at night; their disgusting food doled out to them in such scant measure as wholly to fail to meet the actual demands of nature; without medicines or nurses for the sick; could it be expected that these weary, half-clad men could do otherwise than die by scores? And, indeed, was not death a sweet relief to an honorable heart under such sad trials?

The men, in solemn vow, pledged themselves to stand by their officers and each other to the last extremity. Although separated from their officers, and all conversation with them prohibited, they swore to avenge with their own blood any insult that might be offered to them. Men and officers were alike treated as if they had been felons of the lowest grade, the steadiest watch exercised over them by the low, base minions of an unprincipled tyrant; subject at any moment to be shot or bayoneted by these infidel hirelings, yet they never for a moment lost the consciousness of their superiority, and of the righteousness of their cause, and never would they cower before insolence or insult. Such was their noble bearing, such their dignity, that even the stolid hearts of their guard were moved with respect and admiration.

A few days passed, when suddenly, and wholly unexpected, Major Cassidy was taken sick. This officer, of General Buckner's staff, was a son of one of the oldest and most highly respectable citizens of Louisville. His father, having located in the place before it was yet fully redeemed from the swamps and malaria which made its first settlement so dangerous to life, had amassed a princely fortune. His sons had, from their earliest childhood, been the recipients of all the advantages of education and society that such immense wealth could afford. Major Cassidy was a husband and father, surrounded by all the tender endearments of home. But when the call came to Kentucky's noble sons to arm themselves in defence of liberty and right, he girded on his sword, and bidding farewell to loving wife, prattling children, and gray-haired sire, he nobly went forth to link himself with the cause of the South. He was with General Buckner while at Bowling Green, at Russellville, at Donelson, and in that fearful defeat decided to remain beside him, and share with him his captivity, rather than desert his general and his friend in the hour of overthrow and gloom. And now he was a prisoner, receiving with the others all the insult and trial that malice and fiendishness could heap upon him.

Rapidly he grew worse. At the earnest solicitations of his brother officers, a dispatch was sent to his friends in Louisville, apprising them of his illness. But his disease quickly ran its course, and before his aged father and young and loving wife could reach him, he was dead.

This was the first death among the officers. Its suddenness and mysteriousness gave rise to suspicions of foul play. It was said he had died from congestion, but there lurked in many a mind dark misgivings as to the truth of the statement. The body was placed in a metallic case. Few of the men were permitted to gaze on the noble form now still in death. They could only watch it from afar, as it passed through the outer gate on its way to its last resting-place.

Each day new accessions were made to the already large number of prisoners from among the citizens of Kentucky who were suspected of Southern sympathies. No age nor condition in life was free from the tyranny of arbitrary arrest. Old, gray-haired men with tottering limbs, borne down with the infirmities of age, without any accusation against them save the general charge of disloyalty, were snatched from their homes and families by a ruffianly soldiery, and without a moment's preparation—in many instances not even permitted to bid farewell to their wives and children—were hurried off, frequently at the hour of midnight, transferred across the river, and incarcerated in this noisome prison. Young men, on whom depended the support of their helpless families, as they went about their daily avocations, met the bayonet pointed to their bosoms, and found themselves prisoners in the hands of ignorant Irish and Dutch Lincolnites, who cared no more about the Constitution and the laws, in whose name and by whose authority they claimed a right to practise their outrages, than did the perjured tyrants at Washington.

No class of society was exempt. The learned and unlearned, old and young, the honorable and the obscure—even ministers of the gospel—all alike were the victims of relentless hate and cruelty. Will there not be a day of reckoning for all these deep, dark wrongs, and will it not come speedily? Already the throne of the tyrant begins to totter; already, too, his unprincipled and debased tools begin to feel the coming storm of wrath which most surely will sweep them before it to ruin—fearful, irremediable. An oppressed and outraged people will rise to avenge the high-handed abuses that have been heaped upon them by a base abolition usurpation. And when this hour comes, and come it

4*

must, for justice, though long delayed, will surely overtake the transgressor, ah, will it not be one of fearful moment?

After a few weeks more, in order to effectually remove the influence of the officers from their men, the former were transferred to Johnson's Island. The men were left in their loathsome confinement. The daily round of life was but little varied. Now a familiar face would be missed—a few days more, and a plain pine coffin bore the body to the burial-place. Then a fellow-prisoner, for some imagined offence to the guard, was shot down—before the eyes of his friends. Then would the demon of revenge take possession of the men's hearts, and solemn vows, muttered through clenched teeth, would go up before heaven, to wipe out the shameful crime.

As the spring went by, the character of the prison ground, which was a low, wet swamp, somewhat improved, and the men, to relieve the tediousness of the weary hours, would sometimes indulge in a game of ball, and other such athletic exercises as their limited space would allow.

For two months Charley, with such of his companions as had survived the hardships and deprivations of that horrid prison, had suffered on without one ray of hope. They saw nothing before them but years of close confinement, with all its attendants of insult, want, and *ennui*. The oppressive tedium was sometimes relieved by the presence of a visitor, sometimes by the reception of a letter from absent friends, at others, by the arrival of a memento of love and affection in the form of a box of nice clothes and delicacies. But, oh, it was an irksome existence to men of spirit and daring.

It was in the middle of April. The sun shone brightly down from the clear blue heavens, as if in mockery of the wretched scene beneath. Charley, leaning against a tree that marked the beat of the guard, stood reading a letter from home. He turned the page, and there met his eyes a pressed rose-bud, and written in his sister's own sweet hand, these words: "This is sent you by Mary, Charley."

Our young hero's face brightened into a high flush as he read again and again the charmed line. His heart quickened its beatings, his eyes swam with tears.

"Why, you appear distressed, Charley," said young Reed to him, as walking by he observed his deep emotion. "Is any thing wrong at home, my boy, or are you so glad to get a letter that you can't help shedding a tear over it?"

"Nothing serious, Bob. It is a letter from my sister Lu. I am so overjoyed to hear from my friends, that I could not refrain a slight manifestation of weakness. It is the first I have had for six weeks. And my sister writes, jestingly, of course, that we may look for her soon to make us a visit."

"Does she mention my sister, Charley?" said John, who at this moment joined the two. "I do wish she would come with Miss Lu."

Charley endeavored to conceal his deep feelings at the mention of Mary's name. He did not wish to prevaricate, and yet he felt unwilling, in the presence of Robert, to disclose the message.

"Yes," he answered, after some hesitation, which seemed to arouse the young men's curiosity. "Lu says perhaps your sister will accompany her. But, of course, John, the girls must be quizzing us. They cannot seriously contemplate such a thing."

"Oh, if Mary has any such idea in her head, she will as certainly make us a visit as that I shall shoot that cursed Dutchman yonder, if ever I have a chance. And you know, boys, that I have sworn by the eternal heavens to do this. I tell you, if my sister has made up her mind to it, she will carry it through at all risks. I do hope she has determined to come. I would rather see her than anybody in the world. You do not know her, Bob. I believe she is the sweetest creature living. Ain't she, Charley?"

"Certainly, John," replied the young soldier, with quite a flippant manner, that he might avoid suspicion. "Miss Mary is quite a charming young lady."

"Three cheers for Kentucky and her lovely girls," and John took off his ragged beaver and tossed it high up in the air.

"Three times three," responded his friends.

"Come, Charley, finish your letter, my boy, and give us all the news. You are selfish. When I received the letter from Mary, I read it aloud to all the Kentucky boys, and they enjoyed it as much as I did. What's the matter? I do believe you have got some secret, you blush so. Well, Bob, we'll give him time to read his letter, while we walk round a little. We'll be back this way, after a few minutes, to hear the news. We mustn't be disappointed, you understand."

The two passed on, and in a little while were back again.

"What news, Charley?" asked John, walking up and putting his arm in his for a stroll. "All well, I hope."

"Yes. The only news item is the proposed visit of our sisters, and this is so vaguely expressed, that I am not sure I have rightly interpreted Lu's ambiguous language. So we must not too sanguinely anticipate the happiness."

The three passed on. Charley was silent. They continued walking for some time to and fro in the space allotted for their exercise.

"Why are you so mum, Charley, my boy?" said John, withdrawing his hand and slapping him on the shoulder. "Something's wrong with you. You act so mysteriously. Come, Bob, let's besiege him until we rally his spirits."

"No need of that, John. I'll tell you and Bob all about it, but you must guard my secret as you would your own life, boys. Should I be betrayed, I dare not think of the result. We must speak low, the guard might overhear us. Come aside by this house. We will be free from notice there."

The three stepped aside, and reached a secluded spot. Seating himself between them, Charley undertook to unfold his secret.

"I have been thinking for several days of proposing to you to escape. I cannot stand this life much longer. I would rather die. And this letter from home, together with the shocking death of that young Virginian, has determined me in my purpose. What say you, boys, will you risk it?"

"Wasn't that a brutal murder," interrupted young Lawrence, "to shoot that poor fellow through the heart, just because he accidentally, and in play, crossed the beat? And that poor man who was shot by that Dutch scoundrel last week, merely because he carelessly threw out his arm in the rascal's way. Oh! I tell you, boys, I want to kill every one of them, from Abe Lincoln down to that old fool, Dick, that swaggers around here, with not sense enough to know how to carry his gun. Never mind; if I ever get out of this infernal place, I'll avenge all the murders that have been committed here. I here swear, boys, eternal hate to the Yankees."

"Amen and amen," responded his companions.

"But, tell me, Charley," resumed his friend, "have you decided on any plan? Will you bribe the guard, or try to get out secretly?"

"Secretly, of course. I would never trust those wretches; and then, besides, I have no money. You know they robbed me of it, and they have never allowed me but two dollars at a time since, of all the money father has sent me."

"They are nothing but thieves and murderers, the best of them, Charley. But never mind, the day will soon come when we'll pay off the reckoning. I tell you, I'll never be surrendered again. I do wish to get out of this infernal place, if it is for nothing more than to shoot the Yankees. However, boys, we settled this score with them at Donelson. We swept them down there by hundreds. But tell us, what about getting out? I will share your fate. If you can go, so can I. Bob, what say you? Are you willing to risk the thing?"

"Yes, John, if the plan is at all feasible, I am ready to undertake it with you and Charley."

"I have no settled plan, boys. Several have passed through my mind, but there are difficulties in the way of them all which I do not know how to overcome. We must not go before our sisters come. But hush, boys; see that guard yonder? he's watching us. We'll meet again."

CHAPTER XV.

THE VISIT OF THE NUNS.

Busy were the minds of the prisoners that night in their endeavors to hit upon some practicable method of escape. Long after the hour of midnight, Charley was canvassing the subject with deep and earnest thought. No scheme suggested itself that was not attended with great difficulties. Even should they succeed in clearing the prison walls, what would they do in a strange and hostile country, with enemies on every side? And should they be overtaken, how greatly would their sufferings be increased! But some risk must be run. Surely the object to be secured was worth the hazard. Thus soliloquized Charley to himself, as he tossed on his hard plank bed. But after hours of feverish thought he could decide upon no plan that appeared to him feasible. And he fell into a disturbed sleep, his brain haunted with visions of attempted escape, arrest, bayonets, and death.

No opportunity presented itself during the following morning for consultation. The meeting must seem accidental, otherwise suspicion would be aroused. The boys were several times together, but always in presence of the guard, or their fellow-prisoners.

Charley and John were busily engaged in a game of ball near the entrance of the inclosure, when their attention was suddenly arrested by the appearance of two nuns, who, escorted by the captain of the guard, stood near the plank gateway. Each nun bore a basket on her arm, and a small package in her hand. The players paused a moment to observe them, but as such visitors were by no means unusual, they resumed again the game. The officer, after having shown the sisters in, left them to pursue their mission of charity unattended.

The two females were clad in deep mourning. Their closely fitting bonnets completely shielded their faces. Timidly they moved along towards the play-ground. Bowing to the guard, and handing him a tract, they proceeded hesitatingly towards the prisoners in front of them.

As they approached, the men left off their game to receive them.

"Some more of the sanctimonious sisters, with their little tracts," said John to a young Mississippian by his side. "They are very anxious indeed about our souls, the hypocrites. I wish they would manifest a more tender regard for our bodies. I think we have done penance enough since we came to this place to atone for all past sins. I don't see what more the veriest saint among them could require at our hands. For my part, I am tired to death of their little books, and their holy advice, and I'll end the matter forthwith this time, by distributing the tracts myself. See how gallantly I'll relieve them of their business, boys," and off the young man hastened on his self-imposed mission, to the great amusement of his comrades, who quit their play for the moment to note his success.

As he neared where the two females stood, he observed the half-raised basket-lid fall from the hand of one of them, who fixed her eyes intently upon him. He felt rather abashed to meet her earnest look, but he had undertaken his work, and would not be thwarted. He knew his companions were observing him.

"Good-morning, ladies," he said, at the same time bowing very cavalierly, and tipping his ragged beaver. "Have you any religious books for us poor sinners this morning? We stand sadly in need of your tracts, good sisters, and are most happy to see that you take such an interest in our spiritual welfare. There are but few who seem to care for us poor rebels. But let me relieve you of the very unpleasant task of going round to distribute your books among all these graceless sinners. Just hand them to me. I assure you it will give me the greatest happiness to aid you in your good work," and he extended his hand to receive the packages.

One of the nuns grasped it nervously. He started back amazed.

"John, don't you know me—Mary, your sister? But hush! for your life don't betray us! We have risked every thing to see you."

The boys, who had been remarking his gallant air, at this juncture burst into a merry laugh. "Served him right!" "served him right!" exclaimed several of them. "He should have left the holy sisters alone, to pursue their labor of love. Wasn't he taken back?" and a loud laugh rang out from the amused beholders.

Our hero stood for a few moments perfectly bewildered. He

could not tell what to think of this strange incident. Could it really be Mary? or was some one trying to deceive him? The young nun looked hastily around at the guard, and seeing that he was intent on the tract she had just handed him, she stepped forward to the young man, lifted her bonnet, and threw back the snowy frill of her muslin cap. The dark, auburn ringlets escaped from their hiding, and fell over the beautiful brow.

John was convinced—petrified. He could scarcely credit his senses.

"Mary! Mary!" he exclaimed. "How on earth came you here?"

"Hush, John, hush, I tell you! We'll be arrested and sent away to a dungeon. Can't you take us to some spot where we won't be observed?"

"Anywhere, so that we'll be removed from the eye of the guard. So here is Charley. He must come with you."

"Where is he—my brother?" asked the sister nervously, speeding from the door.

Quick as thought the prisoner comprehended the whole position. He must be calm, or every thing would be lost. The game must be played, and played successfully. Commanding himself, he took a tract from his sister Mary's basket, and slowly turned the leaves, as if closely examining the little work.

"Your brother is with that group to our right, Miss Lu, but you cannot speak to him now. The prisoners must not know who you are. It might lead to trouble."

"But I can see him, can't I?" asked the young girl, eagerly. "I cannot leave this place until I do."

"You shall see him, if possible. But we shall have to be very careful. If you and Mary are discovered, you will certainly be arrested, and perhaps imprisoned."

He mused for a moment, in deep thought, then looking up, he said:

"Do you see that house to the left? You two pass on towards that, give pamphlets to the prisoners as you go, and I will get Charley and join you directly. There we will be safe to say what we please. But give me some tracts to hand to the boys here—that will divert their attention from us."

The two nuns passed on as directed. John took his tracts and returned to the group.

"Why didn't you relieve the sisters of their mission, John?" the boys asked, laughing, and taunting at his failure. "Your gallantry died out in their presence."

"Oh, they are righteous overmuch, boys—hope to get to heaven on their good deeds—and attach great virtue to distributing their pamphlets. I soon saw they were bent on their purpose, and it was no use for me to offer service. But I succeeded in getting these. Come, poor rebels, learn to do right from these holy books," and saying this, he took the wrapper off and handed them round.

"Here, Charley, my boy, here is one that just suits our case. Throw down your bandy, and let's read it. I don't believe you want to learn your duty. Oh, what a wretched sinner you are!"

"I'm tired to death, John, of these Catholic books. I'm a Protestant, and don't believe one word in their holy water, and penance, and purgatory, and saints. I am just as good as any of them, and I don't intend to bother my head with them any longer."

"But this doesn't say a word about saints and crucifixes. It is an appeal to sinners, and you know you are one. Here, look at this first page," and John whispered a word into his ear as he stood beside him. "Are you not convinced? Come, let's go and read it."

The two set out towards the low, wooden house.

"Hold there, boys," called out Bob, who supposed they were going apart for consultation; "wait, and I'll go with you. I'm a sinner, too, and may be your book will do me good."

Joining his friends, he proceeded with them towards the house. He was hurriedly initiated into the secret as they passed along. The two nuns were overtaken just as they reached the door of the building.

"Here, this door, Mary," and the two brothers entered quickly, followed by the sisters, while Bob lingered outside to look out for any danger.

With difficulty Charley mastered his emotion as he beheld the face of his sister and that of Mary. He scarcely knew how to conduct himself, his surprise and joy were so great. But he must not yield to his emotions—the time was short, and he had much to say.

Mutual surprise and embarrassment were soon succeeded by pleasant and joyous conversation. Kind inquiries were made for friends and acquaintances, and many questions asked about the changes that had taken place in the city since the young men left it.

The fight at Donelson was graphically described to the sisters, and some of the horrors of their two months' imprisonment portrayed to their shuddering hearts.

"But, Charley, why don't you get out of this wretched place?" asked his sister Lu, with tears streaming down her face. "I would rather die in the attempt to escape than remain longer here. I have heard of several prisoners who have succeeded. Can't you do so too?"

"We have that very thing under consideration now, Lu—John, Bob, and I; but we don't see how it is to be done. We were trying all last night to decide upon some plan of escape; but there are so many difficulties in the way, it seems almost hopeless to make any attempt. John, did you come to any conclusion, or you, Bob?"

"None as to the *way*. But I have made up my mind to go out. As Miss Lu says, better die trying than live here."

"Can't you bribe the guards?" said Mary, as she opened her basket, and turning up the tracts, drew forth a well-filled portmonnaie. "Here is enough for three, I should think."

"Hazardous experiment, Miss Mary. These creatures are so treacherous. One of the prisoners gave a sentinel a twenty-dollar gold piece to let him pass; the man, after agreeing to do it, fired his gun, and the poor fellow was retaken, placed in chains, and fed on bread and water for days."

"Well, can't you climb over the wall, or dig out?" she asked, laughing.

"The latter is the only method that seems to me at all practicable, and I have decided to try it. The only obstacle is the dirt. I can't see what we will do with it. If left where it can be seen, it will create suspicion, and every inch around the inclosure would be thoroughly examined."

"Why, the dirt—that's but a small matter, Charley. Put it in your hats and pockets until you get out," suggested Mary, laughingly.

"Capital idea, Mary," exclaimed her brother, springing to his feet. "That's just the thing. The way is open before us. We'll be free, Charley, won't we?"

"But once out, John, how are we to get through to Kentucky? There we would be safe. But how are we to pass through this abolition State without detection?"

"That is a question, Charley, that must be met before we set out. Mary, can you and Miss Lu solve this difficulty for us? Woman's wit is always ready for any emergency."

"Charley, we have a relation, Cousin Sam Lightfoot, living near the railroad, about fifteen miles from Columbus. He is as good a Southern man as you are, and I know he will be glad to assist you. You can go there, and he will direct you how to get through."

"Ah, Miss Lu, I felt sure you could devise some plan for us. If we can get that far out safely, we'll certainly make good our escape."

As the quartette were thus busily engaged in completing these arrangements, Bob suddenly thrust his head in at the door and called out, "Guard."

In a moment the two gay ones subsided into meek and quiet nuns, and with their books presented, were most earnestly urging on their silent listeners the necessity of giving heed to the things pertaining to the world to come.

"I think these two young fellows are in a fair way to become religious," said Bob to the guard, who was an Irishman and a Catholic. "See how penitent they look, while those two good sisters are telling them their duty. I have been reading one of their good little books myself," and he displayed the one John had left with him, "and I do believe the Catholic church is the only true church, after all."

"To be sure it is, sir. It is, indade, the only thrue church, an' there ain't none beside it, at all, at all."

The bait had taken. The man's face lighted into a regular Irish smile. He looked pleasantly into the door, and without comment passed on.

"Here, my friend, you must read this most excellent work," said Bob, calling out to him as he walked off. "I know you'll be delighted with it."

"No, no, thank ye, sir. Kape it yourself. I cannot rade."

"And yet you are called loyal, you old fool, you, and are placed here to guard me, when you know no more about constitution and law than the vile numsculls that put you here," muttered Bob between his teeth, as he looked after the ignorant old man, who, "clothed in a little brief authority," strutted on, as *à la* soldier as it was possible for one of his calibre to do.

The mementoes of love, provided by the hand of affection at home, were given to the young men. Full arrangements for escape were made, hasty adieus given, and the two young girls, with bonnets drawn closely over their faces, sought the door.

"We shall expect you at the appointed time. Success to your undertaking," and with meek, bowed mien the two nuns passed out, distributing their tracts as they went.

Their *ruse* had succeeded fully. Not a suspicion had been aroused, and the two girls returned to Columbus.

CHAPTER XV.

HOW THE PLAN OF ESCAPE SUCCEEDED.

"We must begin our work to-night, Charley. By Saturday morning we are to be at your cousin's. This is Thursday, and if we are entirely successful, we cannot more than accomplish our purpose. But we must tell Bob about it, and see if he approves of our plan."

The young friend was called in, and the matter laid before him. He indorsed it fully, and coincided in the view of promptly beginning the work.

"But, boys, we cannot dig out to-night, and what are we to do with the hole to-morrow? We can carry the dirt in our pockets, as Mary suggested; but who will take care of the opening?"

"We can put our dirty clothes over it, John. You know it is our custom to throw them beside the fence to be washed. This, as it is usual, will create no suspicion."

"Yes, I must have a pair of new pants and shoes; and so must you, Charley. How would we look, my boy, in your cousin's parlor, with this garb on? And, moreover, this will be a good way to save our money. Bob, there, appears quite like a gentleman, with his new suit from top to toe."

"I was fortunate, you see, boys, in getting mine when I did. They still have twenty dollars of my money; but that's a small matter. The rascals are welcome to it, if I can only be allowed to bid them an eternal farewell."

The three young men separated—Charley and Bob returned to the playground, while John went to make application for the pants and shoes.

Night came. Under cover of its thick darkness the three prisoners entered upon their hazardous undertaking. In breathless silence they pursued their work, using only their penknives and three sharp sticks which they had fashioned for the purpose. Not a word was spoken, as assiduously they labored on.

The earth, as fast as removed, was carefully piled together, to be placed in their hats and pockets when the night's work was over. It was a tedious process, but the three prisoners applied themselves like men determined to conquer.

The enclosure, embracing several acres of ground, was surrounded by a high, wooden fence, on top of which were placed planks, at regular intervals, where the guard kept watch, so as to have a view without, as well as within. As with bated breath the three young men worked on, the heavy tramp of the sentinel overhead keeping his lonely watch was distinctly heard. At first his marked footstep struck terror to the hearts of the midnight workmen; but as hour after hour they toiled on, it became familiar music, and it was only its cessation that awoke forebodings.

The night was starless, which greatly favored their purpose, as it shielded them from discovery on every hand.

Hour after hour they toiled on, never for a moment pausing in their undertaking. At three o'clock in the morning, as the first faint beams of the rising morn, struggling through the rifted clouds, began to light up the dark landscape, they carefully gathered up the new earth, filled their hats, pockets, shoes, socks, etc., threw the heap of soiled clothing over the opening, and stealthily crept away and secreted themselves until morning.

Finding their weight of dirt burdensome, they deposited it under some loose planks in their sleeping-room.

Early application was made for the new outfits that had been selected the previous evening. They were furnished during the afternoon. Immediately the old garments were doffed in favor of their successful rivals. The remaining hours of the day were spent in sleep.

It is ten o'clock at night. Most of the prisoners have retired to rest—some on the floor of their rude plank house; others, preferring the open air to the noisome rooms, have thrown themselves on the ground, with no covering save a blanket. The sentries are on duty. No sound is heard but the dead monotone of their heavy tramp. The stars are out to-night, but their radiance, soft and mild, throws but a dreamy light over the scene.

Noiselessly the prisoners arise from their pallets. Not a word is spoken as they pass on among their sleepy companions. They gain the open air, and pause to look about them that they may be assured of their safety. Charley ventures first, the two follow, each several paces behind the other, so that if one shall be discovered it may not involve his companions. Breathlessly they steal along like shadows in the faint starlight. Charley is within a few paces of the outlet. The sentinel halts in his round and pauses to listen. The prisoner crouches to the ground, and screens himself in the dark shadow of a house. His comrades mark his movement and follow his example.

A moment more the sentry, reassured, resumes his round. Charley glides back to where his friends are in their hiding-places, whispers to them the incident and his fears. The **three crouch together near the** house, and in low tones canvass the **prospect before them.** It is at length decided to remain in their present position until the guard, weary **with** watching, shall slumber at his post.

Eleven o'clock. They **rise and** stealthily approach the **scene of** their last night's labors. The sentinel no longer treads his weary beat; his eyes have become heavy with his night-watching, and he leans upon his gun. Now is their time for action. In one hour, and the guard will be relieved. Before that time their work must be accomplished, if at all.

The prisoners gain the spot, throw aside the heap of clothing, and apply themselves to the removal of the earth that intervenes **between them and the world without. They** work with silent desperation. A half hour more and the task is accomplished. **Who shall venture first?** The moments flee—there is no time for parley.

John shall lead, as he is smallest. With difficulty he makes his way through. But he is at last successful, and stands outside the prison walls. The two within enlarge the opening with their sharp sticks. A few moments more, and they are beside their comrade. Novel position—they can scarcely **realize it.** Once more at liberty, beyond the pale of that high frowning wall, which, for two long weary months has shut them in from freedom.

They pause **a** moment to assure themselves that they are not discovered. **All is unbroken stillness. The sentinel** sleeps on. Thank God, they are free!

"Come, boys, profound silence, as you value your lives. **Follow me,"** and Charley leads the way through the buildings without. They gain the open ground, and set out in the direction of the railroad.

CHAPTER XVI.

THE MEETING—HOME VISIT.

Rapidly as they could, and avoiding the city, the three soldiers made their onward way. A few miles passed, and they had reached the road. Following its track, they proceeded several miles at a quick pace, when, feeling that they were fully beyond the reach of danger, as their escape could not be discovered before the morning, they halted to rest. Hungry and weary were they, but they had nothing to eat, nor could they spare time to sleep.

"We must reach our destination before morning, boys. There may be Abolition enemies in the neighborhood, who would certainly inform against us, if they knew we were there, and cause our arrest."

"And then the girls are anxiously looking for us now, Charley," added John. "And I fancy we will not be averse to meeting them. We promised them, if we could get out, we would reach your cousins before morning. How happy they will be when they see we are safe!"

After resting themselves a while they resumed their journey, beguiling the long dark hours with bright plans for the future.

"We talk, boys, as if we were surely out of the reach of the lion's paw. For my part, I cannot see how we are to get from here to Louisville, and from there to our army," said Bob, whose usually hopeful nature seemed to have yielded to a certain degree of timidity, which prevented him from indulging in any bright anticipations.

"Oh, if we can but reach the city, Bob, I do not fear beyond that. All southern Kentucky is right, and every man we meet will befriend us. We will have to trust ourselves to the ingenuity of the girls to provide for our safety to Louisville. I am sure they can manage the case for us. Don't you think so, Charley?"

"I am confident of it, John. I would not hesitate for a moment to trust them for a release from Fort Lafayette itself. Their visit to us proves them equal to any emergency. It was a novel affair, really. Who would have thought that those two demure-looking nuns, with their baskets of tracts, were our merry, timid sisters, come to plan our escape from prison? If I were a writer I'd immortalize these heroines."

"Your sisters deserve immortality and fame, boys. I do believe we should now and forever have been in that miserable place if they had not encouraged us in our undertaking."

"You are right, Bob. And yet, what an easy matter it was after all!"

"And how sad a matter it would have been, Charley, if we had been discovered! The fates were propitious, and the Dutchman was sleepy, so we made our way out; and now we shall be breveted among our friends for gallant conduct and heroic daring, when really I do not believe our emotions ever rose a whit above selfishness."

The three indulged in a hearty laugh over their success, and humming a verse or two of Dixie, they pursued their way cheerily on.

"I have been thinking, boys," said John, breaking the silence, "that if we could procure a genteel coat and hat each, we might take the cars to-morrow for Cincinnati, and go from there to Louisville by boat. Wouldn't it be pleasant once more to act the gentleman and be in society?"

"You are right, John. It would be delightful, indeed, to see ourselves acknowledged gentlemen, we have so long been treated as brutes. But getting the clothes is the rub. We are gentlemen now, forsooth, but unfortunately minus the cash; and how to supply this very sad need, I must acknowledge myself wholly inadequate to suggest. Can you give me any light, boys?"

"Oh, leave that to the girls, Bob; they will meet the case. I am sure they have discussed every possible plan, and I'll venture they have already selected the one most likely to succeed."

The faint gleams of morning were just beginning to tinge the eastern sky. The pedestrians, weary and worn, were looking out with longing hearts for their destination.

"That must be the house, boys, there to the left. Look! don't you see the light in the front windows? That was the signal the girls agreed upon, and surely we have come fifteen miles since we struck the railroad."

Charley was right. That was the house, and the two sisters, with Cousin Sam and his wife, were in the parlor awaiting them.

Joyous was the meeting between the young girls and the escaped prisoners. Very little like nuns did the two glad young creatures look as they welcomed their brothers and their friend to liberty. A lunch had been prepared by the kind hostess, and never was food more enjoyed than by these three half-starved men. It had been many a month since they had enjoyed the luxury of a private table, and they declared that, in honor to their hostess and their own appetites, they must make amends for past neglect.

It was very soon determined—for no time could be lost—that Charley, with the addition of a coat and hat to his toilet, should accompany the young ladies to Louisville, while his companions, under such directions as Mr. Lightfoot could give them, should make their way on foot to Cincinnati; there cross the Ohio river into Boone county, where Bob had friends, who would provide them safe conduct to the city. Accordingly, the morning found the two young ladies, with their escort, looking quite à la mode, seated in the cars bound for Cincinnati. The following night they were safely landed at Louisville. Here, to avoid any possibility of exposure, a hack was taken, and at that late hour the party drove out to Mr. R.'s.

Words are powerless to express the joy in the homestead when Charley was welcomed back to its affection and comforts. The mother's heart overflowed with tenderness as she pressed him to her bosom, while great tears of joy streamed down her face; and the father's soul swelled high with grateful pride as he clasped his noble boy in his arms, while the sisters and brother heaped upon him affectionate caresses, and were never weary of lingering near him to listen to the recital of his varied adventures. And our young hero, amid the happiness which surrounded him, forgot for the time the trials and sufferings of the past two months. Mary remained with the family to await the arrival of her brother, and her presence was to Charley as that of an angel visitant. Vows of love, long ago given, were renewed, to be consummated when independence and peace should bless the Southern Confederacy. There was but one shadow resting over the sunny scene. It was the sad thought, that hid itself away in the bosom of each, that soon—ah! too soon—must come the bitter parting.

CHAPTER XVII.

THE PEDESTRIANS.

Beneath the old oak-tree, whose bursting buds were unfolding tender leaves of green, sat Mary and Charley. It was the last evening of his stay at home. To-morrow, ere the sun should begin its daily circuit, he must bid farewell to loved ones, and go to seek a life of exile and danger.

The evening sun, declining low in the west, threw its golden glory in long lines of living light back upon the earth, now springing into life and beauty. Fleecy clouds of white floated lazily through the azure heavens, catching upon their western margins the radiant hues of the departing sun; and as the eye looked up into the vault above, the soul could fancy itself gazing up—up through the blue empyrean—beyond sun and moon and remotest star—into the glorious splendor of the New Jerusalem, whose sapphirine beauties beamed from out their far-off heavenly home down upon the emerald earth. The evening wind swept gently by, kissing the grass-blades and the tender leaflets, and bearing the sweet breath of the lovely violet that nestled in its modest loneliness beside the field fence-row and at the foot of the giant forest-tree.

Before them lay the city, its distant spires gleaming in the gorgeous rays of the setting sun, its busy hum falling on the listening ear like the dull monotone of a mournful dirge. Beyond it rose the dark blue outline of the hills which skirt the northern bank of the beautiful Ohio. It was a charming scene. One that might invite the pencil of Claude Lorraine. The lovers had long been seated at the foot of the old familiar tree, talking over their present, past, and future, and sealing in words of love's own eloquent truth the vows long ago pledged. To their young and bursting hearts the coming years gave promise of joy and gladness. Yet over that radiant pathway there could be discovered, even by their inexperienced vision, the shadow—aye, the gloom.

Why is it thus, that even in our most joyous moments the heart is ever aware of these gathering clouds, which, though all unseen, throw their darkling shade over our life-path? Is it that the malediction pronounced upon our first parents, as they turned their weeping eyes for the last time upon their lost Eden, and bent their burdened step out into the unknown waste before them, has found lodgment in our fallen nature—is so burnt in upon the struggling soul of man, that he needs not bitter experience to teach him that the evil ever accompanies the good?

As the dancing wind lifted the dark auburn ringlets from the passive brow of Mary, and kissed with its cooling breath her cheek, flushing with love's own holy kindlings, Charley gazed upon her with silent admiration. Tears started to his eyes, and his oppressed heart sighed heavily.

Mary turned her eyes with a look of sorrow upward to his.

"Why do you sigh, Charley?" she asked in tones of tenderness. "It is sad to part, but you know there is no safety here for you. They would take you from us, and put you in prison. We must bear this trial as heroically as we can. It is a deep, deep one, but there is no other hope."

"I feel reproved, Mary," he replied, "by your words of truth and courage. It is not the parting—and God knows this is bitter enough—neither is it dread of the battle-field that thus oppresses me; but—" and he paused, as if unwilling to proceed; "but—Mary, pardon me, I would not do you injustice—you are young, you will be courted, flattered, tempted. I do not doubt your truth—heaven knows I do not—and yet—and yet—I cannot tell why, when I think on this, my brain burns, my heart throbs with the wildest torment. Young Morton—Mary, do not, I beseech you, trust him. He is made to win—and to deceive."

"Oh, Charley, Charley! how can you do me this great wrong? Why do you doubt me? Have you not proved my love, and found it constant, undying? Am I younger now than when we last parted? Did I prove faithless? why should I now?" And the young girl burst into a flood of tears.

"Oh, forgive me, Mary," said Charley, tenderly, gently drawing her towards him, and kissing her burning cheek. "I do not doubt you, and yet—and yet my heart thrills with a strange emotion, when I think of the future. The form of Morton haunts me."

"You need not torture yourself with apprehensions of him,' said Mary, looking confidingly up into her lover's face. "Our love was merely the fancy of our childish hearts, a wild, foolish admiration for each other, because we called each other sweethearts. I may never see him again. You know he is speaking of joining the Federal army."

"God grant he may," was Charley's earnest response.

The two arose, and walked towards the house. In the front yard they were met by Lu, whose saddened face told of the sorrow of her loving heart.

"Mother has sent me to seek you two. She wishes Charley to supervise some little preparation she is making for him."

Charley, resigning Mary to his sister, who conducted her to the parlor, passed to his mother's room to furnish any necessary suggestions.

An hour later, and the family, grouped in the parlor, were discussing the probability of the recapture of the two young soldiers, when a loud and hasty knock at the door interrupted the conversation for a moment. The servant announced two gentlemen. They were shown into the parlor. Mr. R. rose, bowed politely, and asked them forward to the fire. The visitors returned the salutation without speaking, and advanced.

"It is brother!" exclaimed Mary, springing from her seat on the sofa, and throwing her arms around the young man's neck.

"Why, John and Bob, can it be you?" said Charley, seizing a hand of each. "We were just speaking of you. Didn't know but that the Yankees had you again; we were fearful we should never see you."

The two heroes were heartily welcomed by all, and many were the congratulations offered on their safe arrival.

"Well, John, if you and Mr. Reed had suffered yourselves to be again taken by the Yankees, we should have left you to your fate. Wouldn't we, Lu? Couldn't turn nun again, and run all the risk of being discovered a second time to effect an escape for you." And Mary laughed one of her sweet, merry laughs, while she looked archly first at her brother, and then at her friend, whose cheeks were suffused with crimson blushes.

"Indeed, Miss Mary, I do not think we should be deserted by the ladies in our misfortunes," replied young Reed. "You know it would be no fault of ours, if we were even now within the gloomy walls of Camp Chase, instead of being here in this most delectable society: and I feel assured that you would again, in the generousness of your heart, rush to our rescue. Don't you think so, Charley?" and Reed looked quizzically at the young lover, whose eyes were riveted on the bright, smiling face of Mary.

It was now Charley's time to blush, which he did deeply, notwithstanding his efforts to subdue his rising emotion.

"Indeed, indeed, Mr. Reed, you are mistaken!" exclaimed Mary, animatedly, at the same time manifesting the embarrassment which seemed to be becoming general among the young members of the circle. "I advise you, gentlemen, to avoid, at all hazards, another introduction to a Federal prison, lest, unhappily, no angels of mercy should come to your rescue."

"A word to the wise man is sufficient, Mr. Reed," interposed Lu, pleasantly, who had been silently listening to the badinage. "I am sure you will never again thus test our courage and kindness."

"But tell us, young gentlemen," said Mr. R., who was impatient to hear the young men's story, "how you succeeded in getting through to Kentucky. We have been in a most anxious state of mind, with regard to your welfare. I suppose you have had some adventures by the way—perhaps some narrow escapes from the Yankees."

"We feared that they had caught you," said Mrs. R., her kind, motherly face speaking more than her words the interest of her heart. "And Charley had decided to leave to-morrow, lest he should share the same fate."

"How do you go, Charley?" asked young Lawrence. "I suppose you have some plan marked out for getting through?"

"None, John; I must trust to my wits. Several friends have suggested to me methods, but all of them are alike full of risk. I think I know enough of the country through which I am to pass, and enough of Yankee character, to make good my way to Colonel Morgan."

"Ah, you intend to join Morgan, do you? John, that will be the idea for us. I am heartily tired of infantry life. And, moreover, we need the exercise and dash of cavalry-men to restore us to our former vigor. Do we not, young ladies?" said Reed, with a polite bow to his fair listeners.

"Most assuredly," they both replied. "Life with Morgan for health and fame."

"But how do you propose to get through, gentlemen?" asked Charley. "Now that you are so experienced in eluding the vigilance of the foe, doubtless, you can aid me on my way."

"We go through like gentlemen, Charley," responded young Reed, laughing. "Do you not think we are entitled to this privilege, in virtue of these handsome new suits?" he added, at the same time rising from his chair, and displaying his finished **suit of** black clothes.

"Undoubtedly, you deserve all the privileges due to gentlemen," responded Charley, looking somewhat bewildered at young Reed's manner and remark, "but I fear me you will find your new suit of black but a poor safeguard against Yankee watchfulness and hate."

"Oh, my friend, we by no means depend on our attire for passport through the lines; only look to it to secure us the civilities by the way due to Kentucky gentlemen. We take the boat to-morrow or next day, provided these officials do not have us in the military prison before then, and shall depend on our permits to secure us safe transit to Dixie."

"Permits, Bob; what do you mean?" and Charley's look of wonder and perplexity increased.

"Oh, we go out as **cotton agents, duly authorized.** Here, examine our papers, and see **if it is not so,**" and Reed took from his pocket and handed to Charley some **papers,** which the latter took and examined carefully; then, with an expression of mingled surprise and doubt, gazed up into the face of his facetious friend, who, with young Lawrence, was highly enjoying Charley's entanglement. This last **remark of Reed's** had aroused the inquisitiveness of every one present, and a look of curious inquiry rested on each face.

Charley opened the permits, and read them a second time.

"Boys, are these genuine?" he asked, after duly scrutinizing them again and again. "Or do you design to attempt to out-Herod Herod?"

"Genuine! of course," replied Reed, with an assumed air of insulted dignity, at this insinuation against his honor, and that of his friend. "Do you not see they are duly signed?"

"But, if genuine, how did you obtain them? Certainly, you must have in some way imposed on somebody."

"Why, Charley, my friend, have not James Safford, Esq., and John Livingston, ditto, true and loyal men, who have endured long and dreary exile from home and friends beloved, because of their ardent devotion to this glorious 'Union,' 'the dear old flag,' and 'the best government in the world,' have not these patriots, so distinguished for their sufferings, a right to the protection of that government, and a small share of its profits?"

This pseudo-panegyric on his own patriotism was delivered in such a farcical manner, that the whole company burst into laughter. Charley shared the merriment, but with less zest than the others.

"Well, boys," said he, "**you** puzzle me more and more."

"Do tell us the meaning of these official documents, and explain to us how they were procured."

"**Oh,** do tell us the whole story," cried **out several** voices. "We would **hear** all your adventures through **Ohio and** Kentucky to Louisville."

"Our **hegira** from Camp **Chase** was attended by no incidents worth the mention until we came to Cincinnati. We traveled on like two common workmen, avoiding every thing that looked suspicious, stopping at night wherever darkness overtook **us, behaving** very much like poor men all unused to society—that is, **playing** *mum* on all subjects until we ascertained **the sentiments of our** host; if adverse to **ours, we declared lustily in favor of the glorious** Union, *tiraded* against **the rebels, and after that played mum for** the remainder of the night.

"If, however, we discovered that we were in congenial society, and this was our good fortune two nights out of four, we gave full rein to our powers of entertainment, related all our adventures, answered the many hundred questions propounded to us by our eager listeners, and in our turn gained all the intelligence we could about the Yankees and their movements.

"Tuesday night, **weary and** worn with our **tramp, we** halted with an old avaricious Jew, just outside Cincinnati. **We told him** we were from Tennessee. He immediately asked if we knew **any** thing **about** the cotton section. John caught his idea in **a moment, and,** determining to make capital **out of it,** readily answered that **we were well** acquainted with all **the cotton** region of that State; **that** our fathers **were** heavy **planters, and now** had on hand a very large **amount of that very desirable article.** The bait had taken. The old man's eye flashed with delight under this intelligence, and he hinted his desire to buy **cotton, intimating his fear to be found in Tennessee, lest** he should **be overtaken by the rebels.** We cautiously proposed to act as his agents should he desire it.

"His **keen** black eye twinkled with **the** joy that filled his bosom, **and** he unhesitatingly accepted our **offer.** He agreed to pay us a commission on delivery of the **cotton** at Cincinnati. We acceded to this, **and the** contract was immediately drawn and duly signed.

"The next morning he took us to headquarters in the city, procured for us permits, and seeing **we** were in rather a sorry plight, **opened his** narrow Jewish heart sufficiently to give **us a** new hat and coat each, paid **our** passage to Louisville, and sent **us out on** our most lucrative agency. And here we are to prosecute our undertaking like gentlemen **of** the strictest integrity and highest business ability."

"Bravo!" exclaimed one and all, as **Bob finished his story,** "you deserve a medal for your triumph."

"Or to be brevetted," added Charley.

"So you see our stay among the Hoosiers has rather sharpened our wits, and Bob and I feel that no emergency can arise in the future that will seriously trouble us."

"And **you leave to-morrow, do you, boys?" asked Mr. R.** "I wish Charley **would go with you. I do not at all like the thought** of his setting **out alone to travel so far through the enemy's** territory."

"Yes, sir," responded young Lawrence; "we shall take the first Cincinnati boat. This will obviate the necessity of renewing our permits. Charley," said he, turning and addressing his young friend, "cannot we devise some plan that will insure your safety **with us?"**

"I fear not, John. We should have to practice so much deception, **and I should be so much more** public than in a land trip, I think **I prefer the risks of the latter.** I shall leave very early to-morrow morning, and hope soon **to join you** and Bob in Dixie **land, where, under the** victorious banner of Colonel Morgan, we **shall avenge our wrongs and the wrongs** of the noble fellows who **yet pine** amid the cruelty of Camp Chase."

Supper was announced, after which the **family** reassembled in the parlor, where music and cheerful conversation made pleasant the fast fleeting hours. **Southern songs were** sung by the young people, in which Mr. and Mrs. **R. joined with** that zest which told, in word and **look, their devotion to** the cause to which they had yielded up **their son. The** hours tripped **by** with rosy feet. Yet there **were moments when** the heart, leaving behind the delights **of the present, looked out with** trembling on the sad parting of the morrow.

The hour came **for** the young men to leave, as it was necessary for them to be in the city, that they might avail themselves of the first Cincinnati packet. With renewed pledges of friendship and mutual wishes for safety and success, the three young men bade **each** other adieu.

CHAPTER XVIII.

THE NASHVILLE PENITENTIARY.

The morning came. Charley was ready to set out on his perilous journey. We need not describe the parting. Ah, has not every homestead throughout the land witnessed the same sad scene? And the heart has but to recall its own bitter experience to realize the gloom of that darkened household, as the angel of grief folded its wing over each stricken bosom.

We would not invade the sacred sorrow of the young loving heart of her who was now called upon to yield up to the dread chances of war that heart's idol. It were sacrilegious to invade the hallowed temple where, mid the purity of such deathless affection and the clinging memories of the years gone by, the beloved image sat enshrined.

Ah, how very poor is all language to express the keen emotions of joy and sorrow that the human heart is capable of experiencing! No analysis can do justice to the varied shades of feeling that move its inmost springs, and full often, even in a moment of time, give rise to thoughts and emotions that influence the life throughout all coming time.

Circumstances light as straws are levers in the building up of character.

Fired with a loftier devotion to the cause he had embraced, since by sore experience he had become acquainted with the infamy and injustice of those who opposed it, inured to deprivations and sufferings, with a score of deep personal wrongs to avenge, our young hero left home a second time to engage in the great struggle a wiser and a more determined man.

By the exercise of his ingenuity and daring, both of which had greatly developed under the stern teachings of the last eight months, he succeeded in reaching Gallatin, Tennessee. From here it was his intention to proceed to the vicinity of Nashville, hoping that, as Colonel Morgan was frequently dashing around in the neighborhood of that city, he should be able to join his command without delay.

Leaving Gallatin, he crossed the Cumberland, and was proceeding towards Nashville, when one morning about 6 o'clock he was accosted by a squad of Lincolnites, who imperatively bade him halt. His astonishment was so great at this unexpected meeting with the enemy, that for the moment **he lost** his self-possession, **and before he could** recover his equipoise, **he** found himself surrounded **by six burly** Indianians, who, seizing his bridal-rein and presenting their pistols to his breast, claimed him as their prisoner.

Recovering himself, he manifested great surprise and indignation, protesting against their act, alleging that they had **no right to arrest him, an unarmed** citizen, who was passing **through the** country on business of his own.

They questioned him closely, evidently not at all satisfied **with** his story, and his answers, ambiguous and indefinite as they necessarily were, fixed their suspicions. **He was arrested, sent under** guard to Nashville, where, refusing to take the oath, he was committed to prison as a spy. And thus in a few brief hours were all his bright expectations, all his joyous hopes, dashed as by the hand of some pitiless divinity, and he whose soul had panted for the contest and the fray, whose thoughts had dwelt but upon **glory and** revenge, **found himself a helpless,** hopeless prisoner in the power of his detested foe.

Ah, **how bitter were his reflections as** he lay in his narrow cell, isolated from the world without, friendless, devoid of hope! Despair came to be a guest with him, overshadowing, with its leaden wing, both present and future, and the two sat down together over the grave of buried joy and blighted hope, to mourn unavailingly.

After a few days passed in this deep **despondency, our young** hero rallied, and, with that desperation that impels to the most daring exertions, he roused himself, resolving to escape or perish in the attempt.

He soon managed through another prisoner, a young Tennesseean, who enjoyed **more privileges than did** Charley, to make **known** his condition to some Southern gentleman of the city, who undertook to effect his **release.** His case underwent investigation; nothing could be substantiated against him, and he was offered liberty on condition that he would take the oath. This he peremptorily refused to do, urging that they had no right thus to question his loyalty, and, unless they could satisfactorily establish that he had compromised it, it was an insult to his honor to require him to take any **oath.**

This course of reasoning being by no means convincing to the obtuse minds of his judges, he was remanded to prison.

Loathsome, beyond the power of words to portray, was the cell allotted to him. Filled with vermin of all kinds, with a negro on one side and a criminal on the other; shut out from the light of day, damp and noisome, it would have been cruelty to have immured a felon of the most atrocious character within its dreadful walls. Added to this, the meagre exercise he was permitted to take was insufficient to preserve his health, and his food, of the coarsest and most unwholesome nature, was furnished in such scant quantities, as scarcely to support life. All he had undergone at Camp Chase was as nothing compared to his present tortures. He soon became convinced that without a change he must die—yet he would not take the oath.

Charley had been in **prison about a** week, when one morning early he was suddenly **aroused by a noise** in front of his cell. **Starting to his feet, he peered through the iron bars of** his grate, **to endeavor to ascertain the cause.**

By the flickering light of the lamp, he saw a young man forced **along by** two of the guard, who held him on either side. He was **tall,** handsome, and **wore the defiant look of one** who had made **up his** mind never to yield. The prisoner was dressed in citizen's **garb, but his sun-browned** brow and military air bespoke him a **soldier.**

With a brutal oath he was rudely thrust by the coarse, unfeeling men into the second cell from Charley.

"Who can this be?" soliloquized Charley, as he threw himself **back** upon his iron bed, and passed his hand over his forehead, **as** if to collect his scattered thoughts. "He cannot be a convict? No, no. That fine face, and manly form, and air of *hauteur*, can belong to none other than a gentleman. How defiantly he scowled on the guard that bore him **along. There is spirit not to be** subdued in that breast. The true, genuine soul that defies time **and** circumstance, and acknowledges no **conqueror but death.** I **almost fancy I have seen that face before, and that proud form looks strangely familiar. He must be a** Kentuckian—one of Morgan's men. Looks something like Colonel Morgan himself—so brave, so noble, so daring. Can it be he? Oh, no; *he* would die first. I do wish I knew who it is. I'll make his acquaintance the first opportunity. **Wonder if he would take** that oath—*that vile, detestable oath!* I'm sure he will **not.** No one with that look would ever submit **to such degradation!** So we shall be fellow-prisoners for a long time. Perhaps"—and Charley shuddered at the dark thought—"perhaps for life. We may both die **in this** horrid place."

Charley made his plain toilet with a degree of animation he had never before felt since he entered that dark and noisome abode. **While** he was thus engaged, a strain of music arrested his attention. **He pressed his ear** close **to** the iron bars to catch the words—

> " Awake and to horse, my brothers—
> Look up to the rising sun,
> And ask of the God that shines there,
> If deeds like these shall be done?"

He listened. The thrilling words were repeated. The **voice** was clear and musical, and, although somewhat subdued, **the expression** bespoke the strong, deep feeling of the heart that **gave** utterance to the stirring words.

"Hush your singing there, fellow, and behave yourself," said the guard, in a coarse, gruff tone, as he passed by. The music ceased. Charley fancied he heard a suppressed oath. But he was mistaken. **The dark** vow of vengeance was uttered only by the bursting heart. It needed not words to give it strength of purpose or remembrance.

"**I go from here at all hazards. I go to be avenged.** This insult shall be atoned for by blood."

Thus vowed the prisoner, as, with fury-lit eyes and **elevated** hands, he stood beside his barred door, and **looked upon the wretch** who had insulted him. And fearfully has that **vow been kept.** Beside the low Muskingum, where the evening winds wail through the forest-trees a sad requiem for the slain, in the desolate **cottage** sits the lone widow, with her three little children, mourning over the lost husband. She knows not where he lies. But this she has heard, " He was killed by **one of Morgan's men.**"

CHAPTER XIX.

THE PRISON CHAT.

At breakfast the two prisoners met. Glances were exchanged. It was enough. They understood each other, and as they filed out, Charley touched the young man on the shoulder, and whispered "Southern?"

A slight nod of the head, and a smile was the only reply.

"Meet me in the courtyard," Charley said, in an undertone; "I want to talk with you."

It was several days before the proposed interview took place, for at first the young man was not permitted to leave his cell, except to come to his meals. In the mean time Charley had learned, from snatches of conversation in going to and from the table, that the prisoner was one of Morgan's men, caught within the Federal lines. But as he was in civilian's garb when arrested, and not known to any one in Nashville, it was not likely his punishment would be any thing more than imprisonment.

At length, after a week's close confinement, the young man was permitted to walk in the open court with the other political prisoners.

The first opportunity that offered for conversation was eagerly seized upon by the two Kentuckians, to inquire into the past history of each other, and lay plans for future action.

"I came out from Kentucky last September with Colonel Morgan, and have been with him since until a few weeks ago," replied the young man to Charley's interrogatory.

"Then we have met before. I, too, was in 'Camp Secret,' and came through with that fearful expedition to Green River. There I joined Colonel Hanson's regiment—"

"And were taken prisoner at Donelson?" interrupted the listener, eagerly.

"Yes, and sent with others to Camp Chase."

"And escaped from prison? How did you succeed in doing it,

and how came you here?" asked the young man, hurriedly, his face brightening with the interest he felt in the fate of his new acquaintance.

Charley briefly and graphically recounted his story. His companion listened with breathless attention.

"Quite an adventure, indeed. You are already a hero. How unfortunate that after all your trials, and your successful escape, you should again be taken and lodged in this disgusting place. Better by far be in Camp Chase than in this miserable place. Surely no other prison-house in all the range of Yankeedom can be as horrid as this!"

"That is wretched enough, I assure you, but this is far worse. But I find the same brutality and coarseness characterize their officers and guard everywhere; in this respect I discover no difference."

"Can this be so? I had supposed that on their own soil, removed from any apprehension of danger, and free from the provoking influences of daily contact with Southern people, they would manifest some degree of humanity. I know they are everywhere cold, heartless, and overbearing; but I thought they must be more brutal here than there."

"No better there than here. Vulgarity, coarseness, I might say fiendishness, are each day experienced by the prisoners at Camp Chase, and there remains to them no redress. I will give you an illustration of their savage cruelty in one of the most heartless incidents that ever blackened the record of any people, however savage. It took place while I was a prisoner there.

"A poor man was arrested in Western Virginia for alleged disloyalty. As usual, no charge was brought against him, save this general one. He was told that he must go to prison with the guard. 'To what prison?' he asked. 'No matter to what prison,' they answered with an oath. 'You must go with us, and that right away. We have no time to wait.' It was night. The wretched man knew not what to do, for in the low bed beside him slept his three motherless children. He felt he must obey the inhuman order, but how could he leave his little ones without protection, without any one to care for them? The eldest was nine, the youngest only three years old. An old negro woman, who attended to the children, was the only being about the house, and she was no safeguard against the brutal soldiery that infested the neighborhood. In his great extremity, not knowing what else to do, the wretched father besought his captors to allow his children to go with him to prison. The request, strange to say, was granted. The four were brought to Camp Chase. The poor man was placed in strict confinement; his children were imprisoned in another part of the ground. They were never permitted to see **each other.** With the most heart-rending entreaties the stricken father implored to see his children—only once. The children wept and prayed to see the father. Day after day, week after week, **were** entreaties, groans, and cries poured into the deaf ear of the **hellish** guard. But all was useless. Their **hearts were** harder than the adamant—the permission was never granted.

"The health of the heart-broken man gave way under his heavy grief and close confinement. He languished on amid his dark sorrows, and then died. In his **last moments he prayed, entreated,** besought them just to let him see his children once, that he might bless them before he closed **his eyes in death. He was** told his **children were doing very** well, but he could not see them.

"And thus, calling for 'his children,' his 'poor little children,' his 'motherless children,' the agonized spirit of that poor outraged father went up with its tale of deep, damning wrong before the tribunal of the Lord Jehovah."

The young man grew pale as he listened. "My God!" exclaimed he, springing to his feet and clenching his hands, as if in a paroxysm, "was there ever, ever such brutality, such dark, hellish cruelty. God in heaven will avenge that injured man. I swear by all that's holy, that if ever again I meet these fiends on the battle-field, the thoughts of that poor man's wrongs shall move my heart to do, and dare, and die, that he and his helpless children may be avenged."

"And I have seen the guard shoot a man dead merely because in play he had accidentally stepped beyond the limits assigned him. And again, another was shot by a vile Dutchman because he carelessly threw his arm across the wretch's path."

"And what, sir, have we to hope from such a people?" exclaimed the young man, clenching his teeth, while his face assumed a **look of desperate** revenge. "Call them brothers, friends? They are devils incarnate—fiends from the lowest pit. Never, never could I recognize them in any other light than foes, enemies that must be defeated, swept from the face of the earth. Oh, that every Southern man could hear that tale of cruelty, that it might nerve his arm in the day of conflict! Blood for blood, life for life! They drive us to it, sir, and I take the issue."

The young man's face was flushed with the wildest excitement.

His whole frame trembled—he started forward as if to meet the dastard foe.

For several minutes not a word was spoken. The resolves of that fearful moment were never forgotten.

The bell rang that summoned the prisoners to their wretched supper.

In a few days the two met again. The conversation turned upon the feasibility of escape, and joining Colonel Morgan.

"I have heard of many wonderful feats performed by **Colonel Morgan** in the vicinity of this place," said Charley to his new-formed acquaintance, **as the two seated** themselves on some loose stones, beneath the shadow of the frowning wall. I suppose his daring is remarkable?"

"There is not, sir, a braver or more resolute man living. I have been with him in most of his adventures, and such courage, combined with foresight and caution, I have never in my life witnessed. On one occasion, very soon after the Yankees took possession of this place, few, about thirty in number, dressed in Federal uniform, under the direction of Colonel Morgan, swept **round** the city, and, obtaining a good position on the other side of **the river,** halted for a few minutes to plan an attack. Our object **was to set** fire to two boats which were above the fleet in the river, and send them enveloped in flames to communicate the fire to the **others. As I** remarked, we halted some little distance out from the city. Colonel Morgan then dispatched five of us into **town to fire the boats.** Uniformed like the Yankees, we passed along the streets unnoticed."

"Did you do this during the day?" asked Charley, in surprise.

"Oh, yes, it was early in the evening. **Following Colonel Morgan's** instructions, we crossed the river to this side, the boats being at the main landing, walked leisurely through the streets, encountering everywhere Yankee soldiers and civilians, gained the point nearest the lower boat, which stood out a little way in the **river.** It was an old affair, and was left in the possession of negroes and three Irish soldiers. Securing a yawl that was near, we put out for the boat. On reaching it, young Winfield, from Lexington, took command of the arrangements. We boarded the boat, **and** ordered off to shore the three Irish soldiers and a portion of the negroes, with instructions that they should be landed and the yawl brought back to the boat. Winfield ordered every man remaining on board to get into the yawl. He then proceeded alone to fire the boat at four different points. This done, he left the vessel, from which the flames were already bursting, and jumping into the yawl, commanded the boatmen, at the peril of their lives, to row to the opposite side. Before we reached the bank the boat, which was now slowly floating down the river, was discovered by the Yankees to be on fire. Great was the consternation in their ranks when this became known, as the fleet below contained many sick soldiers. We reached the bank, waved our hats at the affrighted Yankees congregated on the opposite side, bade them adieu, and, finding our horses, returned safely to the command."

"And did your plan succeed? It certainly was full of daring."

"We have learned from the Yankee papers that the boat was arrested in its downward course in time to save the other boats. What damage they suffered we did not learn. A few days after this, as Colonel Morgan was riding in advance of the body of his men, accompanied by only two others, he met a Yankee colonel and his staff trotting along very leisurely. 'Halt,' said Morgan.

"'I'll be d—d if I do,' was the reply; 'I have already been halted a half dozen times since I left Nashville, and I'll submit to it no longer. Who are you, any how?'

"Morgan quickly drew out his pistol and presented it. 'Morgan,' he very quietly replied to the Yankee's interrogatory. 'And you are my prisoner.'

"The Yankee made no further resistance. He and his escort, beside a considerable force which followed in the rear, were made prisoners by Morgan and his men. We were pursued by a heavy Federal force, and young Winfield, who was guiding the rear detachment, after having two horses shot under him, was taken prisoner. The remainder escaped."

"And where is he now?" asked Charley.

"In Camp Douglas. He was for a long time confined here, but they fearing he would be rescued finally sent him north.

"On another occasion, about forty of us in number, headed by Morgan, dashed in upon their pickets one morning early, and captured eighteen out of thirty. At another time, a few days afterwards, learning by some means that General McCook and staff would pass out on the Murfreesboro road, Colonel Morgan placed some fifty of us in ambush, at a point just beyond the toll-gate, to capture the Yankee general and his whole staff. The old gate-keeper, who had observed our movements, informed McCook that there were about one hundred armed men in the woods ahead of them. McCook soon became convinced of the danger, and putting spurs to their horses, the whole party proceeded, at Gilpin speed, never for a moment halting, until they reached the city. The gate-keeper paid the penalty of his treachery. The boys seized upon him and hung him before Colonel Morgan could interfere in his behalf.

"Not long after this, General Buell was accosted as he went out from dinner on the landing of the hotel by a wagoner, who informed him that the next day a squad of rebels was coming into his (the wagoner's) neighborhood to procure provisions, and that if the general would send out some cavalry the whole force might be captured. Buell asked the wagoner his name. He gave it, and told the Yankee general that he would keep him posted with regard to the movements of the secesh. Buell, suspecting there might be some trick in the matter, inquired into it. To his surprise, he was convinced it was a verity, as there was just such a man living in the designated neighborhood who was a wagoner, well known to the community for his honesty and probity.

"The wagoner, who in reality was no other than Colonel Morgan, duly disguised, soon disappeared from the hotel. After he had looked round the streets to his satisfaction, and heard all the news, he left one of our men behind to spy their movements and apprise him of the starting of the expedition, and regained the camp in safety.

"The next evening the Lincolnites set out, highly elated with the glory and success that their enterprise promised. Just before they left Nashville, the man who had been keeping a strict watch over their movements, mounted his horse, and following the nearest route to our encampment, gave Colonel Morgan the information.

"Immediately the colonel prepared for the capture of the whole force. The men were so arranged and instructed that the escape of the Yankees was impossible. On they came, dashing like mailed horsemen of the olden time, their clanking sabres and tramping horses making the earth to resound with mighty reverberations. When they were sufficiently ensnared, the signal was given, and we rushed upon their front and rear. Our success was complete. Out of eighty that came to our overthrow, there escaped but four or five to tell the tale of their surprise and defeat."

"I cannot remain here in captivity, while my comrades are covering themselves with glory!" exclaimed Charley, his enthusiasm roused to the highest degree under the young man's thrilling recital. "I must go from here—go where I can raise my arm in my country's cause. But, alas! how can I get out from this loathsome place?" he added, sighing deeply.

"There is but one way, my friend."

"And what is that?" asked Charley, his face growing instantly animated at the bare mention of escape.

"Take the oath. There is no other way to escape."

"Take the oath!" he exclaimed, starting from his seat. "Take that infamous oath? Never—never! Death, a thousand deaths, first!"

"It is humiliating in one view of the case; but in this instance, I have decided 'to stoop to conquer,' and I shall take the oath to-morrow. Were there any other alternative, I would not resort to this means of escape. But there remains to me nothing but this or death. I choose the former."

The guard approached where the two were sitting. It was the same who had so abruptly hushed the prisoner's song. The young man recognized him. His brow became dark and knitted, and his lips firmly compressed. He gazed a moment upon his foe and passed to another part of the inclosure.

"Have you decided the question of taking the oath?" asked the young man, as he encountered Charley in the long, dark passage that led to the cell.

"Oh, no, no—I cannot. I was offered my liberty when I came here, if I would but swear to its detestable requirements. I refused. I would rather perish than do it."

"I appreciate your sentiments. They have been mine; but my views have changed. Of what avail will it be to me or my country, if I lie here and rot, merely to gratify the cruel hate of these wretches? I'll take their oath, and then go forth to slay them; and in so doing I shall not feel that I have sinned against God, or sacrificed my honor. It is this or death here. They force me to it. I take what appears to me the less of two evils. They have proved nothing against me. They will not bring me to trial, that I may have justice, and they shall not keep me here to die."

"You speak truly," replied Charley; "we shall have no show of justice. I know that I must take the vile oath or die here, amid wretchedness and filth. I cannot escape—they will never bring me to trial. And yet, in view of all this," he added, after a few moment's pause, "I cannot see how I can take that oath."

"I do not advise you to act against your convictions of honor. You must decide for yourself. I have fully made up my mind, and shall take the oath to-morrow. I think it is the wisest thing you can do. But you must rely on your own judgment."

The two separated, each to his noisome cell.

CHAPTER XX.

THE REFLECTION AND ITS RESULTS.

Charley lay in his dark and narrow cell that night, **his mind** perplexed with the question before him. Hour after hour passed on, the silence all unbroken, save by the dull tramp of the sentry, and yet the decision was not reached. **His noble nature revolted** at the idea of the **humiliating act.** How could he sacrifice his honor by **pledging** himself to do **that which his** soul detested? **How could he again meet his parents and friends** with that burning curse in his heart?

"Had I better die a wretched death than cover myself with this deep infamy?" he said to himself, as he turned uneasily on his iron bed. I do not regard it as a sin. God will not hold me responsible for saving my life by any means from the hands of these heartless tyrants. Oh, no, a just Maker will not condemn. Life or death, which shall I have? Shall I languish here for months, and then go down to the grave, while my country needs my services, or shall I accept the only method of escape that is offered me, and go forth to vindicate justice and truth against hellish wrong and fanatical error? Here I can do *nothing*,—in the battle-field I might avenge some wrong that my people have suffered, strike some blow that will aid in their redemption. Others have taken this oath—men of high and noble sentiments—rather than die, as I must do, in a horrid prison. If I could but escape; but this I cannot do, it is utterly impossible—impossible."

Thus, until the night watches were far spent, did he debate the knotty question. Sleep overtook him, and found him yet undetermined. He awoke from his fitful slumbers, which had been haunted by horrid dreams. He felt all the wretchedness of the low, damp cell, filled with every variety of disgusting vermin. His brain reeled with exhaustion, his whole frame trembled with feebleness, which every day must increase. He looked hastily back upon all he had endured, then forward to all he must yet suffer, and, clasping his hands to his burning forehead, he exclaimed, "I cannot endure this! I will go—I *must* go!" It was all he said. The decision had been made, and he drove the detested subject from his mind. It had been a fearful struggle, but it was over, and forever.

"I go," he said to the young man, as they met at the door of the dining-room. "Ask me no questions, but make known my request with yours, and we will go out together."

Let us kindly throw a vail over this scene of deep humiliation through which these two proud, honorable spirits were called to pass, and shut out forever from remembrance the narrow, disgusting room, with its low-browed, arrogant official, and his train of base attendants; the taunt, the jeer of the mocking crowd; the burning cheek, the trembling frame, moved by the deep indignation that heaved within; the defiant eye, the compressed mouth; the deep, dark oath which the proud heart took, while the lips were speaking strange words; the look of scorn and bitter detestation, as they turned to seek the streets—all this we pass, as far too sad to dwell upon.

The trying ordeal is over. The two young men are once more free.

CHAPTER XXI.

SEARCH FOR COLONEL MORGAN'S CAMP.

"And now for Morgan!" said George Irving, as the two gained the street.

"But how shall we get there? You who know this country, Irving, must devise the plan."

"The first thing to be done is to visit a barber; the next, to obtain a disguise."

"But how is this latter to be procured, Irving? Every cent I had was taken from me when they put me in prison, and I have not a friend to whom I would dare to apply."

"You mentioned to me a gentleman who interested himself for you when you were first committed. Do you know where he resides? I would not for a moment hesitate to make known our circumstances to any true Southern man. I am sure such a one could not be addressed in vain."

"Indeed, I cannot find him. I have no idea where he is. I saw him but for a few minutes, and did not so much as learn his name."

"Well, we must trust to our wits. I do not fear. Let's seek the barber, and trust, like Micawber, for 'something to turn up' for our relief. Perhaps it will be better if we separate. I will go ahead of you a few paces, keeping always in sight; and as I have been here several times before, and have a pretty good acquaintance with the streets, I think we will avoid suspicion."

The two proceeded, as agreed on, to the barber's, from whence, relieved of their hirsute appearance, they emerged so metamorphosed as to defy recognition.

They were walking leisurely along the street, scarcely knowing whither to direct their steps, when Charley, grasping the arm of his friend, ejaculated—

"There he is! I am sure I am not deceived."

"Who, your friend?"

"Yes; let's follow him."

The two turned, and walked after the gentleman, until they

reached his business house. It was the dinner-hour, and no one was in. They entered, and approached his office, where the merchant was sitting with one of his clerks.

The young man rose to bid them enter. As he encountered Irving, he started, and gazed earnestly upon the visitor.

"Irving!" he exclaimed, "is that you?"

The soldier, surprised to find himself recognized, **fixed a look of searching inquiry on the stranger.** A moment's scrutiny sufficed.

"Why, Arthur, how you have changed since last we met! I did not **expect to** find you here."

Introductions followed, to which ensued a **long conversation**, wherein the individual story of the friends was rehearsed. **Every assistance** that Charley and Irving needed was afforded, and a few hours found them with their preparations for leaving the city entirely perfected.

Wholly changed in *personelle*, and provided with some whiskey to treat any pickets they might encounter, **and** a few trifling articles of trade, the two set out late in the afternoon of the following day, on their perilous search for Morgan.

They eluded the first line of pickets by crossing fields, thus altogether avoiding the public road. As night was overtaking them, they came, unexpectedly, **on the** outer pickets. Retreat or escape was impossible. They were discovered: already the cry of "Halt!" rung out from the sentinel.

"We must trust to *finesse* and our bottles, Charley."

"All right," and the two obeyed the summons, and with a very nonchalant air stood waiting the approach of the three pickets that advanced to meet them.

"How d'ye do, friend?" said Irving blandly, **stepping forward,** and extending his hand to the one in front.

The Federal was **an Irishman, and quite pleased with Irving's** cordial manner, returned the salutation quite heartily.

"An' whar is yer pass, friend?" asked the picket, as Charley explained to him that they wished to go beyond the lines for the purpose of making a little money out of the secesh.

"Oh, we didn't think it was necessary to get a pass—loyal men **like ourselves—who are** just **going out** a few miles to sell some **little articles by** way of turning a penny or two."

"We felt sure we should meet with friends like yourself, and so we brought along a little of the needful," and Irving took out his bottle, and seated himself with perfect *sangfroid* on an old log by the wayside, beckoning to the Irishman and his two companions to do likewise.

"I feel pretty tired. Don't you, Michael?" said he, addressing Charley, who by this time had produced his bottle and handed it to the Irishman on his left.

"Yaas, an' I do," was the reply, as the bottle was turned up to his mouth, and then passed on.

"Any rich secesh below here?" asked Irving of the picket on his right. "Me and Mike want to sell out our little stock as soon as we can, for I left a sick wife at home, and you know it won't do to leave her too long. Have you a family, friend? Here, take a little more; you need it; hard work standing picket," and he passed the bottle round. "Pretty good," he added, as he put it to his mouth for a second drink.

"An' it is, an' shure," said the Irishman next him, who was just ready to apply Charley's bottle for a third drink.

"Do you watch all night?" asked Irving, and without waiting for a reply, he turned to Charley and said, "Come, Mike, we can't get on much to-night; let's turn in with our friends here," and he commenced to unstrap his budget, and make preparations for the proposed stay. "Here, boys, you must take a little more. Nothing like it to keep up the spirits these long nights," and the bottle was again passed.

"We don't stand here all night; we gets relieved in half an hour," responded a little red-headed Irishman, one of the three who had taken but little part in the scene, save to do duty at the bottle. "We goes off now, d'rectly."

"Well, then, Mike, we'll go on. If we can't have good company here, we had better find a better lodging-place. Any house near, friend? Here, take this, it will help to steady your nerves," and he handed him the bottle. "Maybe you'll go along and show us the way?"

"There is a house just a little ahead to the right. Maybe you'll get rest there. We must go back to camp."

Irving rebuckled his strap, rose to his feet, swaggered round a few minutes, talking about the horrors of war and the trials of the poor soldier, bade the three *friends* good-by, expressing a hope they might meet again, and, followed by Charley, walked on, whistling Rory O'More.

"Well done!" said Charley, when they were out of hearing of the pickets. "We are now safe, thank God! and will soon be with Morgan."

"'Count no man happy until he is dead,' said the old philosopher, and we cannot count ourselves safe until with Morgan. However, I regard the greatest danger past. Most of the citizens in this part of the State are Southerners, and should we cross some Yankee sympathizer, we can very readily cajole him. But, see, yonder is the house. Shall we turn in here for the night, or drive on a few miles further?"

"Turn in, I decide. We are both weary and hungry. Should we go on we may not meet with another house in some distance, and without blankets as we are, we should find it rather disagreeable sleeping out in the dew and chill night-air. I say, run the risk—let's apply at the mansion for supper and lodging."

"Remember, we are peddlers, Irving," said Charley, as the two gained the front yard gate. "And do not forget that a peddler's chief characteristic is asking high prices and selling for nothing. I have no doubt but these people will be glad to get our needles and thread. We must drive a pretty good bargain with them, that they may believe we are really what we profess to be. You must do the trading, Irving. I do not know the price of a single article that we have in our budgets."

"Oh, I can do that, Charley. I sold goods for three years, when I was a chap, and I well remember the price of needles, pins, tapes, combs, etc. I'll multiply these old prices by six, and then I'll be sure to have them high enough. But if we find these people true to our cause, and they treat us pretty kindly, we will just make a lump bargain with them, and say no more about it."

"That would do, Irving, if we were entirely beyond Federal limits. But we must keep some things to preserve appearances, should we fall into the hands of the blue-coats. And by all means we must hold fast to our bottles. It will not do to let them slip."

"But what will we do with them now, Charley? They will make us suspicious if they are seen."

"Oh, give them to me; I'll secure them," and Charley stepped aside from the pathway that led to the house, and threw the two remaining bottles into a clump of evergreens. "There," said he, "*requiescat in pace* until the morning."

The two approached the house, reached the door, and knocked for admittance. After waiting a few minutes, a servant came to the door, who invited them to walk in.

"Ask your mistress if two—shall I say gentlemen or fellows?" whispered Irving to Charley.

"Peddlers, of course."

The negro heard the question, and giggled outright.

"Ask your mistress if two peddlers can stay all night."

The girl went into her mistress's room, and soon returned, accompanied by the master of the house.

"Walk in, walk in," said the old man, after he had thoroughly surveyed the two strangers, by the dim light of the flickering candle. "I see you are no plaguy Yankees. Walk in."

After conversing with the old gentleman for a short time, the two dared to inform him who they were. Supper was immediately ordered, and partaken of with fine zest by the hungry travellers.

The next morning the old gentleman gave them some valuable directions to guide them on their journey. He would receive no compensation, but he was amply rewarded for his hospitality in the quantity of pins, needles, and thread left with his grateful wife.

CHAPTER XXII.

LEBANON, TENNESSEE.

After travelling for five days over fields and through lanes and by-roads the two soldiers came, after many delays, upon Morgan's camp just as the men were preparing their supper. The old woods rang with cheers and applause when it was ascertained who the newly arrived visitors were.

The boys gathered around Irving to welcome him back again; and as they shook his hand their beaming faces and kind words fully attested the high estimate in which he was held by his comrades. And Charley, who was known to not a few, was received with the warmest expressions of friendship.

"How do you do, Charley?" and our young hero felt both hands clasped in kindly gratulation, and recognized the familiar voices of his two old friends, John and Bob.

"We thought you were dead, old fellow, picked off by some vile Yankee rifle," said one; "or perhaps had fallen alive into their clutches, and sent to Camp Chase for the improvement of your morals," said another; "or had taken life-long lodgings in some Nashville prison, where we should never be able to visit nor even hear how you were faring, laughingly remarked a third.

"You are right, Brent; there's just where I have been accommodated. But, I am happy to say, not for a lifetime, though it looked very much like it at first."

"Tell us all about it, Irving, do—all your experience with the cut-throat Yankees," exclaimed a dozen voices.

"How did you get out, and how have you made your way through to us?" and the boys, forgetting their supper, crowded round him to hear his story.

He told them all: how he had been captured in his attempt to get within the Federal lines; of his being accused as a spy, and without trial offered the alternative of the oath or imprisonment; how he had chosen the latter, but had been made to repent his choice by the wretchedness of his condition and the daily insults he received; then of his change of purpose, taking the oath, release, and subsequent tramp from Nashville to the camp.

"Bravo, bravo, my boy!" filled the air as the hero concluded his narrative. "You have out-Yankeed them. Bravo! bravo for old Kentucky!" and the boys threw their caps up in the air, and huzzaed, until the whole camp resounded with their cheers.

"Why, how you have changed, Charley! We scarcely knew you, old friend. You look pale and thin. But never mind, you'll soon rally again. Come with us," and Lawrence, taking him by the arm, led him away to his mess, where, amid the aroma of the steaming coffee, and the no less grateful odor of the smoking fried ham, they too related in turn their hairbreadth escapes since last they parted.

Irving reported to **Colonel Morgan the success** of his undertaking, and was informed by the colonel that he should set out on the second day following on an expedition to visit some of the Yankee garrisons.

"Hold yourself in readiness, Irving. I want you to be one of the number."

"Certainly, colonel," was the reply; "nothing would give me greater pleasure than to pay off a small portion of the score I have against the Feds."

Charley, who had no idea of being left idle and inactive, immediately began preparation for joining the proposed expedition. He went out that evening into the neighborhood of the encampment, and through the assistance of his two friends, John and Bob, who were well known in the vicinity, and who were already well provided for, he succeeded in procuring from a friendly farmer a good horse, and Colonel Morgan furnished him with saddle and bridle and arms, so that by nightfall he was pretty well equipped.

The expedition, numbering one hundred and fifty men, headed by their gallant leader, all well mounted and armed, set out the following morning at daylight. They travelled rapidly all day, and late in the evening came upon Lebanon, where a small detachment of a Federal regiment was stationed. Their capture was a matter of easy achievement, mere sport for the gallant lads who knew no fear in the presence of the foe. The prisoners were paroled, their arms distributed among the captors, and the stores in the place secured. Every thing went "merry as a marriage-bell." The boys congratulated each other on their success, and only regretted that the enemy had yielded without being made to "taste gunpowder." Horses were fed, stabled, and the victors retired to rest after their brilliant *coup de main*, feeling perfectly secure from all danger.

The night wore on. The weary men slept peacefully. Just as the day was dawning, the alarm rang out. "The enemy is upon us." Men started hastily from their beds and rushed into the streets. Every thing was wild confusion. The order was given by Colonel Morgan to defend themselves and escape as best they could. This, under the suddenness of the surprise, was all that could be done. Some seized their guns and prepared for the attack; others ran to secure their horses.

The enemy, headed by Dumont, drove in upon them in overwhelming numbers. Resistance was useless. Order could not be brought out of the sad confusion that everywhere reigned. They were surprised by thrice their number, and surrounded on all sides by the foe, who pressed in upon them, confident of an easy triumph. Seeing the hopelessness of an attempt at defence, the order was a second time given to cut their way through, each man to depend upon himself for his own safety.

Morgan mounted his beautiful mare, and, regardless of consequences, dashed through the advancing ranks. It was a miracle that he escaped. His noble animal was shot under him, and it was only by the most reckless daring and courageous self-possession that he saved his life. Some of his men essaying to follow his example were wounded, others were killed. Among the latter was our young friend Bob, who, in attempting to escape from three Yankees, two of whom he had shot, was struck by a ball in the heart, and fell just as he felt himself securely beyond the range of their guns. Most of those who had succeeded in mounting escaped, but about eighty fell into the hands of the enemy—among them, sad to say, Charley and Irving. These two men, failing to receive the warning in time, had found it impossible to reach their horses, and had to yield to the numbers who, rushing upon them, seized them and forced away their arms before they could prepare for any resistance. The prisoners were assembled in a large unoccupied building, and a strong guard placed round it.

"Ho, for Camp Chase," said one of the victors, as they closed the door upon the captives.

"Never for me," said Charley to Irving, his brow darkening and his eye flashing with the thought. "Death, but not Camp Chase."

"Amen," responded Irving. "A short imprisonment for me, or death to end the scene."

They could see from the windows of the house in which they were confined their dead comrades borne along the streets.

"There goes poor Bob Reed—dead! dead!" exclaimed Charley, starting back from the window at which he had been standing. "I wonder what has become of Lawrence and Brent; perhaps they have met the same fate with Reed," and Charley heaved a bitter sigh, and the tears, despite the efforts to suppress them, rushed to his eyes.

"Would I were in poor Bob's place," he added after a few moments' silence. "Misfortune attends me on every side. This is my third imprisonment, and I have been in the service but nine months. Better be dead than thus doomed."

As he spoke, his eye rested on the plain gold ring that encircled his finger—Mary's gift—and dashing the unbidden tears away, he settled himself on an old box in the corner of the room and covered his face with his hands.

"We'll outwit these infernal Yankees yet. Camp Chase will never have the honor of holding Colonel John Morgan's men, rest assured of that."

"You are right, Irving," interposed Cal. Morgan, a younger brother of the colonel. "It will be but rare sport for my brother to rescue us from these scoundrels. I have no more fear of Camp Chase than I have of the gallows."

But Charley could not feel assured that so happy a fate awaited them. He felt he was doomed, and that it was useless to struggle against his destiny. Dark thoughts entered and took possession of his soul. He could see no light before him. He dwelt on the horrors of his former imprisonment, on the degradation, insult, and suffering that awaited him.

"I will never again pass Louisville a prisoner," he said to himself, sadly. "The cold waves of the Ohio shall roll over me first."

The next day active arrangements were made to convey the men to the river, in order that they might be transported by boat to Cincinnati.

CHAPTER XXIII.

PROPOSED PLAN FOR ESCAPE.

It was a great trial to these noble spirits to have to submit to imprisonment, aggravated as it was by the coarse taunts and brutal jeers of the unfeeling guard, who appeared to take increased delight in tormenting their unfortunate victims, because they were Morgan's men.

The position to these proud Kentuckians was one of the deepest humiliation—one that each man of them had vowed never to occupy. But the alarm was so sudden, the surprise so unexpected and complete, that it was impossible to make any successful resistance. They were overpowered and robbed of their arms almost before they knew the enemy were in the town. And, to add to their distress, they were told that Colonel Morgan was killed in his attempt to cut his way out. This was to them the saddest feature of the whole matter. Many of them had confidently expected, throughout the long hours of the weary night, that their brave leader would gather together a force, and return to their rescue.

They felt fully assured that never would one of his men be permitted to enter the walls of any Northern prison, if it were in the power of mortal man to avert it. But when they heard that Morgan was dead, this hope forsook them, and they saw their inevitable doom was protracted imprisonment, unless they could extricate themselves, by their own effort, from their captive condition.

It was proposed to bribe the guard, but there were so many difficulties in the way of successful escape, even if beyond the prison walls, as the enemy, in large force, entirely surrounded the town, that this project had to be abandoned. Many favored it; among these were Charley and young Irving, who believed there would be comparatively little risk in it.

"Do not give yourself any uneasiness, boys," said young Morgan, a brother of the colonel, who had listened with an air of nonchalance to the animated debate; "my brother is not dead—there is no Yankee bullet that can kill him. Be quiet, and let things take their way. We'll be attended to in proper time. My life as the forfeit, if we ever pass the gates of a Yankee prison."

"You speak very confidently, Cal.," replied young Irving; "but, for my part, I do not feel quite so well assured. I know what is before us. I have recently had a bit of experience in prison life, and I am perfectly willing to dispense with the tender mercies of the Yankees for all future time. I vote for bribing the guard."

"We have only a hundred and fifty dollars, all told, Irving—not two dollars apiece—and it is folly to talk of bribing the guard with that meagre sum. Moreover, he would not dare to let us all go, and who among us would be willing to remain? And even if we were out, the great probability is that half of us would be caught again. I think we had better remain together, and when the time comes, our combined force can strike a heavy blow."

"Thou reasonest well, Cal., my friend, and we will have to decide the question by vote. All favoring the plan of bribing the guard, hold up the right hand."

"Only twenty. The majority is against us, Charley. Like good democrats, we will yield to its voice."

Charley assented, but it was in sadness. "The bitter fruit of taking that oath," he murmured to himself, and turned to the window to look out. The house opposite had been appropriated to the slain. It was through that faded brown door that he had seen the dead body of his friend borne.

"I wish I was in poor Bob's place," he said again to himself, as he gazed fixedly at the old frame house. Tears rushed to his eyes, but quickly he dashed them away—he would not be seen unnerved—and commenced to hum the air of "Auld Lang Syne."

It was a most unfortunate selection. It brought to his sad heart cherished and touching memories. It was Mary's favorite air, and many an hour he had sat beside her listening to the sweet music of its variations, which she performed with exquisite taste and skill. The lovely girl, who had risked so much for him, to secure whose happiness he felt no sacrifice was too great—home, with all its tender associations—came before him, and, in spite of himself, the big tears would flow. He looked at the delicate gold ring, the pledge of love. "I will live for her sake," he said to himself, "for her, the idol of my heart, the light, the star of my life," and he choked down his emotion, nerved his heart, and began to whistle in a lively manner, "Cheer, boys, cheer."

It was known among the prisoners that they were to leave

early the following morning for Nashville—whether to proceed from there by boat or railroad, they could not learn.

"It doesn't matter, boys, how they start us on our way to Yankeedom. We'll **never reach there.** The stars may fall, or the Yankee nation turn respectable, but never will any of **us** breathe the air of their infernal Northern slaughter-pens."

"Hope you are right, Cal.," **ejaculated all present.**

"**My** head for a football, if I **have not spoken truly.**"

The next day the prisoners, **eighty in** number, were sent to Nashville, there to take boat for Cincinnati, the rumor having obtained among the enemy that Colonel Morgan intended to release **his men at all** hazards, if **sent by rail.**

CHAPTER XXIV.

AN EPISODE.

The operator sat in his office silent and grum. He had just completed the forwarding of a dispatch from Louisville to Nashville, relative to Morgan's captured men, to the effect that they must be sent immediately to the former city by rail. The reason assigned was that Morgan could at any time enter Nashville, and, with the assistance he would there obtain from rebel sympathizers, could force the prison and liberate the prisoners.

"Confound Morgan and his men!" said the operator to himself, biting his lips in rage. "I wish the last one of them was at Old Nick this very minute. They are always doing some devilment to make trouble. Who knows but what they may pounce down on me some of these days, and take me off to some of their cursed prisons? Confound the whole batch of them, I say. I wish I had Morgan here; I'd soon put an end to his villany—the cursed rebel!"

Just at this juncture of the soliloquy, a horseman alighted in front of the door, and, with whip in hand, walked carelessly in. The surly operator scarcely raised his head to speak to the intruder, as he caught a glimpse of his butternut suit, all bespattered with mud, and the old slouched hat with rim partly torn off. But the visitor was not to be repulsed by this very uncivil reception. Stepping forward towards a vacant chair, which stood beside the window in the further side of the room, he seated himself, and asked for the news.

"No news," was the curt reply.

There was a morning *Journal* on the desk. The stranger reached out his hand, and, with the most perfect *sangfroid*, took the paper, and, opening it, commenced to read.

"John Morgan at work again," he said, as he glanced down the first column; "great pity that man can't be caught—he plays the wild with every thing."

At the mention of Morgan's name, the operator, as if suddenly seized by his Satanic Majesty himself, sprang from his chair, doubled up his fist, and then with a sudden jerk withdrawing it again, as if practising the pugilistic art on some hapless victim, and then thrusting his arm out at full length, while his eyes darted vengeful fire, exclaimed:

"Yes, the scoundrel, villain—I wish I had him here. I'd blow his brains out, this very moment. I'd show him. Just let him come in reach of me, and he'll soon get a ball put through his cursed body. No more pranks from him, the mighty John Morgan, I tell you!" And the infuriated man went through all the gestures of shooting his hated foe.

"You wouldn't kill him, would you?" asked the stranger, quietly looking up from his paper, and lifting the torn brim of his old white hat.

"Kill him? aye, and I would, sooner than I'd shoot a mad dog. I just dare him, at any time, to cross that door, and if he isn't a dead man in five minutes, there's no truth in me."

The stranger rose, took off his hat, and stood before the bloodthirsty operator, and with a quiet mien and voice gentle as a maiden's, said:

"I am John Morgan, sir; execute your threat. Here is a pistol—you are entirely welcome to use it!"

As he spoke, he fixed his large, piercing eyes steadfastly on the operator. Every feature of that noble face bespoke daring and defiance.

"Here is a pistol, use it!"

"Oh! thank you; I—I—didn't know—I hadn't any idea—that you were—Colonel Morgan, sir—indeed I didn't—beg pardon, sir—so much annoyed to-day—every thing gone topsy-turvy. Man gets so fretted—excuse me—really didn't mean what I said—wouldn't have any man's blood on my conscience—oh, no—remember the commandment—thousand pardons, sir—hope you'll forgive"—and the frightened man bowed himself quite back to the wall, where he stood, pale and trembling.

"You have my pardon, sir," replied Morgan, in a firm, gentlemanly tone. "Another time I advise you to be less boastful of your courage and veracity. I have but little time to stay. Seat yourself, and send the messages that I shall dictate to Louisville. Make no mistake; if you do, your life is the forfeit."

The bewildered man, but too glad to escape so easily, obeyed the order of the colonel with alacrity.

"I understand this operation, sir; don't you attempt to give any information but what I instruct you to do."

Had the trembling man felt disposed to disobey the warning, the close proximity to his head of that formidable pistol would have forever lulled all such desire.

"Now," said Colonel Morgan, "show me all the dispatches that have passed through this office in the last twenty-four hours."

The man sprang from his seat, and with a most obsequious air obeyed the bidding.

"That will do, sir," said Morgan, bowing politely, and bidding the pusillanimous wretch "Good-morning." Reaching his horse, he mounted, and rode away, leaving the confused operator dumb with wonder and surprise at the strange and startling occurrence.

It was a beautiful Sabbath morning in May, 1862. Lovely as a poet's dream rested the flower-mantled earth beneath the soft warm sunlight. The cars, laden with passengers, were wending their way at full speed from Louisville to Bowling Green. There was to be a "*Union* mass-meeting" in Nashville the following day, and the zealots of Kentucky, determined that it should have at least the appearance of power, and its proceedings be noised abroad through the land, had turned out in numbers to attend it. There were on board politicians, speculators, Federal officers, curiosity seekers, and hangers-on, besides a few private travellers.

Prentice, of the "Journal," had fully purposed to be present, but "owing," as one of his friends said to another, "to the fuddled condition of his brain, he was unable to make the time, and most unfortunately for the incidents of the day, was left behind."

The whistle had sounded, and the train was slowly nearing the depot at Cave City, when a dozen armed horsemen suddenly appearing in front of the locomotive, called out "Halt!" accompanying the command with a wave of the hand, a signal to the engineer to stop.

This functionary appearing but little inclined to obey the order —his movements indicating a determination to proceed—the command was repeated, and at the same moment about thirty other horsemen, armed to the teeth, dashed in view, and dozens of bullets shredded the air, whizzing alarmingly about the ears of the frantic passengers.

"Morgan! Morgan!" was uttered by a dozen voices. "Morgan! Morgan!" was caught up and re-echoed by all. Then followed a scene of the wildest confusion, which was at the same time both ludicrous and serious.

The engineer now seeing the folly of attempting to proceed, quickly brought the cars to a stand-still.

Some of the horsemen immediately sprang from their saddles to obstruct the track with rails, lest he should reverse the cars, and endeavor to return to Elizabethtown. Others rode up to the side of the cars, and, with pistols presented, demanded a full surrender of all soldiers and freight belonging to the government.

Wild was the tumult among the loyal ladies, profound the panic that had seized officers, politicians, and speculators. Each was endeavoring as best he could to secure his own safety and interest. Private purses rapidly passed from the hands of *loyal men* to those of disloyal ladies, in order to preserve them from the hands of the rebels.

Amid the fright and confusion Colonel Morgan entered the ladies' car. As he stood for a moment, every eye was fixed upon him.

"Be quiet, ladies," said he, with a pleasant smile, as their cries of terror fell upon his ear. "Be quiet, none of you shall be hurt, I only want the blue-coated gentlemen."

Instantly there was profound silence. His words acted like a spell in calming the tumult.

He approached one of the "blue-coated gentry," whose wife sat beside him.

"Oh, spare my husband, Colonel Morgan! Don't take him from me," screamed out the frightened wife. "For God's sake, don't take him. Have mercy—mercy on me, colonel, and spare him to me. I appeal to you as a gentleman—to your clemency—your generosity—your kindness—for my sake, for God's sake, for the sake of mercy, don't take him away."

"I do not wish to take your husband from you, madam," he replied, amused at the woman's importunity. "Take him yourself, and teach him better behavior than to come down here to kill Southern people. This is all I ask. Will you promise me this?"

The grateful woman, in the joy of her heart, grasped the knees of the noble benefactor, and thanked him in the most passionate strains.

A low-browed Dutchman, who had been a music teacher in Lexington, Kentucky, but who now enjoyed the most impressive sobriquet of Major Helveti, was taken by some of the Louisville boys from the cars, mounted upon a shabby trotting mule, and spirited away under an escort in the direction of Dixie.

"I have thirty thousand dollars in that safe," said the cotton agent of one of the large firms in Louisville, to Colonel Morgan, who was quietly examining Uncle Sam's treasures. "It is private funds, colonel. I hope it will not be appropriated. Here is my receipt for its deposit from the agent, colonel."

"Give yourself no uneasiness, sir," was the quiet response, while Colonel Morgan continued his operations. "My men are not thieves. Be assured, not one cent of private property shall be touched."

After making such disposition of government funds and stores as he deemed proper, Colonel Morgan surrendered the cars to the conductor, **under strict** orders **to return to** Louisville without attempting to **proceed to** Bowling Green.

Colonel Morgan, with his force, immediately dashed down the road to the depot below, to intercept the upward train, on board of which **were his men, proceeding** to Louisville. Unfortunately for his plan, a courier, unobserved by him, had left the scene of action during the *melée*, **and reaching** the nearest depot below, had **telegraphed to the** conductor, by all means, to return to Nashville, **as Morgan and his men were** awaiting the train to seize it.

Sad were the hearts of the prisoners, as the cars reversed their movement, and steamed back to Nashville. They understood it all in a moment, and felt that all escape by liberation at the hands of their noble chief was at an end. Their disappointment and chagrin were unspeakable. There was no hope left them now, save in their own skill and **management.** But they did not despair. They were determined on one thing—and that was, come life or death, they would never enter a Northern dungeon. How they succeeded in averting this detested fate remains to be seen.

CHAPTER XXV.

HOW THE PROPOSED PLAN SUCCEEDED.

"Played out—played out, boys!" said Charley, despondingly. "No hope of rescue now—prison or death—we must choose between the two."

"There, Charley, croaking again. Why, my boy, this is only a pleasing variety. What is life without diversity? Come, cheer up! be a hero—with a heart for any fate. If Colonel Morgan doesn't rescue us, we'll rescue ourselves. That's all."

"You are very hopeful, to be sure. You have had no experience in prison. Wait until you have groaned beneath their iron rule for a few months. Then we shall see if you regard it as a pleasing diversity."

"But there's no use despairing, even in the face of the most unpromising circumstances. Be patient. My word on it, Morgan will outwit these Yankees yet. They will not dare to keep us here in Nashville. Why, they wouldn't even risk us in Louisville. Don't you know that these cowardly wretches believe that Morgan can do just what he pleases? I'll wager they are trembling now for fear he will rush upon them and spirit us away. They will never feel safe until we are beyond the Ohio river."

"But what does all this argue? Simply that they won't imprison us here."

"And that they will have to ship us to Camp Chase. And you know it's a long way from here to Cincinnati, and there will be many chances for us to escape. I, for one, will never see the inside of one of their dens, take my word for that. Indeed, I have a great mind to dodge them right here in Nashville. But then, it would be so much trouble to get out of their lines; and, moreover, I shouldn't like to leave any of my friends behind me."

"They will take us by boat now, I suppose," said Charley, his voice assuming a rather more cheerful tone.

"Oh, yes! that will be their plan. They will not try railroad shipment again, and they won't dare to keep us here; so you see there is no other alternative."

The prisoners were marched from the depot, and huddled together in the close, damp jail for the night, without supper and without beds.

The next day they were taken on board a small boat, lying at the wharf, to be sent to Clarksville, where they were to be transferred to a large vessel, and forwarded immediately to Cincinnati.

It was night—a soft May night. The young moon, from amid her throng of starry worshippers, beamed tenderly down on the sleeping earth, which lay reposing in her soft, warm rays like a glad babe on its mother's loving bosom. The radiant stars looked down with their spiritual eyes from out their far-off home in the blue vault above. And gentle breezes, wooed into life by the moon's soft kiss, sported caressingly among the fragrance-breathing flowers.

It was the hour of midnight. Over the still bosom of the Cumberland, the cliffs, with their wooded brows, threw a deep, dark shadow, here and there lighted up by the sparkling moonbeams as they stole through the young and tender foliage of the overhanging forests, and fell in streams of silver sheen on the rippling waters.

No sound was heard, save the low, irregular splashing of the waters, as the wheel of the little boat drove the tiny craft along over the river's still, smooth bosom.

"Now is our time," said Morgan, quickly. yet stealthily, approaching the spot where young Irving and Charley were standing on the guard, looking over into the river below.

"Pass the signal; let each man but do his part, and we are free. You and Charley will attend to disarming the drunken guard. You, Irving, pass the word."

The signal was given. Quietly, yet with lightning-speed, the prisoners hastened to the work assigned them. The officers and boat-hands were seized, and before they could recover from their consternation, they were bound and put under guard. The sentinels, overcome by too deep libations from rebel bottles, lay senseless on the guards. To relieve them of their arms, was but the work of a moment.

It was a daring undertaking,—one that required great tact and adroitness. But the plan had been well arranged, and its *denouement* was eminently successful. The captain plead to be released, offering to convey them to any point on the river, if they would only allow him to keep his boat.

"On these conditions," said young Morgan, "you must surrender to us all the arms you have; give us rations for two days; all the money you have in your safe; then land us above here, on the east bank of the river, and **we** will spare your life and release your boat. But **as** you value your head, captain, don't you attempt **to** trick us in any way. And another thing, you must go on to Clarksville, and remain there until we shall have time to get beyond danger. Will you promise me this?"

The captain, but too glad to save his head on any terms, readily assented to the proposition.

"Swear him," said Irving; "**swear** him, **Morgan.** Excuse me, sir," he added, turning to **the captain**; "but you Yankees have such unreliable memories. **The** penalty for perjury under our oath **is death at first sight.** You'll remember? Here, Charley, get out your Bible, and let **the captain take the oath on that.**"

The little pocket-book **was produced, and the captain duly** sworn.

"Now, go with us, boss, and give directions to your engineer to wheel about and take us back a few miles; after this, sir, we will attend to the pantry and money-box. Boys, keep a sharp lookout **over your** prisoners, and if these drunken soldiers dare to move, just throw them overboard."

The necessary directions were given to the engineer. The safe **was then visited, and relieved** of its treasures; after which, Morgan, **calling to his aid a number** of the boys, stormed the pantry, **and emptied it of its edibles.**

"Come, cook," said he to the mulatto, who had stood beside him eyeing the movement with a look of wonder, mingled with admiration; "**come**, be quick, get to work immediately, and fry these steaks and this ham, and make up all that flour and meal into bread. Here, boys, you **that** know how, fall to work and grind this coffee, slice the light-bread and butter it, and roll up sandwiches for yourselves—here's a nice cold ham. Each one take as much sugar and tea as he wants."

"Come, steward, **bring paper to these gentlemen.**"

"None on board, sir, **I** believe," and the darkey trembled with **fright at having** to disobey **orders.**

"**Well, well,** never mind. **Get your towels and** tablecloths; **no matter** what, so it will do to wrap up victuals in."

The steward darted like lightning, and in a moment was back with the necessary articles.

There was **a** general jubilee on board the boat. The boys laughed, and danced, and sung. They had not had such a merry time since the fated night at Lebanon. Morgan, Charley, and Irving took the management of affairs upon themselves, and superintended all the preparations. Every thing was carried forward with the greatest dispatch.

The pilot was commanded to land them at the first safe point on the eastern bank of the river. Just as day was dawning over the earth, the boat was rounded to, and the boys, enforcing remembrance of their instructions on the captain and crew, equipped themselves with the few arms they had obtained, secured their edibles, and with one long, loud, ringing shout, sprang from the boat, and dashed into the woods.

"Didn't I tell you that we would out-general these Yankees?" said young Morgan to Charley, as he stepped up to his side, and slapped him on the shoulder. "But you wouldn't believe me. Did I not speak truly?"

"You did. Your plan has succeeded well, and you deserve all praise. We are once more free, thank God. Never let us again fall into the enemy's hands."

"Ah, we will never be caught napping again, Charley. Eternal vigilance is the price of liberty these days. How would it do, Irving, for us all to vow that we will never be taken prisoners again? What say you, Charley?"

"Amen, amen!" responded the two young men.

"Come to a halt, Morgan," said Charley, "and let us all swear that the Yankees shall never again claim us as captives."

The column was halted, the proposition submitted to the men, which was received with loud and protracted cheers, throughout the whole line.

The oath was administered, Irving holding up the small pocket-Bible, upon which each man was commanded to look, while he repeated the form of words after young Morgan.

"What do you say to breakfast now, boys, and a division of our money? Come forward, treasurer, and disburse your funds *per capita*."

A young man stepped forward from the ranks, and drew forth from his pocket a roll of notes.

"Two hundred and forty dollars—just three dollars apiece. Come forward, boys, and each one receive his quota."

A council of war was then called to decide whether the company should divide into squads, and thus endeavor to make their way to Colonel Morgan. or should, *en masse*, proceed to join him.

The subject was gravely discussed, pro and con.

"Most of us know every mile of this country," said Irving, the chief speaker. "We have travelled over it often. It is inhabited only by friends. We have provisions enough to last us twenty-four hours, and if at the expiration of that time we shall find it expedient, in order to procure food, to divide out, we can do so."

"But perhaps we shall encounter the Feds," suggested the treasurer, "and we have not arms enough to defend ourselves."

"That is **not** at all probable, Carter. There are no Yankees in **this** section. You know that we have kept them too badly scared to venture out in small squads, and if they have thrown a large force anywhere near, we will soon learn it. Let us send out an advance whose duty it will be to apprise us of any danger ahead."

"Boys, all in favor of moving on together, call out aye," **said** he, leaving it to the decision of a vote.

"Aye," rang out from every man.

About an hour was spent in eating breakfast, which was greatly enlivened by the recital of many a laughable incident that occurred **while** taking possession of the boat. The old woods were resonant with their mirth and hilarity, as they ate of their fried ham and steaks, with the buttered light-bread and fresh biscuits. It was far superior fare to any they had enjoyed in a long while, and their heightened appetite did ample justice to its acknowledged merits.

"Well, boys," **said** Irving, rising, and depositing the remainder of his roll in his pocket, "if **we** are through with breakfast, we'll take up our line of march. Our course is southeast. The Cumberland may give us some trouble, but we will find friends who will assist **us, and** we shall soon make our way to Morgan. Three cheers for our colonel, boys!" and the speaker flourished his old white hat vigorously around his head. The example was followed by every man, and loud and lusty cheers went up from the moving column, which were echoed and re-echoed among the leafy recesses of **the forest until they gradually died** away in the distance.

CHAPTER XXVI.

FINDING MORGAN.

The party travelled a day and a half before they could obtain any reliable intelligence of Colonel Morgan's whereabouts. They were then informed that he had a few days before passed within twenty miles of Carthage, going north. They could not learn whether he was accompanied by his whole force or not. The rumors were conflicting. One story said that he had certainly gone to Gallatin; another, that he had undoubtedly proceeded to Kentucky.

"If we cannot overtake Colonel Morgan," said Irving, after listening to the various contradictory rumors that met them on every side, "we must go where he can find us. Our present business is to get beyond the reach of the Federals. We can then wait until we can ascertain where he is. This done, our troubles are at an end."

They marched on for two successive days. No certain intelligence of Morgan could be gained. Hearing of no enemy in that portion of the State, they decided to halt and establish a camp. A fine position was selected for this purpose in a skirt of woods, bounded by a beautiful stream. They purchased such necessary articles as their limited means would allow. The people in the neighborhood of the encampment generously assisted them with provisions and blankets. After remaining a few days here, and ascertaining nothing of Colonel Morgan, it was proposed to procure some horses, and start a party in search of him. The proposition was favorably received by the whole encampment, and Irving, Charley, young Curd, and Johnson were selected to go,— Morgan remaining behind to look after the camp. He had already become quite popular in the neighborhood, partly because he was a brother of the favorite hero of the West, but quite as much on account of his agreeable manner and daring spirit. The project was made known to a few of the farmers, who readily furnished horses and every thing necessary for their equipment. The outfit was complete, and the four set forward on their search, under the direction they had received. After a day's **travel northward, they** obtained such intelligence of Colonel Morgan's recent movements as they could credit. Two **days more, and they** had reached his camp.

Information was given him of all **that had occurred.** He had **heard,** while passing through the country from **Cave City to his** headquarters via Knoxville, that his men had **escaped.** Immediately he turned about, **and sent up into the region of** Clarksville, for the purpose of rendering them **assistance; but he was too late,** and learned on reaching there that they had set out on foot to overtake him. He dispatched Irving, Curd, **and** others back to **the camp** for their comrades, with instructions for as many as could to join him immediately.

CHAPTER XXVII.

THE DARK SHADOW.

The morning after the men reached Colonel Morgan's encampment, Charley was very leisurely sauntering around objectless, further than to indulge his general habit of activity, when, in passing near a clump of undergrowth on the outskirts of the camp, his attention was arrested by the earnest **voice of some** one who seemed to be reading. As he neared the spot from whence the sound proceeded, **he heard the speaker** pronounce the name of Mary Lawrence. Suddenly he **paused, as** if transfixed to the spot. The blood mounted to his temples—his heart beat audibly—his **frame grew rigid under** the power of his strong emotion. A **moment more, and the name of Arthur** Morton reached his ear, **and** then the words "Federal officer," and "undivided attention."

As one who is suddenly seized by some demoniac passion, he exclaimed, "Oh, my God!" and sprang forward. Then, as if impelled by the magic of an invisible power, he paused and strained **his ears to listen.** It was the voice of young Brent, who was evidently reading a letter from some friend in Louisville.

As Charley stood breathless—trembling in every nerve, his hands clenched in the agony of dreadful apprehension, while his face, which for a moment before was crimson, was now livid as death, his bloodless lips apart as one who listens with his soul as well as ears—these maddening words were plainly heard: "Rumor says they are to be married. I do not myself know, for I have not seen Mary in many weeks."

He **could** bear no more. Frenzied, **he turned and** rushed away, walking as if pursued by a demon.

"Where on earth are you going, at that break-neck speed, Charley?" hallooed young Lawrence to him, as with great strides he pushed by the spot where a group had gathered around Captain Hawkins to hear him read a Louisville *Journal*, which had found its way into the camp.

Charley paused, and looked wildly around.

"Come here, Charley," exclaimed a dozen voices. "Come, and

hear," added young Lawrence, "what old Prentice says about our capture at Lebanon. He gloats over the idea of our surprise and imprisonment. Little does the old wretch think we are here free as air, laughing over his fiendishness."

Charley, as if incapable of exercising his own will, obeyed the summons, but it was as one who acts devoid of thought and object.

He took his place amid the group, listless; as one in a strange, wild dream, he stood, his eyes gazing out into vacuity—his face wearing that peculiarly sad expression which results from sudden grief; while his heart—ah, how can we describe its tumultuous heavings!

"Look, boys, Charley lives the whole scene over again!" exclaimed young Morgan. "He is even now, in thought and feeling, the inmate of a Yankee prison. Indeed, Charley, my friend, you do not regard yourself safe from the clutches of the villains, do you?" and Morgan slapped him on the shoulder pleasantly. Come, this won't do. You are as free as the bird of the wildwood—as safe, Charley, as though all the Yankees had been ferried over Styx by the good Charon, who of late must have been kept very busy at his work."

"No, no, Cal., I have no fear of the Yankees. I have seen them too often, and am too familiar with their face," responded Charley, endeavoring to assume an air of cheerfulness.

"Then why so melancholic? Disappointed that you did not get a letter from home, eh?"

"Yes, partly that; and partly indi-position."

"Oh, you mustn't get sick, Charley," interposed young Lawrence. "We are going to make Louisville a visit soon."

"Just at this point in the conversation, Captain Hawkins, who had been silently scanning the paper, read aloud one of Prentice's witticisms, which caused them all to break out in a fit of the most uproarious laughter.

Charley essayed to join them; but what a mockery to laugh, when the heart is breaking! His effort was fruitless—only a wan, ghastly smile was the result.

Attracted by the shouting, Brent and his cousin, young Arnold, to whom he had been reading his letter, came rushing to the group, Brent holding the yet open letter in his hand.

As Charley looked towards the young men, who were advancing at full speed, crying out. "What's the joke? what's the joke? Do let us share it?" he perceived the unfolded sheet. His first impulse was to meet Brent, and ask him to permit him to read his letter. But this would necessarily involve the betrayal of his secret, and, restraining himself, he simply said to young Brent, in passing, "One of Prentice's lucky hits, that's all," and walked on in the direction of the woodland which flanked the encampment.

Seeking its cool recesses, he seated himself upon an old log, around which the mushrooms had thickly grown, and burying his face in his hands, gave himself up to the tortures of the demon jealousy. And who that has felt his wasting fires, consuming, as it were, the very life of the soul, but can exclaim, "Death, death, give me death!" So felt Charley. The world to him was one wide-spread void, over which rested the blackness of darkness. Despair, deep, fearful, had unfolded her sombrous wings over his heart, shutting out all hope—all joy. Gladly would he have lost his weary weight of anguish in that long sleep where dreams do never come. He prayed for the fierce conflict, that he might yield up that life which in a few short hours had become to him only a meaningless existence.

There are moments in life when the soul, bowed down beneath its weight of disappointment and despondence, fearfully strives to discern one gleam of hope, to find one promise of good, in all the vast universe spread out so illimitably around it. It turns to present, past, and future—but ah, how vainly! and the recoil upon itself is but the mightier for the effort made.

In such moments, did the will but control the pulsations of the heart, what an array of self-murderers would stand in the last day before the final tribunal!

After remaining in this frenzied frame of mind, more intolerable than that which prompted the beautiful priestess of Venus to throw herself into the deep, dark sea, our hero arose, determined to seek out young Brent, obtain the letter, and if it confirmed his fearful apprehensions, to procure a furlough and leave immediately for Kentucky, and if his troth had been betrayed, to wipe out the wrong in the blood of the hated rival.

He sought the camp. But, as he bent his steps thitherward, his resolution began to falter. He could not make known the secret of his love to another; and how could the letter be procured without an explanation that must necessarily lead to disclosure on this point? He racked his brain for a plan, but the knot could not be untied—he had not determination to cut it asunder. So, avoiding young Brent, whom he met midway the inclosure, he turned aside with agitated look, and passed on with rapid pace towards his own tent.

The evening and night were passed amid the tortures of jealousy and despair. Sleep visited not the restless, tossing frame, and the aching brain, racked with fearful thought, throbbed wildly, while the blood-shot eyes looked out into the gloom of the rayless tent strainingly, as if the sinking soul sought to catch some ray of hope from the outer world. It was the small hours of the morning before that exhaustion consequent upon such intense and continued excitement of mind induced a fitful, feverish slumber; and this unsatisfying rest was haunted by fearful dreams, wherein specters of frightful form and fiercest mien unrelentingly pursued him through all the winding way, from which he saw no way of escape. He awoke to a realization of his wretchedness, and, springing to his feet, rushed frantically into the open air, and paced back and forth before his tent, goaded on by the increasing intensity of his emotion.

The morning came, but morning brought no relief. Pale and dejected, he pursued his walk.

"Why, Charley, you look sick to-day!" exclaimed his messmates, as he seated himself to attempt a breakfast. He made no reply, but, sipping his coffee listlessly, and scarcely partaking of the bread and fried ham before him, he sat silently brooding over his grief.

"Why, Charley, my friend, what is the matter with you?" remarked young Lawrence, with manifest astonishment, as returning from guard he seated himself at the mess-table. "You look as if the Furies had been tormenting you. Are you suffering from the scorpion whip of conscience for not going to church yesterday?"

"I slept but badly last night, and this morning my head aches violently. Altogether, I am not well," replied our hero, endeavoring to rally himself, so as to avoid renewed inquiry and remark; but the effort was futile—the smile too painfully sad.

"Oh, indeed, you must rally. It will not do to get sick now. Rumor says we go into Kentucky in a few days. Come, let's go and see some pretty girls to-day; that is, if we get permission. A sweet face is always a sovereign catholicon for the blues. Come, what say you? I saw several interesting demoiselles yesterday at the old country church, and two of them live near here. Hughes, there, fell in love with one, and Brent with the other."

"Not in love at all, Charley. Lawrence is exaggerating. We admired the young ladies; they were quite beautiful, I assure you; but for me, I must wed a Kentucky girl, or die a Benedict."

"You are right, Hughes; I say so too. A Kentucky girl for me. They are the fairest and best of all earth's daughters, and one of them for me or none," exclaimed Brent, accompanying the remark with a very enthusiastic gesticulation, which upset the cup of hot coffee on his knee, and imminently endangered the breakfast table, which was a camp-stool; and notwithstanding it boasted of four legs, instead of three, they were so unsteady as to jeopardize its uprightness under a sudden smart blow.

The boys roared with laughter at poor Brent's plight, which was really not enviable, as the hot coffee was by no means a pleasant *douche*. Charley joined in the merriment, for a moment forgetting his woe, but it was like the fitful gleam of sunlight bursting through the slightly riven cloud.

"Irving," said Charley to his friend, as soon as he could meet him after breakfast, "I wish you to take a walk with me; I have something to tell you."

"I hope you are not in trouble, Charley, though one to see you would imagine you had again fallen into the hands of the Yankees, you look so grief-stricken. I will walk with you in a few minutes, just as soon as I can deliver this note to Major Duke. Wait here," and Irving passed rapidly on, and in a very short time returned to rejoin Charley. The two walked towards the dense woodland which flanked the rear of the encampment. Seated on the old log, around which the mushrooms had gathered, with the sweet music of spring-birds gushing out from amid the dense overhanging foliage, Charley unbosomed his grief to his friend.

"I trust you, Irving, because I feel I can rely on your sympathy and *finesse*. I must obtain that letter from Brent, at all hazard. Would you undertake to procure it for me, pledging me to keep my secret most fiducially?"

"I think so. Trust me, I will not betray you. If possible, I will secure the letter this evening. Join me about four o'clock, and we will together find Brent; and if I succeed in my purpose, you can either read it, or hear it read."

The two parted;—Charley to attend to his daily duties, and find, as best he might, relief from his goading grief; while Irving, who had been intrusted with the secret of the expedition so soon to be undertaken, was busily engaged in such preparations as were necessary for the purpose of carrying out the commands of the morning.

Punctually, at the designated hour, Charley sought Irving. He found him earnestly engaged in a conversation with Hawkins, one of the command upon whom Colonel Morgan greatly relied in all matters that required energy and tact.

Pausing beneath the shade of a tree against which he leaned

with the air of one aweary, Charley awaited his friend. A few minutes, and he was by his side, and the two set out to overtake Brent. Their search was for some time unrewarded. At length he was seen with Lawrence and Hughes, emerging from the lane which led from the encampment into the main road.

"We are just from seeing the young ladies with whom these gallants fell in love yesterday," said Lawrence to Charley, as the two met, "and I do wish you could have been there to have witnessed the gaucherie of these noble Kentuckians. It would have cured you of your blues eternally. It was serio-comic, I assure you."

"No such thing, boys; Lawrence is exaggerating the whole affair. We conducted ourselves right nobly, like gentlemen to the manor born. Didn't we, Hughes?"

"Undoubtedly. Lawrence embarrassed us by telling the ladies we had fallen most deeply in love with them at first sight, and would not wait longer than to-day to make a call, when really, as you know, Charley, we went at his most earnest persuasion. Didn't Brent and I declare this morning that none but a daughter of Kentucky should capture us?"

"Oh, that vow, like woman's, 'was traced in sand.' Charley, you and Irving would so decide, could you have but seen the earnest, loving looks, and heard the soft, tender words which were inflicted upon those two beautiful Tennessee damsels, by these amorous swains."

"Come, Brent," said Irving, taking him by the arm, and leading him off, "come with me. You must make confession. I chance to know, gentlemen, something of this gallant knight's lady love," said Irving, looking back over his shoulder, and addressing the trio, now heartily laughing at something said by Lawrence.

"Your company, boys, if you please," and Charley left Hughes and Lawrence, and hastened to follow Irving and Brent, who were seeking a rude seat which the boys had constructed beneath a large oak tree, and to which they had given the name of My Lady's Bower.

"Is she your sweetheart?" were the words that met Charley, as he found himself beside Irving. It was an inquiry of surprise from Brent.

"Oh, no," replied the young man; "not exactly a sweetheart, but a young lady in whom, from my first acquaintance, I have felt a deep interest. I knew her in Lexington, and she is the sweetheart of one of my particular friends."

"Is Morton, of Louisville, a friend of yours, Irving? Do you know he is now in the Federal army? He and Miss Lawrence are to be married soon."

"Married to young Morton, Brent! That cannot be. She is, undoubtedly, engaged to a young friend of mine. There must be some mistake. Where did you get your information? Surely, it can be nothing more than rumor."

During this conversation, Charley's face was flushed almost to crimson. His pulse throbbed violently.

"Oh, no; it is not mere rumor. A letter just received from my sister in Louisville, says the marriage is certainly to take place."

Charley clutched young Irving's arm convulsively.

"I should like to see the statement, Brent. As you may well conceive, I feel a deep interest for this friend of mine, who I know to have acted honorably and sincerely throughout. Would there be any impropriety in my reading here in the presence of our friend, Charley, as much of the letter as is pertinent to the subject?"

"None in the world. I will step to the tent and get the letter. You and Charley remain here."

Charley had scarcely time to request his friend to read the paragraph carefully and a second time, before Brent returned and handed him the letter, pointing out the fearful passage. Irving took it, read it slowly to himself, and, shaking his head rather ominously, began to read aloud:

"Oh, I had almost neglected to mention," the young girl wrote to her brother, "the strangest item of news, and one that creates the greatest sensation among our young friends. It is said, and generally believed, that Mary Lawrence and Fred. Morton are to be married very soon. Lizzie Hutton told me yesterday there was no doubt of it. And you know Mary and Lizzie are old friends. Yet I scarcely know how to credit the statement, I have so often heard Mary declare she would not marry a Union man, if her life depended upon it. And Fred. Morton is now a Federal officer, dressed in his uniform. I met him on the street this morning. We passed without speaking. You know I have no admiration for blue-coats, and so I dropped my veil as I approached him. I do not think he recognized me. I have not seen Mary myself for weeks. I have been out at sister Sue's for a long time, and have not, indeed, seen any of my friends. I shall go round this evening, and if there is any truth in the report, Mary will surely tell me. I cannot believe it unless she informs me of it herself, even if rumor does say it's a certainty."

Irving folded the letter and returned it to Brent, remarking, "I do not understand this, surely there must be an error somewhere."

Charley rose and walked away.

CHAPTER XXVIII.

IS SHE FAITHLESS?

BEFORE a large mirror, which reached from ceiling to floor, Mary Lawrence stood, while her maid fastened the last white rose-bud amid the rich auburn curls.

A perfect picture of loveliness was she as she stood there, arrayed in that soft white silk muslin, threaded with silver, fitting so *recherché* her exquisitely moulded figure; while the elegant point-lace *berthe*, with its sprigs *d'argent*, the late gift of the fond mother, graced so charmingly the full drooping shoulders, and fell in gauzy softness over the rounded arms, which were encircled by a pair of bracelets, carbuncles set with pearls. A sash of white, spotted with silver, to correspond with dress and *berthe*, was fastened round the delicate waist by a simple *nœud* to the left. A pair of white kid gloves, perfectly fitting the small plump hand, and a costly pearl fan, completed the toilet. A few half-blown rose-buds looked out from the rich luxuriance of the lustrous curls. The last bud was secured by the hand of the admiring waiting-maid, who stood motionless, gazing on the angelic vision before her. Mary took a survey of herself. The blood rushed to the roots of the soft, dark hair. She threw herself on the sofa, and buried her face in her hands.

"Oh, indeed, Miss Mary, you'll mash your dress and all, all to pieces," ejaculated the maid, with a look of horror. Do get up, and let me straighten it for you."

The young girl heeded not the request, but sat still as death, her head bowed in her hands.

The door-bell rang. Mary sprang to her feet.

"Go, Maria, see who it is," she said, nervously, to the girl, who stood gazing upon her with astonishment.

"It is Captain Morton, I'm sure, Miss Mary. See, it is nine o'clock. You know he was to be for you at that hour."

"Go, Maria," and she waved the servant to the door, who, with a feeling of curious wonder at her young mistress's strange manner, descended the hall stairway, and, opening the front door, ushered the Federal officer into the parlor.

With rapid step Mary paced the floor **for a few** moments, her agitation constantly increasing. **Then, leaning** her elbow on the dressing-stand, she toyed with the exquisite bouquet which stood in the vase before her, and which Captain Morton had sent with **compliments** but a few hours before.

Maria returned, and announced Captain Morton.

Murmuring some indistinct words to herself, while the **color** deepened in her cheek, Mary seized the fan from the stand, cast a hasty glance into the mirror, and beckoning to Maria, who stood holding her nubia, to follow her, with trembling she sought her mother's room.

Bending over the couch of the pale invalid, she printed an affectionate kiss on the wan cheek.

"You look worried to-night, my daughter. What is the matter with you?" asked the anxious parent, in a soft, tender tone. "Your face is flushed and feverish."

"Oh, nothing, mother," replied the young girl. "Only excitement." And stooping over the low couch, she kissed her mother a second time, and passed to the parlor.

"God shield my child!" murmured the mother, earnestly, as the form of her only, her darling daughter disappeared through the door. Then clasping her hands, the mother offered up for her child's safety such a prayer as only the heart of a mother could give utterance to.

With a sweet, affable smile, Mary bade the young captain good-evening, which was returned by him with a most gracious air. He was charmed to see her looking so beautiful, and he stood gazing upon her with an expression of fond delight.

He observed she did not wear the flowers he had sent her. For a minute he felt chagrined, but in a moment the thought occurred to him, she regards them too highly to waste them on this evening. She keeps them in her room, that she may enjoy them. His rising fears were subdued, his self-conceit highly flattered.

"**You are** appearing most charmingly to-night, Miss Mary. Your **color** is unusually beautiful. Nature's own cosmetic. I am sure that you will be the cynosure of all eyes, and I the envied of all the beaux. The party is to be one of the largest ones we **have** had in the city since the war began; indeed, I doubt whether we have ever had any thing that will excel it. The most costly and extensive preparations have been made, and all the *élite* are invited. It is rather strange, is it not, that one who is generally known as a Southern man, should have invited so many of us officers? Almost every one I have seen is expected to attend."

"Indeed! I had scarcely supposed this would be so. But then, Mr. and Mrs. H. love popularity. They would sacrifice a great deal to secure it. And they have succeeded well. Their names are on the lips of both parties. Everybody speaks approvingly of them, as generous, affable, polite. And yet, I doubt—"

The young girl paused, and taking the nubia from the servant, threw it around her shoulders.

"Doubt what, Miss Mary?"

"I will not finish the sentence. I fear I might, perchance, do some one injustice."

"Shall we go?" and the gallant captain, with all the air of one who has a position and feels it, offered his arm to escort the trembling girl to the carriage, which stood at the door awaiting them.

It was a splendid scene. The gorgeously furnished rooms were brilliantly lighted, and thronged with the beauty and elegance of the city. Bright eyes flashed, and diamonds gleamed, and smile answered smile, and greeting and congratulations were everywhere given and returned throughout that gay multitude, where each heart seemed to have forgotten forever all sorrow, where each face was radiant with smiles, and every tongue was voluble with utterances of joy and gladness.

Near the door of the conservatory, where rich, rare flowers breathed out fragrant perfumes, and where a hundred lights threw a flood of dazzling splendor over these mute but eloquent representatives of every clime, stood Mary Lawrence, leaning on the arm of young Morton. He was speaking in a low but earnest tone, and his attitude and manner betrayed the depth of his feeling. With half-averted face, now flushed to crimson, and eyes bent to the ground, she listened to the fervent words. Her bosom heaved with deep emotion, her hand trembled as it clasped the fan which she vainly endeavored to use to cool her burning cheeks. She felt that the eyes of all who passed were fastened upon her, and this served to increase her embarrassment.

"What can be the matter with Mary Lawrence to-night?" asked Miss Whitmore of Lieutenant Dickinson, as the two stood in a position in the parlor that commanded a full view of the conservatory door. She appears so excited. I have never seen her half so gay as she seems this evening, nor yet half so beautiful. Is not she a perfect picture of loveliness, as she stands yonder beside that large orange-tree? She looks a fairy 'mid the flowers. Indeed, no idea that I have ever formed of the ancient goddesses could at all equal my realization of beauty in that form and face. I do not wonder Captain Morton worships her. Look how earnestly he bends to catch her slightest word, and how admiringly he gazes upon her! His soul is wrapt in devotion at the shrine of her charms."

"Busy-mouthed rumor says they are engaged to be married in September next. I know not whether the statement be true. I have heard it from various sources, and I opine no one who has observed his devotion to her to-night will for a moment doubt it. You regard the engagement as being a matter of certainty, do you not, Miss Lu?" said the lieutenant, turning to address Charley's sister, who, but a few minutes before, in company with Miss Brent and two young gentlemen, had taken a position near Miss Whitmore and Lieutenant Dickinson, and who, interested in the officer's remarks, had turned to give him attention.

"Mr. Shirley and I were but a few minutes ago discussing that question," she replied, assuming as much calmness as she could command. "He took the affirmative. I differed in opinion."

"It is certainly so, Miss Lu!" exclaimed young Shirley. "Fred is one of my friends. I cannot be mistaken."

"No one doubts it now," added Mr. Grayson. "The evidences are conclusive."

"It has been believed for weeks," interposed Miss Brent. "Three weeks since the rumor was so rife, I felt justifiable in writing the report to my brother who is with Colonel Morgan, and since then I have had such frequent intimations of it that I have learned to regard it as a fixed fact."

"He has scarcely left her side during the evening. I have observed several gentlemen endeavor to win her from him. I myself thought to do so; but after using all the strategy that I could master, I had at last to acknowledge myself foiled."

"Ah, Grayson! we unstarred, buttonless wights stand but a poor chance now in winning the hearts of the ladies fair. 'Our occupation's gone.' There is something about the stripes and tinsel that charms the girls. We shall have to don *les habits militaire*, or make up our minds to be Benedicts," said Shirley with an air of badinage, at the same time looking with an expression of mock grief upon the three ladies present.

"Come, come, Shirley, you do the ladies injustice," responded the lieutenant. "I appeal to the three present to support me in a denial of the charge. Say, ladies, is there an attraction about the trappings of war to win your hearts and fix your affections?"

"By no means," responded Miss Whitmore; "if a man is a patriot, I care not whether he wears the insignia of the battle-field or not," and she smiled very complacently on the officer by her side.

"There is a wide difference in our views of patriotism, lieutenant," replied Miss Brent, spiritedly, yet with no manifestation of unkind feeling. "I deem it far more noble, far more patriotic to oppose the wrong than to perpetrate it: to fight for freedom and liberty than for subjugation."

"Oh, we will not argue this question now, Miss Brent. Our views are diverse, and I suppose irreconcilable," responded the Federal officer, reddening over the position in which the young lady's remarks placed him.

A smile of satisfaction gleamed on the face of Grayson and Shirley at the embarrassment of the lieutenant. They were at heart Southern, and were only awaiting an opportunity to get through the lines to join Colonel Morgan.

"Will it not be the Union of the white and red roses when Miss Lawrence and young Morton marry?" remarked young Grayson to Miss Brent, as they withdrew to a position nearer the door which led out to the conservatory. "You know she was always regarded as one of our most patriotic Southern ladies. Indeed, it is said that she had a lover who was taken at Donelson. It is no other than our old friend, Charley R., and that she went in disguise of a nun to Camp Chase to visit him."

"And so she did, though it is not generally known. Lou. R., Charley's sister, accompanied her, and she will not believe that Mary and Fred Morton will ever be married. You see she will not be convinced. But certainly she is the only one that doubts. And she can no longer disbelieve after what she must have observed this evening."

Supper was announced, and the guests were ushered into the large and brilliantly lighted dining-room, where tables, laden with every delicacy that could please the eye or tempt the palate, were spread out in luxurious bounty and elegance before the charmed eye; sparkling wines, every variety of confection, in style *à la Parisienne*, ices, sherbets, noyaus, jellies, cakes of magnificent size and proportion, with every variety of iced ornament that the imagination could conceive, with fruits of all climes, were arranged with such artistic taste and skill as to give an air of magic grandeur to this splendid collation.

It so chanced that at the table Lou. R. found herself *vis-à-vis* to Miss Lawrence and the young captain, while to her left stood Miss Brent with Mr. Spalding, an old friend of her brother Charley, and now a devoted admirer of **Miss R.**

Mr. Spalding, a young man of twenty-seven, handsome and intelligent, was the son of a wealthy farmer near Lebanon, Kentucky. Having met Miss R. during the winter while on a visit to her aunt, who resided in the vicinity of his father, he had formed a warm attachment for her, and during the spring and summer had become quite a frequent visitor at her father's.

Having been, from his earliest childhood, a great favorite with the family of Mr. H., with whom he was distantly connected, he was ever a guest in the house while visiting the city. As soon as he received his invitation to the party, he hastened to Louisville to secure the company of Lou. R., but found, on arriving, that Mr. Shirley, who was also an admirer of the young lady, had previously engaged it.

Opposed to Miss Brent and Mr. Spalding were Miss H., the daughter of the generous host, and young Quimby, a cousin of Captain Morton's, who had formerly been a lover of Miss Brent, but, owing to political differences, they had become estranged, and the young gentleman now vied with Lieutenant Dickinson in his attentions to Miss Whitmore, one of the belles of the occasion.

Conversation flowed freely between the friends across the table. Only young Quimby seemed averse to enjoy the dashes of witty and brilliant repartee which were giving zest to the charming viands. He was piqued at his proximity to Miss Brent, and assumed an expression of contempt for what he chose to denominate persiflage. Captain Morton appeared the very embodiment of happiness. He had a smile and bow for every one, and a satisfactory air which seemed to say I possess all my heart desires.

Mary Lawrence was gay, unusually so, but her friend Lou. R. thought she discovered in her conduct something which pronounced her buoyancy an effort. There was an expression of *subduedness* in her manner and on her face which, to the sister's eager searching interest, appeared the index of that soft and tender emotion, the consciousness of loving and being loved. And as the thought of her friend's falsity to her brother settled into a conviction in the sister's heart, she grew pale with the feeling of the deep wrong done that noble soul, of the agony and sorrow that must wring his heart with anguish unutterable.

The remainder of the evening was passed by her in alternate

hope and fear. Every movement of Mary Lawrence received her searching scrutiny. But amid the whirl and excitement of the moving multitude she could form no just conclusion. Often, as she passed amid the throng, her ear was greeted with the fearful announcement of the certainty of the approaching marriage.

Once she thought to take Mary aside, and ask her if it could be true that she had deceived Charley. But why ask her, she said to herself; if she is false, will she not deny it? I could not expect her to confess to me.

Bewildered, chagrined, grieved, jealous of her brother's honor and happiness, and yet unwilling to inflict an injustice, even in thought, upon the friend of her childhood, Lou. R. left the gay assemblage, at the close of the evening, with feelings to which she had hitherto been a stranger—feelings that she could not analyze.

"You are sad to-night, Miss Lu," said Mr. Spalding to her, as he accompanied her and Mr. Shirley to the house of a friend on Broadway.

"A perceptible change has passed over you in the last two hours, Miss Lu," interposed Mr. Shirley. "Did you lose your heart in the gay throng of cavaliers, to-night? I observed the admiring and very devoted manner of the gay Lothario from Lexington, Mr. Grigsby. Was he really successful in making an ineffaceable impression?"

"Oh, by no means, Mr. Shirley," she replied, with that frankness so characteristic of her heart. "He is a pleasant, agreeable gentleman; but I shall have no remembrance of him beyond an evening acquaintance."

"I would not be bold or inquisitive, Miss Lu," said Spalding, in a serious tone, "but I will dare to ask, as a friend, why it is you have been so sad for the last few hours?"

"What, have I been sad? I fancied I was very *glad* and happy. You gentlemen must be deceived. Have I not been full of smiles and laughter?"

"Rather of thought and sadness. It could be read in your face; was echoed in your tone—spoke in every movement."

"All a mistake, gentlemen. Allow me to say to you, you have greatly deceived yourselves."

"Happy to hear you so declare, Miss Lu," replied Spalding "Better that we should be deceived than you grieved."

"How very brilliant your friend Miss Lawrence was to-night!" he added, after a pause. "And so beautiful! I presume there is no doubt but that she is engaged to young Morton. His attentions to her to-night were vexingly devoted. I but bowed to her. I had desired to converse with her, for I wished to hear her describe her visit to Camp Chase. She is *au fait* in description. Captain Morton will secure a lovely and charming prize when he claims her as his own."

The young girl made no reply.

"He is a lucky fellow, indeed," interposed Shirley. "Miss Mary is one of the most beautiful girls of our city, and as good as she is beautiful."

The party had reached the steps as Mr. Shirley concluded his remark. Waiting to see the young lady safely in, they bade her good-night, and left.

To describe the sister's emotions, as she lay thinking over the strange, inexplicable question before her, would be impossible. Her soul was stirred to its depths at the thought of the deep injury her brother had received, and her indignation against the author of the crime changed her love to hatred.

"I will write to Charley!" she exclaimed, as she lay tossing on her pillow. "I will tell him he has been deceived—wronged—cursed—in bestowing his wealth of love on this unworthy girl."

CHAPTER XXIX.

THE SURPRISE.

It had for some time been the intention of Colonel Morgan to advance into Kentucky, for the purpose of recruiting his forces, and of harassing and damaging the enemy, by cutting off transportation, capturing his detached troops, and destroying his stores at such points as he should find imperfectly protected. The sad disaster at Lebanon, Tennessee, had delayed the accomplishment of his plan, but though postponed it had never been abandoned.

His designs had been imparted to his staff, and their advice and co-operation solicited. They fully coincided in his views, deeming the undertaking one that, if properly conducted, would necessarily result in great benefit to the Confederate cause.

His adjutant, Major Basil Duke, a man of cool judgment and undaunted courage, together with Colonel St. Leger Grenfel, an English officer, who had attached himself to Colonel Morgan, and who, from his experience and skill, was peculiarly fitted to accompany such an expedition, were his chief advisers.

One of the objects of the expedition—indeed, the main one—was the destruction of the Louisville and Nashville railroad, upon which the enemy in Tennessee, owing to the low stage of the Cumberland river, was almost wholly dependent for supplies. Could the road be effectually destroyed, it would necessarily greatly embarrass him for the present, and certainly retard his advance.

After the return of the eighty prisoners, the first thing to be attended to was the arming and equipping of as many as it was possible to attend to under the circumstances. Most of them were veterans who could be relied on in any emergency.

Many of them were natives of the State, perfectly familiar with its roads and streams, and consequently peculiarly fitted for an advance, and for reconnoitring.

Colonel Morgan, after having matured his plan, and made such preparations as he deemed necessary, determined to move into

Kentucky. It was about the 4th of July when he set out on his undertaking.

Leaving his headquarters in the vicinity of Knoxville, he made a dash through Middle Tennessee, crossed the Cumberland river near Hartsville, and entered the State south of Scottsville, to which point he proceeded with the main body of his force, numbering about one thousand men.

Meanwhile, he sent Colonel Stearnes, with a detachment of about two hundred and fifty men, to capture Tompkinsville, and destroy what stores might be found there. There were stationed at this town four companies of a Pennsylvania cavalry regiment. Not supposing that the enemy was within hundreds of miles, the Yankees were completely surprised, and after a short and bloodless contest, were fully routed, with the loss of forty prisoners and as many horses and guns.

It was an entire defeat to the Federals, and so rapid were the movements of the Confederates, that before the routed foe could recover from their consternation and rally reinforcements for an attack, the enemy had fled, they knew not whither.

Colonel Morgan, at the head of his command, then dashed into Glasgow, where, after capturing the place and its provost-guard, and releasing some Southern men whom he found imprisoned for their opinions, he issued a proclamation explaining his object in invading the State, and called on all true Kentuckians, who regarded freedom as a birthright, and were unwilling to bow the knee before usurpation and tyranny, to join his standard and assist in redeeming their beloved State from the vile thraldom under which she now groaned.

A little incident occurred here worthy of notice, since it illustrates the difference between the *animus* of Southern men and so-styled Union men.

There was in Glasgow a Judge McFerrin, a prominent member of the Baptist Church, now an old man; his head was whitened by age, his litheness and buoyancy were long since gone. When the question of North and South was introduced into Kentucky, he took a very decided stand in favor of what he called "*the Government.*" Some of his friends, more far-sighted than himself, endeavored to convince him of his error in supposing an abolition administration ever was or ever could be the constitutional government of the United States. But the old man, never distinguished for quick perception and correct conclusions, with his faculties blinded by years, could not be made to discriminate between the two. And with a zeal all untempered by judgment, he espoused the "*union cause*," and became the bitter opponent of all who dared to entertain a contrary opinion. With that intolerance characteristic of narrow minds governed by prejudice and passion rather than right reason, he denounced all who opposed his mistaken views as destitute of all religion, and wholly debarred forever from entering the kingdom of heaven. Thus, with Jesuitical zeal, he became the persecutor of his brethren. For months he had been active in finding out who, in his vicinity, were "vile secesh," as he contemptuously branded them, and whenever a fitting opportunity offered, he would "bring them to justice," as he denominated searching out innocent neighbors, and having them imprisoned.

His zeal equalled that of Paul, when breathing out threatenings and slaughter against the disciples of the Lord. He persecuted this way unto death, binding and delivering into prison both men women.

And all this was done to support the "best government in the world," it was alleged, as if the precepts of the Divine Teacher were no longer binding on the consciences of those who had espoused the cause of the civil magistrate.

Colonel Morgan's men had been informed of the course pursued by the old judge. Partly by way of retaliation, and partly for amusing variety, they determined on his arrest.

It was high noon. The old judge, sitting in his office, in all the assumption of judicial dignity, was conversing with two or three friends, like-minded with himself, on the "wicked rebellion," and the doom that ought to be meted out to every traitor in the land, be he young or old, distinguished or obscure.

His wrath waxed hot as he dwelt on the "high crime of trying to overthrow the best government, in the act of endeavoring to break up the glorious Union for which our forefathers bled;" and as he warmed with his subject, his righteous indignation would vent itself in sundry hard thumps on the red cherry table at his side, which served with him to give emphasis to his loud and bitter words. While the old judge was thus in the very height of his abusive tirade, a young man, breathless with excitement, rushed to the door of the office, and calling out, "Morgan's men! Morgan's men in town!" disappeared down the street. Suddenly the scene changed. The question was now, not how he should defend his country against the vile secesh invader, but how he could save his own important person.

A fearful silence quickly succeeded the loud rant of the moment before, and the crimson of fierce passion died out in the wrinkled face of the old man, over which the deadly pallor of fear now spread itself. This violent denouncer of "traitors and rebels," like Felix, was seized with sudden trembling in view of his high misdemeanor. His ardent patriotism vaporized in a moment at the mere mention of the enemy's presence. Not waiting for any further assurance of danger, he cast one wild, blank look on his horror-stricken companions, and seizing his hat with the desperation of a man who seeks to free himself from impending destruction, he rushed through the back door of his office, and with rapid strides sought his home. Reaching the house, he dashed frantically in, and exclaimed with gasping breath, "Morgan, Morgan, Morgan!" and without pausing to answer any of the many inquiries proposed by his affrighted family, he dashed out of the door through which he had entered, hastened down the street as if pursued by the vengeful Furies, never pausing a moment to look to the right or left until he reached the outskirts of the little town. He was making his way with all possible celerity to a field of corn which stood to the left of the main road, hoping to secrete himself therein until he could pass unobserved to the house of a friend two miles distant in the country. But, alas for his vision of escape, just as he gained the fence a voice cried out—

"There he goes, boys; see him, see him; catch him!"

"Where, where?" cried out a dozen voices at once.

Like a death-knell the words fell on the ear of the old man, now vainly essaying to climb the fence. He was perched target-like on the topmost rail, his hair streaming out on the breeze (he had lost his hat in his desperate plunge at the fence), his face pale with affright, while he shook from head to foot with trepidation and alarm.

"Where, where?" the boys repeated.

"Yonder on that fence, behind that large tree. Don't you see him?" and young Leslie, who knew the old man well, dashed on towards the spot, followed by his comrades, shouting like madmen.

"Our prisoner, judge," said he, as he sprang forward towards the old man. "Turn about is fair play, you know. You have been persecuting our friends; we must now avenge their wrongs. Come with us, if you please." The old man was assisted from his perch, placed between two of the boys and marched back to town, his guard in the mean time preserving the greatest gravity, while the boys behind were convulsed with laughter.

"And the day of retribution has at last come, and woe to the offenders I tell you, boys. They must now endure something more than the lashings of conscience," responded Morgan in a solemn voice, at the same time looking most mischievously at Charley.

"Ah! most fearful indeed must be their doom. Ours is the Draconian code—death by the law for every crime," added Charley impressively, catching in a moment young Morgan's meaning.

Leslie and Irving, scarcely able to contain themselves, glanced round with an approving smile upon their companions, while the boys behind them laughed outright at the farce.

The boys knew that Colonel Morgan would release the old judge after scaring him a while, and they were determined to punish him a little on their own score.

So Charley and young Morgan, assisted by several others who crowded round the trembling culprit, continued their ominous remarks, preserving all the while a most serious tone.

The old judge looked nervously first on one side and then on the other. He would have defended himself, but he could not think what to say. He knew he was guilty of all the charges the boys so adroitly brought against "offenders," and he was left without one plea to argue in his own behalf. He was thinking, as well as the confused state of his mind would allow, of throwing himself on the clemency of Colonel Morgan, who he had often heard was full of magnanimity, when Charley remarked to the boys in a loud, distinct tone—

"Our colonel is always ready to forgive a personal wrong, boys, you know; but when his *friends* have suffered at the hands of Union men, he never fails to redress their grievances in the most summary manner."

The old man's heart sunk within him. His last hope was gone. His knees trembled violently—the deadly pallor of his face increased—he stared wildly upon his tormentors. Soon he would be in the presence of his inexorable judge, to await his fearful sentence. "What would that sentence be?" his fearful heart asked. What could it be but the severest punishment!

"Oh, that I had but pursued a different course!" he said to himself. "My country did not require all this at my hands. Oh that I had minded my own business and left these matters alone!"

"There are Southern men in jail in this town now, I hear," replied Morgan, "placed here through the efforts of Union men. They must be avenged."

"Some of our friends and relatives are in prison, Jones," said Leslie to one of the young men near him. "We must see that they are released, and their persecutors sent down to Dixie to try the charms of imprisonment there."

These two young men were from the vicinity of Glasgow. Their relatives were all Southern in sentiment, and with others had shared the injustice of the mob.

"They will be fully avenged now, Leslie. Those who have placed them there will have to suffer for it. Colonel Morgan will ferret out the whole matter, and when he finds the guilty one, I tell you, woe be to him."

"It were better that a millstone were hung about his neck, and he cast into the depths of the Mississippi."

"And it is but just that they should suffer," responded Charley, preserving his solemn air and impressive tone. "Nothing but just. It is a crying sin, that should meet with the severest penalty, this thing of taking up a man and putting him in prison merely because he can't think as another man does. We don't imprison men for their opinions, and woe to the Union man when he falls into our hands who has been the cause of hunting out his Southern neighbors and putting them in jail."

Thus regaling the ears of their conscience-stricken prisoner, the boys bore him along to the presence of Colonel Morgan. Leslie introduced the judge.

"Judge McFerrin," observed the colonel, eyeing closely the trembling old man: "I think I have heard of you, judge. Not very friendly to us 'vile secesh,' I believe—have had something to do with arresting those gentlemen there whom I have just released," said he, pointing to the five citizens of the place who had but a few minutes before stepped forth from the county jail.

The old man could not reply. He stood as if spell-bound, looking upon his accuser.

"Take care of the judge, boys. I will attend to his case another time," and Colonel Morgan having very politely waved to the boys to remove the prisoner, it was done with all possible solemnity.

The old man, trembling from head to foot, was conducted to his office, the door locked, and a guard stationed round the house.

The boys, who had entered into the scene with great zeal, and who had derived no little merriment from the ludicrous fright of the old judge, determined not to release him until he was sworn to good behavior for the future. So after keeping him in prison for full three hours, dinnerless and quaking with alarm, they brought him forth and duly administered the oath of allegiance to the Southern Confederacy, to which the old judge, happy for any means of escape, subscribed, albeit his self-pride brought certain contortions to his face, which the boys, divining the cause, enjoyed most fully.

"Go, sin no more. We'll be round about here soon again, and hope to have a good report from you," said Irving, taking upon himself the dignity of a magistrate. The old judge turned, and hastened away from this improvised court of justice a wiser if not a better man.

In a few short hours fear had so far overcome his *patriotism* that he has never since manifested any lingering of his Jesuitical propensity.

That evening Colonel Morgan, with his command, set out on a rapid march to central Kentucky.

"I wonder," said Charley to young Lawrence, as the two rode on in the soft moonlight, "if we shall really reach Louisville?"

The interrogatory was propounded in a tone so full of melancholy that Lawrence looked up in surprise, and fixed his eyes full upon the face of his friend, which was plainly visible in the moonlight, its sadness deepened by the pale, soft light.

"Indeed, I cannot tell, Charley, but suppose we will if it is practicable. But one would think from your look that you would prefer death to a return to your old home. What is the matter with you, anyhow? You have looked as if, Atlas-like, you had the whole world on your shoulders. I have noticed it ever since this expedition was projected. Surely you are not seriously opposed to a visit to our dear old city, if it does wear the gyves of the 'Old Baboon.'"

"No, no, John; of course I do not object to returning to Louisville."

The lips uttered the words—the conscience questioned their truth.

"If she is false," he exclaimed to himself, "why should I desire to return? Death—the cold, lone grave—eternity with all its dread uncertainties—any thing—any thing rather than see her—she, the light of my life, another's!"

"Charley, you puzzle me, old fellow. You act like one in a strange, wild dream. I have noticed it for several days. What on earth can be the matter with you? When we are all so delighted with the thought of being once more on old Kentucky soil, so wild with the hope of getting back to Louisville, to greet our friends and punish our foes, to find you sad and gloomy, is anomalous. I can't tell how to interpret it. You must have something on your mind, that you haven't told me of. Out with it. If it is a secret, I will keep it for you most masonically—that you know. If you have sins to atone for, let me be your father confessor. It will do you good to unbosom yourself. Come, let's have it."

The words of avowal struggled up to our young hero's lips. He was about to disclose his consuming grief. He paused a moment, choked down the words with a mighty effort, and replied, with as much *nonchalance* as his feelings would admit—

"You must be mistaken, John. I am sure I act very naturally. I am not well, to be sure, and this no doubt affects me. Perhaps I do seem dull—I certainly feel so."

"I am glad to hear that, my old boy. This trip will cure any indisposition you may have, I'll wager. Won't it be too fine, if we can pounce down on old Prentice, Jerry Boyle, and a few others of the same calibre, and whip them off to Dixie? But the cowards, they'll run. I'll venture old Prentice is already sleeping of nights in Jeffersonville or New Albany. We'll never get him, I'm afraid; he will always manage to keep out of harm's way."

Charley made no answer to his friend's remarks, but rode along silent and thoughtful. After several fruitless efforts to engage him in conversation, Lawrence desisted, and gave himself to humming snatches of Southern airs, and indulging in bright dreams—many of which, like the dreamings of us all, were never to be realized.

About ten o'clock the column reached Barren river, where they halted for the night. Pickets were thrown out—scouts sent forward—every precaution was taken to avoid surprise by the foe. The remembrance of Lebanon, Tennessee, was yet fresh in their memories.

Charley was required to do picket duty. The lonely hours of the night rolled wearily on, as sullenly he brooded over his great grief. How mockingly every sound fell on his ear! how mockingly every sight met his eye! The moonbeams, quivering **in** silver sheen on the bosom of the quiet-moving river; the nodding star of **heaven;** the deep, dark forest; **the** breeze that through its silence crept; the low monotone of the cricket; the baying of the watch-dog;—all seemed to whisper to his soul tales of disappointment and **woe.**

> "Scenes that are brightest awhile may beguile
> Hearts that are lightest, and eyes that smile;
> And o'er them, above us, Nature may **beam**--
> But **with none** to *love* us, how dark they seem!"

CHAPTER XXX.

LEBANON, KENTUCKY.

It was Friday morning, July 11th, when Colonel Morgan, with about seven hundred men, set out for Lebanon, distant thirty-five miles from Barren river. The day was hot and dry; the burning summer's sun looked down from the cloudless heavens above upon the parched earth, which reflected back his scorching beams into the heated air, until **the breath of the** Simoom seemed to sweep over the land. But the men, neither unnerved by scorching sun or winter's icy breath, rode cheerily on. And one, to have seen them with their coats off, carelessly hanging from the arm or thrown across the horse before them, while they jauntily sped along, and listened to their gay conversation and merry laughter, would have thought it a jocund hunting-party, rather than a band of soldiers, far away from friendly assistance, in the heart of an enemy's country. Honor, all honor, to those brave men and their gallant chieftain, who thus boldly penetrated the lines of the foe, and carried terror and destruction throughout his borders!

Twenty-nine miles of the rough, weary road had been passed. Eleven o'clock at night found this handful of brave men at the New Market bridge, on Rolling Fork, six miles from Lebanon. Up to this point they had encountered no difficulty. The enemy had wisely withdrawn from their path.

And here they were, hundreds of miles from any force that **could give** them relief—in a hostile country, surrounded on all **sides by a vengeful foe**—everywhere beset by those whose chief joy it would be **to betray them into the** hands of that foe—they braved **danger in every form**, encountered hardship in every phase, that they **might serve the cause of right and** human liberty.

Lebanon, **the** county seat of Marion, is a well-located town, with a population **of several hundreds.** It is the terminus of a branch of the Louisville and Nashville railroad, and the thoroughfare for all the travel and produce from the large extent of country surrounding it, which finds outlet at Louisville. It was regarded as a point of great importance by the Federal government, and was one of the first places in Kentucky permanently occupied by their troops. At the time of which we write, they had concentrated at this point a large amount of stores of every description. A commodious hospital had been erected near the town, and the large wagon-yards were filled with wagons, ambulances, and all vehicle paraphernalia. It was a tempting prize to the Confederates, and their brave leader decided to secure it.

Two companies of the Twenty-eighth Kentucky, under the Federal officer, Lieutenant-colonel A. T. Johnston, held **the place.** So rapid had been the movements of Colonel Morgan since he entered the State, that but little respecting them could be ascertained with certainty.

The excitement and indignation consequent on the occupation of this town by the Federal troops, had subsided. All was now peace and quiet—the villagers had grown accustomed to the "blue-coated gentry," and those who detested them and the principles they represented, had learned to regard them with contemptuous silence.

Suddenly, on the 11th of July, the town was thrown into a state of the wildest confusion and alarm. Rumors spread through **the streets** that John Morgan and his men, having driven before **them** all the Federal forces in the southern part of the State, routing **and** slaying them at every point, were now marching rapidly **on** Lebanon. Every tongue caught up the fearful intelligence—from house to house the news was borne—each repetition giving a widely exaggerated margin, until the story was indeed one of fearful import. **Shortly,** a dispatch came—*this was authentic* —and never did questioner of oracular divinity wait with more eager fear the decisive response, than did the terrified crowd the unfolding of the lightning's message. Alas! it was but little calculated to still their consternation.

About noon, the following dispatch was received—

"John Morgan is twenty miles southwest of Lebanon, near the little village of 'Pinch 'Em Slyly,' and will take Lebanon to-night."

This confirmation of their fears sped on the wings of the wind, **and** like the morning rumors was soon added to, and so highly colored, that the six hours' future became the fearful *now*.

Every moment Morgan was expected to rush through the streets. What was to follow his *début*, no one *knew*—each one imagined as suited his preconceived opinions and desires.

The military partook deeply of the fright. Runners were dispatched here, there, everywhere, to warn the Home Guards to hold themselves in readiness for a most fearful attack. One company of the Twenty-eighth Kentucky was placed in position for offensive operations, under command of Captain Barth. Dispatches were sent to Louisville and other points for reinforcements to be forwarded immediately; the town was but feebly defended, and unless assistance was received, it must certainly surrender.

Evening came, but brought no reinforcements. The commander, Lieutenant-colonel Johnston, was in a sad dilemma. Every moment the dreaded foe was expected to bear down upon his feeble band with an overwhelming force of veterans. In the consternation, the bridge across the Rolling Fork was forgotten. It was a point of some importance, and might be defended. Some one mentioned its strength to the terrified commander. Immediately a squadron of men, composed of volunteers and Home Guard, under young Lieutenant Vatlin, was sent out to guard the bridge. Pickets were stationed on all the roads leading into the town, for no one seemed to have the least idea from what direction Morgan would approach.

Men, women, and children thronged the streets, hurrying to and fro with no definite object in view, except to hear the news. Stores, groceries, shops, all were closed—their alarmed proprietors swaying to and fro with the moving crowd. It is doubtful whether a drachm of medicine could have been secured for a dying man.

Hour after hour of fearful suspense rolled by, and yet no enemy came. Half-past eleven o'clock at night a man dashed into the town, saying Morgan was at the bridge, only six miles out. The guard had fired upon him, and he was in full retreat. This calmed the fears of the over-credulous, and some of the weary watchers ventured to retire.

But the Federal commander had too high an appreciation of Colonel Morgan's courage to suppose that the force at the bridge could thus easily put him to flight. So he ordered two men to accompany Lieutenant Fiddler to the bridge, and ascertain the true state of affairs and report immediately.

This Lieutenant Fiddler, a pettifogging lawyer, who used to "fiddle" on every possible occasion in all matters, whether of church or State, finding his profession wholly unremunerative, "had enlisted," to use his own words, "under his country's glorious banner, to serve his country's glorious cause." He was of medium height, slim, red-haired, and self-important. He had volunteered his services on this momentous occasion as aid to Colonel Johnston.

Mounted upon his charger, with a splendid navy pistol at his side, he dashed off amid the darkness, accompanied by his body-guard of two, to see how matters stood at the bridge. Inflated with a sense of his own importance, he spurred on at break-neck speed towards the accomplishment of his momentous mission.

He, with his two aids close beside him, was ascending a hill a few hundred yards from New Market, when the three were very unexpectedly ordered to halt by the advance guard of Morgan's brigade. The fiddling lieutenant debated not a moment. Wheeling his horse about, he started out under whip and spur for Lebanon, followed by his panting attendants. Shots came whizzing around their ears. The clatter of the pursuing horsemen grew every moment nearer. He strained his failing steed to the utmost. Already he was distanced by his body-guard, and solus he was urging on his fearful gallop, when two of the dreaded foe dashed by him and cut off further retreat. Appropriating horse, equipments, and revolver, they gave him parole and left him to his fate.

Two miles from this the Confederates encountered the pickets, which were readily driven back upon the main body. Morgan sent forward scouts to ascertain the enemy's position and numbers. They reported a small force drawn up in line of battle two miles ahead. Advancing, he dismounted and deployed two companies to attack the enemy on the left and right.

Rapidly, yet silently, the men marched on. They were not discovered until they were within a few hundred yards of Johnston's command, when they were fired upon by the Federals. They rushed forward and returned the fire with a well-directed volley, and at the same time the mounted men dashed up in front.

A general panic seized the enemy, and casting aside guns and every thing that could impede their race, they set out, pell-mell, in full retreat along the road, over fences, through fields and woodlands, each one striving with strained nerve to make the best time back to the town. Two of their men lay dead upon the field, others were wounded so severely that they had to be left. The Confederates pressed on after the fleeing enemy. In a few minutes Colonel Johnston and sixty-five out of his force of eighty men were prisoners. Only thirteen escaped.

Colonel Morgan, at the head of his brigade, entered the town without further opposition. He was welcomed by many with evident manifestations of joy. **Taking** immediate possession of the telegraph office, he learned that the 60th Indiana, under Colonel Owens, had been dispatched from the Junction to reinforce Johnston.

An order was given to **Major Gano, of the Texas** Rangers, to proceed **with a** company and **destroy the railroad** bridge on the Lebanon branch, thus preventing **the troops from** reaching the town. This was successfully accomplished **by this young** and daring officer.

They were now fully secured from all attacks, and the few remaining hours of the night were spent in rest.

Early next morning Morgan threw out pickets **on every road,** and then proceeded to the work of inspecting the depots, **with their** stores of sugar, coffee, flour, bread, guns, caps, cartridges, powder, boots, shoes, hats, etc. Not wishing wilfully **to** sacrifice these immense commissary stores, **he made known to the** people his intention **to divide, among those** that needed, such portions of the **captured articles as they might desire. Great** was the rush to the depots from every quarter. Men, women, and children, with wheelbarrows, baskets, buckets, and every available means of transportation, **crowded the depot to receive a share** of the general spoil. Sugar, **coffee, and flour** were distributed with a generous hand by the soldiers appointed for the purpose.

"Come, boys," said Colonel St. Ledger Grenfel, who was charged with the burning of **the depots;** "come, we must do our work, the day passes. Get your torches. We are going to have a grand bonfire, of which Uncle Sam will pay **the expenses.** We have fed the hungry and administered to the **wants of** the needy, and now we must commit this surplus to **the flames.** But first, boys, take for yourselves all you **desire. You** are entitled to it by right of capture. Come, boys, to **work.**"

The order was scarcely given, before the boys, eager for the undertaking, rushed in and fired the building at a dozen points.

"Now, Captain Roberts, you proceed with **your men to** the ordnance department, and do likewise."

With alacrity the command followed their leader, and, after having secured such arms as the colonel had designated, for the arming of new recruits, the men dashed into the depot, gathered up armfuls of guns, and proceeding with them to the nearest available point, **would batter** them over rocks until they were bent double; others would pound them with heavy stones, thus rendering the locks entirely useless. It was a scene of the greatest activity. The boys would cheer each other with song and jest, and kindly word, while the citizens who grouped round them, joined in the merriment and laughter, irrespective of old prejudices. Cartridge-boxes, kegs of powder, cases of caps and guns, were indiscriminately thrown into a stream that run outside of the town, which precluded forever their recovery by the Yankees.

It was laughable to see the many and ready transformations effected by the boys, who, amid the roaring of laughter, stepped forth metamorphosed into Lincoln soldiers. Every man who desired, provided himself with a full Yankee outfit—pants, coat, hat, boots, and gun.

All instructions having been obeyed, the order rang out, "Now fire the buildings, boys." In an instant, twenty men rushed in and applied the burning brand.

A few moments more, and the flames, crackling and hissing, leaped from point to point, until the two large houses were wrapped in a glaring sheet of fire. As the boys stood gazing on the fearful and sublime scene, they sent up shout after shout of triumph, their pealing voices rising high above the crashing noise of falling timbers and the hissing tongues of fiery flame.

Colonel Morgan had reserved for himself the superintendence of the destruction of the large hospital with its stores. Taking with him a detachment of picked men, among whom were Charley, Brent, Curd, Irving, and Hawkins, he proceeded to have removed to places of safety and comfort, the few Federal sick that there were contained in it. Gently, as a brother, he provided for their wants. He remembered that, though foes, they were helpless; though seeking to destroy his life, they were suffering human beings. When the last man was beyond danger, the hospital was fired. Simultaneously with this, the torch was applied to the wagons and ambulances, and the flames from these two points, combined with those from the burning depots, gave to the scene an aspect of wild and terrible sublimity. Colonel Morgan remained long enough to see that his purposes were fully executed. Then, mounting his horse, he dashed out of the devoted town, followed by his jubilant command, and, lighted by the wild, red flames, pursued his way to Springfield.

Charley obtained permission to pass the night with his aunt, Mrs. Payne, who resided a few miles from Lebanon. There he met with young Spalding, who had just returned from Louisville.

The two being old, tried friends, having been educated together at Bardston, were delighted to meet again. Spalding, in the ingennousness of his soul, recited to Charley all the intelligence he possessed, giving a lengthy and most minute description of the elegant party at Mr. H.'s. Most of Charley's friends had been present on that occasion, and the gay young man deemed he could select no topic of equal interest. When he dwelt on the increasing devotion of Captain Morton to Mary Lawrence, and the certainty of their speedy marriage, Charley's heart ceased its beatings, his soul was pierced as with barbed arrows.

"And so you think they will be married, Ben?" he asked, with a mighty effort to control himself, while he felt as one who asked for his own death-sentence.

"No doubt of it, Charley. The city is full of the rumor; indeed, it creates a great deal of gossip, as Miss Mary has hitherto been considered unalterably opposed to every thing Federal, even so stringent in her views, as to seek the middle of the street, rather than walk under the old flag. And then she has a brother John, her only brother—by the by, is he here with you?—in the Confederate service. Her friends are astonished at her course, and some blame her in unsparing terms. But Morton is rich, you know, and a very fascinating fellow in his manner; but, in my judgment, by no means worthy of Miss Lawrence. You know his habits are very loose, and no one gives him credit for patriotism in donning the Yankee uniform. He only desired to be important, the world says."

Charley made no reply to the remarks of his friend. He dare not trust himself with words. The last ray of hope was gone. Shipwrecked on life's sea, he was lost, forever lost. The future, rayless darkness; the present, a Promethean fire; the past, a tantalizing dream. Deceived, betrayed, wrecked by the beautiful idol of his soul, whom his pure, trusting heart had worshipped with more than earthly devotion, henceforth, the world to him must prove a cold, barren waste, life a weary weight, which must be borne as the prisoner does his galling, clanking chains.

In torturing thought the night was spent. The following morning found him in the saddle, ready to start forward to join the command. He waited not to bid adieu to his friends. He felt all earthly ties snapped forever. Henceforth, he would court death.

CHAPTER XXXI.

ONWARD MOVEMENTS.

Captain Jack Allen had been dispatched from Barren river with three companies, to destroy the bridge over Salt river at Shepardsville. But, before reaching his destination, he was encountered by a force that had been sent from the Lebanon Junction to reinforce Johnston at Lebanon. After a sharp engagement, he was repulsed with the loss of one man killed. He then proceeded to Springfield, where he rejoined Colonel Morgan, who had moved to this point after the capture of Lebanon. From here Captain Allen advanced with a squad of men to Taylorsville, from whence he sent forward a small force under Captain Champ Ferguson in the direction of Shelbyville, in order to menace Frankfort, thereby preventing reinforcements being sent from this place to Lexington or Paris.

At Shelbyville, when it became known that Morgan's men were in the vicinity, the wildest confusion prevailed. Here, as at Lebanon, the most conflicting rumors ran riot through the streets.

"Morgan is assuredly marching on Shelbyville," cried out one.

"It is so, for a reliable gentleman has just seen his men only a few miles from the town."

"He is coming from Taylorsville on the Mount Eden road, and no mistake," asserted another.

A few minutes more, and a man, breathless with excitement, dashed into the town, declaring "he himself had seen Morgan's men, and their horses' heads were set towards Shelbyville, and they would be there in a few minutes—half an hour at the outside." This time he was approaching from the direction of Louisville.

"He is on his way to Frankfort, and must necessarily pass through here," argued another. And thus it was settled, Shelbyville, par nécessité, must receive a visit from the dreaded chieftain.

The funds were hastily extracted from the bank vault, and dispatched under strong escort to Louisville. The Home Guard were called upon to defend the place. In the most hurry-skurry manner that could be conceived, they hastened to arm themselves, and after much more noise and confusion than a skilful general would have made in preparing an army for battle, they finally succeeded in forming themselves into something like an orderly line, and stood prepared to meet the impending crisis.

Men flocked to the town to hear the news, each one receiving a different statement from every informant he met. The day wore on—every hour the excitement grew more and more intense. And by the early evening it was asserted as a fact, beyond the shadow of doubt, that Morgan, with hundreds of men, was within a few miles of the place, and would be upon it directly. At this intelligence the Home Guard suddenly broke ranks, and fled in every possible direction, never for a moment slackening their pace until they were assured that danger no longer beset them.

Henry F. Middleton, a most rabid Lincolnite, editor of the town sheet called the Weekly News—every issue of which dealt out the most unsparing abuse of the North, and of all that pertained thereto—hastily gathered up his family and valuables, and, without waiting to procure a more suitable conveyance, jumped into a furniture car, with some free darkies, drove off at lightning speed, and never halted until he was fifteen miles from the enemy.

A council was called to see what was best to be done under this most alarming exigency. The *defenders* of the town had fled—the editor was off with his valuables, many of the prominent Union men of all ages were gone, no one knew whither—everybody was panic-striken. What could be done but surrender the place to this formidable chieftain? After much debate, it was decided that this should be done, and two of the council were proposed as fit personages to set out under a flag of truce, to meet the dreaded hero, and tender him possession of the place.

And now the question arose, "who should go?" Here was a dilemma. Union men were afraid to venture. Southern men said it was a matter of no moment to them whether the town was given up or not. They did not fear John Morgan and his men, and if he chose to take the place, they were content.

Finally, after much ado, a Southern man, who had enjoyed the sport to his greatest satisfaction, and who felt his heart moved with compassion for the helpless women and children so nearly dead with fright, consented to be one of the flag-bearers. But now a new difficulty arose. The few *loyal* men left did not know how to get up a flag for the occasion. "They wanted no mistake about it—Morgan was a terrible man, mighty particular, and must have things done upon the square."

The ladies were importuned to assist in finding a suitable emblem of submission, and finally succeeded in procuring one that satisfied the most faint-hearted Union coward.

Out went the truce-bearers, followed by the prayers and tears of the anxious multitude. On they rode, bearing high aloft their immaculate ensign.

Pursuing the route of the reported approach, they passed on, mile after mile; but no enemy appeared. Strange, wild stories met them at every step. But nothing could be credited. Feeling, at last, that they had pursued the fleeing phantom far enough, they wheeled their horses, and galloped back to town to relieve the fears of the friends who awaited their return in torturing suspense.

Meanwhile, Colonel Morgan was quietly pursuing his way through Springfield to Macksville, where he arrived late in the evening. Here he rested for a while, and here was attacked by the Home Guard, who, after the exchange of a few shots, were routed—not, however, until they had severely wounded one of his men, and taken two others prisoners.

Morgan, finding two of his boys captives in the hands of the enemy, determined not to leave the place until they were recovered. Seizing upon two of the most prominent Union men in the little town, he made it known that they should not be released until his men were restored. This had the expected effect, and early the next morning the two missing men found their way to camp.

From Macksville a detachment was thrown across the country to the Lebanon pike, to threaten Danville from the southwest.

"This looks but little like getting to Louisville," said Charley, despairingly, to Lawrence and Brent, as the three paused for a few minutes' rest beneath the shade of an old sycamore-tree that stood by the roadside. He sighed deeply, while his expression grew noticeably sad.

"Oh, don't be so down-hearted," remonstrated Brent. "Why, Charley, you have grown to be the unhappiest of luckless wights. What has wrought such a change in you? You were formerly full of spirit and fun, but now you are spiritless, and full of sighs and sorrows. You haven't smiled half a dozen times since it was known that we were turning back into Kentucky. You must be sorry at the promise of getting home. Come, come, you must rally, my friend. Never mind the sweetheart now. We must whip the Yankees first, achieve our independence, and then woo and win the fair Desdemona."

Charley paled, then reddened at the remarks of his friend. Did Brent know his secret? How could he have heard it? If not, why should he have spoken as he had just done? He endeavored to reply, but could only stammer out a few incoherent words, while his color deepened, and his whole manner became confused.

"Caught, Charley, caught, my boy," exclaimed young Morgan, who, with Curd and Irving and two others, had joined the group under the tree. "You need not deny it. We all see you are in love, and desperately too. Now make a clean breast of it, and tell us all about the fair one. We will sit here on this grass, and listen to your tale of love and trial, and perhaps we will all relate our stories."

"Capital suggestion, Cal. What say you, Charley?" called out young Curd, as he dismounted, and throwing his bridle rein over his horse's neck, seated himself on a projecting root of the tree. "I sympathize with you, Charley, for I too remember well a dark eyed girl of Lexington. Cal., you can't appropriately laugh at Charley. You are wild now to get back to see your lady-love. Remember your fancies at Lebanon."

"Come, Ed., you are not going to betray me. Don't you know you are masonically bound to keep my love affairs secret?"

"Oh no, Cal., I'll not betray you; but I have no idea of laughing Charley out of his spurs, when I'd venture, if the truth was known, we are all in the same fix."

"Don't doubt," interposed Irving. "I own up to the weakness."

"But, boys, you have the advantage of Charley and myself," interposed Lawrence. "You expect very soon to be at home, where you can enjoy the delectable society of your lady-loves, while we have not the most remote prospect of such happiness."

"Oh, don't speak so discouragingly of our chances, Lawrence," ejaculated Brent, rising from his seat. "There is hope for us. What shall we do when we get to Frankfort, but sweep down on Louisville? The good people there will wake up some morning to the clatter of our horses' hoofs, as we dash along its sounding streets, and the cry will ring out from square to square, 'Louisville is fallen! Louisville is fallen! John Morgan and his men have got possession of us sinners!'"

The boys shouted in wild merriment as young Brent closed his description.

"Come, boys, dismount, and refresh yourselves in this grateful shade. Why do you set perched up there on your horses in that burning sun?"

"Indeed, boys, we must hasten on," replied young Morgan, taking out his watch, and looking at the hour. "You know we must pay our respects to the Danville Home Guard before dinner."

With jest and laughter the detachment of thirty sped along, little dreaming of the wild dread their approach was sending into the hearts of the good people of Danville.

CHAPTER XXXII.

DANVILLE AND ITS DEFENDERS.

If the consternation of Lebanon and Shelbyville was great, what shall be said of Danville, that seething cauldron of Unionism?—the birthplace of Colonel Smith Fry, who, with brutal coarseness, boasted that " *he killed Zollicoffer!*" and of General Jeremiah S. Boyle, who has publicly asserted that "he would wade through the blood of his wife and children rather than this rebellion should succeed." *Glorious patriots!* How approvingly humanity must laud your noble sentiments!

Colonel Morgan's deeds at Lebanon had reached the anxious ears of the Danvilians, and filled their hearts with terror. They knew their guilt in oppressing the Southern men in their midst, and while, like the Babylonian king, they saw the handwriting on the wall, fear seized their souls. There was alarm, anxiety, consternation, depicted on every face. Fear and confusion characterized every movement.

The cry went out for "help, help!" The captain of the Guard, who lived two miles out in the country, on receiving the frightful news of Morgan's approach, galloped into town with all the dignity befitting his position and the momentous crisis, although it required but a glance to perceive that he was quaking within. Runners were sent to and fro to inform the Home Guard to assemble immediately.

The money was taken from the bank, deposited in an express-wagon, placed in charge of Mr. Rice, a rabid old Unionist, who, mounting the seat, dashed off as fast as the horses could go towards Lexington, with instructions not to stop short of Cincinnati. Ladies gathered together their silver and other valuables, and boxing them up, dispatched them, post-haste, to a place of safety in the country. They buried their linen and bedding, and bidding a hurried adieu to their homes, jumped into carriages, wagons, and every available vehicle, and left for safer points.

Old men, whose heads were bleached by age, suddenly fired

with patriotism, seized their guns, and rushed out "to defend their homes from the lawless invader."

Some wag facetiously named the heroic band of venerable sires "The Silver Grays," and it was serio-comic to see them strutting around armed *cap-à-pie*.

Through the desperate exertions of the bustling captain, matters at last assumed somewhat of form. About sixty men were assembled, armed, and ready for the fray. Pickets were thrown forward on the Lebanon, Perryville, and Harrodsburg roads.

Morgan was advancing upon the city, no one knew from what point. Here, as at Shelbyville, the wildest and most contradictory rumors filled the streets. Finally, scouts were sent out to ascertain the truth of the matter. The one sent forward on the Lebanon pike, came dashing into town after a half hour, in the highest degree of excitement, breathless with fear, his eyes starting from their sockets, and his whole appearance that of a madman. "He had seen Morgan, no doubt about it, and his men covered the whole face of the earth. No use trying to hold the town— men enough to take away every house, not to talk about people."

When this most alarming intelligence was received, the town became frantic. Men hurried to and fro as if an evil deity had imposed on them this fearful penance to expiate some dreadful crime. Women, pale with affright, dashed through their houses, seizing on any thing that met their hands, to bear it off to some secure point, or stood hopelessly despairing at front doors and windows to hear the latest news. Children, following the example of the men and women, drove about like masqueraders at carnival. Hurried consultations were held at every corner of the streets, but no one could tell what was best to be done. At length, after much general debate, it was decided to move out the armed force to Dix River Cliffs, and there fortify.

This point was six miles from the town, and in a direction diametrically opposite to the one from which Morgan was expected. Accordingly, this gallant band of patriots darted out pell-mell, some mounted, some on foot, to begin their all-important work of "*fortifying Danville,*" six miles out, and fully twelve miles from the nearest advance of the enemy.

During this last scene, to the ludicrousness of which no language could do justice, some Southern boys, who had been hugely enjoying the fright of their Union neighbors throughout the day, conceived the idea of heightening the effect of the drama.

Understanding that the "*noble defenders*" were to march out and begin active preparations for the erection of suitable fortifications, they hired some negroes to follow after them at rapid pace with empty wagons. Then setting out before the armed heroes, the boys reached the Cliffs first, and secreted themselves where they could hear all that passed, without being themselves observed.

On, amid the deepening twilight, at break-neck speed, the brave band moved towards the river, each one discoursing on the momentous crisis that had overtaken them. Suddenly, as they were nearing their Thermopylæ, a strange and fearful sound met their ears. What could it be? they asked each other in breathless anxiety. Were they pursued? Was the dread enemy hard after them? It must be so. Dreadful thought!

"Hist! Hist, boys, be quiet; let me listen," said one of their number—Jack Webb, by name—a very important personage, indeed, since he had been at the battle of Fishing Creek. "I know all these war sounds, and can tell in a minute the noise of cannons, and horses, and infantry, and all such things. Stop, men, and be right still while I listen. I can soon tell whether it is the enemy or not."

Every thing halted in breathless suspense. Jack stooped down and placed his ear close to the pike. It was a moment of fearful expectation.

"Can't tell, boys, yet; sounds mighty like the enemy: wait a moment till it comes a little nearer."

It was asking a great deal of these patriots to wait until the enemy should get a little nearer, but they submitted most heroically.

"You stop here, boys, and I'll go back to the top of the hill yonder. Maybe I can hear better there."

Jack had gone but a minute, when he came rushing wildly back, crying out at the top of his voice, "Enemy, boys—flying artillery—enemy upon us fast as they can dash; no mistake!"

Just then the report of several pistol-shots reverberated along the cliffs to their right.

"The enemy is upon us—every man look out for himself!" was the order of the terrified captain.

In a moment, the men were scattered in wild confusion, each one rushing for dear life along the road that led to Nicholasville, twenty miles distant; nor did they stop until that point was gained. Never was there a more inglorious *finale* of warlike preparation for defence. Surely the bards of Danville, through all coming time, will delight to sing in stirring verse the heroic deeds of her brave defenders.

CHAPTER XXXIII.

A LOOK AT LOUISVILLE.

"FATHER, father! do see here!" exclaimed Mary Lawrence, eagerly, as she rushed into the breakfast-room, a few mornings after the party at Mr. H.'s. Her face was beaming with delight. The soft, auburn curls were thrown back from the blue-veined temples, her cheeks were of the brightest rose-hue, while her large, blue eyes spoke out from their soft depths, as gladly as if the soul within had received a heavenly inspiration. With her bright, airy morning-wrapper, confined at the waist with a simple sash of blue ribbon, floating out on the breeze as she entered through the open door, she looked more like a Hebe than a child of human mould. "Here, father, here, do read that," and holding the paper before him, while she threw an arm around his neck, she called his attention to an editorial paragraph. Pausing a moment for the father to read the announcement, she exclaimed, "Isn't that glorious news? John Morgan coming into Kentucky—coming right here to Louisville, and will bring brother and all our friends with him! Oh, I am wild with delight. What a blissful time we shall have!"

"But, perhaps, Colonel Morgan will not reach Louisville, my child, even if he should come into the State."

"Oh, yes he will, father. Don't you see old Prentice is scared out of his wits; and that, you know, is a fine indication. I am sure the Confederates will come to Louisville!" And Mary clapped her hands and commenced to waltz gracefully round the breakfast-table.

"Oh, my child, do not grow too ecstatic," said the mother, gazing with a look of tender, reproachful love upon her beautiful daughter. "It is scarcely possible that Colonel Morgan will reach Louisville. His force cannot be sufficient to take the city; and, moreover, there is nothing here to induce him to come. I judge the object of his visit to our State is to obtain recruits and horses, neither of which he would find here."

An expression of sad disappointment, in a moment, overspread the young girl's face and manner. She threw herself into her accustomed seat at her mother's right, and supporting her head with her hand, while her elbow rested on the table, looked inquiringly into her mother's face.

Mrs. Lawrence was a woman of most excellent judgment, and her word had ever been law with her household, because every member of the family daily felt her superior wisdom and justice. She was one of the loveliest of women, gentle, kind, thoughtful, and, at the same time, firm, decided, even unyielding in a matter of *right*. She had been deeply pious from her earliest girlhood, and the Spirit of all grace in her heart, had molded her manner and expression of face into sweet conformity to its own gentle teachings. She had, for a long while, been a great sufferer, her bodily infirmities increasing with each year, and now she was so enfeebled as scarcely to be able to leave her house. But, while thus slowly passing to the far-off land, mid pain and weakness, she grew day by day strong in faith, and that abiding hope which irradiates with heavenly beauty the darkest path ever pressed by the weary feet of the earth-pilgrim.

"O, father, don't *you* think Colonel Morgan will come here? He has so many Louisville boys with him; and then it would be such a satisfaction to us Southern people. He ought to come to release us from bondage, if nothing more. And there is old Prentice. Morgan ought to have him and ride him down to Dixie. A trip of this kind, I am sure, would improve his morals. Don't *you* think it is *possible* that the Southerners may come here, father?"

"No, my daughter. You need not revel in that anticipation. I am convinced they will visit central Kentucky, remain there a short time, and then leave the State."

"Too bad—too bad!" ejaculated Mary, as she raised the cup of coffee to her lips and sipped it. Placing it nervously back in the saucer, she looked thoughtful for a few moments, and then her face lighted up with the new ideas that flashed through her mind, and, smiling to herself, she again sipped the coffee, and glancing up to her mother, was about to speak, when she suddenly checked herself and remained silent.

The mother's sweet, sad face was very thoughtful. Her heart was with her boy. She longed to see him once more before her eyes should close in death. She knew her stay on earth must be brief: that before the flowers should fade, and nature clothe herself again in the emblems of death, she might be quietly resting from her labors beneath the green hillock.

The father folded the paper, and mechanically placing it beside him, fell into a grave, quiet mood.

The door-bell rang. Mary started nervously. The servant entered, bearing a card from Captain Morton, and handed it to her young mistress. It was a request for the pleasure of Miss Lawrence's company for an evening ride. An apology for the early intrusion accompanied the note. He was going immediately to the country, and would not be back until the afternoon.

"Bring me my escritoir, Maria." The girl obeyed the bidding. The mother looked at her daughter for an explanation. Mary never had any secrets from her loved parent—only one thing, her engagement with **Charley R.**, had she ever withheld.

"From Captain Morton," she answered to her mother's interrogatory look. "He wishes me to ride with him this evening at five o'clock."

"And will you go?"

"I cannot, mother; I have other plans." The servant returned with the writing-desk. Mary took from it a card, penned a delicate refusal, and enveloping it, dispatched it to the servant in waiting at the door.

"Mother," said the young girl, breaking the silence that had reigned for several minutes, "I should like to go to Frankfort this **evening.**"

The mother looked up astonished at the request.

"Go to Frankfort, Mary! when that country will be filled with armed men **in conflict!**"

"Ah, they **will not** hurt me, mother; **I have** no fear. I wish so much to see brother; and I am sure I shall do so, if I can only **get into central Kentucky.**"

"Would you go alone, my daughter?"

"Oh, no; I am sure cousin Frank will gladly accompany me. May I go if he will? Say, father, won't you consent? You know cousin will take good care of me."

"I don't know, Mary, that you **will be in any** danger in going to Frankfort; but I do not think you will get to see your brother."

"But let me go. May I, mother? What do you say? You won't object, I **know?**"

"You must first see **if your cousin** Frank will go with you. I **could not** permit you **to set out** without him."

"Oh, I will go and see him. I am sure he will be delighted to have an opportunity to take a little recreation."

Mary sprang from the table and ran to her own room, enthusiastic **at the** thought of accomplishing the plan that had so forcibly presented itself to her as she sat tasting her coffee.

In an incredibly short time she was bonneted and ready to set out. As she reached the door, she encountered Captain Morton.

His face was clouded, and his look one of unusual sternness. Mary started back as she beheld him. Recovering herself, she invited him into the parlor.

"I wish to see you for a few minutes only."

She motioned him to the hall sofa.

"I called, Miss Mary, to see why you refused to ride with me this evening. It is the first time, and I, of course, felt surprised." He fixed a penetrating look upon her as he spoke.

Feeling that he had no right to address her thus, the young girl straightened herself up, and with most perfect calmness replied:

"I have other engagements for the evening, Captain Morton. I presume this explanation will suffice," and she compressed her lips and assumed an air of hanteur which repelled further inquiry.

The color rushed to the face of the excited captain. He was foiled. Seeing and fully appreciating the hopelessness of any further attempt to secure a satisfactory explanation, he took his hat from the stand, and, bowing stiffly, left.

Two o'clock came. The hour found Mary, escorted by "cousin" Frank, at the depot, ready to take the cars.

"Poor Lu! She will be so sorry that she went to visit her friends in Ohio, when she hears that Morgan has been in the State. She set out yesterday morning for Cincinnati. Did you see her, Frank?"

"Only in passing. She has not been to see us since the party at Mr. H.'s. I have met her on the street once since then, and she only bowed coldly and passed on. Something is wrong with her, I am sure. I intended to go out and see her, and ask her what it is; but mother, you know, has been so feeble most of the time. I did not wish to leave her. Oh, I am so happy she is better now!"

The car-whistle sounded. Mary and her cousin entered and seated themselves. A few minutes more, and they were merrily speeding their way to the "City of Hills."

CHAPTER XXIV.

THE PANIC INCREASES.

Leaving Macksville on Sunday morning, Colonel Morgan pressed forward to Harrodsburg, which point he reached about noon.

As the column rode listlessly along, the colonel conversing with Captain Duke and Colonel St. Ledger, on their recent successes and future plans, Morgan's keen eye discerned in the distance two suspicious-looking horsemen. Calling upon Captain Castleman, he ordered him to take four men with him and pursue.

The five, driving the rowels deep into the sides of their horses, dashed forward. They had been gone but a short time before they were seen returning, bearing with them as prisoners a Federal captain and lieutenant.

On reaching Harrodsburg, Colonel Morgan found that the Home Guard from all that section of the country had fled to Lexington. Receiving no encouragement from the citizens to protect them, and deeming their own personal safety could be far better secured by flight than fight, they had precipitately set off at the first note of alarm.

The whole population of the town turned out to welcome Morgan and his gallant men. Ladies and children appeared on the streets to hail them as friends. Handkerchiefs were waved from every window, and bouquets, arranged with artistic taste, were showered upon their passing ranks. Smiles, cheers, and pleasant words met them everywhere.

Gaining the public square, Colonel Morgan ordered his men to halt and alight. In a moment the boys were surrounded by men, women, and children, eager to shake their hands and present them with every token of sympathy and respect.

The few Union individuals in the town, whether from policy or admiration, vied with their neighbors in acts of kindness and regard.

The scene was like a grand holiday occasion, where every one, happy himself, felt it a pleasure to contribute to the happiness of every one he met.

The men were invited into private houses to dine, and when they refused, because of their dusty and neglected appearance, baskets, laden with the nicest edibles, were sent out in the greatest profusion. There was scarce a housekeeper in all the town who did not that day prepare some dainty for "Morgan's men." And an old Union man, who had hitherto trembled at the very name of Morgan, providing himself with a basket of the best his wife's pantry could afford, went in person to present it to the dreaded chieftain, who received it with such a pleasant smile and polite bow, as completely won the lifelong admiration of old Mr. Savant.

After having partaken of the kindly cheer of the good people of Harrodsburg, Colonel Morgan set out for Lawrenceburg, twenty miles distant. In the mean time, he had sent forward a detachment to threaten Frankfort on the left, and another to menace Nicholasville on the right.

The whole country was in an uproar—Frankfort, Lexington, Nicholasville, Lawrenceburg, Versailles, were all seriously menaced. The Home Guard had fled in the wildest confusion from the minor towns, and concentrated in Lexington and Frankfort. At the latter point there was assembled a force of about three thousand Home Guards and regular troops. Nicholasville and Versailles were deserted. The shops were all closed, and the citizens awaited in anxious suspense the approach of the formidable column.

In Lexington the scene was widely different. Dispatches had been sent to Cincinnati for troops to assist in defending the place. All business was suspended—the stores shut up. Persons might be seen hurrying to and fro through the streets, as if bestirred by the fearful voice of an earthquake. Martial law was proclaimed, and every man found on the street was immediately placed under arms.

It was more than a man's life was worth to whisper the name of Morgan. A citizens' guard was organized, and authorized to arrest or shoot down any man found unarmed on the streets, so eager was their thirst for the blood of Southern sympathizers.

Various rumors, wholly conflicting with each other, were caught up and repeated at every corner of the streets by men whose fanaticism manifested itself alone in curiosity and excitement.

"Morgan was at Midway! Morgan was at Nicholasville! Morgan was approaching the town from Versailles! Morgan was entering Harrodsburg! Morgan was within six miles of the city with ten thousand men!"

Then came the thrilling tidings that the fight had commenced at Frankfort. What should be done? Could troops be spared for poor besieged Frankfort? If men were sent, might not the ubiquitous Morgan suddenly swoop down upon Lexington? The Eighty-fifth Ohio, under Colonel Sowers, had just reached the city from Camp Chase. It was decided to dispatch this regiment to the relief of Frankfort. But one company mutinied outright. It was more than they had bargained for. They had set out for Lexington, and would not go a mile further. The officers took the matter in hand, and after some coaxing, mixed with threats and curses, they succeeded in bringing the men to the point of acquiescence, and off the troops set, at railroad dash, for Frankfort.

All these movements being made known by telegraph in Louisville, that great city was thrown into a state of the most ludicrous confusion. Troops were ordered over from Jeffersonville; regiments were recalled from the Nashville road; bank vaults were robbed of their contents, which were inclosed in strong boxes for ready shipment across the river. Drays were kept in readiness for this purpose before the bank doors. The greater portion of the type of the daily press was packed up, and landed safely on Indiana soil. Armed men were rushing about, seemingly with no other object in view than to scare timid men and women out of their senses. Forces were hastened to the Lexington depot, but scarcely had they reached there before the order was countermanded, and they were marched back again. Headquarters were besieged by crowds of pale and anxious citizens, eager to catch one item of reliable information. The streets were literally blockaded by the rushing mass, all on the *qui vive* for intelligence from Morgan.

Cavalry from Nashville dashed through the crowded streets, their headlong speed and clanging swords adding to the already wild furore.

News came that Morgan was at Shelbyville, and would be at Louisville that night. Then ran along the seething multitude the rumor that martial law had been proclaimed, and every man capable of bearing arms was to be called out in defence of the city. This soon silenced, to a great extent, the crowded streets. Many of the Union patriots were unwilling to risk themselves in the presence of Confederate bullets, and deemed it more prudent to retire to their own peaceful dwellings, and there keep as quiet as their excited nerves would permit them to do.

During the grand *melée* Southern sympathizers looked on at the farce with inward satisfaction. They did not for a moment believe that Morgan would attack the city, but they were quite willing that their Union friends should think so.

While this fearful panic was shaking Louisville, Frankfort, and Lexington to their centre, giving rise to numberless ridiculous scenes, Colonel Morgan was quietly pursuing his way, as we have said, from Macksville, through Harrodsburg to Lawrenceburg.

Reaching this latter place Sunday night, Morgan remained until his scouts came in from Frankfort and other points. He then proceeded to Versailles, crossing the Kentucky river at Shryock's ferry. Here he found the boat sunken in the stream by the Home Guard as they moved on in their ignominious flight to Lexington.

About sunset on Monday evening Colonel Morgan, at the head of his command, entered the streets of Versailles, twelve miles distant from Lexington, and about as far from Georgetown.

"Here, boys, is a rich prize," said the colonel to his men, as dashing along the street he discovered about three hundred horses and mules belonging to the Federal government. "If any of you have sorry horses, here is a fine opportunity to exchange them for better ones. Help yourselves. Uncle Sam will not dare to enter a protest, I presume."

The little band was now situated in the midst of the enemy. At Lexington, on their immediate right, and only twelve miles distant, there was a considerable force under the commandant of the post, Brigadier-general Ward. At Frankfort, about equidistant on their left, were three times their number of men, some of them regular troops. Either point could be reinforced at a few hours' warning.

Colonel Morgan fully appreciated the danger. He ordered pickets thrown out on every outlet from the town, and commanded that his men should hold themselves in readiness for attack at any moment. The men sat sleeping on the pavements, their bridles resting in their hand, their arms beside them, ready at a moment's warning to mount and meet the foe. But no foe came. He was glad enough to be left to act on the defensive.

At dawn on the following morning, the command was ordered to be ready in an hour to set out for some other point. Promptly the command was obeyed, and as the sun, climbing up the sides of the morning, threw his first beams over the summer's landscape, the whole force set out at a brisk pace for their unknown destination. The Lexington boys hoped to be led to their homes and friends; the Louisville boys turned their anxious, longing thoughts towards that city.

"Not to Lexington to-day, boys," said Captain Castleman, with a sigh, as the column advanced along the road leading to Midway. "But, I do hope we shall yet have an opportunity to look in on our friends and sweethearts before we leave this part of the State."

"Really, it doesn't look much as if we shall, Castleman," replied Irving. For my part, I think I shall don my '*Lincoln blue*,' and try my hand at deceiving the Yankee pickets. What say you, Curd and Morgan? Wouldn't you venture this much to see those lovely girls you were speaking of a day or two ago?"

"Aye, and more than this, Irving, for the accomplishment of an object so desirable. Just insure us we shall see those angelic beings, and get back with whole bones, and we'll risk every thing. Won't we, Cal.?"

"Any thing, Curd, short of grim death itself," responded young Morgan.

"But, Morgan, how is it—"

"Halt!" rang along the line, suddenly breaking in upon the young men's fancies and earnest conversation.

"Morgan!" called out an aid, dashing to the rear. "The colonel wants his brother immediately."

The column was rapidly nearing the Lexington and Louisville railroad. Colonel Morgan had been informed that the train from Frankfort, having on board two regiments of Federals, would be due in a few minutes, and he determined to secure it.

Accordingly, he dispatched a squad of men to tear up the track in front. Another force was ordered to look to their guns and station themselves in position on either side of the road; while yet another company was given charge of the howitzers, which were so placed as to fully command the road at the point where it was supposed the cars should stop.

Colonel Morgan, with his operator, Mr. Ellsworth, repaired to the telegraph office, and took possession. They had been but a few minutes there, when a telegram from Lexington came flashing along the wires.

"Is it safe to start the train from Lexington? We hear Morgan is on the road."

"All safe—let the train come," was Ellsworth's answer.

Immediately preparations were made to give the train due reception. Breathlessly the men waited. Drawn up in line of battle, for one hour they stood momentarily expecting the prize. But the alarm had been given, and the trains retraced their steps in hot haste—one to Lexington, the other to Frankfort.

Being convinced that the enemy had been warned, and that nothing could be gained by longer delay, Colonel Morgan moved on towards Georgetown. As he neared the town, he was informed that some Home Guards had assembled to dispute his entrance. He halted, and sent in a demand for surrender. But nowhere were armed men to be found. Like their copatriots of other places, they had precipitately fled to Lexington for safety.

At Georgetown, as in Harrodsburg, shouts of welcome greeted the approach of the Confederates. Every preparation was made by the citizens to entertain them in a manner worthy of their chivalrous deeds and gallant daring.

All knew and appreciated the brilliant record these noble men had made in defence of liberty and right, and they dared to manifest their approbation, though it might cost them their freedom and property.

Union men were everywhere left unmolested. Many had fled, leaving their families behind them. Some remained, willing to trust the magnanimity of Colonel Morgan, whose conduct on all occasions had taught them that they had nothing to fear at the hands of Kentucky's noble son.

CHAPTER XXXV.

UNEXPECTED HAPPINESS.

As the troops were passing in column along the main street of the town, amid the glad cheers of the ladies and children who everywhere thronged the pavement, Charley's attention was suddenly arrested by hearing his name pronounced in soft, clear tones.

He looked in the direction from whence the sound proceeded, and discovered a group of females standing on the front balcony of one of the houses to his right. One was slightly in advance of the others, leaning over the banister and waving a handkerchief to the soldiers, as they slowly filed along.

She was dressed in a simple white muslin, confined at the waist by a long sash of blue ribbon. A wreath of natural flowers garlanded her soft auburn curls.

Charley's heart stood still as his eye rested on this beautiful female figure, so like that of Mary. Bending forward, he gazed earnestly upon it. His eyes dilated to their fullest extent, and his lips paled with fearful anxiety. Could it be Mary? Ah, no—it was impossible. Surely he was mistaken! And yet so like—that form, those curls, that sweet, glad face. It must be—and yet how was it possible? He gazed, and gazed, as one bewildered by some bright, fascinating object, which he could not comprehend, and yet from which he dare not turn.

"Charley, Charley! don't you know me?" spoke the same sweet tones.

Ah, that voice—he could not mistake it. It must be Mary. It could be none other.

His first impulse was to spring from his horse and clasp her to his bosom—his heart's own idol—the day-star of his destiny. But, with more than rush of Alpine torrent, came the frantic thought, "Perhaps she is already another's!" and, turning in his saddle, without even a bow, or look of recognition, he passed on.

Ah, the anguish of that moment! What words can portray it? The hopelessness of despair crushes the human heart, and wraps in rayless gloom our human life; we sink—we fall—prostrate, wo lie bleeding—but, ah, can the sufferer tell you what he feels? No human utterances can describe the weight of unutterable woe that chains the victim down to misery worse than death itself.

As may be imagined, our young hero knew but little of what transpired after this. What to him was the gay pageant, the loud acclaim of the joyous multitude? What to him that men, impelled by admiration for all that ennobles our nature, all that elicits true and undying praise, were now regarding him as hero-deliverer? No eulogy, not the battle-trump could have aroused him from his deep, dull apathy. He moved amid the living throng insensate to its tumultuous applause.

An hour later, and Charley lay outstretched on the college-green, as one haunted by a strange, wild dream. He looked out on the beautiful town spread out before him; on the clear, smiling sky above; and then away on the charming landscape, bounded by its margin of green woodland that encircled the town. But none of these things gave him pleasure, or abated for a moment his deep, mental suffering.

"Come, Charley, come; what are you doing here? You look more dead than alive, my boy. What's the matter with you? Get up, get up. Mary says she wants to see you, as soon as you can get there."

Charley gazed with an expression of perplexed inquiry up into his friend's face, as if he did not fully comprehend the meaning of his words.

"Wants to see me, John? Are you not mistaken?" Then, pausing a moment, he asked, slowly, "Is your sister married?"

"Married, Charley!" and John burst into a loud laugh. "Preposterous, boy! You are certainly crazy. Here, let me feel your pulse and forehead. You must have brain-fever, from your appearance. This July sun has been too hot for you. Come, get up, and take a refreshing bath at that spring yonder, and prepare as fast as you can to accompany me to see two of the most charming girls in the world."

Charley looked up again into the face of his friend with an expression of doubt and anxious inquiry. He made no effort to arise.

"You are too weary to go, Charley. I will excuse you to Mary; but I know she will be sorely disappointed in not seeing you."

"Do you really think so, John? Don't deceive me," said Charley, springing up as if animated by a new life. "I had thought your sister was engaged to be married, and would not care to see an old friend."

"Engaged to be married to whom?" exclaimed the brother, in astonishment.

"To Fred Morton."

"Fred Morton, Charley! that Lincoln sycophant. Do you think Mary Lawrence would thus disgrace her brother? Ah, I understand it all; yes—yes," and young Lawrence shook his head knowingly; "it's all plain to me now. But we won't stop to discuss this subject, my boy. Rest assured, Mary wishes to see you—and I am sure she will never marry Fred Morton. Come, we have no time to lose. Time is fleeing, and the girls await us."

Charley could not divest himself of the sad apprehension that, deepening into conviction, had so long hung like a death-pall over his soul. And yet, with that readiness to seize upon the faintest promise of good, so inherent in the young heart, he suffered himself to hope that his friend's words were true, and that Mary might yet be his own.

Hastening to improve his friend's suggestions, he was soon transformed in appearance, and ready to set out to meet Mary at the residence of Mr. Johnson, whose daughters had been her schoolmates and intimate associates. With trembling footsteps, and with conflicting emotions and thoughts filling his bosom and racking his brain, he ascended the steps of the front balcony, and stood before the door.

What years of dread and misgiving he lived in the few moments that intervened between the ringing of the door-bell and the appearance of the servant to usher them into the parlor! Charley deposited his cap on the hat-rack in the hall, and followed his friend to the room. There, on the divan before him, sat Mary, more beautiful than Peri of ancient Parsee faith. She was robed in a simple dress of white muslin, with a chaplet of roses and myrtle encircling her brow. As Charley entered the room, she sprang forward with all the love-look of old, heightened and intensified by the joy of meeting.

The lover's doubts and fears were gone. It was the Mary of yore, the idol of his heart, that stood, in her purity and loveliness, before him. He could not be deceived. She was true to him—faithful and constant as when they two had sat together beneath the old elm-tree, and plighted their vows. The shadows suddenly lifted from his heart—his doubt and dread gone—his fearful apprehensions forever dead.

His whole frame trembled with the intensity of his feelings. Happiness, such as the beings of a higher and brighter abode experience, thrilled his soul, and awakened therein the most rapturous delight.

How deeply he upbraided himself, as he sat beside her, and gazed into that beautiful face, and felt his whole being stirred by the soft, sweet tones of that gentle voice, that he had ever, even for a moment, indulged a suspicion of her truth! He wondered at himself to think that he should have credited idle rumors, when he had received from her whom he had known from childhood vows of eternal faith.

An hour later, and the lovers sat on the balcony, in the soft moonlight. Never were there two happier hearts. Not a shade intervened to cloud their joy. Mary had fully explained why it was she had received the attentions of Fred Morton, the Federal captain. Their mothers had been intimate friends from childhood. The young man was the nephew of her mother's physician, to whose solicitous care and tender watching she believed she owed the possession of that inestimable boon, a mother's love. And, in addition to this, Mr. Morton, the father, had kindly aided her father at a time when, but for this opportune assistance, he would have failed in business and been hopelessly ruined.

"I never loved Fred Mroton, Charley, you know this; but I have known him ever since I knew any one, and the considerations I have mentioned I deemed sufficiently binding upon me to compel me to courtesy in my demeanor towards the young gentleman. I know what the world said. I know my friends censured me. Your sister, Charley, whom I have ever loved as *my* sister, turns coldly from me. Often has my heart bled, often have I wept at being thus situated. But I did what I was convinced was my duty. But had I known—had I thought it possible that you, Charley, would have distrusted me for a moment, I would have hazarded all old family friendships, and rejected the attentions of Captain Morton. But I did not dream that you, Charley, could ever have cherished a doubt of me,—you who have known me so long and so well, to whom I have ever shown kindness and truth."

The large tears that had been gathering in the liquid depths of those soft, blue eyes, rolled down the burning cheek and choked the young girl's utterance.

"Forgive me, Mary; forgive me that I have thus sinned against you," and Charley knelt before her, and clasped the soft, dimpled hand in his, while his broken words full well attested the strength of his emotions. "I have wronged you, my angel—my life: have doubted you, when I should have hurled from me the vile slanders on your pure fidelity: have blamed you, when I should have loved. Forgive me, Mary—oh, forgive me my folly, and remember not against me this horrid weakness, this irreparable guilt."

The fast-flowing tears fell on his hand. He had but to read the sweet words of full forgiveness in that tear-dewed face, as the moonlight revealed it in all its living beauty.

He clasped her in his arms, and pressed his lips to her flushing cheek.

They were reconciled, forever reconciled—full atonement had been made, and thenceforth there should never arise one thought to mar their perfect love. So felt those two young hearts, as they sat there wrapt in the bliss of confidence restored, of forgiveness granted. Ah, alas! how poorly did they understand their own hearts—how little appreciate the influences of time and circumstances! They forgot, while plucking the fair and blooming flowers of Eden, that "the trail of the serpent is over it all."

For several moments both were silent. Each bosom was too filled with bliss to find language.

"But you did not tell me, Mary, how you chanced to be here in this little country town," said Charley, breaking the stillness.

"Why, in this wise, Charley," she replied, something of her wonted vivacity speaking out in look and gesture. "Convinced by father's arguments that it would be wholly impossible for Colonel Morgan to reach Louisville, I importuned mother to permit me to come to Frankfort, under the protection of my cousin. She consented. When we reached Frankfort, we were persuaded, from the information we received there from Southern men, that you would certainly pass through this place, and cousin Frank took a carriage and brought me here."

"And where is he to-night, Mary?"

"Oh, you know he has a sweetheart out in the country about three miles from town. Notwithstanding we were hourly expecting you, he could not resist the magnet, and he is now with Miss Appleton. I look for him back every moment."

"I thank God that we have met once more, Mary. Oh, you cannot tell what unutterable anguish I have endured under the belief that another had won from me that love which I hold as above life itself. I have told you of Mary Brent's letter to her brother. This was the first intimation I received of the attentions of Captain Morton, and the consequent rumor that you were to marry him. It came with such assurance of its truth, that I could not—pardon me, Mary, I did you a great wrong, I know—could not doubt it. Love is jealous, you know, Mary, and the thought of another, a hated rival, coming in **between me and** the being of all others to me most dear, drove me to distraction. I sank as one suddenly overtaken by a fearful disease. **Life lost all** charms to me. I wandered as one demented, pursued by an evil spirit. The **prospect of return to** Kentucky gave me no joy, no hope. It was like saying to the criminal,—Come, walk and take the fresh air, we will go by the gallows whereon you must be executed on the morrow. I came, because it was unavoidable. When I reached Lebanon, Ben Spalding, all unconscious that he was thrusting poisoned barbs into my very soul, repeated to me the rumor, asserting on his own knowledge its truthfulness. **I rose,** dressed myself, and fled the house, unable to rest a moment longer beneath a roof where I had endured such agony of mind. And when, three hours ago, I saw you standing on this balcony, and heard you call my name, **I looked** coldly, distractedly upon you, and said to myself, "What is she to me? Even while **I behold** her, another may call **her his own," and** I resolved to die. **I felt** that I could not bear the insupportable burden of an existence **that** had been forever robbed of its light and joy. But, thank God, I now know that you are mine; that no image of another has ever, even for a moment, enshrined itself in **the** temple of your affections. And now, Mary, I again beseech you to forgive and forget this deep, **unfounded** wrong **done you** by my black, my infamous suspicions. God forgive me, Mary—I feel that I have sinned against heaven in thus sinning against you!"

"Forgive you, Charley? My heart tells me that I should rather plead with you for forgiveness. I now see, that, while doing what I believed to be a right, **I did, all** unnecessarily it is true, but, nevertheless, did surely **lay the foundation of all your unhappiness.** I have learned a lesson, sad and **deep, which no** coming time shall ever wear out from my heart."

She paused, and looked up into Charley's face with an expression so pleading, so full of tenderness and truth, that—soldier as he was, all unused to tears—he could not restrain the big, burning drops that gushed to his eyes and rolled down his manly cheeks. He pressed her more closely to him. He was about to speak, when a footfall on the steps attracted their attention. It was Frank Carter, Mary's cousin, just returned from the country.

"And Morgan has come, cousin!" he exclaimed, as soon as he

caught a glimpse of Mary. "Where is John? I am almost crazy to see him. I understood he was here."

Charley stepped forward. Young Carter recognized him instantly.

"Why, Charley, my friend, is this you? How do you do? I am so glad to see you!" and he stood shaking the young soldier by both hands, looking him intently in the eye, his face beaming with the happiness the meeting with his old friend gave him. "And where is John, Charley? Isn't he with you?"

"He accompanied Miss May to the ice-cream saloon a short time since, but will be back in a few minutes, I suppose."

The three passed into the parlor. In a few minutes, Miss Jenny May and young Lawrence returned.

Carter sprang from his seat, and clasped his cousin in his arms. They had been playmates in childhood, and the love of brothers characterized their whole life.

"O, John, I am so glad to see you once more safely back in old Kentucky! In the name of all the true hearts in our once proud, but now degraded State, I welcome you. May you be one of the noble braves to drive the hordes of abolition invaders from her bosom."

"Join us, Frank; we need strong, young arms and nerved souls, to aid us in our work."

"Have you a gun for me, John?"

"Yes; can give you a complete outfit. Will you accept it, and cast your lot with us?"

"With right good-will, John. I set out from home with that expectation. I have long desired a fitting opportunity to join you, and I am now ready. I go with you to-night."

"And what will become of me, Frank? You know mother intrusted me to you."

"Oh, you will be taken care of. I shall assuredly provide for you."

"Patriotism first, gallantry afterwards—first our country, then our sweethearts. This should be the motto now, Mary; don't you think so, gentlemen?" asked Miss May.

"Our country and our sweethearts, first and forever, Miss May, is the watchword of Kentucky soldiers. We fight for both, for both we die, but never yield either to the foe."

The evening was spent most delightfully in song, music, and cheerful conversation. Southern songs were sung without restraint. No blue-coated spy paced the streets to search out "*treason*."

Charley and Mary again found the balcony. Love seeks no society save its own. Time sped by with nimble feet. Charley lingered. **To-morrow he might be torn away** for the rapid march or bloody skirmish. Sweet were the words of love interchanged by these two young, trusting hearts. How brightly, wreathed with the halo of hopeful promise and joy, did the future outspread before them! Love is a kaleidoscope which, however many new and rare combinations are presented, none are devoid of beautiful colors or symmetrical forms.

"Time for us to leave, isn't it, Charley?" said young Lawrence, appearing on the balcony, accompanied by his cousin, Mr. Carter. "Can you guess the hour, my friend?"

"Ten o'clock, I suppose," replied Charley, taking out his watch for the first time during the evening.

"*Ten* o'clock, Charley!" cried Lawrence, laughing heartily. "Time must have passed pleasantly with you, truly. Wouldn't you think so, Miss Jenny and Frank? Charley says ten, my watch says five minutes to twelve. Charley has taken no note of time, the watch has measured every minute, so I suppose we shall have to take the testimony of the latter, and bid you ladies good-night."

"We soldiers don't often have the pleasure of ladies' society," responded Charley to his friend's badinage. "This must plead our apology for the present trespass. When we call again, we hope to be more thoughtful of your comfort and the prescribed forms of etiquette. Good-night, ladies," and, bowing politely, he descended the steps.

His two friends, after promising to return on the morrow, "*if circumstances would permit*," bade the young ladies good-night, and followed his example.

Descending the steps, and turning the corner of the street, they were soon lost to sight.

CHAPTER XXXVI.

SUCCESS OF AN ATTEMPT TO VISIT LEXINGTON.

It had been concerted by Curd, Irving, Castleman, and young Morgan, to visit Lexington in disguise, if they could obtain leave of absence until the following evening. This done, the four dressed themselves up in a full suit of Lincoln blue, and about nine o'clock they set out on their perilous undertaking. They knew every mile of the way, having often travelled it, and they were also fully acquainted with the sentiments of every individual on the road-side, so that they had nothing to apprehend on the score of falling into Union hands. Their only danger on the way was the Federal pickets, which must, *par nécessité*, be either evaded or deceived. But they also ran the further risk of being recognized by every individual whom they might meet in the city, and thereby be betrayed into Federal hands.

But these young men were fond of adventure, and they cared not a whit how narrow the escape was, so they escaped. Indeed, the very danger they must be subject to throughout, only served to add zest to the scheme.

The four, mounted on fleet horses and completely disguised, set out amid the shouts and cheers of their comrades, on their rather dubious expedition. Many were the wagers laid by the boys that they would be nabbed by the Yankees, and sent to the military prison at Louisville; but the young adventurers, confident of success, in every instance doubled the sum that they would return the following night, with all the items of news known in the besieged city of Lexington.

"Present our regards to our friends in the city," shouted a dozen voices, as, laying whip to their horses, the merry quartette dashed off on their excursion. They rode at a rapid pace for five or six miles, heeding neither toll-gate nor the groups of two and three Federal soldiers which they passed on their way.

When within five miles of Lexington, they halted to discuss and decide upon the best plan to be pursued. Morgan and Curd were in favor of attempting to pass the pickets on horseback. Irving and Castleman thought it best to dismount, leave their horses at the house of a friend, and, avoiding the pickets, enter the city by a by-path.

"We can deceive them, Irving, rest assured we can," argued Morgan. "They'll never suspect us. I'll give the Yankee twang so completely, they'll swear I am a regular Down-Easter, and no mistake."

"But, Cal., is it not better to avoid them altogether? Then we shall certainly be safe."

"But how can this be done, and where shall we leave our horses, Irving? I would as soon the wretches would get me as my horse."

"Ah, I can manage that, Cal. There is an old friend of mine, just across the way here, that will take good care of them until we come back. Once in his hands, and I'll wager my head the Feds will never get them."

"But how shall we avoid the pickets? They are as thick about the city as leaves in Vallambrosa, no doubt."

"But certainly we can shun them better as pedestrians than we could on horseback."

"But in the latter case, if we could neither deceive nor shun them, we could effect an escape; while if on foot, they might shoot us and we could make no effort to get away."

"I will take the chances on foot, Cal. I am convinced it is the safer plan."

"And I will trust to my ingenuity, blarney, and this good steed of mine to secure me a safe passage through, or a safe exit from the rascals."

After a lengthy discussion on the subject it was finally agreed, as a test of the judgment of the respective parties, that Morgan and Curd should attempt the trip on horseback, while Irving and Castleman would essay it on foot. It was arranged that they should meet the next day, at two o'clock, to dine at Mrs. Morgan's, mother of the colonel, provided they succeeded in the attempt.

Irving and Castleman turned through a gate to the right, to seek the house of the friend with whom the horses were to be left. Morgan and Curd, bidding them good-night, pursued their way along the pike. They rode on about a mile, planning their passage through the lines, when suddenly they came upon the pickets, seven or eight strong. Morgan rode forward.

"Halt!" called out a Hoosier, thrusting his bayonet across the road. "Halt! I tell you, or I'll blow out your brains in a minute!"

"Two of the 51st Ohio," answered Morgan, with the veritable Yankee drawl, "trying to escape from Morgan's men. Got caught out here, and came within an ace of being made prisoners. Had a hard time to get off. I tell you, these rebels are regular dare-devils. Bully fellows, they."

"Where's your pass? Let me see that."

"**Pass,** my friend? How do you suppose we could get a pass, **when there was nobody to give us one?** Our pass to-night were these two good steeds."

Just **at this juncture, four or five others,** that **had** been sitting by the road-side, about half asleep, came up and joined the Hoosier, who explained **the** matter to them, and a**sked** their advice.

"Our orders are to let no one pass in or out," spoke a **red-hair**ed man, whom Morgan immediately recognized as Bill Green, of the Lexington Home **Guard.** "And we can't disobey orders, if Morgan's men do catch you," added another voice, perfectly familiar to his ear. He looked over the group. There were four there that knew him well—the least circumstance might betray him.

What should he do? To attempt to deceive them was risking **every** thing. They might recognize him at any moment. And how gladly would they seize upon him. What a prize! "Cal. Morgan, the brother of John Morgan!" All the papers in the land would be filled with the glad intelligence.

They debated but a moment. Giving Curd the signal, he wheeled his horse, and started off at full speed.

"Rebels! rebels!" and a half dozen bullets shredded the air around their head. **One** passed through young Curd's Lincoln cap. **One glanced by** Morgan's right foot, but no damage was received **by either,** as they dashed on as rapidly as their horses could bear them, pursued by four of the picket-guard, who, mounting their steeds, set out to catch the rebels.

The horses of the pursuers were fresh, **and they were fast gain**ing on the two fugitives.

"Fire, Curd," said Morgan. "**Maybe we can kill one of them** This will put an end to the chase."

Curd obeyed the bidding, and fired. The shot was harmless. It was immediately replied to.

Morgan turned himself in his saddle, and aimed at the man nearest him.

"Oh, **God!** I am shot—I'm killed!" cried out the Yankee. His companions halted.

Morgan and Curd took advantage of the confusion, and spurring their horses forward to their fullest speed, dashed over the hill and out of sight. Nor did they stop until they were assured they were beyond the guns of their enemies.

There was high merriment in camp as they told over the story of their escape, and many a joke was perpetrated at their expense.

It was one o'clock the following day. A young female, closely veiled, rang the door-bell of Mrs. Morgan's residence. A servant quickly appeared.

"Hand your mistress this card."

In a few minutes Mrs. Morgan entered the parlor.

"Is your son at home, Mrs. Morgan?" asked the girl in a whisper, as the two seated themselves on the sofa.

"Which one, Belle? What do you mean?" asked the old lady in a voice of surprise.

"Cal., Mrs. Morgan."

"No, my dear. You surprise me by your question. What do you mean? You did not expect to find him here, did you?" asked the old lady, trembling from head to foot.

"Get your bonnet, Mrs. Morgan, and go with me. My brother and young Irving are at my mother's, and want to see you. Be quiet; I'll tell you when we reach the carriage. Let me call the servant," added the young girl, as she saw the nervous state of Mrs. M., who, unable to control herself, stood leaning on the table. The young girl placed the bonnet and shawl on the trembling mother, and led her to the carriage, ordering the driver to take the most private way home. The young girl turned to Mrs. Morgan, and said, "My brother and Mr. Irving reached home this morning about three o'clock. They avoided the pickets, and got in without difficulty. Your son and—"

"Which son, Belle?" gasped the agitated mother, seizing her arm. "God grant John has not fallen into their bloody hands!"

"No, no, Mrs. Morgan; it was not Colonel Morgan, but your younger son, Cal. It was agreed that he and Jack Curd should attempt to pass the Federal pickets in the dress of Lincoln soldiers. They were on horseback. My brother and Mr. Irving set out on foot, and succeeded in getting safely through, and are now at my mother's. They were all to dine with you to-day; this was the agreement when they parted. But brother thinks our house is watched, and he and Mr. Irving are afraid to leave. They sent me to see if your son and young Curd were with you, and if they were not, I was instructed to bring you home with me."

"Oh, my child, my poor son! I am afraid the Yankees have

got him. How shamefully they will use him, merely because he is a Morgan! My cup of grief is full—it overflows. Surely, I am stricken—afflicted. But I must not falter. These are no times for fear and irresolution. My children fight for a just cause; I must trust them in the hands of God. Have you seen the morning paper, my child? If they are captured, that, no doubt, contains the intelligence."

"I have not, Mrs. Morgan. We do not take the *Observer;* but there is a boy with some papers. I will call him, and get one."

The carriage was stopped; the boy called; the paper purchased.

Eagerly the young girl looked over its columns, while Mrs. Morgan sat in breathless suspense at her side.

"They were not caught, Mrs. Morgan. Here, listen how narrowly they escaped. I know this must be the account of it," and the young girl read the description of the scene as it had occurred the night before. "They were dressed in Federal uniform, Mrs. Morgan. I know they were so; there can be no mistake about it. My brother and Mr. Irving are thus attired, and they told us your son and young Curd used the same means to avoid detection."

"Thank God! my child is safe. I should be very glad to see him, but I would not have him risk his life to come to me. I have been trying all the morning to get a pass out of the city, but they would not grant me one. I feel I would risk every thing to see my children; but, with their brutal cruelty, they deny me this poor request, just because they know it almost breaks my heart."

The ladies alighted at Mrs. Castleman's door. Mrs. Morgan was shown up stairs into a private room, where she was welcomed by the two soldiers, who sat enjoying themselves in the midst of friends of both sexes, and of all ages.

The heroes soon related to Mrs. Morgan's anxious mind the whole story, and assured her that the statement in the morning paper must be correct, as the description of the two men accorded precisely with the appearance of her son and his friend.

Most happily the evening passed to these two men, prisoners as they were in the home of their birth; their rights as freemen trampled into the earth by a horde of Abolitionists, who had no more right on Kentucky soil than Caffres or Bushmen.

Friend after friend called in, until the large room was filled with the young, the old, the gay, the sober, all anxious to see old acquaintances who now enjoyed the high reputation of being Morgan's men.

Having seen their sweethearts and friends, and obtained all the **information they could, the two set out** to retrace their steps, and **heroes they were dubbed, as at one o'clock** that night they entered their camp at Georgetown, without a scratch or any such memento of an affray **with the Yankees.**

Ah, what lasting memories gather around that midnight excursion!

CHAPTER XXXVII.

STAY OF THE CONFEDERATES IN GEORGETOWN.

Colonel Morgan took possession of Georgetown on Tuesday evening, July 15th. The same evening, he issued the following proclamation to the people of Kentucky:

"Kentuckians! I come to liberate you from the despotism of tyrannical fanaticism, and to rescue my native State from the hands of your oppressors. Everywhere the cowardly foes have fled from my avenging arms. My brave army is stigmatized as a band of guerillas and marauders. Believe it not. I point with pride to their deeds as a refutation of this foul assertion.

"We come not to molest peaceable individuals, nor to destroy private property, but guarantee absolute protection to all who are not in arms against us. We ask only to meet the hireling legions of Lincoln. The eyes of your brothers of the South are upon you. Your gallant fellow-citizens are flocking to our standard. Our armies are rapidly advancing to your protection. Then greet them with the willing hands of fifty thousand of Kentucky's bravest sons. Their advance is already with you. Then,

> 'Strike for the green graves of your sires!
> Strike for your altars and your fires!
> God, and your native land!'"

The citizens believed his words, and reinforcements assembled around his standard from Franklin, Scott, Trimble, Owen, and Bourbon counties. Brave hearts and strong arms rallied to swell the number of Kentucky's deliverers.

On entering the town, Colonel Morgan immediately took possession of the press and telegraph office.

The operator, a deep-dyed Lincolnite, declared, on a demand being made for his apparatus, that it had all been packed up and sent to Cincinnati as soon as it was known the Confederates were marching on the place. Colonel Morgan scanned the poor affrighted felon from head to foot. He was a pretty good judge of men and circumstances, and feeling assured that the creature was trying to deceive him, he in a very calm, decided tone, told him he could make his choice of two things: either produce the battery, etc., or take a trip with him South, to share the privileges of a Dixie prison.

The man looked blank with astonishment. This fearful alternative was wholly unexpected. His heart drew back in dread before the horrid picture his excited fancy drew of the miseries of a Castle Thunder. He hesitated—looked confused—paled and reddened by turns. How could he convict himself of falsehood? He cast a furtive glance on the colonel, as he stood there calmly awaiting his decision. He saw the demand was imperative. Moving slowly towards the bed, he stooped down, and, with the look of a criminal, drew from its hiding-place all the missing apparatus. Colonel Morgan received it gracefully, at the same time ordering two of his men to take in charge the poor, trembling operator until further directions.

Situated as Morgan was, in such close proximity to the enemy now assembled in force at Frankfort, seventeen miles in his rear, and at Lexington, only twelve to his right, and also rapidly congregating at Paris in front of him, it became necessary to act with the greatest dispatch and caution.

A company of men, under Captain McMillan, was immediately sent out to effectually destroy the railroad between Midway and Lexington, and Midway and Frankfort, thereby preventing reinforcements from being sent to Lexington.

The boys performed this task with alacrity and success. They tore up the track, blew up the stone bridge, rendering the road wholly useless to the enemy, and returned in triumph to Georgetown.

Scouts were also sent forward towards Paris, to ascertain the number and position of the troops at that point.

The day following Morgan's entrance into Georgetown, as he was sitting in his office with Colonel St. Leger, Major Duke, and others, among whom were many of the first citizens of the place, an old man, of venerable appearance, was conducted in by two of his men, who informed the colonel that the visitor had intelligence of importance to communicate.

The colonel rose, and received the old gentleman with a polite bow and pleasant smile, at the same time requesting him to be seated, which the visitor did with an air of simple modesty. Colonel Morgan scanned him closely from head to foot. He was a plain, unassuming farmer, dressed in homespun, and wearing a low-crowned beaver hat, which he now held in his hand. His countenance was open, and expressive of ingenuousness and truth. Colonel Morgan was satisfied with the scrutiny. It was impossible for such a man to be guilty of a desire to deceive.

Excusing himself to his friends, and leading the visitor into a small ante-room, Colonel Morgan questioned him respecting the intelligence he bore.

"I come, colonel," replied the old man, in a mild, respectful tone, which at once bespoke him a gentleman, "to inform you with regard to a Federal force at Stamping Ground, about twelve miles from here, which I think, sir, you can easily capture, with all their accoutrements."

Convinced that the old man's **story was reliable, Colonel Morgan** asked: "**How many Yankees do you** think there are in **the force** of which you speak?"

"Only about seventy-five, sir. I myself have counted them **twice**, and both times I made that number."

"Are they well armed, sir?"

"Very well, colonel. First-rate guns, and every equipment necessary."

"What have they besides their guns?"

"Tents, wagons, and stores of every kind, which have been sent up recently from Frankfort. And, in addition to these, they have some boxes of guns which have not yet been opened."

"Can they fight pretty well, and have they a brave captain?"

"Can't answer for the men, colonel; but their captain is as brave a man as ever lived."

"Are they looking for my men, and have they made any preparation to receive them; and if so, of what nature, and where?"

"When I left there, late yesterday evening, they were **all in** confusion, every moment looking for you to come down upon them. I judge, colonel, they are looking for you yet. They had no defence then, and I should think, from the scare they were in, that they have found no time for preparation of any kind; your scouts could readily ascertain this, colonel. Any man there would tell them."

Colonel Morgan thanked the old gentleman kindly, and desired him to dine with him at the hotel. But the old farmer declined. "All he desired was, to be permitted to shake hands with the men, and bid them God-speed in their glorious cause."

A guide was appointed to show the old man to the camp and introduce him to the boys.

"Call Captain Hamilton," said Colonel Morgan, to one of his aids.

"Captain," said the colonel, as the young officer stood before him, "take with you one hundred men and proceed to Stamping Ground, break up the Federal encampment there, and capture all their stores, and report to me at this point."

The dashing captain set out with his men about noon. The road was fine, and, after a ride of an hour and a half, they came upon the Federal pickets, who fled at their approach, giving to the encampment the fearful intelligence that Morgan's whole force was marching into the village.

In vain their captain endeavored to rally them for a fight. He told them they could drive back thrice their number. But his arguments could not convince the frightened men that they possessed this wonderful amount of courage. They seized their guns, but, further than this, they manifested no disposition to fight. They stood, fearful and irresolute. He assured them the enemy numbered but about fifty men—that the pickets were scared, and did not remain to see how many there were; plead with them to protect their homes and families—to show themselves worthy supporters of the glorious old flag which their forefathers had so nobly defended.

After much persuasion, he induced them to follow him a few hundred yards from their encampment, where he formed them in line of battle. By this time the enemy could be distinctly heard, rapidly descending the hill into the village. The clattering of their horses' hoofs was fearful to the affrighted ears of the trembling men.

A young man of the place rushed up and cried out that Morgan, at the head of at least five hundred men, was dashing on to attack them. It was enough. The forces broke and ran, scattering in every direction. Each one sought safety where he thought it could best be secured.

Some did not stop until they found themselves lost amid the high hills that bound the village on the north. Others secreted themselves in barns and houses, while others, finding escape impossible, surrendered themselves and received their parole. Captain Hamilton ordered his men to set fire to the tents, and destroy the guns and stores. They then returned to the village, and, amid the wonder of the gaping crowd, took possession of the medical and commissary supplies, which soon shared the fate of the tents and guns.

The victors remained awhile to rest and enjoy the hospitality of the friends who, as soon as they were relieved of the presence of the Lincolnites, hastened to surround them and congratulate them on their bloodless victory.

Recruits, to the number of seven or eight, joined them here, and were provided with guns taken from the vanquished Lincolnites.

A detachment was sent under Captain Castleman, brother to the one who had so successfully entered **Lexington, to destroy the railroad** bridges between Paris and Lexington.

Success having crowned all of Colonel Morgan's plans, the boys felt themselves safe in their present happy position, and gave themselves up to enjoyment. They dashed out into the country, visited the farm-houses, **where they were kindly** received and treated to Kentucky's best cheer; called to **see the ladies;** partook daily of the nicest provisions, **which were sent in** the greatest profusion into the camp; **laughed, danced, and sung.**

Colonel Morgan was waited upon by many of **the best citizens** of the place, who dared thus to speak out their sentiments, **despite** the dark scowls and bitter threats of **the** Union neighbors.

There was a physician in town, uncle to Major **Gano, of the** Texas squadron. This gentleman had been a rabid Unionist from the beginning of the troubles, and was one of the first men **in that** community to advocate the formation and arming of a Home Guard **company.** In consideration of his active services in obtaining arms **and enlistments, he had been** selected as captain of the body, but **with his men he had ingloriously** fled to Lexington, having first sent his family **to the country.** His residence was in the suburbs of the town, and **fronted by a most** beautiful lawn. Into this Major Gano marched his **command and encamped.**

The Texas boys soon **learned** they were on the premises of one of their bitterest foes, and, fired at the thought, they vowed to **destroy every** thing before them.

"**Why** should they protect the property of a man who was then under arms to kill them?" they argued, and with that spirit of "evil for evil" which inhabits the human breast, they set **out to** begin their work of destruction.

The major, hearing of their intention, **forbade** any man's touching any thing on the premises, **and** placed a guard around the house. And, a few **days** after, **when the possessor** returned, he found every thing in *statu quo*, except some forage, which the men had been permitted to appropriate for their horses.

The premises of **other** Union men were everywhere guarded with the same fidelity. And instead of the ravage and ruin which always characterize the progress of the Abolition hordes, they left behind them undisturbed homes and thankful, happy hearts.

CHAPTER XXVIII.

THE PARTING.

It was the evening of the second day of Morgan's occupation of Georgetown. Orders had been given that on the following morning the whole command must be ready to advance at an early hour. Busy preparations for a move were everywhere made throughout the ranks, for the men well knew what Colonel Morgan meant by an early hour.

The dreamy twilight was gliding noiselessly over the earth. The sun declining behind the western horizon, had left in his golden way a flood of light, which fell in mellow radiance over the soft summer's landscape. The stars, one by one, stole out from behind their blue hidings above, and looked quietly down upon the green earth. The moon sent out her silvery beams to add to the heavenly beauty of the scene. The meek-eyed flowers lifted lovingly their tiny heads to catch the kiss of the cooling zephyr as it sported on airy wing across the tufted lawn and waving meadows.

With mingled emotions of joy and sorrow, Charley wended his way over the slope that intervened between the encampment and the town. Old memories rushed through his mind. The past, the present, the future, each crowded upon his thoughts with their promises, their sadness, until, bewildered, he could only feel—not think.

To-night he should see Mary—perhaps for the last time. Should they meet again, it must be after years had run their weary round. Perhaps—and he shuddered at the thought—perhaps the Angel of Death might come and intervene his dark wing—and they should never again meet until they should together stand before the Great White Throne above.

He was passing through the beautiful lawn which bounds that famous stream, the "Big Spring of Georgetown," when he heard a ringing laugh, which was all too familiar to be mistaken. Seeking the point from whence it issued, he found Mary, Jenny, and John reposing on the grassy mound, which rises like a throne above the gurgling spring, the mossy haunt of the guardian naiad of these crystal waters.

Charley approached them, and seating himself on the green carpet beside the group, joined in the merry conversation, which was chiefly supported by Jenny and John. There was a want of interest in his words, and his air was that of one whose thoughts were far removed.

Mary was silent and embarrassed. She, too, had essayed to join in the merry chat, but her words were without interest, her sentences left unfinished. Her eyes sought the ground, or looked listlessly out into vacuity; while the varying shades that passed over her now thoughtful and saddened face told the changeful feelings that thronged her bosom. Her soul was burdened with a fearful sorrow. Afar off in the future she saw the shadow which now fell so ominously about her, deepening and deepening, until it became impenetrable gloom.

She had parted once before with Charley, but *then* she felt no fear. All was bright and hopeful, and adown the opening vista she looked and beheld everywhere sunlight and joy. Why the change—this sad, this fearful change? She could not tell. There was no cause in the present for this dark foreboding. Why should she borrow sombre clouds from the future? She asked herself the question, and her heart answered, "Coming events cast their shadows before." But she would be cheerful; for Charley's sake she would cast away her despondency and be herself again. She made the endeavor, and for a few minutes succeeded in assuming her wonted gayety. But it was a desperate effort, and could not last.

Charley observed the marked change in her manner, and it served to increase the sadness which was brooding so heavily over his own heart. He looked on that sweet face, usually so radiant with smiles, and its thoughtful, pensive cast, rendering it tenfold more beautiful, was as a barbed arrow to his soul.

And those large, lustrous eyes, ever the home of gladness, now, despite herself, suffused with tears, spoke to his trembling, loving heart in tones of resistless eloquence the deep feeling that she was struggling to suppress.

Charley led her slightly apart from the others, and seated her beneath the wide-spread boughs of an old oak-tree that crowned the summit of the gently rising slope. The moon stole through the overhanging arches, and fell in silvery shimmer on the smoothly shorn grass at their feet.

For several moments the two remained silent. Charley felt his heart bursting to tell her all he felt—all he hoped—all he feared—but he knew not where to begin.

"Mary," he said, at length, "I go away from you to-morrow. This is the last time I shall see you for months—perhaps for years —indeed, Mary, we may *never* meet again. You know the chances of war are uncertain;" and he paused, unable to proceed. Suppressing his feelings, he resumed: "We may never meet again on earth, Mary; but let me pledge you once more, here beneath these bending heavens, whose myriad beings witness the vow, that in death as in life my love shall be yours. I need not tell you of that love, Mary; you know its depths—its constancy. But I felt, as I sat beside you on that mossy slope, that it was perhaps asking of you too great a sacrifice to remain pledged to me, when there seems to be so little promise of any consummation of our happiness. And here, Mary, I would say—though it is like driving the cold steel through my own bosom—that if you prefer, I will release you from an engagement which, under the present circumstances, may prove unpleasant to you.

She turned upon him those large soft eyes, now filled with tears, and her voice was low and tremulous. "Charley, do you doubt me? Else why this proposal?" The tears gushed from her eyes, and streamed over her sad face.

"Doubt you, Mary; *doubt you! No! no!*" he replied, with deep earnestness; and he threw his arm around her, and drew her to his bosom. "Doubt you! never, never, Mary! Sooner would I doubt the words of Holy Writ than the love which, amid change and time, has shown itself unchanging—steadfast as the foundations of the earth. I know your love is as true as the heavens themselves. But, Mary, you are young, beautiful, admired, courted, and is it not wrong—ask your own heart, is it not unjust to yourself—to bind yourself to one who has not now the remotest prospect of rendering you happy?"

"If you do not doubt me, Charley, and will promise to love me always, I ask no more;" and she looked up into his face with such a sweet trusting smile, that Charley felt it to live the bliss of years in those few fleeting moments.

"It is enough, Mary!" he exclaimed, while his tears fell thick and fast, "I ask no more. I shall go feeling in the depths of my soul that, come what may, you will prove constant and true. And I pledge you here, before the Great Jehovah, whose eye looks now upon us, and the shining angels around His throne, that never, never, while life lasts, shall your image pass from its sacred temple in my heart."

He drew forth a locket, and threw the chain about her neck. "**Look at** that, Mary, when I am gone, and remember always that I love you." He pressed her to his bosom, and kissed her long and fervently.

"I go now, Mary. **To remain, is but to** torture both your heart and mine. God bless you—God bless you!" He kissed her once more, and leading her back to her brother and friends, bade them farewell, and hastened away.

CHAPTER XXXIX.

THE TRAP—THE TABLES TURNED.

On the velvet grass, beside the Big Spring at Georgetown, lay the manly form of Colonel Morgan, stretched out at full length, reading the Cincinnati and Louisville papers of the previous day.

"The trap has been laid," said the Louisville *Journal*, "and the horse-thief Morgan has fallen into it. He is now at Georgetown, with Frankfort on one side of him, Paris and Cynthiana on the other—with Lexington in his front—each point with as many men as he has in his whole command. There is no way of escape for him, unless he decides to betake himself to the Ohio river, where he will find ample opportunity to cool the ardor of his patriotism. Caught at last, let every loyal heart rejoice that this traitor, thief, and coward, is soon to meet his just doom."

"We may expect to see the reckless guerilla chief, John Morgan, soon a prisoner in our city," said the Cincinnati *Gazette*. "Escape is now impossible. He is surrounded on all sides, and there is no outlet from the mesh which environs him, save through our city to Fort Warren."

"Caught at last," wrote the editor of the *Commercial*. "John Morgan, the noted bandit and horse-thief, is at length entrapped. Reliable information locates him and his dirty followers at Georgetown, completely surrounded by our troops, who, under their gallant leaders, will soon make an easy prey of their victim. He is now just in the situation we have long desired to place him, and the next intelligence we look for will be the announcement that the whole gang is bagged."

"Ha! ha! ha!" broke out the colonel. Dashing the papers from him, he sprang to his feet and approached the murmuring spring.

"What's that, colonel, that pleases you so?" asked his adjutant.

"Nothing, Alston, except that we are now completely entrapped by the Yankees; surrounded on all sides; no way of escape. Here, read for yourself. Great and mighty prophets, these Northern editors. But we'll see," and the colonel stooped and drank a refreshing draught from the cool, crystal waters of the old spring

"Castleman has left?" said the colonel, looking round from his stooping position to the adjutant, who stood reading the papers, highly amused at the startling announcements.

"Two or three hours since, colonel. They have already reached the railroad, and successfully accomplished their business, I hope, and are now menacing Lexington from the Winchester pike."

"We must leave here at an early hour to-morrow morning, before sun-up. Let every thing be ready, Alston. Harrison, with a company of seventy-five men, must menace Lexington from the Georgetown pike, as soon as the day dawns. If necessary, we must drive their pickets into the very town."

The adjutant bowed, and left to carry out the orders. Colonel Morgan threw himself on the green sward to perfect his plans.

The evening was very warm. The thermometer stood at ninety, but the thick foliage of the grand old oak, beneath which the colonel reposed, shut out the sun's scorching rays. The breezes danced among the leaves overhead—the clear, limpid waters gurgled at his feet.

"Dotards!" exclaimed Morgan to himself, laughing. "Do they think I would allow myself to be hemmed in and taken by them? Old Prentice will have another tale to tell his gullible readers before the setting of to-morrow's sun."

Colonel Morgan took a calm survey of the position of affairs. All Indiana, Ohio, and Kentucky were aroused, and from every available point, troops had been forwarded for the purpose of surrounding him and "bagging his whole force."

Heavy reinforcements had been sent from Cincinnati to Cynthiana, and from thence to Paris. A large force was assembled at Lexington, at Frankfort, and at Louisville. But, as the road was destroyed between Lexington and Frankfort, no reinforcements could be furnished the former city by the latter. Lexington, if threatened, must depend for succor on Paris. This would relieve this point, and also greatly weaken Cynthiana.

Castleman, on the morrow, would advance upon Lexington from the direction of Winchester. Harrison, with his men, would, at the same time, threaten the city from Georgetown. This must necessarily create a panic, and the withdrawal of troops from the line of the Lexington and Covington railroad.

"What's the news from Frankfort?" asked Morgan of his courier, as he rode up, covered with dust and perspiration.

"About three thousand troops, colonel, and fortifying. Expecting an attack every hour."

"Ah, hah!" ejaculated the colonel to himself. "All right—just as I desire."

The morning sun was just beginning to beam above the eastern horizon, when Colonel Morgan, at the head of his men, set off at a rapid pace on the road that leads from Georgetown to Cynthiana. They had proceeded but a few yards, when a courier dashed to his side.

"How is Lexington?" inquired the colonel, checking his horse.

"All in consternation, colonel, since yesterday evening. It is believed that our men, to the number of several thousand, are moving on that place from Winchester; that the road to Paris was destroyed, and that you would attack the city early this morning. Couriers were immediately dispatched to Paris for reinforcements just as soon as the news reached Lexington, and troops had already commenced to pour in from that point when I left, about two hours ago."

"Did you meet Captain Harrison and his men?"

"I did, sir, half way to Lexington."

"Trapped, bagged, indeed!" said Morgan. "I'll show them who's bagged."

The July sun poured down his hot, scorching rays on the moving column, as it dashed along the dusty limestone road. The springs and streams were dry, and not a drop of water could be obtained for man or horse, after leaving Elkhorn creek at Georgetown.

It was just past noon when the wearied and dust-covered column of almost famished men were ordered to halt, three miles from Cynthiana. The scouts that had been sent forward to ascertain the position of affairs at that place, returned, bringing the intelligence that a large force of infantry, cavalry, and artillery was well posted in the town for its defence.

"Call Major Gano," ordered Colonel Morgan. "Major," said he to that officer, who promptly appeared in response to the call, "take your Texas squadron and make your way round so as to enter the town from the right; and you, Colonel Harper, with your regiment of Georgians, cross the river and get into the rear. Lieutenant Harrison, you, with your artillery, accompany me. The attack will be made by me in front in half an hour."

The Texas and Georgia regiments dashed off to take the positions assigned them.

Colonel Morgan, at the head of his men, moved down the pike. When within half a mile of the town, orders were given for four hundred men to dismount and secure their horses in a woodland to the right. The others were to remain mounted, and dash upon the cavalry of the enemy, his infantry being in most excellent position, just outside the town, protected by a stone fence.

The engagement commenced by the firing of a volley from the enemy, upon the advancing column. This was quickly responded to by Harrison's battery.

"Forward!" rang out, and the men, inspired by their leader's presence and daring, rushed on the concealed foe. The Federal cavalry were soon driven back before the impetuous onset of the Confederates. But the infantry, protected by the stone fence, held their position, and continued to pour volley after volley into the advancing ranks.

Here and there fell one and another, killed or wounded. But the moving force pressed steadily on. Showers of bullets cut the air and sped on their work of death. The loud and rapid discharge of artillery stunned the ear with deafening roar. For an hour the contest raged with the wildest fierceness on both sides. The Federals knowing their advantage in position, and stimulated by the cheering words of their commanders, were determined not to yield.

But they could no longer withstand the impetuous charges of Morgan's men, who fought with more than their wonted desperation, and finally they began to retreat. They fell slowly back, taking advantage of every fence and house, to shelter themselves, and fire upon their pursuers. There was a stone wall within the surburbs of the town, behind which a squad of men had taken cover, and from this protected point they poured into the Confederate ranks a sharp and destructive fire. They could be dislodged only by a direct charge upon their position. Private Moore, of Louisiana, heading a company of twenty-five men, rushed upon it in face of a rapid fire of musketry, and, leaping the fence, routed the enemy, who fled in wild confusion, throwing aside guns and haversacks in their precipitate flight.

The Home Guard made a sudden rush for the Court-house, but this movement had been anticipated, and a detachment of Confederate cavalry swept round and cut off their retreat. The regulars were hemmed in between Morgan in front and Gano on the right, while the Georgians moved up in the rear. Thus completely surrounded, they saw nothing before them but a hand to hand fight.

Suddenly white handkerchiefs were observed streaming from

the points of many bayonets, and waving from windows. The battle was over. The vanquished enemy had surrendered.

Four hundred and twenty persons were soon paraded in front of the Court-house for parole, among whom were seventy Home Guards.

Colonel Morgan, while crossing the street, had his attention arrested by a little girl who ran wildly along shrieking with fright. He caught the child in his arms, and asked her what was the matter.

She laid her little bare head on his shoulder, and sobbed wildly. He smoothed her tangled hair, patted her stained cheeks, and with soothing voice endeavored to assuage her grief.

It was several moments before she could speak.

"Oh, my father—my dear father! They have got him! I will never see him no more!" And the little, trembling creature burst into a fresh paroxysm of tears.

"Where is your father, my child?" asked the colonel, in a soft tone, at the same time continuing his caresses.

"The Secesh has got him, sir. They'll put him in the big prison. Aunt Nancy told me so."

"And where is your mother, my child?"

"I haven't got no mother, sir. She's went up to heaven, when I was a little baby."

Colonel Morgan felt the tears rush to his eyes. He thought of his own little girl and her mother now in heaven. He understood the whole case, and bearing the child in his arms, he moved into the midst of the prisoners.

"Whose child is this?" asked the colonel. "Is her father here?"

A man—one of the Home Guards—rushed forward.

"It is my child, colonel. Thank you—thank you for your kindness," said the grateful father, as the tears streamed down his face.

It was an affecting incident—such a one as sometimes occurs to relieve the horrors of dread-visaged war. And none of those who witnessed it were ever known to call Colonel Morgan harsh names after that.

The men were speedily paroled and sent under an escort to Falmouth, where they took cars for Cincinnati. Colonel Morgan found himself possessor of a fine 12-pounder brass piece of artillery, a large number of small-arms, a great supply of commissary and medical stores, tents, ammunition, and about three hundred government horses. The horses—such as were deemed fit—were selected by the men; the stores of all kinds, together with the ammunition, were destroyed.

The command rested in Cynthiana for the night, ready to set out on their victorious march at an early hour on the following morning.

CHAPTER XLI.

PARIS, RICHMOND, CRAB ORCHARD, SOMERSET.

THE alarm and uncertainty which pervaded the Federal forces in central Kentucky at the brilliant exploits of Colonel Morgan, and the rapidity of his movements, can scarcely be conceived. Lexington and Paris both threatened, Cynthiana taken, no one could decide which would be the next point of attack. Lexington called upon Paris for reinforcements—Paris, in reply, demanded succor of Lexington. But the condition of the latter city became so hazardous, menaced as it was from the direction of Georgetown and Richmond, that it was finally decided to concentrate the troops within its limits for its defence. Accordingly, the forces were ordered from Paris to Lexington, leaving the former town wholly at the mercy of the advancing foe.

On the 19th of July, the day following the capture of Cynthiana, Colonel Morgan moved upon Paris, now entirely undefended. When within a few miles of the city, he met a flag of truce, tendering him the peaceful and quiet possession of the place, and when he entered the streets, cheers and welcomes rang out on the air. Remaining here through the night, Colonel Morgan understood, through his scouts, that very nearly the entire force from Lexington was being moved upon Paris, for the purpose of attacking him. Not desiring an engagement, when it could be avoided, Colonel Morgan determined to fall back upon Richmond, preparatory to leaving the State. Accordingly, orders were issued to the men to be ready to march early the following morning. Meanwhile, pickets kept watch, lest at any time they should be surprised.

As the Confederates were setting out the next day towards Richmond, they discovered the Federals moving towards the town from Lexington. Colonel Morgan called a halt, and, by a little manœuvring, so scared the Yankees, who supposed he intended to flank them, that they wheeled about and made a quick retreat. Thus relieved of their presence, Colonel Morgan was enabled to bring off all his guns and stores without molestation or detriment.

The only loss sustained was that **of one** picket, who, **it was** supposed, was surprised and captured by the enemy in their advance.

From Paris the Confederate force marched to Richmond. Here the warmest enthusiasm greeted them on all sides. Their passage through the town to their encampment beyond, was a grand ovation, each individual vieing with his neighbor in his endeavors to **manifest** his delight and approbation. Ladies showered bouquets **and waved** handkerchiefs—children waved handkerchiefs and smiled—men, old and young, smiled, and bowed, and **hurrahed.** Ample provision was made **for a luxurious** repast for the whole command, who **partook of the kindly cheer** with right good zest, their appetites **being** well developed by their long and weary ride. Several **recruits joined them here,** who were furnished with arms and mounted.

It had been Colonel Morgan's **intention to remain in Richmond** several days, thereby giving an opportunity **for the enrolment of** many who were desirous to enlist under his standard, but being informed that a large cavalry force had been sent out by way of Danville to intercept and cut off his retreat, he determined to thwart their plans by pushing forward to Crab Orchard, which point he reached the 22d July, at daybreak.

There he found **about one hundred and** twenty wagons and about one million dollars' worth of stores, all of which was given into the hands of his **men** to be destroyed, as it was impossible to remove any thing over that **rugged, broken country.** The boys gave themselves **to the work of burning and** breaking with great zest, and soon the gigantic task was accomplished and the whole **column** again on the advance towards Somerset, which **was** reached at sundown of the same day. This point was the **depot** of the Federal army at Cumberland Gap, and contained large stores. Colonel Morgan, feeling entire safety, took possession of the telegraph office, and countermanded every order of General Boyle with regard to the **movement of** the troops **still in pursuit** of him. There another million dollars' worth of Federal property was destroyed, and a thousand **stand of** arms recaptured that had been taken from General Zollicoffer's forces at the memorable and **disastrous engagement** at Fishing **Creek.**

Having here rested his troops, Colonel Morgan moved forward **to** Sparta, which point **he** reached July 24th, having been absent on his expedition **just** twenty days, during which time he "captured **(and** paroled) over twelve hundred prisoners, seven thousand stand of arms, one gun, and destroyed, at lowest computation, seven and a half million dollars' worth of stores, arms, and subsistence, besides hospital buildings, bridges and other property. Besides this, with the loss of only ninety men, he dispersed over seventeen hundred Home Guards, captured seventeen towns, in which he destroyed war material, and marched above one thousand miles, and recruited his force of eight hundred and seventy men to twelve hundred."

After Colonel Morgan's return from Kentucky into Tennessee, the latter part of July, he removed his **headquarters to** Hartsville, a small town on the north bank of the Cumberland, some twelve or fifteen miles from Gallatin, in a direct line, but much further than this by the river.

There was a Federal force, mostly Kentuckians, in possession of Gallatin, commanded by Colonel Bruce. Colonel Morgan **determined to capture the town, Yankees and all, and to this end he** sent a force under Captain Desha to execute his purpose. This was on the morning of the 12th of **August.** The detachment was accompanied **by George A. Ellsworth**, telegraph operator, who **had, on so** many occasions, rendered Colonel Morgan valuable assistance while in Kentucky. The morning was beautifully **bright; the sun** had scarcely risen when the party found themselves within two miles of the town. Dashing **forward** so as to catch the Federal colonel unawares, the Confederates were demanding the surrender of the place before the Yankees knew aught of their unwelcome presence in their vicinity. **The movement was** *comme il faut.* The Federals were completely surprised. No resistance whatever was offered, but surrender came as if it had been a premeditated thing. The men, with their colonel, were paroled by Captain Desha. When, however, the paroled colonel and his men reached Louisville, a few days afterwards, they were arrested on the charge of cowardice, and sent forward to Camp Chase for imprisonment.

Colonel Bruce was severely reprimanded for yielding his command into the hands of the enemy without a struggle; **but he** argued that resistance, under the circumstances, was wholly useless. They were surrounded by the Confederates without a moment's warning. His men were not under arms, there was no organization, nor could any be effected before the rebels were upon them.

While Captain Desha, assisted by Captain McCann, of the Cheatham Rifles, was scaring the Yankee Kentuckians out of all sense of propriety by marching upon them, *sans ceremonie,* and claiming them as prisoners, Mr. Ellsworth was playing his part of the game by annoying the enemy with dispatches. Dashing into Gallatin, on his fine chestnut sorrel steed, booted and spurred like any other brave Knight of the Southern Cross, he rode quickly up to the principal hotel and inquired, in quite a peremptory tone, for the telegraph office.

"At the depot, sir," replied the waiter of the public house, looking at him in blank astonishment.

Ellsworth hesitated no further. Spurring his horse, he galloped off at full dash to the depot. Alighting, hurriedly, and throwing the rein over his horse's head, he burst open the door, and sprung up stairs to the bedroom of the sleeping operator, who, aroused by the dreadful noise, looked up from his bed to see—oh, horror!—a "rebel" standing over him with a six-shooter presented at his head.

Pale with affright at this most fearful apparition, he sat stark upright in the bed. Could it be so? He rubbed his eyes and gazed wildly up. There it stood. Was it ghost or de'il, or what was tenfold worse than either—an avenging rebel? His hair stood on end. His eyes stared fearfully from their sockets; his lips were pale and motionless; he trembled from head to foot, like one suddenly seized with a strong ague.

"Why are you so scared, man?" said Ellsworth to him. "I do not want your life—behave yourself, and you have nothing to fear. Resist, and you are a dead man. Dress yourself and come with me; Colonel Morgan needs your services in the room below."

The poor affrighted operator, somewhat reassured, sprung from his bed at the word of command, and hastily donned his apparel. As he gave the last few hurried strokes to his hair, Ellsworth, impatient of waiting, turned upon him and said:

"Now, follow me, sir, to the room below."

The man seized his hat and obeyed the command with alacrity.

"Now, show me all your signals. Mind, no cheat. I will not be imposed on," said Ellsworth sternly, as the two reached the room and stood beside the desk.

Had the operator thought for a moment of deception, the bloodthirsty look of the huge revolver which Ellsworth still held in his hand, would have dissipated any such intention in a moment.

"Now, let me test the line to Nashville and Louisville."

The Yankee, with a gracious smile, stepped aside.

"O. K.," said Ellsworth; "what is your earliest office hour?"

"Seven-thirty minutes, sir," responded the operator, bowing obsequiously.

"And it is now just five," said Ellsworth, taking out his watch and looking at the time; "two hours and a half before I can begin my work."

Ellsworth ordered breakfast for himself and prisoner, and the two sat down side by side to the steaming coffee and smoking rolls as if they had always been the veriest cronies.

"Seven o'clock! we must to our work, sir!" and Ellsworth escorted his new-found friend from the breakfast-table back to the office.

Placing Mr. Brooks outside the office under guard, Ellsworth entered and took possession, feeling that he sufficiently understood matters to communicate with any point.

The signal was given at seven and ten minutes. It was from the depot office in Nashville.

"Train left here for Louisville on time."

Another signal, and the operator at Franklin, Kentucky, informed Gallatin that the train had left *on time* for the South.

Ellsworth stepped to the door.

"Tell Captain McCann I wish to see him at this place immediately," he said to a Confederate soldier who was standing near.

In a few minutes the captain rushed into the room.

"Any trouble, Ellsworth?"

"The train from Franklin will be due, captain, in a very little while. Had you not as well prepare to take charge of her?"

"Certainly, certainly, Ellsworth. I will do so with pleasure;" and the captain dashed out, called together his men, and posted them in proper position for the proposed business.

Soon the train came steaming on, all unconscious of danger. She had scarcely reached the water-tank, just outside the town, when the Confederates very politely made known their desire to take her in charge.

This was readily assented to by the engineer and conductor, who saw that resistance or escape was not for a moment to be thought of.

The train from Nashville was due, but there were no indications yet of her arrival.

Ellsworth, seating himself, asked of the Nashville operator: "Train No. 6 not yet arrived. What can be the trouble with her?"

The reply soon came. "Guess Morgan's got her; she left on time with twenty-four cars, six loaded."

Bowling Green called Gallatin. "Where is the Nashville train? Heard any thing from her?"

"Not yet arrived," responded Ellsworth.

Bowling Green then called Nashville. "Gallatin says No. 6 not yet arrived; have you heard from it?"

Nashville, in reply, said: "No; they left on time."

Bowling Green, quite perturbed and beginning to suspect foul play, called to Nashville: "Any rumors of the enemy between Nashville and Gallatin?"

"Nary rumor!" was the laconic answer.

Gallatin was then informed by Nashville that the passenger train had left on time, bound North.

Inquiry after inquiry was made of Gallatin with regard to the two trains, both by Nashville and Bowling Green. The invariable response of Gallatin was, "Not yet arrived."

Eleven o'clock came. Nashville, as if aroused by some sudden fury, began to call on Gallatin with great earnestness.

Ellsworth suspected the cause. The cars, having obtained information of the occupancy of Gallatin by the Confederates, had suddenly put back to Nashville and given the alarm. Questions were asked which Ellsworth did not dare to answer, for fear of betrayal.

He stepped to the door and invited in the Federal operator, Mr. Brooks.

"Now, sir," said Ellsworth to him, "I want you to answer Nashville in the most satisfactory manner. I shall listen to your replies, and if there is any thing wrong, it will have to be atoned for by a life during the war in a Dixie prison."

"All shall be right, sir," responded the accommodating operator, glad to be at his old work again.

Nashville, with suspicions highly aroused, called to Gallatin: "What was the name of that young lady you accompanied to Major Foster's?"

"Be careful," enjoined Ellsworth, leaning over the shoulder of the operator. "Give a correct reply!"

"I don't remember of going to Major Foster's with any young lady," was the response.

"What about that nitric acid I sent you the other day?" asked Nashville.

"You sent me no nitric acid."

"Is that correct?" and Ellsworth eyed the operator sternly.

"Correct, sir."

Nashville, yet suspicious: "Mr. Marshall, the Superintendent of Railroads, is not yet satisfied that you are not Morgan's operator, and wishes **you to tell him who you** desired to take your place while you were gone on leave of absence, how long you wished to be gone, and where did you wish to go?"

Gallatin responded: "Tell Mr. Marshall that I wished Mr. Clayton to take my place, while I got a week's leave to go to Cincinnati."

Nashville was convinced, and soon there came over the wires the following order:

"**To Murphy,** Conductor, Gallatin:

"You will run to Edgefield Junction to meet and pass trains Nos. 4 and 6, and pass them both at that point. Answer how you understand. B. Marshall."

The answer was promptly returned, that the instructions would be obeyed.

Nashville informed Ellsworth that "trains Nos. 4 and 6 had left again at eleven fifteen minutes."

About four o'clock in the afternoon, Nashville again called lusti**ly on Gallatin: "Trains Nos. 4 and 6 are** back again the second **time.** We have positive information that the enemy is in possession of Gallatin. **Where is** Murphy?"

It was unnecessary to practise the deception further. The cars would not come.

At five o'clock, Ellsworth sent the following to George D. Prentice:

"**Gallatin,** Aug. 12, 1862.

"George D. Prentice, Louisville, Ky.:

"Your prediction, in yesterday's paper, regarding my whereabouts, is like most of the items from your pen. You had better go to Jeffersonville to sleep to-night.

"John H. Morgan,
Commanding Brigade."

A lady, beautiful and sprightly, accompanied by Captain McCann, and **two other** ladies, made her appearance in the office, and **was introduced to** Mr. Ellsworth.

"Will you, **Mr.** Ellsworth, send a message to Prentice for me?" she said, laughing.

"Assuredly I will, with pleasure."

She turned to the desk, and hurriedly wrote her dispatch:

"GALLATIN, **Aug. 12, 1862.**

"GEORGE D. PRENTICE, LOUISVILLE, KY.:

"Your friend, Colonel John H. Morgan, and his brave followers, are enjoying the hospitalities of this town, to-day.

"Wouldn't you like **to be** here? The colonel **has seen** your $100,000 reward for his head, and offers $100,000 **better** for yours, at short range.

"Wash. Morgan, whom you published in your paper some time ago, when he was in Knoxville, **accompanies** his cousin John, with four hundred Indians. He seeks no scalp but yours.

"A SECESH LADY."

Mr. Brooks, who was now released from his military position, as prisoner, joined in the **conversation** of the merry party, with as much zest as any one. He seemed to enjoy highly the **whole day's** proceedings, and even jested over his morning fright.

The party repaired to the house of the lady, where, with the assembled fair of the good town of Gallatin, the heroes of the day passed the evening with song and dance, and the graphic recital of thrilling adventure. Every manifestation of joy that the citizens of Gallatin could give at their release from Yankee thraldom, was displayed by all classes.

Captains **Desha and** McCann, and their men, were welcomed to the **best cheer the town** could offer—were feted and toasted—and smiled upon by bright eyes, until they were made to appreciate, in some degree, at least, the great favor they had bestowed on the grateful inhabitants.

CHAPTER XLI.

GALLATIN—ITS REVERSES.

The great joy of the good people of Gallatin at being relieved from Federal domination, by the brilliant and successful attack of the Southrons, under Captains Desha and McCann, was soon turned to mourning, by the sudden reoccupation of the town by the enemy.

Nashville was aroused when she heard that Boone and his men had been seized upon by the Confederates, and the Yankees were determined to be avenged for the loss, by repossessing Gallatin, capturing the hated Morgan and his men, if possible to do so, and, in the event of failure in this object, to wreak vengeance on the defenceless inhabitants of the town and country.

Accordingly, an Indiana regiment, headed by one Colonel Hefferen, set out from Nashville to avenge the dignity of the Federal arms on the audacious rebels, who had dared to molest them in their fancied security.

The Federals proceeded to Gallatin, but found no Confederates upon whom to be revenged. But their insatiable cruelty must be gratified, and with that fiendishness characteristic of the Yankee soldier, they sought out the aged and peaceful citizens, and dragged them from their homes, to incarcerate them in their wretched dungeons.

From house to house these armed wretches proceeded, bursting open doors, rushing from room to room, using the most revolting language to unprotected females, dragging forth, with abuse and cruelty, old men whose only crime was daring to oppose such inhuman proceedings, and a government that would sanction and support them.

Store doors were forced by this lawless mob, dressed in the uniform of United States soldiers; the owners were seized and placed under guard, and all their goods either appropriated or wantonly destroyed. A squad of fifteen of these armed ruffians, with demoniac yells and imprecations, rushed upon the Masonic Lodge, drove in the door, and with the fury of madmen, upset and broke chairs, tables, desks, dashed the fragments about the room, threw the Bible from the window, dragged forth the paraphernalia of the order, and scattered it wildly about the street.

The astonished citizens stood aghast in mute horror as this fearful work of destruction progressed, not daring to offer even a word of protest against the brutal outrage. Private property shared the same fate, and those who were known to the desperadoes as Southern men and women, had to behold in silent despair their houses sacked, their valuables destroyed before their eyes, or taken off by the despoilers.

The work of lawless plunder ended, the unholy rioters set out to return to Nashville, carrying with them forty of the best citizens of the place.

They proceeded on foot as far as Sandersville, at which place Colonel Morgan's men had burnt the railroad bridge, only a few days before.

They had not advanced many miles on their way before Colonel Morgan, with twelve hundred men, appeared in the streets of Gallatin. His arrival was greeted with the joyous tears of the grateful citizens, who hailed him as the deliverer of their husbands, sons, and brothers.

He needed not to be importuned to pursue the dastardly foe. Gaining a few points of information, he dashed out after him. He had not gone far before he overtook the retreating column, who, instead of giving battle, fled precipitately in the direction of Nashville.

The Confederates pursued the fleeing Indianians, killing about sixty and taking a large number prisoners.

On they dashed, as if for dear life, the victorious troops driving them everywhere before them with dreadful carnage. At last, the remnant of the fugitives, breathless with affright, threw themselves behind a triangular stockade at the junction of the railroads, and here made a stand. The Confederates made a charge upon the ranks, but it was a strong position, and the few Yankees sheltered behind the walls would not repay for the trouble, so the colonel withdrew and retraced his way to Gallatin, bearing with him the released citizens, who had been rescued from a doom worse than death.

The women rushed into the streets, wild with joy, as they saw the conquerors advance, bringing with them their husbands and sons. They clasped their benefactors in their arms, thanked them with streaming faces, and invoked the blessing of Heaven on them in all their undertakings. Never was there a more affecting scene, and never before had Colonel Morgan and his men felt so grateful for triumph over the foe.

Officers and men were alike welcomed into every house, where repasts were prepared for them with a lavishness that fully bespoke the gratitude of generous hearts. The young ladies played and sang for the gallant heroes who had restored to them their fathers and brothers. A late hour in the night found the festivity and joy unabated.

Early the next morning Colonel Morgan was informed that a large Federal cavalry force, led by R. R. Johnston, formerly a lawyer of Paducah, Kentucky, who had been sent out for the express object of capturing him and his command, was rapidly marching on Gallatin.

With his wonted quickness Colonel Morgan rallied his forces, and set out on the Hartsville road to encounter his sanguine pursuers.

With him were Major Duke, Colonel St. Grenfel, Major Gano, Captains Desha, McCann, Hamilton, Castleman, Harrison, etc., all of them tried men, whose courage and daring were everywhere known and acknowledged. The force of the enemy was reported as very heavy, well armed and equipped.

Nothing daunted by those rumors of superiority, the brave Southrons shouldered their guns, and, mounting their steeds, rushed out to the conflict.

They had proceeded but a mile when the cry ran through the ranks, "The Yankees! the Yankees!"

Instantly orders were given to halt and prepare for an engagement. Colonel Morgan formed his men as rapidly and as well as he could, and opened upon the advancing foe a heavy volley of musketry. The attack was furious; the Yankees replied in a manner which told their determination to fight.

Again and again, in rapid succession, were the Federal ranks assailed by a stunning shower of Minnie balls and bullets, while the men advanced nearer and nearer towards the serried ranks of the enemy. The sharp, quick fire of the guns, mingling with the low bass of the trampling horsemen, filled the air with strange, wild sounds.

"They are determined to give us close quarters," observed Col. Morgan to Major Duke at his side. "See, they are advancing rapidly upon us!"

"But see, colonel," said Duke, "they bring a flag of truce; they will surrender. Cowards!" added Duke, scowling, " thus to yield without a fight."

" They surely will not do that," rejoined Morgan, keeping his eye steadily fixed upon the approaching squad, who bore down upon them at a pretty lively pace. " They would brand themselves with infamy forever to pursue such a course."

The firing ceased as soon as the flag had been observed, and the column, all ready for a renewal of the engagement, stood awaiting the issue of the parley.

Colonel Morgan received the deputation with his usual dignity and grace.

The note was presented, bearing the signature of the Federal colonel. It was a request for an armistice of several hours. Johnston stated that he was surprised; hadn't his men together and was not prepared for battle.

Colonel Morgan read the missive.

"Tell your colonel," said he to the Yankee adjutant, **"that he has been** pursuing me from point to point, eager for a fight. I am now ready, and he can have it. If he can defeat me, very well."

The officer dashed **back to** his colonel with the pithy reply, and **in a few minutes hostilities were resumed.**

The **Confederates, like men in** earnest, pressed upon the foe, sending at **every step a** hail-storm of bullets into his irresolute ranks. **The Federals made but a** feeble reply. Onward drove the inspirited men—onward, onward **to** glorious victory.

Again appeared the truce flag. Johnston had surrendered! Loud and long rose the shout from the joyous hosts of the victors. **The air was rent** with their wild acclamations.

The Federals were surrounded and compelled to lay down their arms. Colonel Johnston, with six hundred of his men, **were made** prisoners. The remainder fled to the Cumberland. **Believing** themselves pursued, they had cast aside every thing that might retard their flight, and actuated by that strongest law of our nature, "self-preservation," had betaken themselves to the river by the shortest available route, thinking if they could but place that stream between them and the pursuing hosts, they had nothing to fear. On reaching the **bank of** the Cumberland, many deserted **their** horses and dashed into the stream to swim to the opposite **shore.** They were bootless, hatless, gunless, horseless—a parcel **of** poor affrighted men, running away as best they could, from the " dreaded Morgan and his dare-devil crew."

Finding themselves on the south bank of the stream with their horses on the wrong side, unable to walk to Nashville, they fell to work to press into service every horse, mule, and vehicle they could find. And it was a rich, rare spectacle to see the motley cavalcade under whip and spur, bound in hot haste for that city of safety.

"What's the matter friends?" asked a traveller, as he encountered them outside of Lebanon, driving on as fast as circumstances would allow towards Nashville.

"Done for—done for," was the response of a little red-haired man, who sat astride a mule, on which there was not even so much as a blanket; "Morgan has cut us all to pieces, taken our colonel and all his men, and we only are left to tell the tale."

"Too bad, my friend! Has Morgan whipped us again? But where did this occur?" interrogated the delighted Southerner, preserving a grave mien and solemn tone.

"At Gallatin!" responded half a dozen voices, as if eager to proclaim their defeat.

"Who commanded you, and how many strong?"

"We were under Colonel Johnston, and numbered eleven hundred."

"And did that desperado Morgan whip you with his handful of ragamuffins?"

"Oh! he had thousands—the earth was perfectly covered with his men. He did whip us, and I believe he can do it again. These Secesh seem to have the devil in them. They fight like the old scratch himself!"

"Bad—bad!" exclaimed the traveller. "Something must be done to put this fellow Morgan out of the way."

"Can't catch him; he's here, and there, and everywhere. We were after him for days, and then met him where we didn't expect to find him. You can't head him; it's no use trying!"

The traveller bowed and rode on. As he passed along the column, he asked several more the same question. All gave a like response. "Morgan had used them up!"

Colonel Morgan again returned in triumph to Gallatin, bearing with him his long line of prisoners. The remainder of the day was occupied in giving them paroles. The next day Morgan and his men, followed by the blessings and prayers of the whole population of the little town, left Gallatin for earnest work elsewhere.

But a few weeks elapsed, before the Yankees were again the

masters of the place, exceeding, if possible, their former cruelty and coarseness.

Thus, in the short space of a few weeks, this little town, **with its** population of true Southern hearts, was thrice in the possession of the diabolical foe—twice relieved by the most opportune **presence** of Colonel Morgan and his men. **Such are the** chances **of war.**

CHAPTER XLII.

NEWS FROM HOME.

AFTER the brilliant victory at Gallatin, the Confederates retired to their headquarters near Hartsville, to wait another favorable opportunity to pounce upon the Yankees. The defeat of Johnston had served to greatly heighten their fear of the invincible and ubiquitous Morgan, teaching them an increased degree of caution, which they evidenced by prudently keeping close to their base of operations. Now and then, an ill-omened squad, venturing out too far, was caught up by the vigilant Southrons and placed beyond the pale of further mischief.

It was a time of activity with the Confederate army in Tennessee. Bragg was busily engaged in preparations to move into Kentucky. Buell, understanding his designs, and desiring to thwart them, was slowly falling back from Deckherd. General Kirby Smith was advancing into Kentucky through Pound Gap, with an army destined to occupy the central portion of the State, and there act in conjunction with General Bragg, whose proposed route was through Glasgow, Mumfordsville, and Bardstown.

Colonel Morgan, with a portion of his force, dashed once more into Glasgow, arrested the provost-marshal of the place, and issued a proclamation, in which he told Union men of the punishment with which they were to be visited for their cruel treatment to his friends.

Then returning into Tennessee, he consummated his arrangements to accompany Bragg on his proposed expedition.

"We are going into Kentucky again, boys," said Lawrence, as the mess sat around the table one morning soon after the return from Glasgow, "and we go this time to stay."

"Three cheers for old Kentucky!" huzzahed a half dozen voices.
"Three cheers for the noble old State; may we win her from Yankee rule!"

"Come, Charley, what are you doing there, moping in that corner?" said young Brent to our hero, as he lay stretched out on his straw pallet, on one side of the tent. "Come, don't you see breakfast is ready? and didn't you hear that glorious news? We **are** going back to old Kentucky to **stay**. Why, Charley, I should think you would jump over the table at that glorious announcement!"

"I am delighted, Brent, at the news, but my head aches so miser**ably**, I don't believe I could sit up. John, are you sure this is **true?** Where did you get your information?"

"**From** headquarters, Charley. It's as true as the Bible, and no **mistake. Major** Duke told Cal. Morgan, and **I** had it from Cal. himself just a few minutes ago. Come, Charley, get up, boy, and drink this cup of coffee. It's some of my own make, and it is most excellent—isn't it, boys?"

"First-rate! first-rate, John!" answered all present. "**Good** enough to make a sick man well."

"Here, Charley, drink this," said Brent, as he moved from **the** table to the side of the straw pallet with a tin cup of smoking coffee in his hand. "Drink it, and if it doesn't cure your head in ten minutes, I am no doctor."

"Charley raised himself up on his elbow, and taking the **cup** from the soldier's hand, sipped a few drops, and handed it back to **his friend.**

"Pshaw, Charley, you haven't taken any. You must drink it all. Two sips won't cure **you! I do believe,** boys," said Brent, turning to the mess, "that Charley has the heartache! Have you been hearing any bad news **from Kentucky lately?** Come, make **a** good confession. Here, let me feel your pulse. Pshaw! just as slow and steady as an old clock. Not a bit **of fever.** Now put out your tongue, Charley. I must examine you thoroughly, and find out your symptoms, before I can prescribe."

Charley, smiling, obeyed the bidding, and turning **his face full** to the light, thrust out his tongue for Brent's inspection.

"Why, your tongue *is* a little coated, **old fellow—but not much.** A good cup of coffee, and you will be well **by dinner. No time to** get sick now; we may be off to Kentucky in **less than twelve** hours. When did you **say we were to set out, John?**"

"**In a** few days, less than a week, I understand. But it may be to-morrow. You know Colonel Morgan gives us but short notice."

"Here, Charley, you must **indeed take this** coffee,—nothing like it for headache and **heartache; indeed,** it will **cure** all kinds of **aches.** Drink it down, and think of the Kentucky girls, and, my word for it, you will be well in two hours."

"No doubt of it, Charley," said John.

"But, here," said Brent, "let me pour you another cup. That's cold."

"Don't put any sugar in it, John; I am sick at my stomach, and can't bear any thing sweet."

The fresh coffee was handed, and Charley drank it down, wearing all the while a martyr look.

"Now, be still a little while," said young Brent, feeling his pulse a second time with mock gravity, "and by dinner you may be up and preparing for your trip to Louisville."

Breakfast being over, young Brent took it upon himself to clear away the table and arrange things generally. He could do this, he said, and at the same time attend to his patient. The other boys went out to learn the news of the day.

They had not been gone more than half an hour, before John rushed back to the tent, his countenance bright with joy, exclaiming: "News from home, Charley—a letter, a letter! Come, my boy, this will make you well, and no mistake."

Young Brent, who sat beside the open tent, motioned to him to be silent.

"What's the matter, Brent?" inquired John, anxiously, as he reached his side and saw his grave expression of countenance.

"Be still—Charley is asleep, and is really quite sick."

"Oh, I hope not, Brent—nothing more than a nervous headache, I judge. You know he has done a great deal of hard work recently. No one fought more bravely at Gallatin than did he, and he has been kept quite busy since we came into camp."

"It may pass off without serious consequences, but I feel anxious. He has a very high fever. Here, look how red his face is, and he complains of severe pain in his side."

John approached the bedside, and stooped down to look at his friend.

The sleeper's lips moved—"Water, water!" he muttered.

"What will you have, Charley?" asked John, bending tenderly over him, and speaking as softly as a woman.

The sound of his voice aroused the sleeper, who, starting, opened his eyes and looked wildly up.

"What did you say, Charley?" repeated John. "Is there any thing you want?"

"I didn't say any thing, did I? I must have been dreaming. But I am intolerably thirsty. Can I have some water, Doctor Brent?" he said, casting a mischievous glance into that personage's face.

Young Brent hastened to procure him a cup of fresh water.

"Charley, what for a letter from old Kentucky?" asked John, quizzically.

"Oh, have you a letter, John?" And Charley sprang up in bed and gazed beseechingly on his friend. "Is it from Louisville? But you haven't got one, John," he added, despondingly. "Why did you tantalize me so?" and he fell back upon his pallet with a sigh. "Oh, my head!" he exclaimed, a moment after, pressing his hands on his temples. "It aches to bursting."

"I am sorry I excited you so, Charley; but here *is* a letter for you, and it is from Louisville, too."

Charley stretched forth his hand eagerly, and grasped the extended missive.

"From Lu—my dear, dear sister. But how did you get it, John?"

"A man came through direct from Louisville—young Mayner. He brought a large lot of letters for our men."

"Did you get one from home, John?" inquired Charley, most earnestly.

"Yes; from Mary—a sweet, loving letter as ever a brother received. You shall read it, Charley, when you get through with yours. You will see Mary has not forgotten you. She mentions your name in every line. And she says, too, as you will see, that she has written you a long letter to be sent out with this. Perhaps it has not yet been distributed."

"Where is Mayner now, John? Do tell him to come here immediately, if you please."

"He is somewhere in camp. I will go directly and bring him here. But let's read our letters first."

"Here is a good, cool drink of water, Charley; I ran all the way from the spring," and Brent put the cup to his fevered lips. He swallowed the draught eagerly.

"I must bathe your head, Charley."

"Oh, wait, Brent, until I read my letter from home," and Charley hastily tore off the envelope. As he opened the letter, a neatly folded sheet of note paper, closely written, fell out. He took it up and examined the signature. As his eyes rested upon it his face flushed crimson.

"Ah, Charley will have no further need of my services now, John. That *billet-doux* will prove a sovereign panacea. Headache and heartache will now be cured. I'll leave you to your happiness, my most happy patient, and go and see if I can't hear of a letter for myself. Surely some friend has remembered me."

Brent stepped outside the tent, leaving Charley to peruse his sheet uninterrupted by his presence.

John sat down beside the straw pallet, and the two read and re-read their letters, and talked of the dear friends at home, whom they hoped so soon to see, until Charley forgot his headache in the joy of glad thoughts and bright anticipations.

"How pleasant it would be, John, if we could but get to Louisville in time for Lu's marriage! It is strange Spalding told me nothing of this, when we met at Lebanon; but then I left so abruptly, and doubtless he had deferred it till morning. And Mary, too, she ought to have known of it."

"She told me, Charley, that for some weeks previous to your sister's visit to Cincinnati—you know Miss Lu was there while we were in Kentucky—they had met only on the street. Lu for some reason had avoided her. May not this account for her want of information?"

With sparkling eyes and throbbing brain, Charley read over and over the letters. Great big tears gathered in his eyes and rolled down his burning cheeks, as he dwelt on the sweet words of love from her who was his heart's idol.

"All well, Charley?" asked John, re-entering, after an absence of several minutes.

"Very well," was the reply, while a happy smile lighted up the fevered face of the speaker.

"Yes, that's it. How sad for us all that that miserably false report should obtain currency! You know to what I allude, John? It caused me such anguish as I could not describe, and produced that temporary estrangement between Mary and Lu—these two, who have been as sisters from their childhood."

"Bad, bad—too bad. But it's all passed now, Charley, my boy, and we won't torment ourselves over it longer. You see, the two girls are reconciled, and I should think that you and Mary were *friends* again. And who knows, Charley, but we may yet be able to accept Miss Lu's invitation? Do you not know, my boy, that we are all going into Kentucky soon? I heard it just before I came to you; but, in our joy over the letters, forgot to mention it. Yes, indeed, it's so. We go to stay this time, and, if I mistake not, I shall have the pleasure of attending more than one wedding," and John looked so significantly at his friend, that Charley, in spite of himself, blushed red, and betrayed deep embarrassment.

"Going into Kentucky! when, John?" and with the excitement of the thought, he sprang from his straw pallet, on which he had been sitting during the conversation, and placed himself on a saddle that stood **near by**. "Can it be possible, John, that this is true? Oh, what joy! But, then," and, sighing, he leaned his aching head on his hand, "I may not be well enough to go."

"Oh, yes, you will, Charley. Why are you so despondent? **All** you need is a little rest. You have been overtaxed of late; indeed, I don't think you have gotten **over** your trip to Kentucky. Come, now, you must lie down and be still; keep quiet, and you will soon be better. I'll go now and see if I can learn any thing respecting our movement."

Charley threw himself on his low bed, in accordance with his friend's desire. But he could not rest. He endeavored to call in his thoughts and compose himself to sleep; but the endeavor was a futile one—his mind would go out to live in the future.

11

CHAPTER XLIII.

DISAPPOINTMENT.

"When do we set out for Kentucky, Irving?" asked young Gray, a member of Charley's mess, as with a group of boys he stood under the wide-spread branches of a sycamore-tree, eagerly listening to Irving's recital of the joy and glory that awaited the command, when, as victors, they should repossess the soil wrenched from them by the oppressive foe.

"Very soon, I understand. Preparations are now being made for the trip. Hawkins, here, thinks it will not be more than a week."

"And it may be earlier than that, Irving. Major Duke told me this morning that we must hold ourselves in readiness to leave at any moment after to-day. I should not be the least astonished if we receive orders in less than an hour to set out to-morrow morning."

"What is that, Hawkins?" asked Lawrence, as he stepped up to the side of the speaker. "Is it certain we are going into Kentucky?"

"No doubt of it, sir. We are to accompany Bragg's army; that is, we are to move simultaneously with them."

"And when will this be?"

"We will leave this point very soon; perhaps in less than twenty-four hours. There may be some work for us to do before we are ready for invasion."

The old woods rang with loud acclaim, when the boys became assured that the rumor which had filled them with such anxious expectations, was really true.

To Kentucky hearts, Kentucky is still dear. Her sons feel deeply the blighting disgrace under which she now rests, but they love her still; and with pity for what she is, and hope for what she yet may be, they stand ready to struggle, to fight, to pour out their best blood, to vindicate her rights and break the base, ignoble shackles that now bind her to the most disgraced, ignominious despotism the world has known for ages.

Noon came. Charley was no better. His fever had increased, and with it the pain in his head. The physician was sent for, but he had rode off to a neighboring farm-house, where one of the men lay ill with fever. Just at night Dr. Lapsley returned to camp. He was immediately called in to see Charley.

After thoroughly examining his symptoms, he prescribed medicine to be taken at intervals of four hours through the entire night.

"What do you think of my case, doctor?" inquired Charley of him, most anxiously, as the physician sat holding his pulse. "I will be well enough to go to Kentucky, won't I?"

"Oh, I hope so, sir," responded the doctor, most encouragingly. "Your fever is pretty high at present. But I think a night's rest and the medicine I have left will greatly restore you. Who will take it upon himself to administer these powders, gentlemen? They must be given regularly."

"I," said John, promptly; "just leave them with me, sir."

"You understand directions?"

John bowed assent.

Next morning found our young friend much better. He had slept well through the night, and the medicine had produced a most happy effect. His head was measurably relieved, the pain from his side gone, and his fever quite abated.

He spoke most hopefully of Kentucky, and, with the others of his mess, longed for the moment of departure to come.

The doctor called early, pronounced him better, but advised quiet through the day.

At noon, it was announced that the whole command must hold itself ready to leave the day after the morrow.

Charley joyously set about preparations for the trip. When evening came, he was weary and exhausted, and his fever quite burning. But he was determined to brave it out, and did not mention it to any one. He spent a restless, wakeful night, and the next morning found him unable to rise from his bed.

Dr. Lapsley was again called in. He examined him and pronounced him worse.

"Oh, can't I go, doctor?" asked Charley, in a most pleading voice.

The doctor hesitated to answer. "I must be candid with you, Charley," he said, after some delay. "I think it will be impossible. I fear you may have a serious attack of fever."

Charley turned himself on his low bed, and burst into tears.

Brave, daring soldier as he was, he could not refrain from this expression of his sore disappointment. The physician left directions and hastened away.

"Brent," and Charley turned his face imploringly up to that of his faithful friend beside him, "I have a favor to ask of you. Will you write me a letter to-day, and take it with you to Kentucky? I feel I shall not go. I trust you as a friend. I know you will not betray me."

"Yes, Charley, I will do any thing I can for you."

"Here, sit down beside me, and I will tell you all."

The young soldier did as he was requested, and Charley told him the story of his love.

"I confide my secret to you, Brent, as I would to a brother. I know you will not deceive me. Now get the paper, and let me tell you what to write."

Brent wiped the tears from his face, and obeying Charley's directions, got paper, pen, and ink.

The letter, full of love and devotion, was penned.

"Tell my friends, Brent, that if I live I will follow the army into Kentucky as soon as I am able."

Dr. Lapsley looked in about noon, to order Charley to be moved to a neighboring house. He had been out and secured a place for him.

The ambulance was provided, and stood ready to carry him to his new home. One by one his friends called to bid him goodby. It was an affecting scene to see those brave men, so unused to weep, wipe away the tears from their sun-burned faces, as one after another took leave of their sick comrade.

"I will stay with you, Charley," said John. "I feel it my duty. I cannot leave you in this condition."

"Oh! no, John, I cannot ask it of you. The doctor informs me that the people where I am going have promised to nurse me, and he himself will board in the same family. No, no, go on, and may you be permitted to reach Louisville and see again all our dear friends there."

John and Brent accompanied Charley, and saw him most comfortably situated at farmer Johnson's.

"Tell my friends all you know I would say, boys; I am too weak to talk now," said Charley to them, as they stood over him to bid him farewell.

The boys shook his hand affectionately, wishing him a speedy recovery; and dashing away their tears they hastened off to camp.

CHAPTER XLIV.

THE MARRIAGE.

The evening came **gloriously down over the earth.** The day had **been one of those soft, mellow days of early autumn,** when the Spirit of Beauty, descending from her empyrean **abode walks** the earth in silent majesty, scattering from her celestial train enchanting loveliness to gladden the soul, permeating it with heavenly inspirations and linking it in hope to the upper world, whose air is beauty and whose soul is infinite love. There is an *intellectuality* in the autumn which belongs to no other season of the year—a **voice which** speaks to man of the higher destiny that awaits him where, unclothed of the materiality that now fetters his thoughts **and** blinds his vision, he shall **rise to the immortality of the just,** and drink of the living fountain of knowledge and goodness that flows from the throne of the Infinite.

Dressed for the altar, the young girl stood amid her bridemaids the very personification of beauty. The natural grace and elegance of her form were charmingly manifested by the dress of rich white silk, with its point-lace flounces. A *berthe* of the same material fell from the tapering shoulders over the full bust. No ornament, **save** the simple wreath of orange bloom which bound the bridal veil, decorated her person.

On the **stand beside** her, in its soft case of white satin, lay a full and handsome set of pearls—the gift of her affianced, Mr. Spalding. Lu R. felt tempted to wear these superb jewels for *his* sake; "But not to-night," she said in reply to Mary Lawrence's earnest request to be permitted to clasp them about her neck and arms. "Not *to-night*, Mary dear; **you know my fancy:** no jewelry for a young bride. I feel he will not disapprove my taste. Nor do you, Mary?—come, **tell me truly.** Do you not think it more befitting to dispense with jewels on such an occasion."

"Yes, Lu; but these are so handsome!"

"And Mr. Spalding's gift," interposed Molly Brent, another attendant.

"I'm sure they would be so becoming, Lu. You would look

like one of the princesses of Oriental story—so majestic, so elegant. I could almost wish you would wear them," added Evangeline Lenoir—a beautiful girl of French descent, who, in early life, had been left an orphan in charge of an uncle, a man of wealth and position. "Just let me try them on you, Lu. There, see how beautiful! Oh! are they not exquisite—perfect? But I see you would rather not wear them to-night; so I'll unclasp them and lay them gently back in their soft bed."

"*When will you wear them, Lu?* I am almost dying to see them on you!" exclaimed Dolly Quitman, as she gazed on the beautiful ornaments. "Oh, how superb they are! I never saw any thing more magnificent. But I agree with you, Lu, in your taste; I am determined when I marry not to wear ornaments, even if they are diamonds themselves."

"Now the queen, and *now* the gentle girl-bride," said Evangeline, as she undid the clasps and placed the ornaments back in the *écrin,* beside which lay two other sets—one of amethyst and pearls, the other a chaste turquoise.

And there she stood, the "girl-bride," as beautiful as a poet's dream. No ornament needed she to enhance her loveliness. Her black hair parted over her forehead, swept back from the full white temples over the delicate ear, and was gathered into a large roll behind, confined by a comb of consummate workmanship, and her face was partly shaded by the gossamer veil that fell sweeping like fancy frost-work over the chiselled shoulders and full bust until it reached the floor.

> "And there were roses on her cheeks
> That came and went like living things."

And her lustrous dark eyes beamed bright with the hope and joy of her swelling bosom.

Below in the large, elegant parlors, numerous guests were assembled, awaiting in breathless expectation the appearance of the bride and bridegroom—for it is now the hour of ten.

A moment more and the throng from the door falls back—a way is open—and the attendants pass in and form themselves on the floor.

Scarcely a moment for a glance at these four lovely creatures, all in virgin white, and their handsome escorts, before the manly form of the bridegroom, bearing on his arm his gentle, blushing bride, enters and fixes the gaze of all beholders. The minister approaches, and standing before them, in a solemn and impressive ceremony unites for life the destiny of these two loving hearts.

The prayer is ended and congratulations and kisses are showered on the happy pair, whose present is perfect happiness, and whose future now wears only the hue of the rose-tint.

Ah! well it is that at such moments one cannot look with unclouded vision adown the way of life. For there must we behold the grief—the disappointment—the anguish—the parting—the pall—the bier—the narrow house which all must meet, and our hearts, aweary with the contemplation, would sit down in silence and in gloom, heeding not the present good. What wisdom, then, that the veil of uncertainty is thrown before our eyes to shut out the ill that soon must come!

It was a joyous company. Ease and genuine hospitality characterized every movement of the kind host and hostess; and that freedom from restraint and mutual interchange of thought and feelings, which always distinguish wedding parties from all others, prevailed among the guests. There was but one cloud that threw its shadow over the bright and gladsome scene—it was the thought of the far-away loved ones.

Many present had friends in the Southern army. Soon they must be exposed to the shock of battle; for it was fully known that General Bragg had taken up his march into Kentucky; and the husbands, and brothers, and sons who accompanied him, with eyes fixed so strainingly on the old homes, and hearts bent so yearningly towards the loved ones there, might never again sit by the hearth-stone, or hold sweet converse with the cherished friends of yore. Ah, no! but it might be that they would fall in the fierce conflict, and insatiate Death batten on their prostrate forms; and amid the merry laugh and joyous conversation the heart would stand still at the dread picture which the imagination called up.

The evening passed pleasantly. The entertainment throughout was marked by the finest taste and the utmost liberality. The table combined elegant profusion and most **exquisite grace**. The wines were of the **finest** flavor, the confections of the most choice kinds: while the polite and agreeable manner of Mr. and Mrs. R., served to heighten the pleasure of the whole.

On the following morning, attended by numerous friends from the city, they proceeded to Lebanon, where several days were to be passed in festive enjoyments. Mary Lawrence was bonneted, all ready to take her seat in the carriage which was to convey the bride and groom to the railroad depot, when a note came summoning her to her mother's bedside.

CHAPTER XLV.

PARTING OF THE FRIENDS.

It was the early morning. The first rays of the sun, struggling through the thin clouds that lay lazily floating in the east, threw a soft, uncertain light over the earth, which was but just awakening from its deep repose, and early morning birds, decking afresh their soft plumage, began **to warble their matinal pæans to** Him who feedeth **the young sparrows and** satisfieth the desires of every living creature.

The hand of autumn was just beginning to touch with mellow dyes the rich foliage of the woodlands. Already her presence had hushed into holy stillness the roystering summer, and filled the soul of nature with calm, contemplative thought.

Beside the uncurtained window, Charley lay on his soft, clean bed, looking out into the gray dawn of the morning. The long, weary hours of the night in which fitful sleep brought only ghastly dreams, were passed at last, and as he caught the first faint beams of the opening day, he thanked God that the dreary nightwatches were over. His head ached—oh, so severely; and his heart sadly—ah, so sadly! Alone—alone! His friends gone—and he in pain and suffering, amid strangers, away, far, far away from home and kindred. No mother to bend over him and soothe his throbbing brain; no father's voice to bid him hope; no sister's gentle hand to smooth his pillow or administer the cooling febrifuge. Alone—alone! Great, scalding tears rushed to his eyes, and chased each other down his face.

He endeavored to disengage his mind from these sad contemplations, and, turning on his pillow, he strained his gaze through the window, to find, if perchance he might, some object to distract his attention. He saw the uprising sun battling with the slothful clouds, sending his golden glory through the ridgy rifts, and heard the birds sing from amid the drooping boughs that came down over his open window, and he thought but the more of home—for often in his careless boyhood had he looked upon the same morning scene, and listened to the sweet songs of early birds. And the tears, a moment before wiped away, now streamed thick and fast.

Just then the loud and ringing shouts of his happy comrades, as they broke up camp and set out on their homeward march, borne on the morning's breeze, came in through the casement and fell on his ear. He sighed deep.

"Gone—gone—to Kentucky!" he sadly murmured to himself. "And I am here alone—left without a friend—perhaps to die! They go to meet with parents and sisters, and mingle with them in joy and gladness amid the haunts of olden times, while I, in sickness and pain, must linger here in a strange land, with strange faces around me, where no one will care for me—and all the kindness I shall receive will be bestowed because I am a Southern soldier. Hard—hard fate! Oh, the horrors of this dreadful strife! When shall it end, and we be permitted to return to homes and friends in peace?"

Just then a gentle rap was heard at his room door. He wiped away his tears, and, assuming as cheerful a tone as he could, replied, "Come in." Supposing it to be one of Mr. Johnson's family, he drew the light spread up so as to conceal his face.

"Good-morning, Charley. How do you do? What, old fellow, here by yourself? Where is Dr. Lapsley? I thought he was going to cure you immediately, so that you might go into Kentucky. Didn't know but that I might find you well enough to set out with us this morning. Came by to see. Say, my boy, can't you be off? I cannot bear the thought of leaving you behind. How do you feel, anyhow? Let me call the doctor; isn't he in the house? Perhaps he will agree for you to go. I don't know but a ride in the cool morning would do you good. You can rest in the heat of the day. I will stay with you, and we can travel when it is cool. What say you, Charley?"

"Oh, John, I wish I could go. But I fear I am too sick. My head aches dreadfully, and I feel feverish and full of pain. But I am tempted to risk it, anyhow. I had just as well die in the effort to return, as to lie here and waste away. I am sure it will kill me to remain after you are all gone. The boys have all left, I suppose?"

"Yes; started out but a little while ago. Didn't you hear their shouts? A force left this morning before daylight—an advance. All of our mess, except myself, and I obtained permission to remain, to come over and see how you did this morning."

"I am very glad you did, John," the sick man replied, looking gratefully up into the face of his friend.

"I have some little keepsakes I wish you to take home for me. I intended to mention it to you and Brent yesterday, but in the confusion of the hour, I entirely forgot it. Look there, John, in that valise, you will find two rings and a breast-pin. Give the one with the three sets in it to my sister; the other, John, with the two hearts, to Mary. The pin I wish my mother to have. And here, John, take your knife, and cut off this lock of hair, and give it to them at home."

"Why, Charley, what do you mean?" asked his friend, in astonishment. "You talk as if you were making your last will and testament. I shan't cut off your hair at all. You will be sure then to think you are going to die, and I shall not be able to persuade the home-folks that you are not dead and buried. No, no. You must make haste and get well, and carry your own love-tokens. When shall I tell them you are coming? I must see the doctor, where is he? I hope he will decide to let you go, now."

"John, I am in earnest. I know you will not refuse me this last request, before we part. I am very sick. I may die. I desire that those three articles may be given as I have said. They are my own work, made, as you know, at Camp Chase. If I should die, and I may, you know, John, they will be little mementoes that my friends will cherish for my sake; and if I should recover—why, it will all be right."

"Oh, well, Charley, I will take them if you wish me to, you know. But there is no need of sending *souvenirs* home, that I can see. You will get there as soon as we do. We go to open the way for you, and there will be nothing left for you to do but follow on."

John stepped to the valise, which stood in the corner of the room, under the stairway, and, unlocking it, drew forth the keepsakes.

"Now, John, the hair," said Charley. "You know that is an item of the request."

"Well, where will I cut it?" inquired John, assuming a gay air, although he felt as if preparing his friend for the coffin. "It will gratify you, and the hair will do for the girls to make rings of, and keep in their memory-boxes. You know all the ladies take a lock of Colonel Morgan's hair. I have seen them myself walk straight up to him with a pair of scissors in hand and clip off a bit without leave or license, and you, Charley, wish to be as renowned in this particular as the colonel. Ah, me, we are all ambitious! But tell me where I must take it off? Here, just behind the ear? It will show less than anywhere else."

"It matters not, John; wherever it suits your fancy."

"See, here, I have got a big lock: this is enough to give you renown throughout all Louisville. The ornamental hair-makers will have enough to do for weeks to manufacture it into charms, and rings, and guards, etc., etc. But where will I find the doctor, Charley? I must see him before I go, and it is high time I was off. The Yanks will catch me, if I don't look out pretty sharply."

"The doctor is up those stairs, John. I don't think he is out of bed yet."

"Well, he must get up and tell me just exactly how you are. That's what I came here for. I wished to know precisely how your case stands. I'll go up and rouse him. It's high time he was out of bed, anyhow."

Without further ceremony John sprang up the stairway, three steps at a time, and, approaching the doctor's bedside, shook him most violently.

"I want to know just how Charley is, doctor, before I set out. His friends will be anxious to hear all the particulars. He is awake now."

The doctor made a hasty toilet and descended to the sick man's room. He examined him closely, and shook his head.

"I must go, Charley," said John, bending over his bedside. "I hope you will soon be well enough to join us in old Kentucky. Don't give up; you are not very sick. He will be well in a few days; won't he, doctor?"

"I hope so, in the course of a week or ten days at the most," replied Dr. Lapsley.

"My love to all Kentucky friends, John," said Charley, in a voice choked with emotion, while his bosom heaved, and his eyes became suffused with tears.

"And shall tell them you will come as soon as you get well?"

Charley bowed assent.

"Good-by, Charley; keep in good spirits," and John shook his friend's hand most affectionately.

Charley returned the kindly grasp, but no words escaped his lips. He dared not trust himself with utterance.

John wiped away the tears with his rough coat-sleeve, and

grasping again the outstretched hand, turned hastily away and passed out of the door.

The doctor followed him to the stile.

"What do you think of Charley's case, doctor?" asked John, as the two walked out.

"He is not very sick, now; but I think, from all his symptoms, that he may have a serious spell. He is greatly threatened with typhoid fever."

"What shall I tell his parents when I see them?"

The doctor, looking down on the ground, hesitated for some time to answer.

"Tell them," he said at length, "that he is quite sick, but not dangerously so. I will give him every attention, and, I think, with careful nursing, he may be up in the course of two weeks, at most."

John shook the doctor's hand warmly, and, mounting his horse, galloped off at full speed to join his command.

CHAPTER XLVI.

THE VISIT OF THE ANGEL OF DEATH.

Low, in that still, dark chamber, the young girl bent over the wasted form of the patient sufferer, as she lay there on the soft, white couch, resignedly awaiting the summons of the messenger that should bear her to the mansion prepared above.

Long had the tried soul looked calmly at death as one who should deliver her from the pain and sorrow of this present time, and anxiously had she desired his guidance into that "world to come," whose heavenly glory from afar had shone in upon her longing spirit, giving it a foretaste of that fruition which awaits the humble child of God in His infinite presence. Day by day had the immortal being been purified, sublimated, and now yet a little while and it should cast off the last lingering remains of earth, and rise to live forever amid joy unspeakable and full of glory!

Faithfully, tenderly, had the daughter watched beside the beloved mother. Gently had her hand smoothed the aching pillow, soothed the fevered temples, wiped the damps of disease from the white, transparent brow; had administered with solicitude to each want, had anticipated every rising desire.

Her form was that of an angel minister, her light foot-fall as sweetest music to the loving mother, whose dimming eye would rest with look of tenderest affection upon her darling child. And often would the mother's heavenly aspirations fall back to earth and linger there, as she thought that soon she should see no more with earthly vision this cherished one, who, bereft of a mother's affection and care, must walk the paths of life alone—no guiding hand to point out to her its hidden snares and pit-falls.

They were together alone one evening—the mother and daughter. The physician had just left, who had confirmed the opinion of Mrs. Lawrence, that a few hours more might end her sufferings.

It was a soft, still, September evening. The golden rays of the departing sun stole faintly in through the draped window, and rested on the couch of the dying woman, and then fretted out in dreamy lines upon the dark carpet of the floor. A fire was flickering in the grate. The mantel clock, with its wonted stroke, measured off the last hours of the waning life. Mary, to whom Dr. Hardin's words were not unexpected, for her quick eye had perceived the change come on which marks mortality for the **tomb, but upon** whose young and devoted heart the announcement of its *certainty* fell as the storm on the crushed flower—the death-knell on the ear of joy—sat weeping beside the bed, holding the cold, **wasted hand in hers.** Her heart was well-nigh breaking, yet she endeavored to suppress her emotion, for she would not disturb, by her grief, the last moments of her beloved parent.

The dying woman fixed her languid eyes, beaming in their wasted light with love to her child, upon the bowed form before her—then closed them—and the thin bloodless lips moved in prayer.

"Mary, my child," she said—her voice was very feeble—"God will protect you, my darling."

The young girl sobbed aloud.

"Weep not, my child. I go to be forever at rest." She paused, for her breath came feebly up. "And you—God will shield and protect you. You have given Him your heart. He will never leave nor forsake you." The eyes closed, and the sufferer lay silent, exhausted. Recovering, she attempted to proceed—it **required great effort.** "Trust in His promises, and seek his guidance. And your brother, Mary, should you ever see him again, tell him my last moments were spent in prayer to God that he might be saved. Urge upon him the necessity of turning to God. Comfort your father, my child. He will be lonely now. Weep not for me, Mary. 'Tis the Lord—He doeth what is right."

The sobbing girl slid from her chair, and, kneeling beside the couch, buried her face in the clothes, and wept convulsively. The mother lifted her feeble hand and rested it amid the luxuriant curls that fell over the bowed face. "God bless you, my child, and give you that consolation which He alone can impart. And be thou, O Eternal Father, her guide and strength through all the coming years of life!"

The husband entered, and seated himself beside his dying wife and sobbing child. His heart was too full for utterance; and as he realized the solemn scene, the tears gathered and swept down his furrowed face. The manly form was buried beneath the weight of anguish that pressed upon the chastened soul.

The wife turned her look to his. Her breathing was growing each moment fainter and more faint.

"I am going, my dear," she said, "but do not grieve for me. It's hard to part with you and my dear children, but God, who does all things well, calls me hence, and I must go." She paused for breath. Her eyes drooped. For many minutes she was silent. Her breathing became more oppressed. The color appeared very faintly in the sunken cheek. She pressed her hand on her heart, and gasped as if struggling for breath.

Some friends entered the room and approached the bedside. "Air, air!" gasped the sufferer. Mary sprang to her feet and threw open the window. "Lift—me—up," she feebly uttered.

Mr. Lawrence, with the assistance of Mrs. Douglas and her sister, Mrs. Grant, raised her from the pillow, and, supported in an upright position, she motioned to be removed to the large chair in which she had so often sat when suffering from this difficulty of respiration. Gently they bore her and placed her in it. She gazed feebly up, while a half-formed smile played round her lips, then closed her eyes, and her head sank on her bosom. Her breathing became more and more labored: the pulse in the fallen hand less and less distinct.

"Oh, the doctor! the doctor! Run, Maria, for Dr. Hardin. Oh, mother, mother!" exclaimed Mary, convulsively, as she threw her arms wildly around the suffering form and pressed it to her bosom. "Oh, mother, mother! can't you speak to me, your child? One word, just one word!"

The husband, trembling in every nerve, stood over his dying wife, bathing the pallid brow. Mrs. Grant and Mrs. Douglas rubbed the cold extremities.

The anguished daughter could do nothing but cling to the loved form of her idolized parent, and give vent to the bursting grief of her heart.

"Oh, mother! don't you know me—your own child, your Mary? Oh, mother, dear mother! speak one word to me—just one word, mother. Oh! you are not dying—you will not leave us. Mother—mother!" and the poor, grief-stricken girl sunk to the floor and clasped her mother's knees, as if, in her frenzied madness, she felt a power to stay life's ebbing tide.

The dying woman opened her eyes feebly, and made an effort to look up. The lids drooped again, the labored breath grew fainter, a short, quick gasp, and the mother's life was done!

It was but a minute—so quickly passed—it was difficult to realize that death, in ghastly form, was in their midst. When the dread reality burst upon them, the father sank on the bed, speechless with grief. Mary uttered one wild, piercing cry, and fell fainting to the floor.

The physician entered. He read, in a moment, the fearful fact. Assisted by the servant, he placed the dead form of Mrs. Lawrence on the bed, and, turning to Mary, proceeded to restore her. It was some minutes before consciousness returned; then, springing to the bedside, she threw herself on the cold, rigid form of her mother, and sobbed as if her heart would break.

It was a sad, solemn scene. Death had come to claim his victim, and though not without warning, it was hard to bow to his stern, relentless will. Oh, how it rends the throbbing heart, to stand and gaze on the cold motionless form of one who but a few moments before was with us—whose eyes looked fondly into our own—whose words of love fell on our ear as whisperings from the upper spheres! We gaze, and fear and wonder mingle with our grief, and the awe-filled soul asks itself,—" Is this death?" Ah, what is this strange, dread power, whose fiat none can withstand? And the spirit—the life that we have loved, with which we have walked and held sweet converse—where has it fled, ah, whither gone?—and shall we be permitted again to meet it and enjoy its companionship?

How often along our pilgrim-path are our most cherished hopes, like the beautiful temple before the whirlwind's wrath, dashed to the earth by this invincible power! We spread out on the glowing canvass of the future our life-pictures, colored in roseate tints of expectancy and joy, and when the scene is complete in beauty, and happiness alone is breathed by every form and feature, then Death comes, and with one bold master-stroke, dashes his pencil, dyed in darkness, over the picture, and with bowed head and breaking heart we stand as in a maze, and gaze on the wrecked loveliness over which despair sits brooding. Ah, what can console the crushed soul under its poignant sorrow? what impart light to it amid its rayless gloom? Naught, naught, save that promise, all radiant with the beams of God's infinite mercy, which for eighteen hundred years of wailing and of gloom has come in tones of heavenly tenderness to the hopeless spirit—" I am the Resurrection and the Life."

Even when we weep over the grave of buried love, and in all the misgiving of our contracted vision we ask, with the patriarch of old, " If a man die, can he live again?" there comes swelling up in tones of celestial harmony the response, " I am the Resurrection and the Life," and our feeble faith "lifts a wing with the angels," and anchors itself hard by the throne of God.

The night wore by. I will **not** attempt to depict the grief **of** the stricken husband and orphaned daughter.

Morning came. In the still, silent chamber, hung with the drapery of death, the lifeless form lay robed in the habiliments of **the grave.** Beside the open coffin the weeping daughter knelt **alone with the** dead. Through streams of blinding tears she gazed on the pale, rigid face, until the accumulated anguish of her soul burst forth in convulsive gasps. She bowed herself, and in the bitterness **of** her soul wept until exhausted, prostrated— her grief found vent only **in sad, low** moans. Rising, she smoothed the marble brow, placed a white rose on the pulseless bosom, then kissing and kissing again the **icy lips, she took one** long, lingering look, and turned away to weep.

It was the daughter's farewell to the **dead mother. Never** again did she behold the sleeping form.

Evening came. Slowly the long procession of mourners moved through the streets, wending its way to the "City of the Dead."

"Dust to dust, ashes to ashes," said the man of God, as the **body was lowered into its** narrow house. Then came the rattling of the clods on **the coffin-lid.** A few minutes of breathless silence, while the hearts of the spectators **commune** with death, and the low tones **of the minister rise in subdued** notes to the throne of God for **mercy** on the dying congregation, which soon, one by one, must turn aside **from life and** come **and** take up their abode in the silent chamber of the grave.

To their darkened home the father and daughter return. Oh, how sadly desolate! How fearfully void! The world, too, is dark, the heavens hung with gloom. Light, light! Ah, it is nowhere to be seen. To the chambers of the soul enshrouded in despair, hope comes not; nor is there a whispering of joy in all the music of the earth. Poor, oppressed mourners! naught save the voice of the Gospel can carry consolation and peace to your stricken bosoms.

CHAPTER XLVII.

GENERAL KIRBY SMITH'S VICTORY AT BIG HILL, KENTUCKY.

It were a work of supererogation to dwell lengthily on the campaign into Kentucky. Every reader is familiar with its most trivial incidents. The battles of Big Hill and Richmond, in which our men drove the flying foe before them with most fearful slaughter—the successful occupation of central Kentucky by General Kirby Smith's army—the victorious assault on the Federal garrison at Mumfordsville by a portion of General Bragg's forces—the race between Bragg and Buell for Louisville, and the great excitement of both parties in Kentucky consequent on the relative movements of these two generals—the great rush of Federal troops into the State to oppose and drive out the Southern army—the bloody battle of Perryville—the retreat of the Confederates—all these stirring circumstances of war are as household words to every Southern heart.

The invasion of Kentucky was a bold, a daring movement. Could it have been made earlier, before the hosts of Lincoln troops were ready for the battle-field, it doubtless would have proved more of a success than it did. As it was, the forces that were sent against the Southern army, although not disciplined, were well armed, and overwhelming in numbers. The movement of the Confederates through the State was so rapid, as to make it an impossibility that large numbers of recruits should join their ranks; and, while in this respect the campaign must be regarded as a failure, the want of success should be attributed to the unfavorableness of the circumstances, and not to the lack of devotion on the part of a large proportion of Kentuckians to the Southern cause.

Kentucky is to-day, if her intelligence and interest were allowed to speak out boldly, Southern, truly Southern. She has been duped, deceived, enslaved; but, seeing the suicidal folly of her former course, she is now beginning to awake to a true sense of her position and her rights; and she will yet, let us hope, stand nobly forth in defence of those great principles for which the South has earnestly and victoriously combated.

The campaign has been pronounced a failure, a sad, sad *faux pas*, and the commanding general has been sorely censured for want of ability and oversight of points which would have insured to the Confederate arms a glorious victory. Were the design of the invasion the permanent occupation of the State by General Bragg's army, then, indeed, did the movement most sadly miscarry.

If the object was to withdraw the Federal forces from their threatening position to north Alabama, relieve eastern Tennessee, obtain a supply of provisions and clothing for the men, and give the Southern sentiment of the State an opportunity to enlist under the Southern flag, then it was not a failure, even though the expectations of the friends of the South might not have been fully realized in any of these particulars.

General Buell was compelled to withdraw his forces from southern Tennessee to northern Kentucky. The Federals, under General Morgan, found themselves forced to abandon Cumberland Gap, and thus was this important point regained to us. Provisions and clothing, to a large extent, were secured, and if recruits did not swell the ranks of the Confederates to meet even our most modest hopes, we must consider all the circumstances, and also remember that General Bragg was clothed with no power of conscription whereby to enlarge his forces to the desired maximum.

That expectations were not met, none can deny. But were not our hopes the offspring of desire, rather than of sound judgment? And even if all was not accomplished that might reasonably have been looked for, let us not *censure* where we do not fully *understand*. Failure does not always argue a want of capacity—and certainly not of *patriotism*. The contingencies of war are so many, and so frequently have the best plans of the best generals been defeated by fortuitous circumstances, that every reasonable mind must admit that "the battle is not always to the strong," but that the hand of the Lord of Hosts guides to results.

The bridal party, after having passed a joyous week at Bardstown and vicinity, returned to the city. In that short time Evangeline Lenoir had become the affianced of Edward Lasley, a dashing young man of twenty-four, who, having been left possessor of a large fortune just as he had attained his majority, had given himself up to the indulgence of every whim and caprice that his versatile nature could suggest. His father had died when Edward was but twelve years of age. His mother, whose wedded life had not been happy, owing to the acerbity of her husband's temper and his continued neglect of her comfort, had never married again, but with the devotion of a tender, loving parent, had given her whole time to the development of her son, devoting herself with the most solicitous care to the cultivation of such traits as her judgment approved, and to the suppression of those characteristics the indulgence of which she felt must lead him to ruin. But despite her vigilant watchfulness, the son had grown up hot-headed, self-willed, and given to self-indulgence. In his early childhood he had manifested this wayward disposition, and shown sad proof at an early age that he had inherited the sporting character of his father. When at school, he was always the leader in all disputes and combats—the agonistarch of the neighborhood. Handsome, fascinating, when he desired to be, he had won the admiration of Evangeline, who, with all the ardor of her French nature, had been captivated by the handsome face, exquisite moustache, and easy *negligé* air of the young man; who, in turn, had yielded to the charms of personal beauty, and the magnetic power of her natural vivacity and grace, so strikingly in contrast with the cold, dead manner of the maiden aunt, who was now the only near relative he had. The aunt, with whom he lived, was about sixteen years his senior, fastidious, imperious, captious. Possessed of ample means, Miss Dorcas Lasley led a life of unhappy indolence and capricious gratification, spending half her time plucking the gray hairs from her head, and the other half in putting them in, by fretting over every thing that came within her purview.

When she heard that "Edward," as she always called her nephew, was devoting his attentions to Miss Lenoir, she fell into a towering passion, declaring that a boy of his age was not capable of judging for himself, and had better be thinking about doing something for himself in the world. Miss Dorcas, in a monetary view, was the antipode of her deceased brother and his son. Frugal almost to parsimoniousness, she had added each year to the comfortable estate left her by her father, until she had grown to be one of the wealthy inhabitants of the neighborhood.

The bride had returned to spend the fall and winter with her mother. This Mr. Spalding had promised the doating parents when they consented to the marriage of their daughter. He had decided to engage in business in the city, and the arrangement was a very happy one to all parties.

Two weeks had passed since the marriage—about the same

length of time since the death of Mrs. Lawrence. During that interval, great changes had been made in the position of the Confederate forces in Tennessee. The plan which had been adopted by the generals as wisest and best for the repossession of that State by the Southern forces, and the occupation of Kentucky, if possible, was hastening to a development.

The family of Mr. R., seated around the fire, were discussing the prospects of the fall campaign, when Mary Lawrence entered, clad in deep mourning, her face expressive of the greatest excitement. Without waiting to bid them good-evening, she exclaimed, breathless with agitation, "Have you heard the news—the glorious news? General Bragg is coming into Kentucky; going to march directly for Louisville! General Kirby Smith is already in the State, as you know, and he has whipped the Federals completely near Richmond, and they are now flying before him as fast as they can run. General Bill Nelson is killed, too, the report says, and the whole army is literally cut to pieces. The Union men in the city are running to and fro, like so many madmen, scared to death for fear the Confederates will march right down on Louisville, and take it before they can get troops across the river to protect it. I never, in all my life, saw such a commotion; the whole town is frantic. They are moving every thing they regard valuable across the river, and they are really making preparations to surrender the city, I believe."

Exhausted, the young girl sank on the sofa beside her. Mrs. R. looked up in amazement, while Mr. Spalding sprang to his feet as if electrified. The young bride remained transfixed to her seat, her face turned with the most earnest look towards her friend, and filled with an expression of wonder: she was the first to speak—

"Oh! Mary, Mary! can all this be true? I fear it is too good to be believed. Have you not been deceived? The city is always so full of rumors that prove so false when you test them; and I fear this is like most of its predecessors."

"True, Lu; of course it is. If you could only be in the city for an hour, you would not be disposed to doubt it!"

"What is the authority, Miss Lawrence? did you understand?" asked Mr. Spalding, eagerly.

"Telegraphic dispatches, sir, from Lexington—dispatches which have been received to-day at headquarters, and which Union men, in their great consternation, could not conceal."

"Oh, that it may be true!" exclaimed the young bride, clasping her hands energetically. "Then shall we once again see our friends."

"Oh, you need not fear, Lu; it is certainly so. The whole town is filled with the intelligence. All the Union men believe it. It has come by telegraph, and will be in to-morrow's papers. You never saw such a stir in all your life. People are thronging the streets, and it looks as if everybody were beside themselves. Pa came rushing in after dinner, his eyes starting from his head, and he was scarcely able to speak. We were all terribly alarmed at his appearance, and could not imagine what was the matter, and it was some time before he was composed enough to tell us. As soon as I understood the story, I called the carriage, and Sunday evening as it is, I drove out here as fast as I could to tell you the good news; and now you are disposed to discredit my whole story. Isn't that too bad!"

"Oh! no, Mary, I would not doubt, but rather fear to believe lest we be sorely disappointed, as we have so often been before."

"Call your father, daughter, and let him hear the glad tidings. He is asleep in the back chamber. Take off your hat, Mary. Did you go to church to-day? Mr. R. was not very well, and we did not go in. Really, Mr. McKee is such a coercionist I cannot enjoy his sermons, and I find that we allow the least thing to keep us at home."

"I was out this morning, Mrs. R., but did not hear Mr. McKee. I go to the Baptist church. Their minister preaches the gospel, and is a good Southern man, though no politician."

"Oh! father, father!" cried out Lu, thumping against the chamber door, where her father was sleeping. "Do get up in a minute, and come and hear the good news. The Southerners are all coming into Kentucky—Bragg, Morgan, Charley, all, going to take Louisville and hold the State."

The old gentleman sprang from his bed, aroused more by his daughter's wild manner than her message.

"Come, father, come to the parlor; Mary Lawrence is just out from the city—come on purpose to tell us all about it. There is no doubt of it—all the Union men believe it, and are scared out of their wits. Mary says they are dashing about the streets like crazy people."

"And what is the news, Lu?" asked the old man, rubbing his eyes to get them fairly open.

"Oh! come, father, and let Mary tell you herself;" and Lu took his hand and led him along the darkened hall into the sitting-room.

"How do you do, Mary?" said the old man, smiling, and extending his hand. "What is all this wonderful news Lu has been trying to tell me about Bragg and Morgan coming into Kentucky, and taking Louisville?"

"Oh! Mr. R., it is all so, sir. Everybody believes it."

"Believes what, Mary?" asked the old gentleman, smiling at his young friend's eager manner.

"Why, that General Smith has whipped the Lincolnites all to pieces at Richmond—that General Bill Nelson was killed in the fight, and Colonel Jacobs either killed or seriously wounded—that the Yankees are retreating as fast as they can to Louisville, and the Confederates have Lexington by this time. And General Bragg is coming into the State at the head of a powerful army, and the Southerners are going to hold Kentucky. It is true, Mr. R., that General Kirby Smith has routed the Federals at Big Hill near Richmond, and is marching victoriously upon Lexington. This part of the story will admit of no doubt. Pa says all the Union men acknowledge it, and are half wild lest he should move on and take possession of Louisville before they can make any preparation for defence.

"And do you think all this can be relied upon?" asked the old man, as much excited as any of the party.

"Oh! there is no doubt of it, sir. Pa had it from the most authentic source. You know, Mr. R., pa is not a very excitable man, and by no means credulous. He has so often been disappointed about the Confederates coming to Louisville, that he is now afraid to believe any thing in our favor. But he thinks every word of this is true; and you would too, Mr. R., if you could be in town half an hour and see the craziness of the Unionists. They are running hither and thither half the time, not knowing what they are about; but all agree in saying that their forces have been butchered—that is the term they use—at Big Hill and Richmond."

"And, what is better than all," further interposed Lilly, who, up to this time, had been a silent but highly interested listener, "Morgan will be here and bring all our friends with him. Oh, won't that be a joyous time! I am sure I shall be too happy. I am going right to work to-morrow morning to prepare for them. All the peaches, and preserves, and jellies that we kept so long last fall, waiting for Buckner's men to come, are nearly gone. I must get to work and bake dozens of big cakes, and make all the nice things I can think of, for brother Charley and his friends. Won't you stay and help me, Miss Mary?" and Lilly sat down beside her visitor and grasped her hand imploringly. The earnestness of her soul spoke out in her large gray eyes, and happy anticipation from every lineament of her face.

"Can't stay to-night, Lilly, but I will come out again to-morrow, and we will then bake the cakes. Pa will look for me to return. He is lonely now," and a sad look stole over Mary's face as she thought of her great bereavement.

"And then suppose, girls, the boys do not come? You will have baked your cakes in vain."

"Oh, but they will come, Mr. R. And if they don't—but I will not allow myself to think they will not. Lu, don't you intend to make some preparation for them? and don't you, Mrs. R.?"

"Oh, indeed I will, Mary, if there is the least prospect of their getting here. I shall prepare every thing good I can think of," responded Mrs. R., with animation. She was quite as enthusiastic as the girls, and ready for any good work.

"Indeed, Lulu, I think you and Miss Mary and Lilly had better prepare lint and bandages for the wounded. They cannot take Louisville without a severe battle, and many a poor fellow must fall before we can welcome our friends back to their homes again."

"That is too true, Mr. Spalding," responded Mary, thoughtfully, "and I shall not forget your suggestion. Oh, my heart bleeds, when I think that perhaps *friends* may fall in the strife. Oh, that this horrid war could end without any further bloodshed! But I must leave, it is growing late, Lilly. Get your hat and ride in with me. Your father can call for you to-morrow—can't you, Mr. R.?"

"I will bring you out after we receive the morning news."

"Can't you remain with us to-night, Mary?"

"No, thank you, Mrs. R.; pa made me promise to be back to-night. He wants the carriage early in the morning for some purpose. I only came out to tell you the good news. I knew you would enjoy it so much. Mr. McKee would be almost tempted to church me, if he knew that I had been engaged in such 'unholy business.' Don't you think he would? Come, Lilly, where is your hat? We have just time to drive to the city before dark."

Bidding the friends good-evening, the two girls entered the carriage and drove rapidly to the city.

CHAPTER XLVIII.

DEPARTURE.

IMMEDIATELY after the death of his wife, Mr. Lawrence gave up his establishment. Bereaved, saddened, he could no longer remain amid the scenes of his former joy and happiness, now so enveloped in gloom. He took boarding for himself and daughter with a friend, a distant relative of his, who had been left a widow about two years before. Her only child was a boy of seventeen, and Mary finding but little companionship in the house, spent as much of her time as her duty to her father would allow with her friend Lu, who, though married, yet found a large place in her heart for the companion of her childhood. They already regarded each other as sisters, and Mary found a solace for her grief in unbosoming her sorrows and anticipations to one who could so readily sympathize with her.

Mr. Lawrence's time was very much occupied in settling up his business, preparatory to moving South. As soon as it was known in Louisville that the Confederate forces, under General Smith, were assuredly moving into Kentucky, he determined, in the event they had to leave the State, to go out with them, and for this purpose he was daily making arrangements for a speedy departure from the city.

When Mary reached his room, she found him sitting in his old arm-chair before the fire, his head resting on his hand, and absorbed in thought. She was pained at the expression of his face, for in addition to its usual sadness, it wore a look of anxiety and gloom.

She approached him, and throwing her arms about his neck, kissed him, and in a sweet, persuasive voice endeavored to win him from his sorrow. He replied tenderly to her caresses, and as he gazed upon her, the large tears started to his eyes and silently coursed down his cheeks. She wiped them away, and inquired the cause.

Seating her on his knee, and throwing his arm around her, he proceeded to unfold to her his plans.

"I have been thinking, daughter, while you were out, that now is my opportunity for throwing off this galling slavery, by going into Confederate lines and remaining there."

Mary looked up astonished.

"Why, father, why need you leave Louisville? The Southerners will certainly take possession of this place. There is no doubt about it, pa. Just wait a little while, and you will see there will be no need for you to seek Confederate protection—it will come to you."

"We cannot now know any thing with certainty respecting the permanent occupation of our State by the Confederates, my daughter, although every thing now looks so promising. They may be able to hold it, and they may not. If they remain, it will be an easy matter for me to return to Louisville; if they do not, I shall be safe in leaving."

Mary looked up earnestly into his face. She did not fully comprehend his meaning. She waited a moment, hoping her father would explain himself. Bending a sad look upon his daughter, Mr. Lawrence resumed:

"The only obstacle in the way, Mary, is leaving you."

"Leaving me, pa!" she exclaimed, with surprise. "You surely wouldn't go and leave me behind? What would I do without you?"

The father scarcely knew how to reply. There were difficulties in either case, which he hardly knew how to meet. After thinking for some moments, during which time Mary gazed beseechingly upon him, he said:

"If I stay here, my daughter, I may be arrested at any moment, and sent to prison. If I go, I shall be free from this dreadful apprehension. If the Confederates remain in Kentucky, I can return to you again; if not, I can send for you at any time. You will be safe here among your friends, in any event, and I may have an opportunity to send for you if the Confederates are driven back. For me to remain longer is to endanger my liberty. And as my preparations are nearly completed, I feel I had better set out the first suitable opportunity."

"You are right, pa," said Mary, throwing her arms about her father. "I would rather you were safe in the Confederacy, than to have you remain here, all the time in fear. And then, as you say, they may arrest you and put you in prison, as they did last summer, when Morgan was here, and perhaps they would not release you in years to come. But, pa, why can't I go with you? You know I'm not afraid of danger."

"But, Mary, you had better wait until I can get through, and secure a home for you. I shall have to go clandestinely; they would not grant me a pass, and I may have to walk half the way to Lexington. The roads are thronged, I suppose, with the Federals retreating upon Louisville."

"But when will you go, pa?"

"To-morrow evening, if I get all arrangements made. I will drive out to Dr. Force's, and send the carriage back, depending on their kindness to convey me beyond danger. It is best that I should go, Mary," added the father, as he saw the flushing face of his child, and readily understood the mighty effort it required for her to suppress her tears. "You understand it all, my child?"

Mary buried her head without speaking. Her judgment approved her father's suggestion—her feelings revolted against it.

"And you will send for me just as soon as you determine what is best to be done—won't you, pa?" she said, as cheerfully as she could.

"Yes, my child; or come after you myself, if circumstances will allow."

"I must go to Lilly, now; I left her down stairs, with cousin Pauline. To-morrow, pa, I will arrange your clothes;" and kissing her father again, she arose from his knee, and went down stairs in search of her friend.

Exhausted from the excitement of the day, Mary sought her room at an early hour. After conversing for some time on the prospects before them, the two girls retired to bed. Lilly, young and free from all care, soon fell asleep; but Mary, to whom the last year had taught many a sad lesson of anxiety and thought, lay, her mind distracted with doubt and apprehension, and many a slowly measured hour wore by before she could calm herself to sleep. She awoke with the early morning light from her unrefreshing slumbers, and, making a hasty toilet, applied herself to preparations for her father's departure. It was a heavy task for her poor breaking heart to accomplish, but amid her dark trial she had one consoling thought which she constantly whispered to herself: I shall soon get within Confederate lines, and then I shall see Charley and my brother!

"I cannot go with you this morning, Lilly, but I will be out late this afternoon or to-morrow. Meanwhile, you and Lu must begin your preparations. You see what Prentice says; and moreover, the whole Legislature from Frankfort reached here a few minutes ago, fleeing in hot haste from the Confederate forces, who, it is said, are now in possession of Lexington."

"Be sure to come this evening, Mary; we shall look for you."

"Lu said I must not fail to bring you out this morning, Miss Mary," said Mr. Spalding, rising to meet them as they entered the parlor. "She is expecting you, and so is Mrs. R. They will be greatly disappointed if I fail to bring you. Come, get your hat; I cannot be denied."

"Thank you, Mr. Spalding; it is impossible for me to go out now. I have an engagement that will keep me in the city until late this evening. If I am well, I will drive out about sundown; but, should I fail to do so, look for me to-morrow. Love to all."

"To-night, Mary, we shall expect you," and Lilly kissed her friend and sprang into the carriage.

"Don't let me look in vain, Miss Mary," said Mr. Spalding, shaking the delicate hand. "Lu is never so happy as when you are with us."

"Ah! Lu needs me not now, Mr. Spalding, to make her happy. You have stolen her from me, and I am left alone."

"Soon to be disposed of in the same way, I judge, if the Confederates reach Louisville," said Mr. Spalding, mischievously, as he seated himself beside Lilly.

Mary blushed: the two, bidding her adieu, drove off.

Mary accompanied her father to make a last visit to the grave of the mother, and place there some tokens of remembrance. Above the hallowed mound the two knelt and silently wept. Their grief was too sacred for words. The heart alone could indite voiceless petitions to the throne of the unseen Father for guidance and consolation. Ah! what pen can describe, what pencil portray the grief of the crushed heart as it bows over the grave of buried love? A mourner on the waste of time, the sad soul wanders, and sees no promise of hope, save in the goal which death offers.

Placing the mementoes of love on the newly made grave, the father and daughter arose and silently wended their way back to the carriage.

Moments there are in the life of every individual, when the heart, communing with itself, holds its joy or grief too holy to mention even to the dearest bosom friend. We would not clothe our emotions in words to whisper even to ourselves.

Evening came. Arrangements were completed: Mr. Lawrence was ready to depart.

"Good-by, my child! God bless you and keep you from all harm," he said, in broken accents, as he pressed Mary to his bosom and kissed her tear-bathed cheek. The sobbing girl clung to her father in silent grief. Oh, how desolate she felt as she stood there leaning against the pillar of the front portico, watching the carriage bear away her loved parent—her last friend! As it disappeared from her view, she burst into a fresh paroxysm of tears, and turned to seek her chamber, that she might weep there alone free from the gaze of human eyes.

There is a luxurious relief in tears, when the stricken soul can weep its fulness of sorrow away unmolested by prying curiosity, or cold, hollow words of sympathy. What can others understand of our grief? Even though another *has felt* what we *now feel*, has not time measurably healed the anguish? The remembrance may remain—the poignancy is gone.

And then, how sad a thing it is to feel ourselves *alone* in this hollow world! *Alone!* How like a death-knell falls this hollow word on the isolated heart! To crowd our sympathies, loves, joys, sorrows, expectations, hopes, into our own bosoms, there to remain—for we are *alone* on the earth—what oppressive anguish! How the poor burdened soul feels like bursting as it vainly seeks relief in tears and sighs! We must have sympathy. Life without friendship is but a miserable groping mid the dark labyrinths of passion and despair. The nature with which God has endowed us requires that heart commune with heart; and the outer life can as well exist without its legitimate nourishment, as the inner life without sympathy and love. Asceticism is an anomaly—a *lusus naturæ*—the contemplation of which should fill every well-poised mind with horror.

Mary Lawrence, as she sat weeping in her chamber, felt the *need* of some congenial spirit to share with her the grief that wrapt her soul. Instinctively her thoughts turned to the friend of her childhood. Bathing her face so as to remove the traces of her bitter tears and cool her fevered brow, she threw on her hat and mantle, and calling the carriage, drove out to Mr. R.'s.

"Why, Mary dear! what is the matter with you?" exclaimed Lu, as she threw her arms about the young girl and kissed her. "You look as if you had been weeping for hours. No bad news I hope. Do tell me, have you heard any bad intelligence?"

Her voice was tremulous, and she grew ashen pale as she looked upon Mary, who had burst into a flood of tears.

"Come into mother's room," she said, as, gently taking her hand, she led her along the hall to the family-room.

"Why, Mary,—Lu,—what is the matter with the girls?" said Mrs. R., as she sprang from her seat, and clasping Mary in her arms, partly bore her to a rocking-chair which stood beside the window, near the fire.

The mother looked inquiringly at her daughter. Mrs. Spalding shook her head.

"Oh, Mary, do tell me, my child, why you weep! Have you heard any bad news from the army? Are any of our friends sick or dead?"

Suppressing her emotion as well as she could, the sobbing girl ejaculated in broken sentences:

"No—no—Mrs. R., not that. Pa has gone—gone—to the army."

"Your father gone to the army, Mary!" exclaimed Mrs. R. and her daughter at the same moment, their voice and manner betraying the greatest surprise.

"Yes, gone—gone—left this morning for Lexington."

"To join General Smith? Why, how can he get there, child?"

Mrs. R., with the gentleness of a mother, removed Mary's hat and mantle, and by kind words endeavored to soothe her.

After a few moments, she sufficiently recovered from her emotion to tell Mrs. R. the sad tale of her sorrow.

The friends were greatly surprised to hear of Mr. Lawrence's sudden departure, but when the reasons were given, his course appeared one of wisdom.

Mr. R. had returned from the city and brought with him the *Bulletin* and the *Evening News.* The latest telegrams were filled with the success of the Confederates, their advance towards Louisville and Cincinnati, and the consequent panic and dismay of Union sympathizers and Yankee soldiery.

It was asserted by Prentice, as a fact incontestable, that General Bragg was marching northward, with the avowed design of taking permanent possession of Kentucky; also, that Colonel John H. Morgan, at the head of a large cavalry force, had been dispatched to intercept the Federal General Morgan, in his retreat from Cumberland Gap. The tone of the editorials was gloomy enough. Unionists were quaking with alarm. The entire State was threatened, a part of it already in the possession of the Confederates, who were daily extending their lines, and daily receiving accessions to their ranks.

"Oh! do you think, Mr. Spalding, that we shall be able to hold Kentucky?" said Mary, as she threw aside the paper, and leaned earnestly forward to catch his reply. "Old Prentice is evidently alarmed, and Harney too. I wonder why they didn't send Colonel Morgan to take Louisville? I am afraid General Smith will wait until the Lincolnites are so strong here it will be difficult to do. They are coming in every day, and I see it is stated in the *News* that General Nelson will take command here in a few days. I thought he was severely wounded?"

"And so he was, Miss Mary, but it has been two weeks, you know, since the battle, and he has measurably recovered."

"Mr. R., do you think the Southerners will hold Kentucky?"

"Indeed, I cannot tell, Mary. That will depend greatly, yes, entirely, on General Bragg. It is impossible for General Smith to do so without assistance. There is a great contrariety of opinion respecting Bragg's intentions; some believing that he designs to remain here through the winter—others that he only wishes to force Buell from Tennessee, and regain Cumberland Gap, by forcing General Morgan to abandon it. I confess, from the confused and contradictory statements of our papers, I am unable to form any just decision. No one can decide fully what will be the end of this mighty movement. We can but hope that it may prove eminently successful; but there are two to play the game, and some of the Unionists are sanguine that the whole thing will prove a failure."

"On what do they base their hopes, Mr. R.?" asked his wife.

"On their numbers, and the hope that Buell, who is moving rapidly on Louisville, will reach here before Bragg. In which event, they feel confident that with his own army, combined with the reinforcements that they can bring to this point from Indiana, Illinois, and Ohio, he will soon drive the Confederates South again."

"I hope the Confederates will not attempt to come to Louisville now," interposed Mr. Spalding.

"Oh! do not say so. Why do you wish this?" exclaimed Mrs. Spalding and Mary.

"For these reasons," replied Mr. Spalding. "It would not be worth the trouble and loss of life, even if they should take it. Every thing of value has been removed beyond the river. They would only get some shoes and clothing which the Southern element now holds, and this they will get anyhow, if they but hold central Kentucky. And, moreover, if they should take the city, they could not hold it against the gunboats and the artillery the enemy could bring to bear against it from the opposite side of the river."

"But would the Yankees shell it, Mr. Spalding, do you think? Is there not too much Union capital here for that?"

"But, even admitting, Mr. R., that this would not be done, it would certainly be too far north for a base of the Confederates. They should be nearer the centre of the State. Remember, the Cumberland and Tennessee rivers are in the hands of the enemy."

"That is very true, sir; and I suppose if the Confederates leave the State, they would go out by way of Cumberland Gap?"

"Undoubtedly so. There is no other safe exit for them. And your father has gone to Lexington, Mary? I was astonished when Mr. Sparke told me of it. What was his idea for leaving?"

"To get into Dixie, Mr. R.," replied Mary, choking down the tears that were ready to overflow at the mere mention of her father's name. "It has been his intention for some time to go South as soon as he could; and regarding this as a fine opportunity to get within Confederate boundary, he determined to avail himself of it, fearing if he should delay he might have difficulty, even if he succeeded at all, and that if he remained he would be imprisoned."

"A very wise decision, I think. And he has left you to us, I hope, Mary?"

"Oh! I am going through, too, just as soon as pa finds out what the Southerners are going to do."

"But you will stay with us, Mary, until you do go through?" said Lilly, beseechingly.

"Oh yes, Lilly, I will stay with you a great deal. This is more like home to me now than any other spot on earth. You know I never go to my old home now that another owns it."

Ten o'clock came. The family retired. Lilly and Mary remained in the sitting-room, as girls are wont to do, after the others had left, to talk over their own particular plans.

"Oh, Mary, how I wish I could go through to Lexington with you! I am almost crazy to see brother Charley. I wonder if pa will let me go? You know he consented for sister Lu to go to Camp Chase."

"We can ask him, Lilly. I hope he will, I should be so glad to have you go with me."

"But how will we get back, Mary, if the Southerners have to leave Kentucky?"

"Oh, Lilly, I am going out with them. Didn't you know that? We are going South to live."

"And what would I do?"

"Can't you go, too? A **winter** South would be fine for your health," replied her friend, pleasantly. "Or, Lilly, if you can't go South, you could remain in Lexington or Georgetown until the railroad communication is established, and **then return** to the city."

"That I could. And I'll ask pa to-morrow to let me go. Sister Lu will be here to keep mother company, and I shan't go to school any more this fall. I expect, Mary, Evangeline Lenoir would **be glad to go with us**. You know her sweetheart, Harry Roberts, is with John Morgan?"

"Oh, my dear girl, you are mistaken. Harry used to be Evangeline's sweetheart, but she has proved false to him. **Don't you** know she is engaged to Edward Lasley, of Bardstown?"

"Oh, I don't believe that, Mary. I have heard it. But, surely she would never think of giving up such a lover as Harry Roberts for young Lasley. Lasley has nothing to recommend him but his fine appearance and his fortune, while Harry is noble, true, brave, one of the finest young men in all this city.

"But Evangeline is assuredly engaged to Ed. Lasley. **I know** it, and they are to be married the 16th of next month. She wished me **to be bridemaid; but you know**, even if I were going to remain here, **I could not accept her invitation. I would not change** my **dress to be married myself.**"

"Oh, is it possible! How shameful in Evangeline to treat Harry so. **He is one of the** noblest young men in the world. She may live to repent her folly. Ed. Lasley is by no means steady in his habits."

"But he has money. **Evangeline has none. And, moreover,** she is fickle."

"Her aunt is wealthy, Mary, and has no children. Of course she will inherit that fortune. She **need not marry for money.**"

"Oh, she is so notional and inconsistent by nature. And what a pity, too; she is so beautiful, so generous and kind. It **will be a sad blow to** Poor Harry, when he hears it, for he idolizes her, and cannot see that she has a defect. **Poor fellow!** it is hard. But then, perhaps she would not make **him happy,** and it may be for the best."

"Oh, if she were married, I am sure she and Harry would **be** happy, she is so affectionate. And she loves him, I know."

Just then a loud knock was heard at the front door.

"What can that mean, Lilly?" said Mary, starting up with fright.

The two girls stared at each other in breathless silence, their hearts beating audibly.

"Perhaps it is some drunken Lincolnite," whispered Lilly, as she moved close up beside Mary, and grasped her arm.

"Perhaps we were mistaken, Lilly. It might have been some other noise. But didn't it sound very much like a rap at the door?"

"Indeed it did; but it might have been some of the servants in the kitchen."

The two girls stood breathless for a moment. Rap, rap, rap, went the door again, louder than before.

The affrighted girls hesitated no longer, but, seizing the lamp, hastened through the hall into Mrs. R.'s sleeping-room.

"Father, father," said Lilly, in a whisper, at the same time shaking her father with all her power; "father, there is somebody at the front door—we have heard them knock twice."

"Oh, you must be mistaken, my daughter, no one could come here without arousing the dogs. Have they been barking?"

"No, sir, I have not heard them."

"Well, then, you are mistaken, daughter. Go to bed. It's too late for you and Mary to be up," and Mr. R. turned over to compose himself again to sleep.

"There it is again, father. Don't you hear it?"

The old gentleman sprang from his bed, and hastening to the window, called out in a stentorian voice: "Whose there, and what do you want at this hour of the night?"

The two girls stood trembling with fear, lest a bullet from some Lincoln gun should speed its way into the room.

"Be still, girls; let's hear what the man says," whispered Mrs. R., as her husband threw open the shutters.

"Who are you?" repeated the old gentleman, as the visitor, forsaking the porch, approached and stood under the window.

"A Southern soldier—one of Morgan's men," was the answer.

"Charley—Charley!" shrieked Lilly, and rushed to the window. Her father caught her and drew her back. "Charley!" she exclaimed, "is that you, my brother—my brother?"

"It is not your brother, but I bring news from him."

"And where is he—oh, tell me, is my brother dead?"

"Be still, my daughter," said Mrs. R., as she drew the pale and trembling girl from the open casement.

Mr. R., having prepared himself, went out, light in hand, to ask the soldier in.

"I have but a few minutes to remain, sir. I must be off again to-night, or the Yankees may catch me," responded the **young man** to Mr. R.'s invitation to enter.

"But you will have time to come in and warm yourself, and take a hasty meal. It is several hours to day yet. Come in, sir; come in."

The soldier followed Mr. R. into the sitting-room, where the fire was still burning in the grate.

"I have a letter for Miss Mary Lawrence. Is she with you, sir?" said the soldier, as he passed through the hall.

At the mention of her name, the **young girl, who stood within** the door, stepped forward.

The letter was handed her. She tore the envelope and glanced at the name. It was from Charley.

"And is he dead?" she gasped convulsively. "This is written in Tennessee. Where, oh, where is he now?"

"He is still there."

"Oh, do not deceive me, I beseech you. Do not deceive me— **tell me truly, is** he dead?" and the young girl, unable longer to **stand, sank on a** sofa beside her, and with ghastly look gazed up into the young man's face.

"**Who, who?" exclaimed the father,** mother, and sister in one breath. "**Who is dead?** your brother, **or—**"

"Charley!" was the scarcely articulate reply.

"Oh, no, no! I assure you he is not dead," exclaimed young Brent, for it was he, faithfully executing the pledge intrusted to him. "He is not dead, sir; I left him quite sick, as he **writes** there to Miss Lawrence; **but his physician assured me he would recover.**"

The burdened **hearts breathed more freely.**

"Thank God! thank God!" **exclaimed** the mother, tears of gratitude streaming from her eyes. "Thank God! my boy yet lives!"

"Be seated, sir," said **Mr.** R., conducting the young man to the fire, and, drawing up a large arm-chair before its genial warmth, led him to it.

At this moment **Mr.** and Mrs. Spalding, who, when aroused by the noise, had made a hasty toilet, descended the stairway and entered the room.

"Why, how do you do, Mr. Brent?" **said Mrs. Spalding,** advancing, and shaking the young man's hand.

"How do you do, Miss Lu?" said the young man, rising.

"Let me introduce to you Mr. Spalding, Mr. Brent."

"Happy to see you, Mr. Brent," said Mr. Spalding, shaking hands with the soldier, who looked at him a moment surprised.

"Ah me, Miss Lu, I understand. Yes, Charley told me you were to be married, and we had hoped to get to Louisville to the wedding."

"And where is my brother, Mr. Brent? isn't he with you?"

"He was not well enough to join the command when we left Tennessee, and we were forced to leave him behind."

"Was he ill?" she asked, quickly.

"Quite sick; but his physician assured me he would recover. He had fever, and was unable to bear the fatigue of so long a trip."

"Had he been long sick, Mr. Brent?" asked the mother.

"Only a few days, madam."

"And was he confined to his bed?"

"Yes, madam. The physician thought he needed rest. He had been taking a great deal of exercise, and was pretty well worn out. Dr. Lapsley, who is a most excellent physician, will stay with him until he recovers."

"And where is my brother, John Lawrence, now, sir?" said Mary, as she folded the letter she had just finished reading.

"I left him with Colonel Duke, near Lexington."

"And will he not come to Louisville?"

"Yes, if we take possession of it; but, otherwise, I think Colonel Morgan's men will be retained around Lexington. It is rather a dangerous experiment for us to come alone into the city. One of our men was caught in the streets this evening, and sent to prison."

"Who was this?" asked Mr. Spalding.

"Harry Roberts, sir, of Colonel Morgan's command. It seems Harry had a sweetheart that he was determined to see, so he came to Louisville at all hazards, and this evening some Union man recognized him on the streets, and he was immediately arrested. I took warning by his fate, and left for the country."

Just at this juncture Mr. R. appeared, followed by a servant, bearing a large waiter of nice lunch, which was placed before the young man, who was pressed to eat.

Mary stood all the while beside the lamp, reading and re-reading the letter, the tears streaming down her cheeks, and all unconscious of the presence of others. Lilly **stole to her side, and** whispered:

"Did you hear that, Mary, **about** poor Harry **Roberts?** Isn't it sad to think he should come to see Evangeline, and **she** engaged to be married to another? **And now** he is in prison—"

"In prison, Lilly, where—how? **I did not** understand," said Mary, looking **on** Lilly abstractedly.

"In prison here in Louisville. Came to see **Evangeline, and** was arrested."

"Poor Harry!" ejaculated Mary. "Sad, sad fate!"

"**I will** go," said Mary **to herself,** as she folded the letter, and replaced it in the envelope.

"Go where, Mary—to prison?" asked Lilly, with surprise.

"Oh, nowhere, Lilly," she replied, coloring **deeply.**

While young Brent was partaking of the timely cheer, he hastily gave to his anxious listeners a brief outline of the Confederate movements in Kentucky since Colonel Morgan had joined General Smith at Lexington.

"*I must go,*" he said, rising to his feet. "I wish I could remain longer, but the hours are swiftly passing, the morning will soon be here, and it will **not do for it to find me within danger.**"

Messages were sent to friends. Thanking them for their kindness, he bade them adieu and departed.

CHAPTER XLIX.

UPBRAIDINGS.

"Oh, Evangeline! Evangeline! how could you thus deceive me!"

"I loved him from my childhood, Edward," she sobbed, passionately. "How could I do otherwise?"

"But you have promised me, Evangeline. Look at this, my token of that pledge."

"And I promised him long years ago—when we were children," she replied, looking up through her streaming tears. "Oh! forgive me; forgive me, Edward! I did not mean to do so! But, Harry, you know I have loved him so long; and now he is in prison, how could I forsake him?"

"And do you mean, Evangeline, to prove false to me? Must I understand that you no longer regard your plighted vows?"

"Oh, Edward! do not ask me! You drive me mad with such questions! I am wild! wild!—my brain aches!" she exclaimed, looking frantically around her.

"You *must answer me*, Evangeline! Will you marry me as you have promised? You know the day is appointed, and preparations are already commenced. Surely, you will not now decline? you cannot, for our position demands that you fulfil your engagement!"

"Oh, public opinion is but a poor solace for a bleeding heart, Edward! When our hearts are breaking, of what matter is it what the world says?"

"But you do not mean to say, Evangeline, that you do not love me—that you hesitate to marry me? Am I to find in you the fickleness and unfaithfulness that characterize your nature. Remember, you have given your word to be mine—have pledged yourself to marry me. This is known to the world, and what will the world say if you fail to keep your word? It will upbraid you as inconstant—full of whim and caprice, and cover your name with reproach!"

"Oh, I know it all, Edward! Do not—do not talk to me

thus! I know I will be called foolish, and perhaps I am. I may be taunted as inconstant, notional, heartless; but God knows I have loved truly, faithfully. Why! oh, why should I have ever forgotten that love!"

"You do not love me, then, Evangeline? You will not marry me?"

She did not answer, but, hiding her face in her hands, wept bitterly.

"Answer me, Evangeline; I will not be thus trifled with!" and a dark scowl gathered over his face as he fixed his eyes on her bowed form. His voice was severe even to harshness. She felt it, and shuddered as she did.

"You will not answer, Evangeline? Why do you treat me thus? I cannot submit to it; I will not longer endure it!" and he sprang from the sofa and paced the room with rapid strides. Evangeline still wept aloud.

"Great God!" he exclaimed, passionately, "am I to be mocked thus? What have I done to deserve such a fate? I will not bear this suspense; she shall answer me!" and he stamped his foot in his rage; then strode on across the floor, his whole manner that of a madman.

His wrath partially exhausted by his rapid exercise, he threw himself on the sofa beside her, and forcing her hands from her face, exclaimed:

"Evangeline, you must tell me—and tell me now!" She started and struggled to free herself; but he held her tightly in his grasp. "Do not strive to go from me, Evangeline. This question must be settled now and forever." She looked at him fiercely, defiantly.

"Loose me, Edward, loose me! I will not be forced!" All the passion of her nature spoke from her face. "Loose me, and I will tell you all; but you cannot extort from me one syllable. I will not be driven!"

The young man dared not disobey. The inferior one always yields to the superior. He relaxed his grasp, and sat eyeing her with a look of mingled wonder and sternness.

Evangeline, nerving herself, drove back her tears, and looking him steadfastly in the face, said, with a degree of calmness quite surprising:

"Edward, I have loved Harry Roberts from my childhood. I love him still. I thought when I promised to marry you that I had forgotten him and loved you. I was mistaken. If I have wronged your heart—forgive me, oh, forgive me! but I cannot marry one I do not love! I cannot forsake one to whom my heart is wedded, now that he is in prison and suffering!"

The noble sentiment of the noble girl fell idly on the ears of young Lasley. He understood but one thing—that Evangeline could not marry him.

"Cannot marry me, Evangeline! Is this your decision? Do you forget that you are bound by a solemn promise to do so? You dare not break that promise; I cannot release you."

"And why, Edward? you do not love me?"

"Yes, but I do love you, and I intend to marry you. All the world knows we are engaged, and I do not choose to be trifled with thus. This passion for Roberts will soon pass away. You only feel sorry for him because he is in prison. A week hence you will feel and think differently. I will give you a week to decide, Evangeline," said he coldly, as he arose to leave.

"Oh! Edward, I want not a week—not a day. I am decided now. I tell you I cannot marry you while I love another! You ought not to wish me to do it! It would only be to render us both miserable forever. I tell you again I cannot marry you, Edward Lasley!"

"You shall never marry Roberts, then, Evangeline!" he said, while his face kindled under the dark working of his fierce passion.

"Then I'll never marry!" she replied determinedly.

Scowling with the fury of a fiend upon the girl he professed to love, he replied in tones of bitter retaliation:

"So let it be!" He paused a moment for a reply; but with the same look of resolution, Evangeline sat silently gazing upon him.

"Do we part forever, Evangeline?" he asked, as he read the meaning of her heart on her fixed, unmoved face.

"Forever!" she answered.

"Ah! say not so. There is a future for me. We will meet again, Evangeline. Then—*then*, perhaps, you will understand me!"

As he finished this ominous sentence he turned from her, and, passing out through the hall, left the house. Evangeline's heart stood still, and her cheek grew pale as those threatening words rang on her ear. She could meet the enraged man with boldness as he stood before her with his words of sarcastic reproach and bitter taunt, but she shuddered with fear, as a feeling of mysterious dread took possession of her bosom.

"What can he mean?" she asked herself, as she revolved his

menacing words in her mind. "What does he intend to do? Surely he does not contemplate being revenged on Harry—and yet what else can it be? His words were so dark, and he looked so fierce as he spoke! But what harm can he do him? Harry is in prison and beyond his reach. But he is a Union man, or professes to be one. Would he use this power against him? Ah! it must be that! It can be nothing else. But what can he do?" she asked herself. "He can have him sent to Camp Chase, perhaps, and kept there. Surely, he cannot mean to take his life; and if he did, how could he accomplish it? He could not shoot him—he would not dare do this. But, perhaps, he could hire the guard to do it. Men have been shot down in that prison without provocation—one, merely because he looked out of the window and waved a handkerchief at some girls who were passing. Oh! if he should do this, how horrid it would be! 'You shall never marry Roberts!' he said. He must mean by this to destroy either Harry or me. Fearful! fearful!" and so Evangeline trembled as she sat there alone on the sofa in the silent parlor.

Long she pondered the last words of Lasley—"There is a future for me; we must meet again, Evangeline. Then—*then*, perhaps, you will understand me!"

"Harry shall be saved!" she said, half aloud to herself, as she rose from the sofa and sought her own room.

CHAPTER L.

A VISIT TO PRISON.

Under the auspices of a Union lady, a friend of her aunt, Evangeline obtained permission to visit the prison where the Southern men were kept, on the day following the remarkable visit of Edward Lasley.

It was ten o'clock in the morning. Evangeline, attired in a plain street suit of green, with a hat trimmed in black velvet, from which hung a veil of green that fully concealed her features, and bearing in her hand a basket of cakes and fruits, with a beautiful bouquet, set out with Mrs. Hanna to visit the prison at the corner of Green and Fifth streets. This building had been, before our peaceful people had learned war, a medical college; but, at the commencement of hostilities it was not used for this purpose. The Abolitionists of Louisville, ready to do the bidding of their dictator at Washington, decided it should be fitted up for prisoners, and accordingly men were engaged to put it in proper condition for this purpose. The whole building, with its small front yard fronting on Green-street, was rapidly inclosed by a high plank fence, and barracks were erected along the west side for the accommodation of the guard.

It was a novel sight to the people of Louisville to see such preparations in their midst. But, notwithstanding the opposition of the Southern people, who believed it an overthrow of all constitutional right to imprison men for opinion's sake, and the wonder of Unionists who had not yet grown altogether accustomed to the attempt to enslave freemen, the work went rapidly on to completion; and the citizens saw in their midst a large building set apart for the incarceration of men who dared to maintain the doctrine that the free people of a sovereign State had a right to decide on the course they, as a free and independent people, should pursue.

As Evangeline pursued her way beside Mrs. Hanna, from Broadway, down Second street to Green, and thence to the prison, she found the streets thronged with men, discussing the startling events of the day. As she passed the custom-house, on the corner of Third and Green streets, and slipped in to ask for a letter for herself and aunt, she heard a gentleman at the door exclaim, with great emphasis: "Yes, Bragg will come; he has got the start of Buell, and is already on his way here, and we have no preparation to meet him. These fortifications they are erecting are mere child's play—only intended to deceive the people into a false idea of security."

She started as the language fell on her ear, fearing lest some Southern man, in the gratification he felt, had so far forgotten himself as to utter "*treasonable sentiments*." She looked hurriedly round, and found to her relief that the words had fallen from a known Union man; of course there was no treason there.

As she passed out, she paused a moment to ask Mr. McAllister, the speaker, when General Bragg would reach Louisville.

"Be here in a few days, 'Vangeline; no help for it, and then the wretches will drive us all from our homes, and burn our property."

"Oh, I hope not, Mr. McAllister," she answered, pleasantly; "Southerners don't do such things, I believe."

"Yes they do; greatest outlaws the world has ever seen—full of revenge and the devil."

Evangeline not deeming it proper to make any further remark to the excited old man, bowed and hastened to overtake Mrs. Hanna, who was a few paces in advance.

"What I do must be done quickly," she said to herself, as she walked rapidly on. "A few days delay, and all is lost."

Overtaking Mrs. Hanna, she repeated the remark of the old gentleman.

"What do you think, Mrs. Hanna? Is it your opinion the Southern army will reach Louisville?"

"Never, never, Evangeline. They wouldn't dare to attempt the thing. Don't you know General Nelson is fortifying every day, and fresh troops are arriving every hour. Old Mr. McAllister is wild, he doesn't know what he is talking about—scared to death, I suppose."

"What am I to believe?" asked Evangeline, mentally. "One tells me Bragg will certainly come. The next moment another says it is impossible. I will execute my plan, anyhow, and then I shall have nothing to fear."

The two females reached the prison gate, and were about to

enter, when the guard, a burly Pennsylvania Dutchman, presented his bayonet across the entrance.

"Where is your pass? You cannot go in without a permit," he said, gruffly.

Mrs. Hanna paused, felt in her pocket, and produced a paper. The man turned it upside down, eyed it very earnestly for a few minutes, wearing all the while a look of great wisdom, and then returned it, saying: "All right, pass in."

Mrs. Hanna smiled, as she replaced the remnant of a gas bill in her pocket, and Evangeline, who had caught a glimpse of it, and understood what it was, laughed outright. The guard looked amazed and somewhat suspicious, but either not fully understanding the cause of the ladies' merriment, or perhaps unwilling to admit his ignorance, allowed them to proceed without further interruption. At the door they encountered another armed man, who, bowing politely, asked them whom they wished to see. They replied they desired to see all the prisoners, but particularly young Roberts.

"You can see Roberts, ladies, and any other prisoner you may wish, if you will but name them; but you cannot be allowed to make a general visit."

"We will see Mr. Roberts, and any other of Morgan's men that you may have here."

The soldier called to one of the attendants of the prison, and instructed him to conduct the visitors up stairs and show them to young Roberts.

The ladies followed the old man. On reaching the landing they found themselves in the presence of several men, all uniformed. They could not tell whether or not they were Southerners. Evangeline thought they were, and eagerly strained her gaze to discover, if possible, young Roberts. The search was fruitless. Only strange faces peered upon her. She looked round for her conductor—he was gone. There the two ladies stood uncertain what to do, wondering if amid that crowd they were to be left to meet the prisoner. Evangeline trembled at the thought, and the basket she held in her hand manifested her perturbation.

At length, after a painful suspense, the old man returned. Evangeline looked up as she heard his voice. Behind him was a young man in prison garb. She thought at first glance it was Harry, and was about to step forward to make herself known. But looking again she encountered the face of a stranger, a handsome man of about twenty-five years of age, who bowed and moved towards them, and stood a moment as if waiting to be addressed.

"Walk in there, ladies," said the conductor, pointing to a long room filled with benches that opened on the landing.

They did as directed, and found themselves in the midst of prisoners. The young man followed. Entering, they bowed. Evangeline knew in a moment that those before her were Confederates, and she lifted her veil, hoping that if she did not recognize Harry, he might see her and come forward to her relief.

"We wish to see Harry Roberts, one of Morgan's men, who was put in prison a few days since," said Mrs. Hanna, turning to the young gentleman who stood beside her.

"Excuse me, ladies," said the young man, bowing politely; "my name is Robertson, and I was told some ladies wished to see me. I'll speak with the guard, and have Roberts sent in."

"And so some ladies do wish to see you," said two females, stepping forward from their seats and confronting the prisoner. He looked at them steadily for a moment.

"Aunt Jane and Cousin Flora!" exclaimed the young man surprised, at the same time grasping their extended hands with all the warmth of his ardent nature. "Why, how did you hear I was in prison?"

"Dr. Henly, of our neighborhood, was in the city when you were brought in, and saw you taken from the cars—he recognized you, having seen you when you were last on a visit to us. As soon as we heard it, we determined to come and see you; but your Uncle James was taken sick the very day we had appointed to set out, and has been so indisposed ever since, that we could not leave him until yesterday."

"And how is Uncle James now?"

"Better; we hope he will soon be well again. He sent you a great deal of love, as did all the children, and says, 'Don't despair, you are in a good cause,'" she added, in a whisper, as she discovered the eye of a Lincoln soldier fixed upon her. The man moved forward and took a nearer position. Mrs. Richey understood the meaning, and quickly changed the conversation to an inquiry for the young man's health.

"Pretty good, Aunt Jane, and spirits fine; we have most excellent company, and as good fare as rebels deserve, I suppose."

"I am glad to see you in such fine spirits, Samuel. It will delight your Uncle James to know you bear your fate so heroically.

He has been greatly distressed since he heard you were here. You know you are his favorite nephew."

"Tell uncle it is not so pleasant as meeting the enemy on the battle-field, but as a soldier I have made up my mind to take whatever chances befall me, and make the best of my fate."

"How long do you expect to remain here, Samuel?"

"Oh, I suppose we shall soon be sent from here to Camp Chase, and perhaps we shall remain there until the war ends. Can't tell; these things are so uncertain."

Mrs. Richey looked up; the guard had moved back to allow a young Confederate to proceed to the two ladies who were sitting beyond her. Seizing the opportune moment, she leaned forward as if to pick up her fallen handkerchief. "Take that, Mr. Richey sent it. Escape if you can, and come to our house." She slipped a roll into his hands, which the prisoner immediately placed in his pocket. The whole movement had escaped the eye of the guard.

"Harry!"

"Evangeline!"

It was all the two lovers could say, as their eyes met. Mrs. Hanna rose, expecting Evangeline to introduce her. But the young girl sat still, overcome by her emotion. Her face was crimson, and she trembled violently. No endeavor to be calm availed.

Mrs. Hanna seeing Evangeline would not introduce her, introduced herself. "I am very glad to see you, Mr. Roberts," she said, endeavoring to relieve the young man's embarrassment. "Your mother and I were schoolmates, and although we did not meet in after life, I have always remembered our girlish association with pleasure, and I am happy to meet you for her sake, though sad to see you in this place."

At the mention of his mother's name the tears started to his eyes. Four years ago she had been laid to rest beneath the green sod in the family burying-ground in the country. Harry had idolized her, for she was to him the very embodiment of all goodness and loveliness. He had heard but the day before that his father had married a second time, and this thought seemed to touch his heart the more deeply.

"You are comfortable here, Mr. Roberts, I suppose?" remarked Mrs. Hanna, desiring to turn the current of his thoughts.

"As well situated as I could expect in a prison, madam; but it can scarcely be styled comfortable. However, I wish not to complain. Soldiers must take the chances of their profession."

"This is a sad and horrid war, Mr. Roberts, and untold suffering must yet be endured before it ends."

"Yes, madam, war is the most dreadful scourge that can be sent on a people, and this war of wars is to us the most dreadful. And it will become more and more so the longer it is protracted."

"Only in one way, Mrs. Hanna."

"And what is that?"

"Acknowledge the independence of the Confederacy!"

"Oh, that will never be done, sir. It cannot be done, for it would never do to sever this great and glorious Union."

"The Union is dissolved already, Mrs. Hanna, and force of arms will never reunite it. But it will not do for me to discuss this subject. You know I am a prisoner in the hands of my enemy—an enemy who thinks that to differ with him is a crime worthy of death."

"How did you know, Evangeline, that I was here? I thought you had not heard it."

"Mary Lawrence told me, Harry. One of Colonel Morgan's men told her—young Brent, I believe. I heard it the morning after you were arrested, but they would not let me come until now." She spoke very low, so that the guard who stood by to overhear their conversation might not catch her words:

"Did Brent escape?"

"Of course he did, or he would be here."

"Oh! yes; he left that night, and I suppose got back safely, as we have heard nothing from him since."

This conversation was conducted in a low tone, and as Harry had moved his seat beside Evangeline, Mrs. Hanna did not understand it. Observing that the two young people desired to interchange some words privately, she engaged the guard by remarking:

"Rather an unpleasant duty, sir, to watch here; but it is a duty that some one 'must discharge.'"

"Oh, yes, mum, as a soldier I have to obey commands; but I would a great deal rather be in the field than here. I don't like the confinement nor the business of keeping men in prison. But these are war times, madam, and the regular order of things is entirely changed."

"Harry," said Evangeline, while this conversation was pending, "you must get out of this prison. Here is my purse—bribe the guard if you can!" As she said this, she drew out of her pocket a small purse filled with gold, and slipped it into Harry's hand.

Scarcely realizing what he did, so surprised was he at Evangeline's words and act, he took the purse and hastily put it into his pocket.

"In this bouquet, Harry, is a note. If you find you can carry out the plan, be at the second window on Third-street Sunday evening, at four o'clock, and give the signal mentioned. Be plain, distinct, so that I can understand you. I will attend to the rest. Understand, Harry?"

He nodded assent.

"Be careful; don't betray yourself. You will be shot if you do!"

Harry gazed at her in wonder. He had always known that she was resolute and fond of daring deeds, yet excitable and frequently overcome by her strong emotion. To behold her so calm, collected, planning his escape from prison, was a manifestation so unexpected he was filled with astonishment.

"Don't look so surprised, Harry; the guard will suspect you."

"Here, Harry," she said, modestly, as she saw the eye of the guard fixed upon her, "is a bouquet of flowers. You allow the prisoner to receive flowers, sir, I suppose," she said, looking up at the man with one of her sweetest smiles. "Won't you have some fruit, sir?" and she extended the basket to him, while she handed the flowers to Harry. "Those apples and oranges are very nice; do take some!"

The man, bowing politely, reached forward and took an apple.

"Have an orange, sir?"

"No, mum, I thank you; this is sufficient."

"Won't you have an orange, Mrs. Hanna?"

The lady declined.

"Well, Harry, I am sure you will not refuse me."

"Thank you," he said.

"This young gentleman may have as much fruit as he pleases, sir! Good for his health."

"Oh! yes, mum; we do not deny the prisoners any little thing to eat that their friends bring them."

"Well, then, Harry, you shall have it all; take the basket!"

As he was receiving it, she leaned forward and whispered, "Take the note from the bouquet; it might fall out." Then turning to the guard, she asked, in order to distract his attention:

"Do you admit ladies every day, sir?"

"No, mum; only on Thursday mornings."

"And can any one come in then who desires to? I have never been here before, and do not understand fully your regulations."

"Any one who has a permit can come; but our orders are strict, and we cannot allow any one who has not a pass."

Mrs. Hanna looked at Evangeline and smiled.

While the soldier was interesting himself to instruct Evangeline, Harry had extracted the note from the bouquet and thrust it down into his pocket with the purse. His manner was nervous. Evangeline observed it; the others, unacquainted with the young man's manner, did not.

Relieved of her great anxiety, Evangeline regained her natural vivacity, and chatted with Harry and the guard with all the ease and naiveté for which she was so remarkable.

Mrs. Richey and Flora rose to leave. Evangeline looked up as they did so. Recognizing the young girl, she rose to meet her.

"Why, Flora! when did you get to the city? I had not heard you were here. Are you staying at your Aunt Ludlow's, and will you be here long?"

Flora answered her questions and then introduced Evangeline to her mother and cousin, young Peterson.

Harry Roberts advanced to speak with her.

"Why, Mr. Roberts! is this you?" exclaimed Flora. "I am surprised to see you here. I thought you were with Colonel Morgan, near Lexington!"

"And so I was, Miss Richey, and ought to be there now. But, anxious to see my friends in Louisville, I yielded to my desires and returned home, and, in an evil hour, I was betrayed by one whom I thought was a friend; and now I am here en route to Camp Chase. You know 'the best laid schemes of mice and men gang aft aglay,' Miss Flora. What can't be avoided must be submitted to; and it is as much a part of a soldier's life to endure hardships as to fight. I have fought, and now I shall bear as best I can whatever is imposed upon me."

"That is true philosophy," replied the young girl, her face growing animated under the expression of such sentiments. "No man is a hero without this element of character. We must learn to suffer and to wait. It matters but little where we are, or how situated, if we but serve the great cause of right."

The guard standing nearest her scowled. Mrs. Richey touched her warningly on the shoulder.

"Good-morning, Mr. Roberts. I hope a brighter fate awaits you."

"Evangeline, come to see me; I shall be in the city but a few days longer."

"If you will be in this afternoon at five, Flora, I will call then."

"You will find me at home and glad to see you."

Bidding farewell to the prisoner, and bowing to Mrs. Hanna, Mrs. Richey and her daughter left the room.

"Your half-hour has expired, mum," said the soldier to Evangeline, who was about to reseat herself beside Mrs. Hanna.

"Do you allow us only a half-hour to see a friend?"

"Had you come earlier you could have remained longer, but our orders are to have no company for the prisoners after this hour."

"We will come earlier next Thursday, Mrs. Hanna. It seems to me we have been here but a short time. But then, all is so novel to me, time has passed quickly by. You will allow me to come in next visiting day, will you not, sir?" she said, turning and addressing the guard. "I shall wish to visit my cousin as often as possible before he goes to Camp Chase."

"Oh, certainly, mum; if you have a permit, you can come in. I may not be here at all then; I am expecting every day to be called out to the field. You know the rebels are marching upon the city, and we shall all have to turn out to defend it."

"Why, do you think General Bragg is coming to Louisville? He will not be rash enough for that, will he?"

"He'll come if he can, mum. It is our business to prevent him. I scarcely think he will get here; but these rebels are a determined people, and no one can tell what they'll attempt."

"Very true," responded Mrs. Hanna, "but I do not think Bragg will ever reach Louisville. There are too many men to oppose him."

"Good-by, Cousin Harry," said Evangeline, gayly. "Keep up your spirits—'tis as well to be merry as sad. You know what uncle always says," and she bent forward and whispered, "Remember Sunday evening, before six o'clock—get out if possible, or you'll be sent to Camp Chase. Pretty good logic, isn't it, Harry?"

"Oh, very fine, and it shall be my motto for the future. I shall, undoubtedly act upon it, let whatever will betide me, rest assured of that."

Mrs. Hanna expressed her hope that the young man's imprisonment might not be long, but that an exchange would soon be effected in his behalf, adding, "I have a son in the Union army, Mr. Roberts, and, as a mother, I can feel for you. Good-morning, sir. I will call again and see you, and if there is any thing you desire, I will bear the request to your father."

"Much obliged to you, madam. The superintendent, Captain

Dillard, kindly forwarded a note for me to pa, yesterday, and although I have not yet had an answer, I know my requests will be attended to."

Mrs. Hanna and Evangeline, accompanied by the guard, who seemed to be quite pleased with the young girl's kind and fascinating manner, passed out into the entry. On the landing, they encountered Mr. Roberts, Harry's father, with Captain Dillard, the Prison Superintendent, and followed by a servant boy bearing a basket of clothing, which showed from its tumbled appearance that it had been very unceremoniously examined by the sentinel. Evangeline bowed to Mr. Roberts and passed on.

Gaining the street, she bade Mrs. Hanna good-morning, thanking her for her kind escort, and engaging to accompany her to the prison on the following Thursday morning, and proceeding down Green-street, past the hospital, turned into Centre and pursued her way to Market-street. She walked up Market until she reached the Brook-street market-house. Discovering here a Jew furnishing store, she entered and examined several suits of dark clothing. Finding one that answered her purpose, she drew forth a roll of Kentucky bills and paid for it: ordering the merchant to send it to Mr. Ludlow's at five o'clock that evening precisely, she turned to leave.

"To whom must I **direct it?**"

"Miss Flora Richey," she replied promptly. "You know Mr. Ludlow's residence, do you? near the corner of Chestnut and Sixth, north side."

The man **made a** memorandum and placed it on the suit, which he had laid aside on the shelf.

On her return home, Evangeline met Mary Lawrence.

"I have just called to see you, Evangeline, and the girl told me you had gone to the prison to see Harry Roberts. Is that true? You *haven't* been there, have you? What will Ed. Lasley say, when he hears you **are** visiting your old sweetheart in prison? Won't it arouse his jealousy a little? **You** know he is a Union man, and it might **be the means of** embittering his feelings."

"Oh, Mr. Lasley must look out for himself. You know it is my duty—so aunt has always taught me—to visit the sick and those that are in prison."

Her manner was so full of meaning, that her young friend could not conceal her surprise.

"Come, Mary, go back home with me, and I will tell you all. You know I was engaged to Lasley, and asked you to attend me?"

"*Was* engaged, Evangeline! What do you mean? You have not broken your engagement, have you? He is in town now. Took dinner with Mr. Spalding yesterday at Mr. R.'s. I was present. He did not act like a rejected lover. Was gayer and more animated than when I met him before. Have you seen him since?"

"Yes, I saw him last evening, and for the last time, Mary."

"Why, Evangeline, do explain yourself. Surely you are trying to hoax me. *For the last time?* You haven't discarded him, have you?"

"Hush, Mary, yonder he comes, now. I do not wish to meet him again. Look! I do believe he reels. Come, quick, quick, into this store, and I'll shut the door, so that he can't see us."

The two girls stepped into Mrs. Le Compte's fancy store, on Fourth-street, and immediately closed the door. Mrs. Le Compte looked up from behind her counter rather surprised.

"What's the matter, Miss Evangeline, with you and Miss Lawrence this morning?" asked the shopkeeper, looking out from under her nicely plaited French cap-border.

"A drunken man, Mrs. Le Compte, and I am so afraid of drunken men," and the young girl held tightly to the door knob, at the same time peering curiously out into the street, through the glass door.

Just then young Lasley, leaning on the arm of a young man whom neither of the girls recognized, passed the door. His face was flushed, his eyes red, his hat slouched—his whole manner evidenced his condition. It was with difficulty his friend could keep him steady. He was talking in an earnest tone, and Evangeline fancied she heard him say, "And I will be revenged, Nick, see if I ain't."

The two young girls looked at each other in mute wonder.

"What was that he said, Mary? did you hear him?" whispered Evangeline.

"Something about being revenged, I believe it was. I could not hear distinctly."

"I thought so, Mary. Ah, I know what he means. He is threatening Harry. I will tell you all when I get home. Look out, Mary, see if they have turned the corner of Market."

"They have turned, but are walking out towards Main-street."

"We can go then. I didn't know but that he had recognized me, and would wait until we came out."

The two girls left, and pursued their way rapidly towards

Broadway. Reaching the house of her aunt, Evangeline rang the bell, and ordering some lemonade, conducted Mary up stairs to her own room.

Closing the door, and securing it so that there might be no intrusion, the two girls seated themselves on the sofa, and Evangeline told Mary all that had occurred the evening before with young Lasley, and of his threat that she should never marry Harry Roberts.

"I do not know, Mary, whether the threat was against me or Harry. He may take my life if an opportunity should offer. I have already heard that he possessed a violent temper, and when once excited he is desperate. But I never realized how violent his temper was until I saw him last evening. Why, I tell you, he acted the madman. If I did not love Harry Roberts, I would never marry him now. I would be afraid to do it."

"Well, Evangeline, this is all very strange to me, wholly unexpected. When I met you this morning, I supposed you had been out making preparations for your wedding. You know everybody believes it is to take place on the 10th of next month. I have heard it half a dozen times since I came in this morning. Does your aunt know your decision?"

"No one but yourself and Ed. Lasley, and he doesn't believe it. He said among the last things before he left, that he would give me one week to decide. I fear to tell my aunt. This is the only dread I have on my mind. If she but knew it and was reconciled to it, I would be so relieved. But my aunt, Mary, is so anxious that I should marry Ed. Lasley. He is rich, you know, and an only child, and will doubtless be the heir to his old maiden aunt's fortune. And my aunt wishes me to make what she calls "a handsome establishment" when I marry. She never favored Harry Roberts, and now that he is a rebel, she would be more opposed to it than ever. Oh, I dread to tell her, and yet I must do it. I will never marry Lasley. I love Harry, have always loved him, and if he ever gets out of that prison, I will go to the ends of the earth to marry him. He is brave, noble, honorable, Mary, one that I could love if we had to live in a cottage. Wealth does not bring happiness, Mary. Look at Aunt Cecilia. What is there on earth that she desires, that she does not have, and yet where will you find a more wretched woman? Her fashionable friends think she is blessed beyond most human beings, and no doubt many of them envy her her position. But could they lift the curtain and see behind the scenes, how differently would they feel and judge!"

"Your views are correct, Evangeline, and you talk quite like a philosopher. But have you considered this matter well? Do you know all it involves?"

"I have considered it this far, Mary; I love Harry, and I do not love Lasley. I thought I did, but it was mere fancy. As soon as I heard Harry was here in prison, I felt I should die if I did not get to see him, and I have walked by that prison a hundred times in the last two days, hoping I might catch a glimpse of his form. I see that wealth does not purchase happiness, and I choose the latter. And besides, Harry will have a maintenance, and a handsome one, too, if this war leaves Southern people with any thing; and if it does not, why I will love him still, and we will live in poverty."

"You are decided, then, Evangeline?"

"I am, Mary."

"But do you not think it may be sympathy for Harry, rather than love, that has decided you thus? May you not change your views if he should be removed from you again?"

"Oh! but I do not intend he shall be removed, Mary, unless they take him to Camp Chase. I am afraid to tell you what I have decided to do. I know you will think it so rash, so wild. But, Mary, you know I have but few in this world to love me; no one loves me as Harry does. Aunt Cecilia admires me because I afford her pleasure and draw around her young and gay society, of which she is very fond; and then, you know, she has no child of her own to bestow her caresses upon. This is the extent of her affection for me. But Harry would lay down his life for me, Mary; he is my best, my truest friend. Why should I not cling to him, even if I yield up every thing to do it? Will you betray me if I trust you? I have always told you every secret of my heart, but this is one more momentous than all others. Will you promise to hide it away in your own bosom and never speak of it to any one?"

"Have I ever forgotten my trust, Evangeline?"

Just then the servant knocked at the door with a waiter of ice-cream and cakes.

Evangeline rose to open the door.

"No lemons, Miss Vangy, and Miss Cilla told me to bring you some cream and cakes."

"Very well, Emily; bring it in and put it on the stand, and tell aunt I am much obliged to her. You must not come again until I ring for you."

The girl passed out and closed the door. Evangeline, throwing off her hat and taking Mary's, resumed her seat beside her friend on the sofa.

"I have decided to do this, Mary: first, to effect Harry's escape; and then, if he has to leave Kentucky, to go with him."

"But, Evangeline, how are you to accomplish these two hazardous undertakings? You cannot get Harry out of prison; and if you did, how will you get through to the Confederate lines?"

"Mary, my belief is that any thing can be accomplished, if you only determine it shall be done. These are times when the very foundations of society are moved, and what would be regarded under ordinary circumstances as insanity, will pass current now for heroism. Many females in every age have dared every thing for their lovers' sake; why may not I do the same? If I can once get within the Confederate limits, I shall have nothing to fear."

"But how is Harry to escape?"

"Oh! I don't know that he will, Mary; that is yet to be tested. His attempt may prove successful; it may not. But you know several have escaped from that as well as from other prisons. I do not see why he cannot do so too. He has promised me he will try."

"You saw him then this morning and mentioned it to him? How did you find an opportunity? I have heard that all visitors are so closely watched by a guard stationed in the room for that purpose, that no private conversation at all can pass between them and their friends."

"Oh, I whispered to Harry, who sat beside me, while the guard was talking to Mrs. Hanna. He looked suspiciously upon me once or twice, but I paid no attention to it. Moreover, I carried Harry a bouquet of flowers that had a note concealed in it, proposing a plan of my own, and this I gave him and in a few words explained the outline, so that when he had read it he would understand what I meant."

"Why, Evangeline, you astonish me! You are really a heroine. Who could have thought that you—always so thoughtless, so gay—would have ventured upon an experiment so full of danger and requiring so much thought and courage?"

"Ah, Mary, love is a powerful incentive—a great teacher."

"And did you consult no one, Evangeline?"

"No one, Mary; I have told no one but Harry and you. It

must be kept very secret, or the whole thing may fail and Harry's life be the forfeit."

Mary sat a few moments absorbed in deep thought. Two or three times she looked at Evangeline as if she wished to tell her something she dared not communicate, and then, lowering her eyes, relapsed into thought again.

"Evangeline," she said at length, looking up through her curls, "you have confided in me; I will confide in you. I need not ask you to keep faithfully what I tell you from the ears of every human being. I know that under the present circumstances you could not divulge it. You know, Evangeline, that, like you, I am pretty much alone in the world. All my relations, save my father and some cousins, are in the South; and Charley R. is there, too, Evangeline—they left him sick in Tennessee. My father has gone through to Lexington, and I am left alone."

"Has your father gone, Mary? How did he get through, and when did he leave? I had not heard a word of his going."

"Of course it was best to keep it secret. He has been gone a week, and as I have heard nothing from him, I am led to hope that he has reached Lexington safely. He went from here to a friend's six miles out in the country, in a carriage; from there he proposed to get forward as best he could. Did not know but that he would have to walk most of the way."

Mary paused as if uncertain whether to proceed.

"And do you propose to follow your father in the event the Confederates do not come to Louisville?" asked Evangeline, understanding the cause of her hesitation.

"Yes, Evangeline, that is my determination. I am now waiting to see what will be the issue of General Bragg's movements as regards this city, and also the permanent occupation of the State. This is all that keeps me here now. Pa said he would send for me just as soon as it was decided what the Confederates would do; but I shall not wait for him to do this, if General Bragg passes into the interior of the State. If he does not come and take me, I will immediately make my way through, lest it be too late if I wait for pa to send some one for me."

"Was Charley very sick, Mary? and how did you know it? and where is your brother? You, of course, have not seen him yet?"

"No; John is with Colonel Duke at Lexington. Young Brent, who came to Louisville, left him the very night Harry Roberts was arrested and put in prison. He brought me a letter from

Charley, and came all the way out to Mr. R.'s, where I was spending a few days, to deliver it to me."

"And how was Charley when Brent left him?"

"Quite sick; had typhoid fever, but his physician did not consider his case dangerous. He was in Tennessee, not far from Knoxville, in a private house, where the family would take the tenderest care of him. The physician boarded in the house, so that he will need for nothing that kindness and medical skill can afford. But, oh! Evangeline, you cannot tell how miserable I am; I fancy all the time he is dead; dream at night of his sufferings and death! It is horrible, this agonizing suspense. I feel at times I shall go mad. And I cannot hear from him! It will be weeks —perhaps months—before I know whether he is dead or living."

"Oh, the horrors of this war, Mary! what tongue can describe them? I shudder when I think of the suffering we have yet to endure. Surely, a just God will punish these Northern fanatics for the misery and death they are spreading over the land! Yes, a day of retribution must come when they shall be made to feel the curse of their own evil doings. I sometimes think I could rejoice if the earth would open and swallow them up, as it did those people of old that Mr. Young preached about two or three Sabbaths ago. But, Mary, if you have determined to go to your father, why cannot we go together?"

"Oh! I would be so glad of your company, Evangeline, and we will go together if it is possible. But will you go out to the Confederates if Harry is sent to Camp Chase?"

"No, Mary; if he should fail to escape and be kept here, or be forwarded to any other Northern prison, I would remain here. You know I could but be miserable in the Confederacy where I should never hear from him. There is nothing to take me South but Harry."

"How soon will you—can you—decide, Evangeline?"

"In a few days, Mary. I can let you know on Monday morning. You will not leave before then, will you?"

"Oh, no! General Bragg could not get here before that time. My going depends on his movements. I shall see you before Monday. I am coming to town again Saturday evening to stay all night; call and see me at my boarding-house."

"Oh, come and stay with me, Mary! Do not think of going to your room—so lonely, so cheerless it must be, now your father is gone!"

"Thank you, Evangie; I shall be compelled to remain at home to make some preparations that will be necessary if I leave."

"Then stay with me to-day, Mary."

"Cannot to-day. I came in with Lu and Mrs. Spalding, and shall have to return with them. They leave at two; it is now half-past one," she said, looking at her watch. "We will meet at church—but you come to see me Saturday."

"Very well; I'll do so."

Throwing on her hat, Mary hastened to her friends at the appointed place of meeting, and they had not yet arrived. Stepping into a store for a few moments to buy a mourning collar, she heard one of the clerks remark to an elderly gentleman, who stood in front of the counter examining some cassimere, and whose face was turned from her so that she could not see it:

"Will they not send our prisoners across the river before Bragg can get here?"

She did not hear the gentleman's reply distinctly. The words, "Harry, haste, and pantaloons," met her ear, and she quickly concluded that it must be Mr. Roberts, who was anxious to get suitable clothing prepared for his son, before he should be sent to Camp Chase.

Ordering one pair of pantaloons cut off and trimmed, the old gentleman then asked for some pocket-handkerchiefs. In turning to look after the clerk, who proceeded to the front of the store, Mary caught a glance of his features. It was, as she had supposed, Harry's father. Ah, how sad was that usually mild, genial face! What an expression of sorrow haunted the deep, gray eyes and rested around the mouth!

"How do you do, Mr. Roberts?" said Mary, as cheerfully as she could, advancing towards him and offering her hand.

He looked at her a moment intently.

"Why, I did not recognize you at first, Mary. How do you do? You look changed, my child, in your mourning dress. How is your father? I have not seen him for several days. I used to meet him almost daily. I thought, perhaps, he had gone from the city."

"He has, Mr. Roberts," replied Mary, lowering her voice. "Pa left several days since to join the Confederates at Lexington."

"He is not going into the army, child, an old man as he is!" exclaimed Mr. Roberts, in astonishment.

"No, sir; but he desires, in the event the Confederates have to leave Kentucky, to go out with them, and he felt the surest way to secure his object was to get into their lines while the army was stationary."

"Ah, I wish I could go, Mary. But they have got poor Harry here in prison, and I could not leave him. Too bad that he should have run so much risk to see us and be caught. We did not get to see him before he was arrested. He had been in town but a half hour when an old schoolmate of his, a Union spy, met him and recognized him, and had him immediately put in prison."

"And haven't you seen him at all, Mr. Roberts?"

"Yes, this morning for a short time, just long enough to ascertain what he needs to make him comfortable. He left all his clothes at Lexington, putting on the worst he had to avoid detection. I am out trying to get him clothing ready before he is sent to Camp Chase."

"Have they decided to send our men there?"

"I don't know that they have; but of course they will do it if there is any certain promise that Bragg will get here. I would not be surprised if they were ordered off to-morrow morning."

Mary's heart beat quickly as she listened to these words. "Poor Evangeline—poor Harry!" she said to herself. "Wouldn't it be too dreadful if they should send him away! Oh, poor girl, her heart would break, she is so sanguine now of his escape. I wish I could go and tell her what I have heard. But, then, what good would result from it? She could not communicate with Harry, even if she knew it, and the dread would only be a source of misery."

"Have you been long waiting, Mary?" said Mrs. Spalding, entering the store and laying her hand on her shoulder. "Why, how do you do, Mr. Roberts? I did not observe it was you; the room is so dark after coming out of the bright sunshine. And how is Harry? I suppose you have seen him."

"He is well and in fine spirits, poor fellow. He bears his imprisonment like a hero. Where is Charley? I did not ask for John, Mary; I suppose they are both with Morgan at Lexington?"

"Charley was left very sick in Tennessee, Mr. Roberts. Was wholly unable to come with his command into Kentucky. Had typhoid fever."

"Indeed! I am sorry to hear it. And did John stay with him? I know they have always been great friends from their boyhood."

"No, Mr. Roberts, my brother came into Kentucky with Colonel Morgan, and is now near Lexington. Pa expected to meet him as soon as he reached there."

"Colonel Morgan, with a portion of his command, have been sent out to intercept General Morgan's retreat from Cumberland Gap, Harry told me. Is your brother in that expedition, Mary?"

"Indeed, I do not know, sir. Mr. Brent, one of Morgan's men, who was in Louisville a few days ago, told me that John was with Colonel Duke, somewhere in the vicinity of Lexington, and was well. This is the only intelligence we have had from him since the Confederates entered the State."

"Mr. Spalding is waiting for us at the door, Mary."

The two bade Mr. Roberts good-by, and seating themselves in the carriage, drove out into the country.

CHAPTER LI.

Mary had scarcely left Evangeline's room before her aunt sent up Emily to tell her young mistress to come to her room for a few minutes, as she wished to see her.

"What does Aunt Cecilia want with me, Emily?"

"Indeed I don't know, Miss 'Vangy. She told me to make haste; had sumthin' of importance to tell you."

Evangeline trembled from head to foot. Her heart foreboded evil. Smoothing her hair and taking off her basque, she descended the stairway and sought her aunt's room.

"Evangeline," said Mrs. Terrant, "every thing is in such confusion here, I have decided to go to Indianapolis for a few days, and shall leave this evening on the cars. You must get ready immediately. Emily will pack your trunks while you go out with me to do a little shopping. Emily, tell the cook to have dinner on the table as soon as she can, and Henry must have the carriage at the door in half an hour. Your uncle cannot go with us, so we shall have to take care of ourselves. You know we should not dare to take Emily or Pauline. We no doubt shall have a pleasant visit. It will at least be a recreation, and we can remain until the fate of Louisville is sealed. God grant it may never fall into the hands of the rebels, though it looks as if it might. Mr. Knott told me there was some danger of such a disaster, and I heard a gentleman remark that the authorities had ordered every thing valuable to be removed to the other side of the river, and the prisoners to be sent to Camp Chase. They seem to be preparing for Bragg."

"But, come, Evangeline, we have no time to discuss these matters now. You had better go to your room and take out such clothes, Evangeline, as you wish to carry with you. Do not leave any of your valuables behind. Use three trunks if necessary."

"Dinner is ready, mistress," said Pauline, appearing at the door of Mrs. Terrant's room.

"Well, come, Evangeline, we will take our dinner; you will then have time to select such clothing as you propose to take.

Come, we will not wait for your uncle, to-day. It is a half-hour earlier than he usually comes here."

Evangeline mechanically followed her aunt to the dining-room. She had not once essayed to speak. Her aunt attributed her silence to her unwillingness to go on account of her **approaching marriage**, and accordingly said, as soon as the servant had left the room:

"You must write a note, Evangeline, to Mr. Lasley, postponing **your marriage at least one month.** Perhaps he may call in this **evening.** He has not been here to-day, has he? You had better write the note as soon as dinner is over. I will tell your uncle **to** have it handed to him, if he has not left the city; and if he has, **to** have it forwarded without delay to Bardstown. Matters are in such a confused condition now, that it would be **impossible** to make preparations for any thing of **the kind. Invite him to visit** you at Indianapolis; and if **you choose, you can marry** him there."

Evangeline sat like some **one petrified. Her heart was bursting** with fear and anxiety. **How** could she relieve herself from this dreadful position? She could not leave Louisville, that was **impossible. But what** valid excuse could she offer to her aunt **for desiring to stay? Once she** thought she would acknowledge all, and throw herself on her aunt's clemency. But she could not do this. It would be to ask too great a favor. And then she remembered her aunt's antipathy to Harry Roberts, and her utter dislike to all secessionists. She dared not make the appeal, so she sat still and silent, her heart beating violently. The color came and went in her cheeks, and the tears would rush up to her eyes, but she would force them down again and endeavor to appear unmoved.

"You do not seem to be pleased **with the prospect of your visit,** Evangeline," said Mrs. Terrant, "**I thought you** would be **delighted to have a short** respite from this ruinous **excitement. For** my part, I am almost dead. I do **not believe I could live unless I can** escape from it awhile. **If I find Indianapolis in such a tumult, I shall** leave my sister's and **go into the** country, to some **quiet village, if such** a place **can** be found."

"Indeed, aunt, I do **not wish to go,**" said Evangeline, summoning all her resolution for the fearful task. "Do let me stay with Uncle Terrant, and keep house **for** him while you are gone. I will get Mary Lawrence and Mrs. Davy to stay with me."

"Why, Evangeline, don't you wish to go? What strange freak

has come over you? You are usually desirous to travel. And who will go with me? I cannot go alone; never travelled by myself in all my life. But why don't you wish to go, Evangeline? What reason can you have for desiring to stay here?"

"Oh, aunt, I could not leave Louisville now. I like the excitement. It would take my life to have to go and stay among the Yankees now. You know, Aunt Cecilia, I never did like them."

"Oh, you needn't trouble yourself about the Yankees; you shall not be annoyed by them."

"But, aunt, I hope you will excuse me this once. If it were any other time in the world, I should take pleasure in accompanying you. Let Uncle Terrant go with you, and then he can return; and if you desire it, I can come out as soon as the fate of Louisville is decided. Won't you excuse me this time, dear aunt, and allow me to stay?" said Evangeline, most coaxingly, quite reassured by the kind, considerate manner in which her aunt received her refusal.

"I do not wish to force you, Evangeline, but should be very glad to have you with me."

"Oh, aunty, you will have company enough when you get there. Your nieces will go with you wherever you wish, and they are most charming society, you know. I will pack all your trunks while you are down town, and will insure that Uncle Terrant will go with you. Had you not better take most of your silver, aunt? or will you leave it all ready packed to be sent across the river as soon as it is ascertained that the Confederates will certainly reach here?"

"I believe I will leave it, Evangeline. It would be a great burden to me to take it with me, and you will keep it in readiness to be moved at any moment, won't you?"

"Indeed I will, aunty. It shall be the first thing attended to by me to-morrow. I will have it all nicely rubbed, and securely put away."

"Get my bonnet and mantle, Pauline," said Mrs. Terrant to the girl, as she arose from the table. "Evangeline, put all my best dresses in one trunk, with my jewelry and velvet cloak, and fill another with plainer wear, and yet another with underclothing. Pauline and Emily must do the packing—you supervise. I shall leave for Jeffersonville at half-past four o'clock."

"Oh, I will have every thing ready, aunt," said Evangeline, gayly, feeling as light as a fairy.

Leaving a few directions with the servants, Mrs. Terrant then threw on her bonnet and silk mantle, and drove down the street to shop.

Evangeline applied herself most energetically to the task before her. Wardrobes, drawers, boxes, were robbed of their contents to fill the three ponderous trunks, that stood open in the middle of the room, awaiting their filling. Evangeline had scarcely begun operations before her Uncle Terrant came in.

"Heigh-day, Evangie, ain't you and your aunt ready to be off yet? Oh, this trunk-packing—what a nuisance to the world! I don't see what women want with such an interminable quantity of clothing, anyhow. Come, come, make haste, you will not be ready in time. We must cross the river at precisely half-past four."

"Go, Emily, tell cook to bring in uncle's dinner directly. Here, uncle, come lie down on the lounge and rest. I want to talk with you awhile," and Evangeline prepared the pillows in her sweetest manner, and drew down the shade at the head of the couch, so that the light would not fall too glaringly on the merchant's face.

"Now, uncle, I have a little kindness to ask of you," said Evangeline, with one of her charming smiles, as she threw her aunt's large plaid shawl over his shoulders, and smoothed back his hair from his forehead.

"And what is it, child?" asked the old gentleman, in a gentle tone.

Evangeline knew her uncle's heart was all right. He had called her "child," with him the most endearing epithet, and so she knelt beside him, and said:

"Uncle, I do wish you would go with aunty to Indianapolis, to-night. Now, won't you just for my sake, uncle? I cannot leave Louisville now, and you know she cannot travel by herself. And aunty is so worn out with the excitement, she really needs a little rest—and then her heart is so bent on going. I shall have to go, if you don't, and stay there with the Yankees until aunty gets ready to come home again. And I would sooner be in Fort Warren; for then I wouldn't be annoyed by them, you know. I never did like the Yankees. I would so much rather stay with you. Now won't you go, just for me?" and Evangeline stroked back the silver-threaded hair, and patted her uncle's cheek most caressingly."

"Oh, my child, I don't see how I can go, I am so busy. Heels over head, scarcely time to draw my breath; large government contract—*must* be attended to, and it keeps me so busy, busy, busy!"

"But you will soon be back again, uncle. Only one day and night, and the relaxation from business will do you good. I am sure it will, and then I shall keep such a nice house for you. I am to be your housekeeper while aunty's gone! You didn't know that, did you? And you shall have such good coffee every morning, and such excellent dinners just when you please, and nice lunch at your store every day at eleven, and music in the evening to drive away care and trouble, and every thing pleasant and nice. Now, won't you go? Oh, I am sure you won't say no, uncle!"

"Oh, you women! Evangie, you women! How you do have every thing your own way! There is no managing you at all. No wonder poor old Adam fell, if Eve was half as persuasive as you women are now-a-days. I am most outrageously busy, but I suppose I shall have to go, just to please you, for your aunt is bent on the trip, and somebody must go with her. But what will you do to-night? You can't stay here alone."

"Oh, never mind me, uncle, I can take care of myself to-night. I am going round to Mrs. Ludlow's, to stay with Flora Richey, a friend of mine from the country. Oh, I am so delighted you will go! And when you get back to-morrow, you shall have every thing so nice, and all your own way, and you shall see what a good housekeeper I'll be. But there is Sarah to tell us dinner is ready. I had you a good, strong cup of tea made. I thought you would enjoy it this chilly day. Walk in, uncle," and Evangeline assisted her uncle to rise, and led him to the dining-room.

During dinner she chatted away so gayly, and attended to Mr. Terrant's wishes with such a pleasing, fascinating manner, that that gentleman began to feel that he had made quite a good arrangement in retaining Evangeline during her aunt's absence, even though it should cost him some present inconvenience.

With no child of his own, it was but natural that the uncle should lavish his love on his young and interesting niece. Evangeline was the only child of an only sister, who, at the age of sixteen, had married a Frenchman of some means, and who, immediately after the marriage, had taken his young wife to Rouen, his native city, where misfortune after misfortune beset them, until they were finally left in very limited circumstances.

When Evangeline was four years of age, Monsieur Lenoir died. His widow, gathering together as best she could the remnant of her husband's property, returned with her daughter to America. Two short years found Evangeline an orphan, in charge of her only remaining relative, **Mr. Terrant**. She brought as her dower a few hundred dollars, **which her mother** had scrupulously preserved for her, and **which Mr.** Terrant immediately placed at interest for the benefit of his niece, when she should marry or become of age. She **was** adopted into his own family, and always **regarded by** him as his own child; and although a man of extensive business and of few words, yet he had found both time and means to make Evangeline feel that she was belóved by him.

"I must go to the store, child, and make my arrangements," said Mr. Terrant, as he rose from the table.

"And I shall tell aunt you will be back **in time to go with** her," she said, as she followed him **into the hall, holding to his** hand.

"Yes; I will be here with a hack precisely at four o'clock. Have every thing ready, Evangie, so that there will be no delay."

"Oh, yes, that I will. Every thing shall be *au fait* in time."

Just as Mr. Terrant was about to place his hand on the door-knob to go out, the bell rang. Evangeline, stepping back to the parlor door, paused to see who it was. Mr. Terrant opened the door, and there stood revealed the form of Ed. Lasley. Evangeline caught a glimpse of it, and with one bound rushed into the **parlor. This was the only** way of escape. As she stood there trembling, scarce knowing what to do, she heard her uncle say:

"How do you do to-day, Mr. Lasley? Walk in, sir."

"Is Miss Lenoir in?" the young man asked, as he moved forward to enter the hall.

"Yes, she is at home, sir; walk in, walk in."

The young man entered the hall, and encountering Pauline, who had gone to answer the bell, said:

"Tell Miss Lenoir Mr. Lasley wishes to see her in the parlor."

"I will go and see if she is in, sir."

"Oh, yes she is; Mr. Terrant has just told me so."

Evangeline waited to hear no more. Frightened at the idea of **encountering** the man who had **threatened her, and** whom she saw on the street but a few hours before in such a disgusting plight, she sprang into the back parlor through the open door, and gaining the door that led into the hall, stood trembling with alarm. As soon as she heard the step of the young man in the parlor, she glided across the hall into the dining-room, and from thence she gained her aunt's chamber, where, locking the door behind her, she threw herself on the couch near the window and hid her face in her hands.

"What *is* the matter, Miss 'Vangy?" asked Emily, who was busily engaged packing one of the three large trunks with her mistress's silk dresses and laces. "You look scared to death, Miss 'Vangy—pale as a ghost!"

A knock was heard at the door.

"Oh, do not let any one come in, Emily!" said Evangeline, her voice tremulous with fear. "Keep the door locked, do!"

"It's only Pauline, Miss 'Vangy; don't you hear her voice?" and Emily turned the key and admitted her before the frightened girl could command her not to do it.

"Mr. Lasley wants to see you in the parlor, Miss 'Vangy," said Pauline, as she approached the bedside, and stood over her young mistress, who had not yet dared to look up. "Here is his card, mam."

The young girl started up. "Tell him, Pauline, that I cannot see him; I am engaged making preparations to go to Indianapolis to-night."

The servant bore her young mistress's message to the parlor, and soon returned with one from young Lasley.

"Mr. Lasley says he must see you, Miss 'Vangy; he cannot leave the house until he does. He has something important to say to you, and he must see you now, directly."

"Pauline, tell Mr. Lasley," said the young girl, trembling from head to foot, yet with her eye fixed steadily on the servant that stood awaiting her bidding, "that I cannot see him this evening; it is impossible. Then do you come here and finish putting your mistress's clothes in that trunk. It is now almost three o'clock, and every thing must be in readiness in a half-hour."

"What did he say, Pauline?" asked the young girl, nervously, as the servant returned from the delivery of her last message to the visitor in the parlor.

"He says he is going to stay here until he does see you, Miss 'Vangy; that he won't move one step until you come into that parlor!"

"Then he will weary of waiting," said the young girl to herself, as she rose from the couch and proceeded to attend to her aunt's jewelry.

"Lock that door, immediately, Pauline, and come here and remove these things from the two drawers to that large black trunk by the washstand. And you and Emily make all the haste you can. You have but little time; the hack will be here at four, and they must not be kept waiting. This carpet-bag leave; I'll attend to it myself. Hand me those rubbers; they must go in it. Put those dresses and those mantles in very smoothly, Emily; and Pauline roll those underclothes very tightly."

Evangeline having secured her aunt's jewelry and attended to the important carpet-bag, threw herself on the lounge, where she could superintend the operations of the two girls. Her face was crimson; her heart beat tumultuously, and her temples throbbed violently; yet she felt she must nerve herself to the task, cost what it might. What she had undertaken must be accomplished, and time was pressing.

As she lay there she could occasionally hear across the hall the footsteps of young Lasley, as he moved about the parlor. Every time this noise reached her ears, she started up and looked towards the door. Once she heard him step out into the hall—

"Thank God! thank God! he is going!" she said to herself, and suppressing her breath and ordering the two servants to be silent, she waited in torturing expectation for the hall door to open. But the young man, after walking to the front door and looking out through the side-lights, returned to the parlor and resumed his seat.

"Why don't you go in now, Miss 'Vangy, to see Mr. Lasley? Me an Emily can finish these trunks in time. And you see he is not going until he does see you."

"Attend to your own business, Pauline, and finish those trunks! I do not wish to see Mr. Lasley this evening, and do not intend to do it."

"Oh! if he should remain here until my aunt returns! What shall I do? I cannot explain this thing to her now, and she will be all curious to know about it. Oh, I do wish he would go! What a simpleton to be sitting up there, thinking he will force me to come! I wouldn't go into that parlor now if I suffered death for it! Half an hour he has been here already; he must possess some patience to set up there all that time alone."

"This trunk is as full as it will hold, Miss 'Vangy."

"And have you put in all the handsome dresses, and the mantles, and aunt's velvet cloak?"

"Yes, mam."

"Well, set it to one side—help her there, Pauline—and then go up stairs, Emily, and look in my room and bring your Miss Cecilia's large travelling shawl and that cloth cloak; she may wish them both. Go the back way."

Again Evangeline heard the footfall in the hall, and again she started up and listened breathlessly. The young man repeated the same act of going to the door, peeping out, and then returning, walked into the parlor and strode across the room.

"He is growing restless," said **Evangeline** to herself. "He will go after awhile; another half-hour!" and she again **took out her** watch to consult the time. "Another half-hour and his patience must be exhausted. **God grant he may leave** before my aunt comes!"

Fifteen minutes more had passed. The trunks were ready for strapping. Again **the footfall was heard in the hall.** It passed.

"Thank God—thank God! he is gone at last!" exclaimed Evangeline, as she heard the hall door open. She sprang to the window to see him pass out. **She waited a moment, wondering why he** did not descend the steps. **She heard the door close.** "Now he is gone, surely!" She pressed her face against the glass to **catch** a glimpse of his figure; a moment more and she heard the same detested footfall enter the parlor. Looking towards the front gate, she discovered her aunt alighting from her carriage!

"What shall I do! what shall I do!" she said, wringing her hands in agony. "There is aunty, and that simpleton is still in the parlor! What will she say when she learns he has been here an hour, and I have not been in to see him? I have a great mind to go in now—no, **I won't. He shall not conquer me by his rudeness. Maybe he'll have** sense enough to keep quiet, and aunty will be in such haste that she will not find out he is here. She has **only fifteen minutes. Oh, what will** those fifteen minutes develop!"

"Unlock that door, Emily, and open the hall door, and tell aunty as soon as she comes in that all **her** trunks are ready. Pauline, go and bring those packages from the driver. Did you leave room for them in the brown trunk?"

"Yes, mam!"

"All things ready, Evangie?" said Mrs. Terrant, bursting into the room. I have but fifteen minutes. Your uncle will be here in that time with a carriage, and he says I must not keep him waiting a moment. **He is going with** me, he told me. Bring my large shawl, Emily."

"**Here** it is, aunty, and your cloak too."

"I shall want them both. I will wear the cloak, and Mr. Terrant can take the shawl on his arm. I shall need it to-night. The whole town is in an uproar, Evangeline, about General Bragg's coming. Oh! I am so glad I am getting away from it. I should go crazy to stay here a week longer. Here, Evangeline, you put these things in the trunk, will you, where they won't get mashed. There are some ruches and flowers in that box; I could not get my bonnet trimmed in time, so I bought the materials and will have it done in Indianapolis. Shop-keepers, milliners, mantua-makers —everybody—are beside themselves. If you had seen Mr. Lasley I would take you with me just as you are, and let your trunks be sent after you. Tell him, Evangeline, that the marriage must be postponed a month, until all this noise and confusion are over. It would be impossible to give you a wedding under such circumstances."

"Sit down, aunty, and rest a moment; you look so flurried. You are ready now."

"Every thing in the trunks? Well, then, strap them, and tell Harry to take them out to the front gate. Did you put me up a snack, Evangeline? I may not get any supper."

"No; but I can in a moment."

"Some bread and cheese, child, and some of that cold ham with a few pickles. Where is my palm fan? I may need it. I believe it is in the parlor;" and Mrs. Terrant rose from her seat to get it, as no servant was present to wait on her.

Evangeline, who heard her words and saw her movement through the open door, bounded into the room—

Oh, aunty, do sit still! I will get it for you. See, your collar is on wrong side out; change it, while I get the fan."

She was about to cross the hall to encounter young Lasley in the parlor, when Emily came in from assisting Henry with the trunks."

"Aunt's palm fan, Emily, in the parlor—not a word for your life!"

"It's in the back parlor, Miss 'Vangy; I saw it there when I cleaned up the room this morning."

"Get it quickly—not a word about Mr. Lasley! Do you hear?"

"Yes, mam," replied the girl, whose wonder was every moment increased by her young mistress's strange movements.

Evangeline hastened to the dining-room, and with the assistance of Sarah, the cook, soon returned with a nice package of edibles, which she deposited in her aunt's travelling basket.

"There's your uncle with the carriage. Write me, Evangeline, at least three letters a week—and don't forget to tell Mr. Lasley about the postponement. And attend to the silver. Emily, you and Pauline do what your Miss 'Vangie tells you, and behave yourselves." And Mrs. Terrant walked rapidly out into the hall, followed by her niece and the two servants.

"Oh! will he come out?" asked Evangeline to herself. "If he will only stay a few moments longer, all will be safe."

But the young man, who knew full well how kindly Mrs. Terrant had treated him, was determined to retaliate, if possible, on the young lady who had left him waiting one long, weary hour to catch a glimpse at her person.

And—oh, horrors!—just as Mrs. Terrant stepped into the hall from the room door, he issued from the opposite one and bade her and Evangeline good-evening, and taking his hat from the rack, proceeded to accompany them to the carriage.

"Evangie has told you that I am going to Indianapolis to-night, Mr. Lasley? Scared away by the Confederates."

"This is the first glimpse I have caught of Miss Evangie this evening, Mrs. Terrant."

"Oh! but a short time in, and Evangie has been so busy."

"Have been in the parlor an hour and twenty minutes."

The aunt looked at her niece wonderingly. The girl colored, but made no reply.

"Found Evangie very busy this evening, Mr. Lasley? But I suppose she has had time to say all that was *necessary*," remarked Mr. Terrant, jocularly.

"I have just this moment seen her for the first time, Mr. Terrant," replied the young man surlily.

The uncle cast a penetrating glance on Evangeline. The rose on her cheek blushed itself to crimson. She was about to say to her uncle that she had been so busy as to prevent her appearance in the parlor; but conscience interfered and saved her the sin of prevarication, and smiling a forced smile, she remained silent.

"Evangie is very tired now, Mr. Lasley, and I know cannot prove interesting; so you had better take a seat with us and drive down to the hotel," and Mr. Terrant placed the packages so as to give the young man a comfortable seat. "We have not a moment to lose; it is now four o'clock," said Mr. T., consulting his watch. "Come, Mrs. Terrant, let me assist you in; and you, Mr. Lasley."

The aunt bade Evangeline farewell, whispering in her ear as she kissed her, "Don't forget to speak to Mr. Lasley about the postponement," and stepped into the carriage. The young man hesitated.

"Just as well ride, Mr. Lasley," said Mrs. Terrant as she discovered his pause.

Turning to Evangeline he said, "I shall call and see you at six. Where shall I find you?"

"Not at home," was the low reply.

"Very well!" he remarked, mistaking her answer, and putting his foot in the step, entered and closed the door.

"Good-by, my child; I shall be back to-morrow, without an accident," called out her uncle as the carriage drove off.

CHAPTER LII.

EXCITEMENTS—DISAPPOINTMENTS.

Evangeline hastened to her own room. Closing the door, she threw herself on the bed and gave way to the pent-up excitement of the day in a flood of weeping. It was the outbreak of the tempest that had been silently gathering together its mighty forces. She wept long and bitterly as she thought of all she had endured —all she must yet meet; and as she looked out upon the responsibilities of the coming two weeks, she shuddered and recoiled as one who contemplates a fearful doom. How strange, how wildly strange, to her was her present position! She who had been the petted child of fortune—who had lived so dependent on others, and who, hedged about by kind protection, had never felt otherwise than safe from all danger, free from all care! It was the turning-point in her life. She had now assumed to act for herself, was about to cut adrift from the old moorings and launch out on an unknown sea. Should she succeed, was the question she asked herself; for she did not for a moment swerve from her purpose.

"It is for Harry," she said; "and whether or not I am successful, I must make the attempt. For his sake I will encounter every obstacle, endure every trial, meet every reproach. He is worthy of all this on my part, and I shall not show myself unworthy of him. If I accomplish my purposes, I secure my happiness for life; if I fail, I have done my duty—all—all I could— and this, poor as it is, will be some consolation to me amid my grief and helplessness. If I do not marry Harry, I shall have to marry Lasley. My aunt is determined on it. But—no—I cannot do it! Rather than do this, I will forever immure myself in a convent, where, shut out from the world, I can cherish my own sorrows, indulge my lifelong grief. Oh, should Harry fail to escape! should he be shot, or die in prison! Then—then—what then! God grant he may get out safely!" she ejaculated aloud, as the thought of his death swept through her mind.

"A life of dark trial mine has been. Fatherless, motherless— no brother, no sister—an orphan alone in the wide world. And yet my uncle and aunt have been kind to me—but they could not love me as my poor mother—they could never understand my heart as she could have done. Oh, no one can love us like a mother—none enter into our joys or sorrows as she—none forgive like her own tender heart. Alone, alone, I have been—alone, alone, I am now. None truly loves me but Harry, and he loves me with all my faults; he knows them all, and loves me still! and shall I not risk every thing for him? dare every thing to remove him from the hands of his cruel enemies? Yes, yes, if I perish in the attempt, I'll try it! I will not shrink now, that dangers seem to surround me on every side; I'll nerve this heart of mine to bear all things, that I may accomplish my purpose!" and she sprang from the bed, and dashed away her tears, her large black eyes flushed with the fires of her invincible resolve.

The clock struck the half-hour.

"I must not weep now—no time for tears! Action, action, demands my thoughts, my time, my efforts. I have a great work to perform, and I must lay aside my grief—'tis but a weakness to weep, when duty calls to exertion. Five o'clock, and I must be at Mrs. Ludlow's. What if my plan should be discovered? But, no! this cannot be—they will think it a mistake of the shopman. But I will be there in time."

Throwing back her hair, Evangeline bathed her face until the throbbing of her brain was partially allayed, then combing the rich masses of her black hair, she changed her dress for a dark blue silk, and throwing on her hat and a black silk paletot, she descended to her aunt's room to give directions to the servants about closing the house for the night, telling them she would not return until the following morning, at ten o'clock.

"Be careful, Emily; see that none of the windows are left open, and shut the conservatory doors—it will be cold to-night. And poor little Blanche, give her her supper and breakfast, and put her to sleep in your room," she added, caressing the little poodle that just then sprang up at her side, and commenced jumping around, as if by its gambols it wished to drive the sad, weary look from the face of its young mistress.

"Poor Blanche!" said Evangeline, stooping, and taking up the pet in her arms. "You are so happy, and my poor heart is breaking!"

"You do look so tired, Miss 'Vangy," said Emily to her young mistress, as she came from the dining-room into Mrs. Terrant's room, where Evangeline was standing with the poodle, smoothing its soft, white hair. "You ain't going to walk round to Miss Ludlow's? Let me tell Henry to bring the carriage, he hasn't put it away yet—stopped to eat his dinner first."

"If the carriage is ready, Emily, Henry may bring it round, for I am very weary. But I have no time to lose, I must be **at** Mrs. Ludlow's at five, and it now wants only ten minutes of the **hour.** See to it immediately, Emily."

The girl left the room; in **a** moment she returned to inform her young mistress that Henry was driving round to the front **gate.**

"**Don't** forget what I have told **you, Emily. Attend** carefully to Blanche," she said, handing the dog to her. **Then seeing that** the shutters were closed, she passed through the front hall, followed by the girl.

"Is this a card of Mr. Lasley, Miss 'Vangy," and Emily handed the young girl an envelope, which she had just picked up near the hat-rack.

Evangeline took it, and reaching the hall door, paused to look at the superscription. She recognized the handwriting of Lasley, and saw the note was directed to a young gentleman of Bardstown, a fast young man, but a particular friend and intimate associate of Lasley. Evangeline also discovered that it had been recently penned, and that it was unsealed. **Her** curiosity was excited, but without waiting to give the subject further consideration, she slipped the missive into her pocket, and hastened to the carriage.

In a few minutes she was at Mrs. Ludlow's door. Alighting from the carriage, she rang the bell nervously. A servant ushered her into the parlor, where sat Mrs. Richey and her daughter, and several lady visitors. They were all strangers to Evangeline save Mrs. Dumfries, who was formerly an intimate friend of her aunt; but differing very widely in political sentiment, the two had ceased their friendly visits, and were now so estranged as scarcely to recognize each other in meeting.

After the introduction, Evangeline took a seat by this lady, and the two engaged in conversation. In answer to Mrs. Dumfries inquiry for Mrs. Terrant's health, Evangeline replied that her aunt's health was good, but that, still suffering from nervousness, she had allowed herself to be scared away by the Southerners."

"And you did not go with her, Evangie? Didn't you feel afraid of the '*rebels?*'" asked Mrs. Dumfries, with some surprise.

"Oh, no, madam; I am not afraid of Southern people. I am

Southern myself. I wish General Bragg would come and take possession of the city, and release us all from Yankee rule, I am so tired of it."

"Your aunt is violently opposed to that, isn't she?" asked Mrs. Dumfries, smiling; "and your uncle, too?"

"Aunt is Union; uncle says but little about it. He thinks the whole thing is wrong, both parties are to blame, and wishes the war would end. Do you think, Mrs. Dumfries, that it is possible for General Bragg to come to Louisville?" Evangeline asked, the earnestness of her voice attesting the deep interest she felt.

"It is possible, Evangeline, I think, but perhaps not probable. Unionists are dreadfully alarmed. The rumor this evening is that he is marching direct upon our city with a force of seventy-five thousand veteran troops. If this be true, he can take the place without trouble. The troops already here and those that are pouring in hourly, are wholly undisciplined, and could make but poor resistance to such an army. I have never seen such intense excitement as prevails in the city. The Union men don't know what to do, those I mean who are informed and capable of judging of matters. They are moving all their valuables to Jeffersonville and New Albany. General Nelson, I understand, has ordered all the heaviest guns across the river, to be placed in position to shell the city, in the event Bragg comes. He says he will contest every inch of ground, and if driven across the river he will shell the city from the opposite side; that not one stone shall be left on another, if the rebels get the place."

"General Nelson is a very rash man, Mrs. Dumfries," remarked Mrs. Sedgwick; "I have known him from his boyhood. There is a great deal of bluster about him. I do not regard his threats with much terror."

"The only fear is his extreme recklessness," said Mrs. Miller; "I judge, from what I have learned of his character, that he is a desperado, and would not hesitate to do any thing that would subserve his purposes."

"But even if he were crazy enough to attempt to execute his threat, I feel confident his own party would not allow him to do it. Union men are more avaricious than patriotic, and will never be willing to be reduced to poverty, even to support their 'best government in the world,'" replied Mrs. Dumfries. "I feel no fear that General Nelson will either burn or shell the city. He would be murdered on the streets first by his own party."

After some minutes' conversation on the all-absorbing theme of the war, the ladies rose to leave. As they gained the hall, the door-bell rung. Evangeline consulted her watch. It was fifteen minutes after five. Stepping out with the departing visitors, she encountered the shop-man's errand-boy at the door bearing the package of clothing.

"This is for me, Flora," she said hastily to the young girl beside her. "Have it taken to your room. It is addressed to you, you see. I will explain all after awhile."

Flora ordered the servant to receive the roll and carry it to her room up stairs. The two girls very soon followed. Evangeline in a very few words explained her plan to Flora.

"I know you will not betray me, Flora," she said, as she finished her hasty recital. "It may not succeed, and should it not, you can readily perceive the necessity of the most profound secresy. Put that package away where it will meet no one's eye, not even your mother's, Flora. I will have it taken home to-morrow. I did not know when I ordered it that my aunt would be absent when it was sent, or I should have directed it carried home. But I have to be very cautious; one misstep, and the whole matter is thwarted. Oh, you cannot tell what anxiety I feel. I am almost wild, Flora."

"I should think so, Evangeline. But how I regret I did not propose something of this kind to my cousin. Mother gave him money, and told him to escape if possible and come to us. Perhaps if the two could have concerted together it would have been better for both."

"And they may yet do it, Flora. They observed that we knew each other. This will doubtless lead to a friendly conversation, which may result in some understanding on their part."

"I sincerely hope for this, Evangie. In a matter of escape no prisoner would trust another unless he knew him well."

"Can't you convey your cousin a note privately, Flora?"

"This is impossible. There is no visiting permitted until next Thursday, and your friend is to escape on Sunday, didn't you tell me?"

"Sunday night; but, oh, Flora, if he should fail! Isn't it dreadful to think of!"

"He would be in a worse condition than now, Evangie."

"Oh, he might be shot and killed! You do not know how dangerous it is to attempt to get out. These Dutch guards are so heartless. They don't hesitate a moment to shoot a man down if he offends them in the least thing. How many have been shot at Camp Chase for mere trivialities. Oh, I shudder to think if Harry should meet this sad fate. I should never cease to upbraid myself for his death!" and the excited girl covered her face with her hands and burst into tears.

"We must hope for better things, Evangie. You know a great many escape unhurt," said Flora, cheerfully, endeavoring to win her young friend from her grief.

Tea came. Evangeline felt no disposition to eat. Her head ached violently, and to her highly nervous agitation had succeeded a most depressing languor. Yet she felt she must make her appearance at table, and summoning all her fortitude, and assuming a gayety entirely foreign to her feelings, she descended the stairs with Flora to the supper-room.

The topic of the tea-table chat was, of course, the movement of the Southern army into Kentucky, and the preparations for defence. Various were the opinions expressed relative to the final issue of the invasion, each one being biased in his judgment by desire and fear.

While sitting at the table the bell rang. The servant soon returned bearing a card, which she handed to Evangeline. The young girl looked at it for a moment. Her color rose to her very temples, and her hand trembled with agitation. She appeared confused, irresolute. Turning to the servant, she said, in a low tone, "Tell the gentleman I am at tea."

The girl bowed and bore the message to the parlor.

Evangeline sat and sipped her tea, joining in the conversation whenever it seemed necessary for her to do so; but her manner was constrained, and her words devoid of interest. She plead headache for her want of life and animation, and Mrs. Ludlow insisted she should take a second cup of tea, which, however, she declined, remarking "That tea did not often benefit her headache."

Excusing herself before the family arose, she hastened to the room alone, and, taking a pencil from her pocket, wrote a few words hurriedly on the card, and laid it on the stand beside her to await the coming of a servant to bear it to the parlor. Then, as if suddenly recollecting the note which Emily had found in the hall at home and handed her, she drew it forth and approached the burner as if to read it. In doing so she passed the mirror. Casting a glance into it, she started back at her flushed and wild appearance.

"No wonder the children at the supper-table stared at me so," she said, as she took a second look; "really, the Witch of Endor could not have appeared more frightful!"

Standing beneath the gas-light, she held the missive in her hand, as if uncertain whether or not to read it. Opening it after a minute, she glanced over its contents. She saw in the second line her name, and just below it that of Harry Roberts.

"It concerns me, and Providence has thrown it in my way. I will read it!" and seating herself on the sofa, she ran rapidly over the first page.

"The wretch!" she exclaimed to herself, "does he call this love? No, no! he shall never have the satisfaction of executing his low, base threat. I will release Harry, or die in the effort! But, be his—never, never! I shall neither be threatened, forced, or cajoled into marrying a man whom I detest. How strange that I should ever have fancied I loved this coarse, heartless man—this man who seems bent on my destruction, merely to gratify his pique! He shall never have to boast that he conquered Evangeline Lenoir!" she said, as she arched her neck, and cast a look of contemptuous defiance on the sheet she held in her hand. "Ah, ha! a very fine plan, indeed!" she said, curling her lip in bitter scorn, as she read the second page. "He may succeed in 'putting Harry Roberts out of the way,' but never in 'leading the proud girl to the altar.'"

She read the epistle a second time carefully, then folded it in the envelope. "A very dishonorable act under other circumstances, but, in me, inexcusable *now*. Thank God! I know his plans, they shall be thwarted. He cannot, shall not succeed."

Stepping to the stand, she was about to add something to her reply. She stood thoughtful for a moment, then, putting the pencil back into her pocket, she threw the letter on the stand with the card.

In a few minutes, the servant entered the room bearing a pitcher of water.

"Girl, take that note and card to the young gentleman in the parlor, and then return and let me know what he says," she added, as the servant was leaving the room.

"The young gentleman didn't say any thing, miss," said the girl, opening the door and peeping in. "He looked very mad, ma'am, when he read the note, and took his hat and went out."

"Very well, girl; where is Miss Flora?"

"In the parlor, ma'am. She told me to tell you to excuse her; an old friend had called to see her, and she would be in the parlor some time."

"It is all perfectly right. Tell Miss Flora I would prefer to be alone, my head aches so."

The girl passed out, closing the door behind her. Evangeline threw herself into the large arm-chair that stood beside her, and burying her face in her hands, wept aloud.

Oh, the agony, the utter desolateness of that moment! There are times in the history of every heart, when the sorrows of life crush out for a time every hope, every desire. How wild and meaningless existence then seems! We shrink from the very thought of our own being, and unless the soul can lift the eye of faith to the source whence cometh all consolation, it sinks into the dread wish for annihilation. Life! strange, enigmatical life! who can fathom thy mysteries?

Evangeline wept and wept. The fountain of tears was unsealed and gushed forth in unceasing torrents. No power of will could check them. Sobbing, she threw herself on the sofa, and in a paroxysm of anguish lay like one bereft of reason. Her brain burnt as with fire, and her heart throbbed almost to bursting. She clasped her hands despairingly, and looked up as if imploring aid.

"Oh! God pity me!" she exclaimed, "pity me, pity me! and bring relief to my poor breaking heart!"

A half hour passed. Evangeline was still weeping. Her sobs and moans, so low and piteous, were sad to hear. Flora Richey entered the room. Going to the sofa, she threw her arms around the prostrate form and said soothingly, "Do not weep so, Evangie. It will all come right."

The young girl opened her eyes and put out her arms to clasp the neck of her friend, but they fell powerless at her side, and the large black orbs closed again, while her whole countenance took upon it a look of unutterable woe.

Flora bathed the hot brow and chafed the cold hands, and poured into the distracted ear tender, loving words. But many an hour passed before the tried heart found peace in sleep.

Friday and Saturday were days of restless anxiety, and conflicting doubts and hopes. On Friday night, Mr. Terrant returned from Indianapolis, and the vocation that Evangeline had assumed, that of housekeeper, gave her employment which served measurably to win her from her trouble. Young Lasley did not call again during the time. Evangeline hoped that her note had convinced him that his visits were no longer acceptable.

Sabbath morning came. Evangeline prepared for church. Her uncle was to accompany her. She was donning her bonnet and paletot when the door-bell rang violently. "Who can that be?"

she said, as she sprang to the window to look out. She could not discern who it was, but she could perceive it was a man. Her heart misgave her. Breathlessly she awaited the servant's approach.

"Mr. Lasley is in the parlor, Miss 'Vangie. Called to see if you are going to church this morning."

"Tell Mr. Lasley I have company, Emily, and he must excuse me."

"Has he left, Emily?" she asked of the servant, who returned to announce that the carriage was at the door.

"No, ma'am; he says he'll go with master."

"Go and tell him, Emily, that your master is going with me in the carriage. I have borne this insolence long enough," she said, passionately, to herself. "I will bear it no longer. He cannot be insulted. He is determined to have his own way in this matter, and make me yield in order that he may show his power. But if he has governed his old aunt all the days of his life, he shall not govern me. If he wishes to go with my uncle he can do so, but he shall not go with me."

"What does he say now, Emily?"

"He didn't say any thing, Miss 'Vangie."

"And did he leave?"

"No, ma'am; he is still sitting in the parlor."

"And where is my uncle?"

"In his room, ma'am; he doesn't know Mr. Lasley is in the parlor."

"What shall I do?" she asked herself, perplexed at her disagreeable position; "if I decline going, uncle will think it so strange, and I cannot go with this man."

She bowed her head in her hand as she stood by the bureau and thought for a moment. Then rapidly descending the stairway, she knocked at her uncle's door. In answer to Mr. Terrant's "come in," she entered, and approaching the window where her uncle was standing, she said:

"Uncle, Mr. Lasley is in the parlor—came to go with me to church. What shall I do?"

"Go, child; of course you could not refuse, could you?"

"But, uncle, I do not wish to do so. You know persons always talk so much when a young lady is seen with a gentleman at church in the forenoon!" and Evangeline, despite herself, blushed deeply.

"Oh, well, child," said the indulgent uncle, "if you do not wish

14*

to go with young Lasley; but I can't see why you don't. But you women are strange creatures any how! You needn't do it; he can walk with me and you can go in the carriage."

"That is the very plan, uncle! Please go in the parlor and take him with you. See here, I am not ready to go just now. He will understand it."

The unsuspecting uncle did as he was bid.

"Girls are very modest creatures anyhow you know, Mr. Lasley," said he to the young man, after explaining the matter to him as delicately as he could. "All right, I suppose; the strange creatures must have their own way. No accounting for their whims."

Lasley bowed assent, but he by no means received the case as did his more elderly friend. Not knowing, however, how to object to the proposition, nor to refuse the polite invitation to accompany Mr. Terrant, he found himself reduced to the extremity of seeming to indorse the one and to accept the other.

Evangeline waited until she thought the gentlemen had reached the church, then taking the carriage she drove round for Mary Lawrence, whom she found already gone.

After services, Evangeline and Mary hastened out of the church so as to avoid observation, and drove home quite in advance of Mr. Terrant.

"I do wonder if he will return with my uncle!" said Evangeline, as the two girls seated themselves in the carriage. "Look yonder, Mary, do! he is with him, and I wager he will be bold enough to come to take dinner with us. If he should, what will I do?"

"Oh! treat him with freezing politeness, Evangeline."

"*Politeness*, indeed! I do not believe I could tolerate his presence for a moment. I do not know why I should feel such utter dislike to one whom I so short a time ago fancied I admired; but, Mary, he has haunted me so—has manifested such entire destitution of all noble sentiment, that I am filled with disgust when I contemplate his character."

The two girls reached home and entered the parlor to wait for Mr. Terrant. In a few minutes he entered the room alone, and bidding Mary good-day, seated himself beside her.

"Where is Mr. Lasley, Mr. Terrant?" asked Mary, smiling.

"Oh, he has gone to the hotel, I suppose. Why, girls, how remiss I was; I did not think to invite him to dine with us to-day. He remarked to me, too, that he would call this evening at four o'clock."

The girls exchanged meaning glances.

"What have you two been doing, girls, that you had to run away from church so hastily to-day? I strove to overtake you, and thus caused me to forget to ask Mr. Lasley to dinner. You are after something wrong, Evangie, child; I see it in your face. Haven't you a guilty conscience on some subject? Come, tell me what it is you are about. Some prank I warrant."

"No prank in the world, uncle!" replied the young girl, blushing as she spoke.

"Something is going on, child, with regard to Lasley that isn't right. He has been here twice and you have refused to see him. Be careful—a man won't bear a woman's whims always!"

"But, uncle, I was so busy on Thursday; how could I see any one?"

"And then this morning, Evangie"—

"Well, I gave you my reason, uncle. Now, be candid, wasn't it a very good one?"

"Oh, modest and plausible enough; but if your Aunt Cecilia had been so chary when we were courting, we should never have been married, I can tell you, child! I couldn't have stood all these new-fashioned ideas of modesty; they would have run me crazy."

"Oh! but times have changed since then, Mr. Terrant, haven't they?" remarked Mary Lawrence, laughing, as she rose to follow Evangeline to her room.

"Yes, yes; and for the worse, Mary. I'm sure of that."

"Oh! no, no, Mr. Terrant," remonstrated Mary, as she turned in the doorway to reply. "You know this is an age of improvement in all things."

"Well, well, may be so; you women will always have things your own way," said Mr. Terrant, bowing deferentially. Mary returned the bow with a most bewitching smile on her sweet, sad face, and passed with Evangeline up the stairway.

"I am going out with Mary awhile this evening," said Evangeline to her uncle, as they returned to the parlor after dinner. "You will wish to take your *siesta*, and should Mr. Lasley come before I return—but of course he will not—tell Emily to tell him where I have gone, and he can call at Mrs. Purdy's and see us both."

"Oh! 'Vangie, child! this will not do. Lasley will feel himself insulted. You will lose him, child, I tell you you will. Better stay at home till he comes, and then he can walk round with you girls."

"Oh, uncle! but we may have to wait all the evening. They dine very late at the hotel, and then Mr. Lasley will have to enjoy a cigar, and after this a nap; so you see he is not likely to be around before dark; and even if he should come earlier, it is a pleasant little walk round to Mrs. Purdy's, and I know he wishes to see Mary, any how. Moreover, uncle, I made this engagement with Mary to meet a friend of ours several days ago."

"And I cannot well release Evangie, Mr. Terrant. I am sure Mr. Lasley will excuse us for not awaiting his arrival when he is made to understand the circumstances."

"Well, well, you girls will have every thing your own way! No use for me to interfere in Lasley's behalf. If he should come—and he told me he would—I shall have to send him round to see you."

"Do, Mr. Terrant, if you please! you will confer a favor on us."

"And, uncle, should I fail to be back at ten, won't you tell Henry to drive round for us? We may not have any company to church to-night."

"Better tell Pauline, child. You know I am so forgetful about these little matters."

Evangeline rung the bell, gave Pauline the necessary instructions, then bidding her uncle good-evening, set out with Mary Lawrence for Mrs. Purdy's.

Fifteen minutes to four. The two young girls, deeply veiled, descended the foot steps to the street and directed their way to the prison. As they walked rapidly along, they encountered several of their friends, but they passed them by without recognition, lest they should be betrayed. Street after street was quickly passed, the two girls scarcely daring to interchange a word. Just as they were turning the corner of Third and Green, they met Mr. Roberts in front of the custom-house. He paused as if about to speak. Evangeline trembled as she felt herself recognized; but the gentleman, after casting his eye vacantly up and down the pavement, proceeded in his walk.

"How sad and disturbed Mr. Roberts looks!" whispered Mary to her friend.

"I am afraid something has befallen Harry," was the tremulous reply of Evangeline.

"I wonder," she said, after a short pause, "if he has been to the prison! May be Harry is sick—has gone away!" she added slowly, as if afraid to give voice to her own apprehension.

A few moments more and the two had reached the prison,

Evangeline timidly raised her thick veil and looked hurriedly up and down Green, and in and out Fifth-street. But few persons were passing. The guard **kept watch in front of the great closed gates that opened on Green. A solitary sentinel paced back and forth on Fifth-street. He was a** youth, pleasant, friendly, and genteel in his bearing. **After taking** this furtive **survey,** Evangeline cast her eye up to the designated window. There stood a **prisoner. Was it** Roberts**?** She looked again. **The prisoner bowed, and she knew it was** Harry**!**

"**Mary, you cross the street and engage the sentinel in conversation, while I stand here to receive the signal. Ask him any thing, Mary, any thing; whether the prisoners receive company, and when; if they behave themselves pretty well? You know what to do, Mary. Go, go! we will arouse suspicion if we remain longer here!**"

Mary quickly crossed over, **and** throwing **aside her thick mourning veil, approached towards the guard. She paused as soon as** she found she had attracted his attention. **This she did that he, in advancing to meet her, might leave Evangeline standing on the opposite side, at his back.** The man raised his cap as his eye fell on the graceful form and beautiful face **of the young girl before him.** Mary bowed, and spoke pleasantly **but modestly,** and commenced **to question him, as Evangeline had suggested.**

Evangeline stepped forward, so **as to place herself directly in front of the window where the prisoner stood. She waved her handkerchief, and strained her eyes for the answering signal. A moment passed. Oh, what a moment of suspense that was to the expectant heart of the young** girl, as she **stood there gazing upward towards that window!** It came. **The prisoner's right hand was raised, placed on his brow, then drawn slowly across his face, and rested on his shoulder. It was the indication of suc**cess that Evangeline **had proposed.**

She stood as one **bewildered, stupefied, under the rush of her wild emotion.** Harry would be free—**a few short hours** would restore him to liberty and to her! **The** thought was intoxicating. Yet another sign **was needed:** the hour must be **designated. She** raised and gently waved **it a second** time. The prisoner **bowed** understandingly. Evangeline sent **up** another eager, **fixed look. The left hand was raised, then** slowly lowered. **This gesture was** repeated eight times. "Nine o'clock," said Evangeline to herself. Then raising her left hand she repeated the action of the prisoner nine times. As her hand fell the last time, **the prisoner bowed** twice, and turned from the window. It was the work of but a minute, and yet what mighty results to these two young hearts hung on its fleeting moments!

"Thank God! thank God!" exclaimed Evangeline, "Harry will be safe!" She said no more, but turned to look for Mary. As she turned she encountered Captain Fred. Morton. She had forgotten to lower her veil, and was recognized. She started back as if she had met a spectre. The captain bowed politely, and passed on.

"Mary!" she called, unconscious of what she did. "Mary, Mary, do come on."

"She was ready to sink under her agitation. Had she been discovered by this Federal officer? Had she? And if so, what would be the result? But Harry is safe, she said. Thank God he is not implicated, and as regards myself, I defy Fred. Morton and all the Yankee hosts; they won't dare to annoy me.

Mary responded to her call, and came tripping across the street delighted that she had acted her part so well in the fearful drama. Just as she reached the pavement, on which Evangeline was standing, she met young Morton face to face. She bowed coldly, and as he passed stiffly by, Mary thought she saw on his face a sinister smile. It was the first time they had met in weeks. She had persistently avoided him on all occasions, which avoidance he had deeply felt. He loved her devotedly—hopelessly he knew, yet he could not conquer his affection. And he felt a constant pique that he should at all times be the recipient of marked neglect.

"Will Harry get out, Evangeline? but I need not ask, I read his escape in your face."

"Yes, yes, Mary, he will soon be free. The signals were all right, and to-night at nine o'clock he will meet me at the First Presbyterian Church."

"Oh! Evangeline, we are betrayed, betrayed!" exclaimed Mary, grasping the arm of her young friend. "I am sure we are. Fred. Morton has seen it all—knows it all. We have nothing to hope."

"Why do you think so, Mary? Did you see him observing us?"

"Oh, no! I was busy talking to the guard. But I read it in the expression of his face as he passed me. His look was full of significance and malignity."

"You are excited, Mary," replied Evangeline, endeavoring to

appear calm. "I am confident young Morton could not have seen any one but me. Harry had left the window before he came up. You were on the opposite side of the street, and what could he suspect from seeing me standing gazing up at the prison?"

"Are you sure, Evangeline, that Morton did not see you? Might he not have been where he observed all your movements?"

"I am confident, Mary, that he did not. I heard him approaching me from Walnut-street, and I feel assured he saw only me. Don't be alarmed. You and Harry are safe. If he desires to make mischief, I only am involved, and I bid him defiance. I am not one whit afraid of all the Lincolnites in creation."

"You are protected, Evangeline, by your Union friends. I am so unprotected. You cannot realize what it is to know you are alone without a friend to defend you. Pa is gone; John is gone, and I am alone, isolated; I have no one to look to, to shield me from the violence of a foe: no one, no one," and Mary sighed as if her heart were breaking. "Oh that pa would come,—no, he cannot, dare not do this, but that he would send some one to take me from this horrid place."

"Be patient, Mary; when Harry gets out we will all go beyond Yankee lines and Yankee rule, and be free and happy. I am almost wild with delight at the thought that he will so soon be free. Do you think there is any possibility, Mary, that he will be discovered?"

"He is to bribe the guard, is he not?"

"Yes, that is the plan, and the matter is already arranged between them."

"He *may be betrayed*. There is a *possibility* of this. A man who will suffer himself to be bribed, will betray if he can find it his interest to do so. But let us hope this may not be."

"Oh I do not fear, Mary. Harry is very shrewd and would not allow himself to be imposed upon. But I must secure a hack to take him out of the city."

"Better leave his escape from Louisville to his own management. He has learned to avoid detection, and he will be much safer on foot than in a carriage."

The girls returned to Mrs. Purdy's to await the appointed hour. To their great delight they found that Lasley was not in, nor had he called.

"And did you reach the city, Cousin William?"

"No, it was impossible. They would not allow me to pass their lines."

"Who would not?"

"The Confederate pickets at Shelbyville. I told them the case, and plead with them to let me go, but it was all in vain. Their orders were to permit no one to go out of their lines, and they could not disobey, they said."

"Oh my poor, poor child!" said Mr. Lawrence, as he bowed his head and heaved a deep sigh. "What will become of her? I know that she is almost frantic with grief. Oh, that I could but get her here!" He buried his face in his hands and sat for some minutes engaged in thought. Looking up at the young man before him, he said: "Do you think you could get through by way of Bardstown, Cousin William?"

"I do not know. The effort might be made. It might prove successful."

"Will you try?"

"Most certainly, if you desire it."

"Oh, I should be most thankful if you would make the attempt. It may succeed. I will remunerate you to any extent. I would willingly sacrifice all I have to get my child. It was folly in me to leave her, but I felt so sure I should get back to Louisville and bring her out myself."

"And this you may yet do. The Confederates may take the city."

"I think not. There seems but little promise of it to me. Indeed I am very doubtful about their remaining long in the State. But Bragg's force and success must determine that. This army of General Smith's will soon have to leave this point unless reinforced. But when can you set out again for Louisville by way of Bardstown?"

"Just as soon as I can procure a pass, sir."

"This is Thursday. If you do not succeed you will be back by Sunday, I suppose?"

"Oh yes, sir, that will be ample time to go and return."

"If possible, Cousin William, bring my daughter. God grant you may succeed." The father spoke earnestly. His grief-marked face wore an expression of unusual sadness.

"I will accomplish the object of my mission, if possible, sir."

"Take this letter to Mary, it will tell her what to do; and here is a purse, hand it to her, she may need it."

The young man bade his friend farewell, and leaving the hotel, proceeded to the stable, where, procuring a horse and buggy, he set out once more to endeavor to reach Louisville.

Two days passed—days of anxious suspense to Mr. Lawrence, who, in the uncertainty of his daughter's fate, was the prey of direful apprehension and alarm.

Sunday evening came. It was the 21st of September. General Bragg having defeated the enemy intrenched at Mumfordsville, capturing four thousand prisoners, and heavy stores, was advancing towards Louisville. The news of his successful march had reached Lexington, and every Southern heart was beating high with gratitude and hope. It looked as if Kentucky was, at last, to be redeemed from the hand of Northern rule, and placed where she should be, under the **government of the Confederate States.** General Kirby Smith's army had received many accessions, and throughout that portion of the **State regiments were being organized for** the Southern army. **Every city, town, village and hamlet in the** State was the scene of the **wildest excitement. The two parties,** Southern and Northern, which everywhere existed in **antagonism,** served by conflicting opinions and desires to **keep the flame of** agitation brightly burning. It was a time of comparative liberty for Southern men, a season for fear and trembling with the Northern party. Every thing was forgotten in the one theme, that of the advance of the Confederate army.

Mr. Lawrence was **seated** in his room at the hotel, gloomy and sad, under the weight of his own personal sorrows, which **neither** his faith in God's providences **nor the consolation of divine truth,** so clearly set forth by the minister of God in his morning discourse, could remove. He **was desolate amid the** throng—grief-laden, though surrounded by the rushing whirl of stormy events. His only son, exposed to the calamities and hardships of war, his only daughter separated from **him** within the enemy's power, unprotected and alone. His thoughts were away with her, and he was endeavoring to paint to himself what she was doing this beautiful Sabbath evening. And then he pictured to himself the happiness of the meeting with her, **which he** hoped would not be long deferred.

The sunlight came in through **the uncurtained window, and fell** in rich golden glory over the floor. **Its radiant light reminded him** of the beauty of that heavenly home, where **dwelt** amid the hosts of the redeemed the spirit of his lost **wife, and** his soul lifted its aspirations to that celestial city which needeth not the light of a **candle, nor** yet of **the sun, for the** Lord God giveth it light, and His redeemed ones, clothed in shining garments, worship before the great White Throne, whereon sits the Eternal Father. It was an hour of soul-communion with **the** stricken father. To him the joy of the world had become dimmed—life had lost its charms—the earth its false glare and baneful influence.

The old man took up his Bible and read, and as he read the tears streamed down his face. Yet, while he wept, his soul rejoiced, for by faith he laid hold on the promises of the Gospel, and his spiritual strength was renewed even amid the heart's deep sorrowing. After reading for some time he closed the book, then knelt to pray. Long and fervently did he supplicate God's mercy and guidance, and earnestly ask for submission to His will. Rising, he approached the window, and seating himself, looked out into the busy street below.

While he thus sat, a gentle knock was heard at the door. He rose and opened it.

"Unsuccessful again, Cousin William?" said Mr. Lawrence, calmly, but in a low, deep tone, that told far better than language could have done how bitter was his disappointment.

The young man bowed assent, and moving forward to the seat designated for him, explained the cause of his failure.

"I must bear it, though it is very hard," said Mr. Lawrence, resuming his seat near the window. "If I knew my child was safe, I would ask nothing more. But I have heard nothing from her since I left, and I know not what may have befallen her."

"Oh, I doubt not she is safe, sir. No one is allowed to leave Louisville now for this portion of the State, and letters do not come except by private hand. You could not reasonably hope to hear from her under present circumstances, I think. I sent your letter by a citizen of Louisville, whom I met on my way, and who will go in to-morrow or the next day."

"And they are fortifying the city and have placed it under martial law?"

"That is the statement of all who seem to be at all acquainted with the present position of affairs there."

"And where is General Bragg now?"

"Marching on from Mumfordsville in the direction of Louisville. It is the opinion of many Union men that he will certainly take that city in a few days, notwithstanding their fortifications and reinforcements."

"I should be most happy to see it, but I am by no means sanguine. And yet if he allows them a foothold they will in their turn drive him South again."

"The only danger I see, sir, is that of Buell's getting to Louisville first Both armies are striving with their utmost **power to** beat the other in this closely contested race."

"And where is Buell now?"

"In close pursuit of Bragg, it is said. Only a day behind him."

"And will General Bragg allow himself to be hemmed in by the two forces—the one at Louisville in his front, and Buell in **his rear?** If he does, he will show himself utterly devoid of generalship, I think."

"It is said, sir, that the troops at Louisville will offer no resistance, but fall back across the Ohio river at Bragg's approach."

"**But even** then **he would be, as it were,** flanked, unless Buell should cross the **river into Indiana. And then the gunboats,** together with **heavy ordnance placed on the opposite shore, will** make his position in Louisville **doubtful. I can see but little hope**—very little hope."

"A few days, sir, will determine the issue. Active preparations are being made by the Federals. They are concentrating **large** numbers of the newly enlisted men at Jeffersonville and New Albany, **and** are about to construct pontoon bridges across the river at **Louisville,** I suppose either for advance or retreat, whichever may be their fortune."

"Are the Southern people enthusiastic in the portions of the **State where you have been?**"

"**Very, indeed. They feel** the permanent occupation **of Kentucky** by the Confederates to be a fixed fact. It may be **I have** caught their enthusiasm. I certainly am inclined to hope."

"But should the Confederates **have to** abandon the State, what a sad, sad thing it will be for thousands of Southern men, who will have to leave their homes, their wives and children, and exile **themselves, or** else **remain** to be imprisoned! Oh, if I but had my child with me, I should feel able to defy every fortune! But **the** thought of having to leave her behind **almost breaks my heart. I** may never again see her, and she may fall into the hands **of the** unsparing foe."

"She spoke **of coming out. But how can** she come alone and unprotected? **I would go** for her, but should I be discovered, I **would be immediately sent to** prison, and then she would be left without any hope. Sad, sad fate for any one so young and inexperienced!" he said, while his whole frame heaved with the pressure of his mental distress.

The young man felt it was unnecessary to attempt consolation. He looked upon his relative with deep sympathy. After some minutes' silence on the part of both, Mr. Stanford proposed a walk to the encampment.

While this conversation was taking place between Mr. Lawrence and his young cousin, Mary and Evangeline were standing before the prison, carrying out the bold endeavor of Harry's liberation.

The church-bells rang. Mary and Evangeline put on their bonnets and shaws.

"Who will go with you, girls?" asked Mrs. Purdy, as the two entered the parlor, ready to leave. "I wish I were well enough to accompany you, but really my head aches too severely. It would be doing myself injustice to go out to-night. There is Lewellen, he can escort you. You will feel no fear with him. Come, my son, get on your cap and go with the young ladies to church."

"Oh, no, no, Mrs. Purdy, don't make Lewellen go out, he looks so weary. Uncle will send the carriage for us. If it is not at the door, it will be there in a few minutes. See, girl, if it has not already come."

"Yes, ma'am, Mr. Terrant's carriage has been here for some time."

"We are not at all afraid to go in the carriage alone, Mrs. Purdy. Henry is a very safe driver, and the horses are so gentle."

"Come back with Mary, Evangeline, and pass the night with us."

"I shall either do this or take Mary with me. You know aunty is from home now, and I do not remain at home at night without some company."

The two young ladies bade Mrs. Purdy good-evening, and, getting into the carriage, bade the driver take them to Dr. Hoyt's church.

"Shall we go in, Mary, or remain in the carriage until nine?" asked Evangeline. "I do not know what is best. If we can secure a back seat, so as to leave unnoticed, I should prefer it to staying without. Would not you?"

"Greatly; but then we must avoid observation. Mr. Plumber has a pew in the back of the church. None of the family are in town. Shall we sit in that?"

"Yes, yes, anywhere to be secure from notice."

Bidding the driver to remain at the corner of the street until the services were over, the two girls alighted and entered the church. They found themselves early. As yet but few persons were seated, and the gas was burning at half light. Quietly they made their way to Mr. Plumber's pew, where, seating themselves, they drew down their veils, so as almost wholly **to shut out the** view of their faces. Family by family the congregation came in, until the building was pretty nearly filled. The gas was turned on **to** a full jet, the organ pealed forth a salutatory as the minister appeared in the pulpit, and services commenced.

During the singing, the prayer, and the rather lengthy sermon that succeeded them, Evangeline and Mary remained seated like statues draped from view. They dared not turn their faces right nor left, lest they should be recognized by some friend. As the minister concluded **his** sermon, Evangeline quietly drew forth her watch. **It wanted five minutes to nine.** "We will **go,**" she said to Mary.

As the minister, **uplifting his hands, said, "Let us pray," they** arose and noiselessly left the house.

"Oh, Mary, Mary, if Harry should not come!" said Evangeline, as she nervously handed her friend into the carriage.

"Stay just where you **are,** Henry, until I tell you to leave, church is not out yet." She remained standing on the pavement holding open the door of the carriage, **her eyes fixed on** the dark, grim form of the prison that rose up before her view. "Strange **contrast,**" she said, "this close proximity **of the house of God, where men** assemble to worship Him **according to the dictates of** their own conscience, and the prison-house, where men **made in** His own image and born freemen are shut out from society, abused, insulted, merely because they have dared to exercise their reason and express **their** convictions—dared to enjoy this right that God himself has bestowed on them, and which all liberal governments **guarantee to** their meanest subjects. What a sad comment upon mankind, upon the passions to the behests of which he yields up conscience and judgment, and which, like the brute creation, **he** follows as his guide!"

"Mary, Mary!" **she said excitedly, thrusting her head into the** carriage, "some one **approaches. I can't see him distinctly, but it** looks like Harry."

"Where, where, Evangeline?" replied Mary, springing out and taking position beside the **trembling** girl.

"**Yonder.** Don't you see somebody in the dim gas-light coming this **way? He turned** from Green-street. Look, he is crossing. It **must be** Harry. Oh, Mary!" and Evangeline started hastily forward to meet the approaching figure, and as it neared the pavement she ejaculated, "Harry, Harry!"

The man suddenly stopped, raised his head, and looked inquiringly round. Evangeline advanced to the rear of the carriage, and said more softly than at first:

"Harry, Harry! is that you?"

Again the figure paused, and peered more earnestly in the direction from whence the sound proceeded. Discovering in the dim light only a female figure near the carriage in front of him, he lowered his head, and passed quickly on.

Evangeline sprang to the door-step, and rushed into the carriage, exclaiming, "It was not Harry, Mary. Who could it have been? I hope he did not know me."

Her voice was harsh, her manner bewildered and agitated. She trembled in every limb, her heart beat audibly. The clock of the cathedral sounded out the hour of nine.

"Be still, Evangeline; be composed. You have nothing to fear. The man evidently did not recognize you, or he would have made himself known. I do not suppose he heard your words—only your voice arrested his attention. Be calm, we have nothing to fear."

"But if Harry should not come? It is nine—the hour—and he is not here. I shall die, Mary, if I am disappointed. It is my only hope in life. For days I have lived on the expectation of this moment. And now, if he should not come—"

Just then the organ pealed forth its deep, bass notes. Evangeline threw her arms around her friend, and hid her face on her bosom. "Not come—not come! Oh, how can I bear it?" and she burst into tears.

"You must be calm, Evangeline. You will betray us, if you weep that way. It is not too late. Harry's plans may have been delayed. I shall look yet half an hour for him."

"Oh, will you—do you, Mary?" she sobbed, starting up and gazing into the sweet face bending over her, as if a ray of hope, altogether unlooked for, had that instant found lodgment in her bosom. "Do you really think, Mary, that this is true? Harry is always so punctual!"

"But, Evangeline, Harry is now dependent on circumstances which he cannot master to suit his will and desires. It may be he is watched, or some of the officers of the prison perhaps are in; or the sentinel with whom he has made the arrangement may not have yet entered on his duty."

"True, true, Mary; I see that a hundred things may prevent his being here at the moment. But church will soon be out.

What shall we do then? Will it not be suspicious for us to remain here in this place without any apparent reason?"

"Suppose we drive round the square while the people are leaving the church, and then return to this point?"

"If Harry should come while we are away, Mary! No, no, I cannot leave. But this we can do," she added, after thinking a moment; "I will remain and keep watch for Harry, while Henry drives you round. I will shield myself in that deep shade yonder, and no one will see me; if they do, I will tell them I am awaiting my carriage. If he should come, and I do not see him, he will doubtless remain until after every one is gone, for he will feel sure I am here."

"Tell the driver, Evangeline, to drive slowly around the square, returning just to this point, but not to set off until the congregation is dismissed."

Evangeline gave the order slowly and emphatically to the boy on the box.

"Do you understand me, Henry?"

"Yes, ma'am," was the reply of the drowsy coachman.

A footfall on the pavement. The two girls simultaneously thrust their heads from the carriage window. Breathlessly they awaited the advancing steps. Nearer and nearer they came, until they were distinctly audible just behind the carriage.

The girls grasped each other in silence. Neither spoke, as they caught the dim outline of a man, evidently making his way towards the carriage. He paused near the open door. Evangeline leaned out until their faces almost met. Her eyes searched his features by the pale light. It was not Harry, only some one who had come to escort a wife or sister from church. As she fell back in the carriage, she pressed Mary's hand convulsively, heaved a heavy sigh, but no word escaped her lips.

The audience commenced to leave the church. Evangeline repeated her command to the driver, alighted, quietly closed the door, and sought the deep shade of the building. The carriage drove slowly off. Almost fearing to breathe, lest she might arrest the attention of some one, Evangeline remained motionless, ensconced in her dark hiding-place. Group after group moved off, and she was left alone. She shuddered as she thought of her situation. Dark fears shot through her mind, but she dismissed them in a moment as ill-omened guests. The sexton extinguished the lights, swung to the ponderous front doors, locked them, and descending the steps, walked away humming a low air.

They appeared hours, those few minutes of racking uncertainty. The lone, trembling girl, hid away in the deep shadow of that silent church, experienced the varied emotions of a lifetime, while her throbbing heart pulsated but fleeting moments. Wonder we at that marked stamp of maturity that characterizes the manner and countenance of some young beings who cross our life-path as we journey onward? Ah, the heart doth often write down in its own ineffaceable record the sufferings and experience of many years, while the hand but moves in time's great dial-plate.

What dread, what apprehension, what doubt, what sinking sorrow, swayed the bosom of Evangeline, as she felt the peril of her position? Not for herself cared she. It was for him whom her soul loved with all the intensity of its passionate, clinging ardor. How unselfish is pure, young love! How ready to immolate itself on the altar of its idol's happiness! Building its own pyre, it looks gladly up, and rejoices while it reads in the preparation for its fearful doom the immortality of its own beloved Psyche. To the tear-dimmed eye this earth is waste and barren, and time and selfish interest eat out the good from man's heart as it obdurates under their ossifying touch. But in the fresh, glad spring-time of youth, flowers bud and bloom, and send abroad sweet fragrance, and the whisperings of angels speak to life, in the soul of unsullied innocence, rapturous emotions akin to those that swell the bosoms of celestial beings.

The noise of the carriage-wheels moving slowly over the boldered street caught Evangeline's eager ear. Uncertain whether it was Mary, she remained under cover of the darkness. She listened attentively. It came tardily on to the corner, turned, and Henry's voice called out, " Whoa, whoa!"

She forsook her covert and stepped to the carriage

"Not yet, Evangeline?"

"Not yet, Mary." After a lapse of time she said, "He will not come, Mary. Harry will not come. My heart tells me so. I felt it as I stood yonder beneath that frowning wall."

She spoke with the determination of desperation, and the voice so cold, so hollow, fell fearfully on Mary's ear.

"Oh, do not despair. It is time yet. Get in the carriage, and we will wait here. There are several minutes yet to half-past nine, and I do not expect him before then."

"Don't you, Mary?" asked Evangeline, sadly, as she seated herself in the carriage, and leaned her head on Mary's shoulder.

"Ah me, I fear he will not come," she added hopelessly. "Perhaps—perhaps—"

The words died out on her lips. She could not trust herself with speaking the fears that haunted her soul.

Twice again during the ten minutes of eager expectation that followed, Evangeline's ear was mocked by the sound of some one coming towards the carriage. Each time she started up, waited until the individual passed by, then fell back with a groan into her original position. Mary's arm stole gently around the languid form. She felt how deeply Evangeline needed words of comfort. But how could she, convinced as she now was, that there was no longer hope left, continue to offer words of cheer or consolation?

Minute succeeded minute. Oh, how wearily they dragged themselves across the tortured heart of the expectant girl! The old cathedral clock rung out the hour of ten.

Evangeline fell on her friend's bosom and gasped out—"Too late! too late! he will not come; we must go." Henry was ordered to drive back to Mrs. Purdy's. More dead than living, Evangeline lay, every sense benumbed by the weight of disappointment. She did not attempt to speak. She did not move; her low still breathing was scarcely perceptible. Mary took her icy hands in hers and chafed them gently, and smoothed back from the rigid brow the sheet of raven hair.

"If Mr. Terrant is awaiting Miss Evangeline, tell him she is with me," said Mary to the driver, as she assisted the almost lifeless form of Evangeline to ascend the front steps. Supporting her as well as she could, Mary rang the bell; the servant answered tardily. "Assist me up stairs with Miss Evangeline," she said to the girl in a low tone. "Do not make any noise."

"Is Miss 'Vangie sick, Miss Mary?" asked the girl, rubbing her sleepy eyes.

"She is not well, Kate. Has Mrs. Purdy retired?"

"Oh yes, ma'am, been in bed long time. Missis got such a headache."

Noiselessly Evangeline was conducted along the hall and up the stairway to Mary's room. Reaching it, she threw herself on the bed, but spoke not.

"Some fresh water, Kate; ice-water."

While the girl prepared the cooler for water, Mary raised the form of Evangeline and took off her hat. She then loosed her clothes and removed her shoes, and rubbed her face and hands.

"Here, Evangeline, take this water, it will refresh you;" and she poured a glass of ice-water from the pitcher the girl had brought, and turning into it a tea-spoonful of sal. volatile, she placed it to Evangeline's lips. She drank, and looking up into Mary's face, whispered, "He did not come, Mary, he did not come."

"You can go down now, Kate, Miss Evangeline is better."

"If you need me to-night, Miss Mary, ring the bell, and I'll come;" and the girl placed the water on the washstand and left the room.

As the door closed behind the servant, Evangeline sprang up, and throwing her arms about Mary, who sat on the bed beside her, burst into tears. She wept persistently for some time. Her surcharged heart found relief from its crushing burden, and after a lapse of time, she said, looking sadly, beseechingly at her friend:

"Oh! tell me, tell me, Mary, why did not Harry come?"

"I cannot tell, Evangeline. He could not get out. Perhaps the guard deceived him."

"You did not hear any shooting, Mary, did you?"

"Oh no, Evangeline; Harry is safe, no doubt."

"But in that horrid prison," she responded, shaking her head slowly, and gazing out into the room despairingly. "He said he would come. It was all arranged, I know it was; he understood all the signs, and answered them all. I wonder why he disappointed me?"

"He could not carry out his plans, Mary; he has been deceived in some way."

"And if he was discovered they'll put him in irons, Mary, and send him to Camp Chase. Oh! I shall never again see him! never, never!" and again she wept bitterly.

Mary endeavored to soothe her, to bid her hope. But how can the heart hope when it is breaking?

A thousand reasons presented themselves to the tortured mind of Evangeline, but nothing was satisfactory. Around each suggestion gathered doubt, uncertainty, fear. Over all hovered the incubus of disappointed expectation.

Throughout the night Mary watched beside her. Sometimes she slept fitfully, at others wept, and then again, with seeming composure, she would converse over her bitter trial.

"Could Lasley have thwarted me, Mary?" she asked, as the two lay, at the midnight hour, vainly endeavoring to unravel the mystery.

"No, no, Evangeline; it cannot be. What influence has Ed.

Lasley! And even did he possess the power of the highest official here, could he have known of your **plan?**"

"I cannot tell, Mary. But there comes over me a vague feeling, at times amounting to **conviction,** that he is the author of all this."

"You do him injustice, Evangie. I am assured he has not penetration enough to discover your secret, or ability to overturn your arrangements. No, no; it is not **Ed. Lasley** that has done this. The guard has either deceived or betrayed Harry. Wait, Evangeline, a few hours **may disclose it all.**"

"I *must wait*, Mary. Stern necessity demands it of my breaking heart. But, oh! how dreadful to bear this wasting anxiety! If Harry is killed or sent away, then life to me is worthless—I ask not to live."

CHAPTER LIII.

MONDAY, SEPTEMBER 22, 1862.

Bright, beautifully bright, as if the angel of light and glory had spread her pinions over the earth, opened the morning of this day so memorable in the annals of Louisville. And with the uprising of its multitudes of men, came what hopes, what doubts, what fears!

During the previous week ditches had been dug and guns mounted, so as to circumvallate the city from the river on the east to the river on the west. Thousands of men, impressed into service, had toiled, beside the soldiery, to prepare "defences against the rebels under Bragg." The fears of the near-sighted and unwary had been stilled by this semblance of strength, and many there were who regarded their little treasures as safe from the "vandal foot" of Southrons, as if some genii, in answer to Aladdin's lamp, had transported them to Central Africa. But others—the wise and prudent—knew and felt how little resistance these pits, dug in the very outskirts of the place, would offer to veteran troops determined to secure a foothold in this "Union stronghold." They were not to be misled by this mere show of safety, and fearfully did they open their eyes to the certainty that General Bragg could take Louisville if he desired to do so. With such, all was fearful apprehension. At an early hour the streets were thronged with the unquiet multitude, eager for the morning news.

"Bragg had left Mumfordsville, where he had defeated the Federals, captured over 4,000 prisoners with all their accoutrements, and was marching in heavy force towards the city." This was the news that ran from lip to lip—arousing the hopes of Southern hearts who were panting for deliverance, and filling with gloom and anxiety the bosoms of Lincoln's supporters. Men were at work on the intrenchments; regiments were paraded through the thoroughfares to impress the public with a feeling of security. Forces were constantly being crossed over from Jeffersonville to take position among the defenders of the city. Officers dashed through the streets on horseback, all eager in the accomplishment of suitable preparations to meet the enemy. Cannon rattled along, followed by the shouts and yells of boys and darkies. **Union flags** waved from Union windows. Cavalry, with rushing tramp and clanking swords, swept from **point to** point. Everywhere the **work went** on; everywhere were signs of confusion and fearful **looking** for danger. Men's hearts failed them as they thought of the coming conflict.

Suddenly the news ran through the streets, "General Nelson **has issued an** order for all the women, children, and non-combat**ants to leave the** city." It sped from tongue to tongue, until it **reached** the length and breadth of the town. Had there been written on the clear azure above, in characters of living light, the fearful doom **of all** mankind, darker and more dire panic could not have **seized the hearts of men and women.** What had been painfully contingent before was now a most appalling reality. Bragg was at the very gates of the city, and Nelson declared, rather than it should fall into the hands of the rebels, he would fight hand to **hand** through the streets; and then, if he were compelled to evacuate and cross to the northern bank of the river, he would plant his guns on the Indiana shore and shell it until every house was demolished before the enemy should hold it. Nelson was known **to be a** reckless, desperate man, always ready for any rash, unnatural act, and each individual considered not only his property, but his life, in jeopardy. In less than a half-hour from the first faint rumor of the baneful order, every house seemed to have emptied its inmates into the already thronged streets; men, pale and trembling, eagerly asking of every responsible friend they met if the rumor was really true. Women weeping and wringing their hands in agony; children affrighted, and aroused by that sense of dread and anxiety which the young always feel under excitement, dashed wildly to and fro. Everybody appeared frenzied, devoid of both reason and method.

The order had been **issued. Bragg** was within a few miles of the city, and the battle would begin **in a few** hours. Then came the fearful rush of thousands, eager to escape the dreadful doom of conflict. Every vehicle, from the most superb hack down to the rickety old dray, was impressed into the service of transporting families to a place of refuge. Clothes were hastily thrown into trunks, which trunks were thrown into drays, furniture wagons, omnibuses, carriages, hacks, or whatever vehicle could be obtained, and driven at pell-mell speed to the wharf. Houses, with every thing in them turned upside down, were hastily cleared and consigned by their fleeing owners to the fate of war. Babes were snatched from the cradle, and, wrapped up in any thing that could afford protection from the chill air of autumn, were pressed to the throbbing bosom of the distracted mother, and borne to one of the boats that stood waiting to convey them to the opposite shore. The river-bank was thronged with fearful crowds, all anxious to secure a speedy transit to the opposite side of the Ohio.

As each hour passed, rumors became more and more numerous, more and more terrible. "Bragg had whipped Buell's forces and cut them to pieces, and was now halting outside the city, demanding its surrender. Dozens of persons had seen his truce-flag borne along the streets; others, who had ascended the roof of the Custom-house, had seen, with the aid of glasses, his whole army only a few miles out, awaiting the return of the flag of truce.

As Nelson had sworn he would never surrender, it was believed the city would be immediately attacked, and the expectant ears of the panic-stricken fugitives, as they sped the streets, or lined the wharf, or pursued the various roads that communicated with the country, eagerly listened for the first booming of the death-dealing cannon.

Evening came, but brought no attack. Yet the excitement was not one whit abated. Still the stream continued to outpour. Everywhere new reports sprang into life, and were caught up by eager listeners and repeated as truths, until to walk one square and hear the varied recitals that met you, was to grow bewildered and doubt the truth of all.

At one corner you would hear that Bragg had completely annihilated Buell's army. At the next corner, you would learn from a source equally as veracious, that Buell had encountered Bragg and routed his army, scattering it in every direction. One would assert as a fact wholly unquestionable, that General Bragg would certainly reach the city that night; another would declare that he knew beyond contradiction that Bragg had but twenty-five thousand men, and that he would not dare to venture upon the place. Shops and storehouses of all descriptions were closed, their alarmed owners having fled, leaving behind them every thing that would embarrass their precipitate exodus.

Evening came—yet the frightful rush continued, and when the chill September night fell down over the earth, thousands of the citizens of Louisville, without any comforts, many destitute of even a shelter from the night air, were congregated in Jeffersonville, New Albany, and other points on the Indiana shore.

Many of the more wealthy had gone to Cincinnati and Indianapopolis; while others, unwilling to attempt to seek safety on free soil, had moved out by every possible means into the nearest towns and the contiguous counties. The prisoners had all been forwarded to Camp Chase, and many of the military officials had made full arrangements to depart at the first appearance of necessity.

Meanwhile, General Bragg was quietly pursuing his way to Bardstown, having diverged from the direct route to Louisville at Hodgenville, some thirty miles from the city. Reaching Bardstown in the forenoon of that memorable day, he halted his weary troops for rest, and immediately sent out detachments of cavalry on all the routes leading towards the city; which movement being made known, gave rise to the belief that it was his intention to approach by the various roads that led from the vicinity of Bardstown to Louisville; and all who ventured out in that direction expected to meet the heavy columns of triumphant Confederates marching on to the certain capture of the town. It was also believed by many that General Kirby Smith's forces were advancing from Lexington by way of Shelbyville, to form a junction with Bragg, and thus simultaneously attack the town from two different points.

"What is the news, Mrs. Purdy?" asked Mary and Evangeline in the same breath, as that lady entered the room heated, flushed, and trembling with affright. "Oh, tell me, Mrs. Purdy, tell me!" gasped Evangeline, as she started up in the bed from which she had not yet risen.

It was ten o'clock in the morning, and Mrs. Purdy had just returned from market. Without waiting below to lay aside her bonnet and shawl, she hastened up stairs, sought Mary's room, and disregarding the ceremony of rapping at the door, entered with an expression of terror on her countenance.

Evangeline sat in bed, her hands clasped, and staring up into Mrs. Purdy's face, as if she would read therefrom the dread secret of her alarm. Mary rose and conducted her to the sofa. In interrupted sentences the terrified woman informed the girls of the fearful order and the imminent peril of the city.

Not a word of reply was spoken. The three sat in silence, horror-stricken. After a lapse of some moments, Evangeline exclaimed, "Can this be true, Mrs. Purdy, or is it only a rumor?"

"True, Evangeline—true, child. I saw Mr. Middleton, who had just returned from the office of the *Journal*, and he told me that Shipman told him the order had been issued by General Nelson, and would appear on the bulletin-boards as soon as it could be printed."

"And what shall we do—what shall we do?" asked Evangeline, imploringly, springing from the bed to the side of the yet trembling woman.

"Leave, leave—we must leave!" was the emphatic reply.

"And where must we go, Mrs. Purdy?" asked Mary, quickly, as the hope sprung up in her heart of getting to her father.

"Anywhere, anywhere, where we will be safe. Hundreds are already on their way to Cincinnati and Indiana."

"And would you go across the river, Mrs. Purdy? Would you seek safety in the midst of our enemies?"

"I cannot stop now, Mary, to debate differences. To secure the preservation of my own life and the life of my child is now my first business."

"And is the city certainly to be shelled, Mrs. Purdy?"

"General Nelson says so."

"And what will be done with the prisoners? Are they to be kept shut up to take their chances for life or death?"

"I do not know, Evangeline. I heard no mention of them. Perhaps the morning paper says something about it. Here, I have one in my pocket. Didn't have time to look at it. Maybe you will find there what is to be done with them," she said, as she handed the sheet to Evangeline, who took it, and hastily ran her eye up and down the columns.

"I must go and pack my trunk, and be ready to be off as soon as possible. Mary, will you go with me?"

"Where are you going, Mrs. Purdy?"

"To my cousins, at Hanover, Indiana. It is the only place where I can go."

"No, Mrs. Purdy, I shall never cross the river to seek for safety. I will die on Kentucky soil first."

"But I cannot leave you, Mary."

"Oh, don't give yourself a moment's thought about me. I will take care of myself. I am not afraid of the Confederates, if they should come; and if Nelson should be wild enough to try to shell them out, I will go to the country."

"You are not going to trust yourself here, Mary?" said Mrs. Purdy, in surprise, as she turned from the door to look back upon the heroic girl. "Stay here and be killed! You will have no time to get away when the fight is raging everywhere."

"I cannot go to Indiana, Mrs. Purdy. I will not place myself beyond the reach of my brother and father, and all who are my friends. No, no; I'll remain on my native soil, and take the chances. But do not let me interrupt your arrangements. I will go out to Mr. R.'s, and whatever they think best, I will do."

Mrs. Purdy left the room, wondering that anybody should stand, at a juncture so critical, upon a question of difference of opinion.

As the door closed, Evangeline ejaculated, "To Camp Chase, Mary, to Camp Chase!"

"Who, Evangeline—the prisoners?"

"Yes—to-day, at twelve o'clock. I must see Harry."

"And are you going to remain here, Evangeline?"

"Oh, Mary, Mary, I know not what to do. I am bewildered, my brain reels. My uncle cannot go with me. All the men capable of bearing arms are to be kept for the defence of the city. I cannot go myself. I cannot remain if Harry is taken away. What shall I do—what shall I do?"

"Go with me, Evangeline."

"And where will you go, Mary?"

"Through the Confederate lines to my father and brother."

"But how will you get through, Mary? Who will go with you?"

"I do not know. There will be some way of escape for me."

"But if Harry is to be sent to Camp Chase, I must keep within Federal lines. You know I have no one to rely on, if he cannot escape, but Union friends, who will never go beyond Federal limits. Oh, that Harry had but escaped last night! then would I gladly go with you."

The door-bell rang. Evangeline shuddered.

"Who or what can that be? The least noise affrights me. My heart forebodes evil. What if Harry is dead?"

"Oh, Evangeline, that cannot be. The morning paper would have mentioned any occurrence of the kind, and the streets would be filled with it."

"Not now, Mary. Every one is too much engaged looking to his own welfare to regard the fate of another."

She had scarcely finished the sentence when the door opened, and Mrs. Spalding entered, trembling, as Mrs. Purdy, with alarm, without waiting to bid the girls good-morning, said, "I have called, Mary, to take you home with me. The city is to be shelled in an hour, they say. Get your bonnet on immediately, and go with me. You will then be beyond present danger. And you, too, Evangie, there is room for you. Why, what is the matter, child, are you sick? you look so pale and worn. Don't be alarmed. There is no possibility of your being hurt at pa's, unless the battle should be fought out in that direction, and then we would fall further back—go to Bardstown or Lebanon. Dress yourself quickly. The carriage will be here in a few minutes."

"Do, Evangeline, go with us, I cannot leave you," said Mary, beseechingly, as she hastened from drawer to wardrobe, and from wardrobe to trunk, gathering up a few needed articles of clothing.

Evangeline buried her face in her hands, and remained silent. Then looking up, she said, "No, no, I cannot go. I remain here."

"Stay in the city, Evangeline, and it being shelled! Why this is folly—rashness. You must go with me—must go. There is no choice left. Your aunt is away. Your uncle will not be permitted to leave. You cannot go alone—to remain here is impossible. You must go with me. I cannot leave you here. Come, get on your dress, we have no time to lose, the fight may begin at any hour. Hush! wasn't that the report of cannon?" and Mrs. Spalding sprang to the window, and hastily throwing it up, listened with trembling fear.

A few moments more, and again the report of cannon sounded out on the air.

"It is—it is!" she exclaimed, springing back, her eyes starting from their sockets. "It is cannonading, perhaps the conflict has already begun. Evangeline, Evangeline! do come. Oh, do—in a moment. Don't sit there. See, Mary is almost ready. And Mrs. Purdy has her trunk packed, and has sent out for a carriage to take her to the boat. Dress, dress, or you will be too late."

"I cannot go, Lu. Oh! I cannot," she said, emphatically. "I must stay with my uncle."

"Stay with your uncle, Evangeline! What good can you do? You only endanger your own life. General Nelson says all the women and children must leave the city. It will be shelled, and if necessary, to prevent its falling into our hands, shall be burnt. Come, there is Mr. Spalding. Get up, get up, and dress yourself."

"Oh, Evangie, do go," said Mary, throwing her arms about the neck of the pale, wan girl. "Do go, Evangie. It is of no avail for you to stay here. The matter cannot be altered. We must submit."

Evangeline looked up at her friend. Her eyes were red with

the weeping of the past night, and on her face there rested a sad and anxious expression. But her compressed lips, and the fixed look of those expressive black eyes, told all too plainly of her resolved purpose.

"Do not ask me, Mary. I must remain here. You know my **reasons**. I should be miserable in Confederate lines, where I could hear nothing, and life is not worth preserving now. I cannot go."

"But what will you do, Evangeline?"

"Oh, I cannot tell. There will be some way opened for me."

"**But I cannot leave you so.**"

"Yes, Mary, you must. Do not **delay** a moment for me. Already you may be endangered. Go, go, and leave me. **I will** take care of myself."

"But you will not remain here. Mrs. Purdy **will be off in a** short time, and the house will be closed."

"No, no, I shall go directly home. From there to the prison and the boat," she whispered. "I may perchance see him once more."

Mary threw her arms about her neck and burst into tears. "Oh, Evangie, we may **never meet again.** Good-by," and she kissed her again and again.

Evangeline spoke not. **The tears gushed from her eyes. She** strained Mary to her heart, and imprinted a farewell kiss upon her lips, and the two parted—to meet no more.

Mrs. Spalding bade her good-by. The two left the room, and gaining the carriage, drove rapidly out to the country.

Evangeline dressed herself mechanically, and walked home. She found her uncle gone, and all the servants, save the cook, out **on the street to hear the news.** The clock struck eleven.

"One hour more, and he goes from me forever. Once in that horrid prison, and he will never come out again," she said to herself, mournfully, as she closed the door of her room, and set out alone, to catch, if possible, one more glimpse of the beloved form.

She drew her veil closely over her face, and proceeded in the direction of the prison. Everywhere met her eyes evidences of **the terrible** panic **that had seized the people.** The streets were thronged with vehicles carrying away women, and children, and baggage. The side-walks were crowded with the moving masses, jostling against each other, as each rushed along in pursuit of his own particular phantom.

Quickly, quietly, she threaded her way along the streets, regarding nothing but her own safety from the danger of being thrown down. Her mind was filled with the one dread thought, that of not seeing Harry before he left. As she neared the prison, she saw a great crowd around the gateway. Men were moving about as if some consternation had befallen them, and on lifting her veil to endeavor to ascertain the cause of the commotion, she saw several soldiers pass in and through the dense mass.

"They are taking the prisoners away," she said, and with one bound she pressed forward and forced herself on the corner of the pavement by which they must pass on their way to the river. Almost ready to faint with emotion, she maintained her position as well as she could amid the surging movements of the ever-changing throng. She could not see the door of the prison, nor the great gate guarded by its sentinels. Throwing her thick veil aside, and shielding her face from the peering curiosity of the passer-by as well as she could with her hand, she looked up over the heads of the people to the prison windows. A few forms stood before them. Her heart bounded as she fancied she caught a glimpse of Harry. She looked again—the form was gone. Eagerly she strained her eyes upward, each moment hoping he would reappear.

"What's going on here?" asked one man of another, as the two met on the pavement near where Evangeline was standing beside another female, like herself, closely veiled.

"Going to take the rebel prisoners to Camp Chase. Are afraid Bragg will get them."

"Pshaw! he'll never come here. Buell will cut him all to pieces, and send his starving, naked vandals flying back to Dixie."

"Not so sure of that, Mr. Duncan. Things look mighty doubtful now, I tell you. The order of Nelson means a great deal. Desperate struggle ahead."

"Desperate struggle, Mr. McAllister! Why, you don't think so, do you? Why, the starving, naked, cowardly Southerners won't fight. They haven't got any arms to fight with. Some old flint-lock guns, and now and then a man with a squirrel rifle. What can such a people do? Our men can whip them out in an hour and not half try."

"Don't feel so certain about that," said the old man, looking searchingly into his friend's face to see if he was not quizzing him. "Don't feel certain—not at all certain, sir. I used to believe these tales about these rebels being starved and naked, and having no guns; but I tell you, sir, when they are right here ready to overrun us, and we have got so many men, it looks mighty strange, sir. Makes a man think, I tell you."

"But Prentice tells you not to fear, they are nothing but a handful of men, made desperate because **they have got no bread** and bacon; and he is good authority, sir."

"Confound old Prentice. I used to believe all he said. But I **tell you, sir, he's** lied about these rebels. Needn't tell me any longer they are cowards, when they stand right here threatening this city. All a mistake, sir, all a mistake. They've got plenty of spunk. **I've been down South, and I** know what they are. Prentice needn't tell me they won't fight."

"Oh, but **Buell will whip them out. Don't be alarmed. He** will manage them."

"Not so sure of that either, **sir. He didn't manage them down** in Tennessee. I don't see how he's going to do it now—they've got the start of him. Mighty fearful Bragg will ruin him, and then pounce down on us, and ruin us. Needn't tell me, Mr. Duncan. You're a Southern man, and I don't believe a word you've said. You are only laughing at me. You Southern men are all in fine spirits. Not one of you but what can laugh over this matter, serious as it is."

"I'm only telling you, Mr. McAllister, what Prentice says. "I thought he was the cream of all wisdom and truth. **As to what** I believe, that's a matter of small moment; it can't possibly affect the issue either way."

"Are you going **to leave Louisville, Mr.** Duncan; I mean your family?"

"No, sir; we have decided to remain and take the shelling."

"Yes, that's the way with you rebels; you all believe Bragg's coming. Not one of you is going to budge an inch; this tells the tale. You all think **Bragg will be** here in a few hours. Well, well, it may be so. **Good-by; I** may never see you again, for if the rebels do come, I, for one, will leave; **I shan't** fall into their hands." The two bade each other farewell and parted.

Evangeline had listened attentively to this little by-chat. She would fain catch at any promise of hope, however vague and uncertain. Could the Southerners reach the city before the prisoners were sent away, Harry would be saved. Or could there even spring up an uncontrollable excitement, it would offer some hope of deliverance.

As these thoughts were passing through her mind, her eys were seeking the open window, desirous to catch one view of Harry.

Two men encountered each other on the pavement on her left. Their words, though spoken in an ordinary voice, reached her ear.

"What's all this, going on here?" asked one of the other.

"Going to take the rebel prisoners across the river; afraid Bragg will get them here."

"Ah, yes, yes. One of them attempted to escape last night, I believe, didn't he?" remarked the elder of the two to the other. The speaker was an old man, with white hair, sunken blue eyes, and thin pale face. He leaned on his cane as he walked along, being stooped in the shoulders.

"Did he, indeed? I had not heard of it," was the quick, nervous reply of the younger gentleman.

"Yes—one of Morgan's men; they are perfect dare-devils, you know."

"And did he succeed?" Evangeline's ready ear had caught the words of the speaker. She stepped forward to the front of the pavement, the better to hear the thrilling conversation.

"I heard that—" The old gentleman had proceeded thus far with his reply, when a rough, brawny man knocked up against Evangeline, almost dashing her down. She lost the last words of the answer, for before she could recover herself the gentlemen were bidding each other "good-morning."

Amazed, distracted at the uncertainty in which she found herself, she looked round to see which way the elderly gentleman had proceeded. Her strong impulse was to follow him, but he was lost to her vision amid the throng. Turning to the veiled female who stood near her, who she hoped might have heard the old gentleman's answer, she asked timidly:

"Did you hear whether one of Morgan's men escaped from the prison last night?"

"No!" said the girl, astonishment evident in her tone. "Did one get out?"

"I heard something said about one of them attempting to escape."

"I do hope he succeeded," the female replied, without raising her veil, only turning her face to Evangeline. "I wonder who it was."

"I did not hear his name. Are there more than one of Morgan's men there?"

"Oh, yes; several. I have an acquaintance in prison, young Roberts, who is one of his men."

At the mention of this name, Evangeline started. Did she know the female standing beside her? Did the lady recognize her? No, else she would have assuredly addressed her by name.

"The prisoners go to Cincinnati to-day," said Evangeline, her curiosity excited, and desiring to prolong the conversation, hoping to hear something that would throw light on Harry's dark fate.

"Yes, at twelve o'clock. I have an uncle, from Owen county, among the number, and I am waiting here to see him as he passes. Poor old man! he has been in prison for a month, and his health is so feeble. I went to see him last Thursday, and he looked so pale and thin; he can't live long in Camp Chase. Have you a friend here?" she said, extending a look of anxious inquiry upon Evangeline.

"Yes," said Evangeline, averting her head as she felt the blood rising to her cheeks.

The crowd gave way, and the prisoners, under strong guard, marched from the gateway to the middle of the street and formed in line. Evangeline, from where she stood, could only catch a view of the two who were in front. She scanned their features closely as they stood with bold defiant air bent on the gazing gaping assemblage that lined the sidewalk on either hand.

A few minutes and the last one had fallen into the ranks. Then came the order, "March!" With elastic step and stern unyielding front, the head of the column reached Fifth and turned out towards the river. Scrutinizingly Evangeline searched each face. Pair by pair went on, but Harry was not of them. "He must have escaped," said Evangeline to herself, beginning to feel the risings of hope in her bosom. "Strange I should not have heard it; but perhaps he had no time—had to flee to the country."

She was solacing her heart with this thought, when she heard a voice say "Good-by, good-by." Instantly she pressed nearer to the passing column. It was the old uncle addressing his niece, who had thrown up her veil so as to be recognized, and who by a signal had attracted the attention of the old man.

Scarcely had the young girl recovered from the shock this sudden surprise had given her, when she heard her own name pronounced in tones all too familiar. Harry had seen her, knew her, and had pronounced her name as he passed rapidly by.

"Harry!" was the only response of the excited girl, as she saw the young man in advance of where she stood.

"Come, go with me to the boat," she said to the female beside her, "we shall see our friends there—it will be the last time;" and she seized the arm of the woman convulsively, who, without time to reflect, yielded without remonstrance, and the two set out with the running mass to follow the prisoners.

"Nobody will notice us," said Evangeline, feeling that perhaps the woman might have some reluctance to accompanying her in this strange and summary manner. "The whole city is in an uproar to-day; they will think we are endeavoring to flee."

The female allowed herself to be led along. "Come quickly, we must pass them and reach the boat first. See! it wants only fifteen minutes of the time. We will not get to see."

Pressing on through the moving tide of human beings that crowded every street, Evangeline and her friend succeeded in gaining the wharf in advance of the prisoners. Selecting a position by which the men must pass as they filed on board the boat, which already awaited them, they paused until the column, the front of which was already in view, should reach them. A moment, and the advance had passed. Riveted to the spot, Evangeline gazed on each passing form, until her eyes rested on Harry. Just as he reached her, the column was ordered to halt.

"Harry," she said, as she rushed to his side, "why didn't you come?"

"The guard, Evangeline—the guard deceived me."

"And can't you get away, dear Harry?" she whispered low, as she saw the soldiers nearing the spot where she was.

"Impossible—impossible! I will try at Cincinnati. If I don't succeed there, I will surely get away from Camp Chase."

"Oh, Harry—"

"Don't be distressed, Evangeline," broke in the prisoner, as he saw the look of hopeless despair that gathered on the sad face of Evangeline. "A few weeks more, perhaps a few days, and I shall be in Kentucky again. Tell my father, Evangeline, what I say, but breathe it to none other."

The young girl regarded her lover with amazement,—so calm, so cheerful, so hopeful, while she saw nothing but distress and suffering: she could not realize that the scene before her was reality.

"Bragg will be here in a day or two, Evangeline, then you will have freedom, and we shall meet again. Rest assured I shall get out, and the Confederates will hold the State."

"God grant it, Harry! but, oh, my heart fears. Harry, you don't know what I have suffered since you have been in that prison."

"I know, Evangeline. It is hard to bear, but these are times of trial, and we must not shrink from suffering. God shield you from all harm. Be brave, never yield, Evangeline. We will meet again."

The order was given to advance. Harry grasped the hand of the young girl, looked upon her with an expression so full of love, that, as sad as it was to Evangeline's heart, it thrilled it with glad emotion. And with a "God bless you, my dear girl, I'll write you soon," he followed on. Once he turned to look back, Evangeline's eyes were fixed upon him, and there she remained gazing, gazing, until he mounted the steps to the boat, where, apart from the rest, he stood to bid her a last adieu. She returned his salutation; then tearing herself away, she leaned on the arm of her yet unknown friend, and ascended the slope that led from the river to Main-street, from whence she found her way with slow and pensive step to her now desolate home. In her own room, apart from all society, she remained engaged with her own plans and thoughts throughout the remainder of that eventful day.

CHAPTER LIV.

LEXINGTON—LOUISVILLE.

When, on the morning of the 4th of September, the Confederate army, under General Kirby Smith, consisting of the divisions of Generals Claiborne and Heath, and two brigades, one from Texas, the other from Arkansas, commanded by General Churchill, marched into Lexington and through its streets, it was everywhere received with the loudest attestations of sympathy and welcome. The streets were thronged with thousands of men, women, and children, waving red and blue ribbons, small flags, handkerchiefs, and who with smiles and tears hailed with joyous acclaim the presence of the men who had come to deliver them from the presence of the insolent oppressor. Windows and galleries—indeed, all available points—were filled with delighted spectators, who appeared to rival each other in their manifestations of gratitude and happiness.

It was a glad scene—one well calculated to cheer the hearts of these toil-worn soldiers. Everywhere substantial evidences, in the way of baskets of provisions, and buckets of cool refreshing water, met the hungry, thirsty men, hundreds of whom were, in addition to this, presented with shoes, blankets, hats, overcoats, and tobacco. Their passage through the town was a grand ovation. Never did Roman emperor, on returning from the scene of victorious conflict, laden with the spoils of triumph, meet with more enthusiastic welcome than did those weary, battle-stained men, who had endured every hardship, overcome every obstacle, surmounted every difficulty, that Kentucky might be free. All thanks to them. Let their names be perpetuated in all future history as heroes who dared, and suffered, and bled for the right.

But if the reception of the infantry was enthusiastic, what shall we say of that of Colonel Morgan and his men, who now, for the first time in ten long months of toil and danger, returned to the homes of their childhood, the bosom of their loved families? The scene was one which utterly defies description. The bells throughout the city pealed out joyously—men, women, and young boys and girls, with smiles, tears, shouts, and **cheers** rushed into **the** streets, waving white handkerchiefs and small Southern flags, and making the very air resonant with the strains of wildest **joy.** Wives pressed husbands to their **bosoms;** parents clasped sons in affectionate embrace. General **gladness** reigned throughout the **vast multitude, and for hours** the most intense excitement **everywhere** prevailed. **No class was exempt. Even** the **negroes were eager participants in** the universal enjoyment.

Colonel Morgan's forces were allowed but a short time **to recuperate.** But during this **brief interval,** the boys, forgetting all they had endured, gave themselves **up** unrestrainedly to the joys of home and society. They visited their sweethearts, went riding with old friends, dashed out into **the country,** and were toasted, feted, welcomed, everywhere.

A detachment of Colonel Morgan's forces was then sent forward northward as far as the five-mile house, in front of Covington, where for three days they menaced the enemy, driving up in front of his hastily constructed rifle-pits. Falling back from this point, **they returned** to Georgetown, and from there passed hastily on, **with the** view of intercepting the Federal General Morgan, in his retreat from Cumberland Gap.

The Friday following General Bragg's occupation of **Bardstown and the issuance of** the Federal **General Nelson's** order for the women and children to leave **Louisville, General Buell reached** the city with his **worn and jaded army, and assumed command of the** place. This restored **confidence to a great extent, as** he was regarded by both parties as a wise and prudent man, who would not unnecessarily bring fear and **suffering on** the inhabitants.

A week from the date **of General** Nelson's order, he lay a corpse at the Galt House, having been shot by Jeff. C. Davies, of Indiana, in an altercation provoked by himself. Troops were hourly pouring into the city from across the river, to **swell** the already heavy army of Buell. **The** fortifications were **also being** strengthened in every possible way, **and** the panic which for days had reigned universally **was** but little abated. During all these days of internal suspense, General Bragg **was** quietly resting at Bardstown, seemingly awaiting the development of General Buell's plans. His advance pickets had been thrown forward to within a few miles of Louisville, **and thus the city** was constantly menaced.

Evangeline Lenoir was aroused early on the Saturday morning following her farewell to Harry Roberts, by a messenger bearing the following note:

LOUISVILLE, KY., Sept. 28, 1862.

MY DEAR EVANGELINE:—I have escaped from my captors, and am now safe at my father's house. Were it not for the fear of betrayal, I would call to see you. But my recent sad experience makes me cautious. I shall leave before morning, to endeavor to make my way through to Lexington, to rejoin Colonel Morgan. Dare I ask you—Will you follow me? Will you forsake home and friends, Evangeline, for one who loves you more than life itself, and who will do all a devoted heart can do to secure your happiness? Once in the land of Freedom, we could be united, happy. As it is, we may never meet again. Say, Evangeline, will you meet me at Lexington? I can write no more.

Ever, my dear Evangeline, yours,

HARRY.

Evangeline stood as one electrified, while she read and re-read the note she held in her hand. As the breaking of the morning light to the weary pilgrim, who amid storm and darkness has wandered on through the tangled maze of the trackless wild, was this joyous intelligence to the heart of Evangeline. Since the morning she had bidden Harry adieu, as the boat left the wharf, she had sorrowed hopelessly. All joy had fled her darkened soul —all hope died out in her stricken bosom. Confining herself to her room, avoiding all company, she brooded over her deep grief and bitter disappointment until her brain was frenzied, and life became a weary burden. The wild excitement which prevailed throughout the city failed to win her attention for a moment; and when at table Mr. Terrant would rally her over her silent and despondent appearance, she would only smile faintly, and reply that nothing distressed her but the dreadful condition of the country. Her uncle, unsuspecting man as he was, ascribed her gloom to her disappointment at her delayed marriage with young Lasley.

This gentleman, fearful of being pressed into the ranks of the "refugee defenders" of the city, had wisely availed himself of the *furore* of Monday to return to his home at Bardstown. He remained in Louisville long enough to see his hated rival conveyed to the boat which was to bear him to Ohio. Then, as if satisfied that he was avenged, he hired a buggy and set off at full speed for a place of security.

"I will go," said Evangeline, determinedly, to herself, as she read again Harry's earnest request. A thousand obstacles rose up to prevent the execution of her design, but she heeded them not.

Undaunted she looked at them, and where she **could not devise a plan** to surmount them, she left the difficulty unsolved, **and** trusted herself to some unforeseen interposition in her behalf.

After breakfast, she ordered the carriage, and drove out to Mr. R.'s, to see Mary Lawrence. As soon as she found an opportunity to speak with her alone, she showed her Harry's note, told her of her decision, and requested her advice.

"We will go together, Evangie," said Mary.

"And when shall this be?" asked Evangeline, earnestly.

"Just as soon as it is ascertained that the Confederates are going to leave the State. There is still a hope that they may come to Louisville, and the strong possibility is they will hold Kentucky. The difficulties of getting through are so great, we will not risk the trip until it becomes necessary."

"But, oh, Mary, what if the army should go out, and we be left behind?"

"That can scarcely occur, Evangie. We shall, most undoubtedly, have some warning—sufficient to enable us to prepare and get through."

"Have you spoken to any friend, Mary, of your intention to go to Lexington?"

"Oh, yes."

"And do they approve this plan you have just mentioned?"

"Yes; it is the advice of all my friends. This is why I have adopted it."

"And you will let me know, Mary, when you determine to go? I must make some preparations, and I will attend to it immediately, so as to be ready at a moment's warning. But how shall we go, Mary?"

"In a carriage. There is left to us no other alternative. All the railroads are broken up, and no stages are running now on any of the old routes. We can hire a carriage for the trip, and go by way of Bardstown. I have an aunt there, and a cousin who will go through with us and protect us."

"But who will take care of us to that place, Mary?"

"Lu's brother can go with us. I know the way well, have travelled it often, and would not feel the least afraid."

Evangeline, having arranged the whole plan with her friend, returned to the city to make such preparation as she thought necessary for the trip before her.

On reaching her room, she found a letter on her table from her aunt. It was directed to Mr. Terrant, and in a handwriting she did not recognize. Seizing it, she read it hastily through. It was an urgent request for Mr. Terrant and herself to set out immediately for Indianapolis to see her aunt, who was confined to her bed, seriously disabled by a fall she had received in descending the steps of a hall where she had been in attendance to hear a **war speech. The appeal** was most forcible, the language setting **forth** the extent of the sad accident, and Mrs. Terrant's most earnest desire to see her husband and niece. Looking again at the table, Evangeline discerned a note which had fallen on the carpet. It was addressed to her by her uncle, telling her that he would make every preparation to leave on the evening train for Indianapolis, and she must be ready to accompany him.

"I cannot go," soliloquized Evangeline, as she threw **herself** into **the** large arm-chair that **stood before** the bright coal-fire **that** was blazing in the grate. "**I cannot go, and** it is **no use to talk about it.** The Confederates may **leave the** State while I am away, and then I should never **get South, and** Harry would think I had deceived him, and Lasley will annoy me to death with his importunities; not that he loves me—no, no—the creature is incapable of love—but he is determined to marry me, merely because he cannot bear **to** be disappointed in his desires. Poor, dear aunt, I do wish I could **see** her,—she **has** always been so kind to me; and now she is away from home, and suffering so, **too.** I ought to go. It will be so ungrateful in me to refuse, **when she is so** anxious to **see** me. She knows I can nurse her better than any one else. And what reason can I give for staying at home? I have none. Oh, I will have to go!" she added, after a pause; "and then if the Southerners should go out before I can get back, what shall I do—what shall I do! I can't stay long. But how am I to get back? It will not do to leave her until she is well—this would be so unkind. Oh, me, what shall I do! I cannot go. **But what reason can I offer** uncle for refusing? I cannot tell him I am sick, though mercy knows I have suffered enough in the last week to kill me. I dare not say I am afraid to go, for that is a place of **safety—this of** danger. And to urge any dislike to the Yankees, when my poor aunt needs me! Oh, **that I** was ready to set out for Lexington this very hour! I would run all risks, take all consequences, if I could but get through. The world might say what it could, it could not harm **me then."**

She took up the letter that had been lying on her lap during her soliloquy, and read it again. "I shall have to go to poor, dear aunt. I would never forgive myself if she should die and I not see her. I will stay a few days, and then come back. But how can I get away? Aunt will think so strangely of my wishing to return before she is well. *I must go*, and *I must return* in a few days," she said, energetically, as she arose and walked to the window.

The carriage stood waiting to take her down the street. Pausing a moment to consider, she took her escritoir, wrote a **note to** Mary Lawrence, explanatory of circumstances, and urging upon **her to** write to her at Indianapolis each day, that she might be kept informed of **what was passing, and of** the unfolding of her plans. Then ringing the bell, she ordered Emily to put her clothes in her trunk, and have every thing ready for her departure.

"My small trunk, Emily. I **shall be back in a** few days. **Put** up such dresses as are suitable for a sick-room. I shall have no use for evening and dinner dresses, only wrappers and one or two street suits. Be careful, Emily, heed what I say to you."

With these directions, Evangeline descended the stairway, and taking the carriage drove to one of the most extensive stores on Fourth-street. Alighting, she made **such** purchases as she desired, and ordering the packages done up directly, took them with **her** to her mantua-maker, where she left directions for the making of the dresses, requesting that they should be finished **by** the middle of the following week **and sent** home. **From** the mantua-maker's she drove to Merriman's cloak-store, and quickly selected a very genteel drab cloth travelling-cloak. She then proceeded to her milliner's, ordered a travelling-bonnet, and calling at Mrs. Ritchy's fancy-store, purchased gloves, collars, handkerchiefs, etc., etc. Having bought all she deemed necessary, she returned home, and occupied the time until dinner in preparing her travelling trunk, so that she might be ready on her return to set out for the Confederate lines at an hour's warning. As she placed **in** the last articles, including her morning purchases, she told Emily to be sure to fold the dresses which would be sent home Wednesday evening of the following week, and put them in the trunk.

"Going to travel again, Miss 'Vangie?"

"Perhaps so, Emily," she replied, carelessly. "It may be I shall have to send for my trunk. I wish to have all things ready."

"Yes, Miss 'Vangie, you are very right. These troublesome times it's well to be ready for any thing that turns up."

The evening found her with her uncle, on their way to Indianapolis. On reaching that city, they found Mrs. Terrant far better than was expected. The injury, which at the time of the fall had appeared quite serious, upon further examination had been found to be comparatively slight, and the physician assured Mr. Terrant that his wife would be in a condition to return home in eight or ten days.

On the fifth evening after Evangeline's arrival in Indianapolis, she received a hasty note from Mary Lawrence, informing her that *she* had decided to leave for Bardstown the following week, and urged upon Evangeline to return immediately.

"What shall I do!" exclaimed Evangeline to herself, as the hand that held the letter fell heavily on her lap. "Aunt cannot travel yet; uncle is gone, there is no one to accompany me. What shall I plead as an excuse for returning so soon? and how can I persuade aunt to let me go alone? I must go—this I am determined on, and must leave on the next train. If I delay, Mary may leave without me, and then all hope of getting South is gone—forever gone." Rising from her chair, she passed into her aunt's room and stood beside the large cushioned chair on which that lady was sitting. She bore the letter in her hand.

"What news from Louisville, 'Vangie?" asked her aunt, looking up and seeing the letter.

"Oh, nothing unusual in a military point, aunty. This note is from Mary Lawrence, who urges me to return immediately." Evangeline hushed down her feelings, resolving to be calm. She had a part to play; she must do it well, or all would be lost.

"And what is the matter, Evangie, that Mary should request you to return at a time like this?"

"Some affair of her own, aunty. You know I must not betray confidence," and the gay girl laughed and blushed deeply.

"Ah, you need not try to deceive me, child. Mary Lawrence is going to be married to Fred. Morton. Well, well, that is all right. If she ever intends to marry him she ought to do it now. Then, if he should be wounded, she can wait on him; or if killed, she will have a right to mourn for him. But you cannot go, Evangie, for several days. You know it is impossible for me to accompany you now, and you cannot go alone. When is the wedding to be?"

Evangeline hesitated a moment. Should she continue to deceive her aunt, or, undeceiving her, depend upon her powers of persuasion to influence her to let her undertake the trip alone? Intuitively, for she had not time to reason, she concluded to let her aunt enjoy her own opinion, and looking at the letter again, she answered:

"She says not a word about the day; only urges me to come immediately, not to delay a moment."

"But how are you to go, Evangeline? It is impossible. She had better be married without you than for you to risk yourself alone, now that the country is so filled with soldiers travelling to and fro. Write to her and tell her you cannot come for a few days. As soon as I get well enough, I will go with you. Perhaps the case is not so urgent as she represents it; and, moreover, if she is to be married in a day or two she can do without you; it will be a small wedding, of course—very few present."

"Oh, aunty," said Evangeline most persuasively, "I do wish you could go with me; don't you feel well enough? You know you can be still when you get on the cars; I will attend to you and the baggage; you shall have no occasion to exert yourself at all. I am so anxious to go. You know Mary is one of my dearest friends, and she has no sister, and no mother, aunty. She is so alone in the world, I must go to her now; she would never forgive me if I did not."

"Let me see the letter, child. Does she give no reason why she wishes you to come right away?"

"Oh, it is marked *secret*, aunty," replied Evangeline, her color deepening. "Mary wishes me to show the letter to no one, but says come without delay. Can't you go, aunty? Here is Doctor Floss coming up the avenue—if he says you may go with me, won't you go this very morning?"

"Oh, my child, I cannot; even were I well enough, and I know I am not, I could not get ready this evening."

Dr. Floss entered the room. Evangeline made known her desire. "What do you say, doctor?" she asked eagerly. "Can't aunty go with me? she is well enough for the trip, isn't she?" The old man shook his head—"Not for several days will your aunt be in a condition to travel."

"Well, aunty, I will go this evening, and send uncle after you," she said most determinedly, though her heart beat doubtingly as she spoke. "I am not a bit afraid; and if I were, I would feel it my duty to risk every thing to gratify Mary."

"What do you think, doctor—will it be prudent for my niece to go to Kentucky alone in these troublous times?"

The old man, who had been raised in Connecticut, where females travel unprotected, looked at the matter in a business-like

16

view entirely, not for a moment considering it in the light of propriety.

"I think she might go safely, madam, if she is willing to undertake the trip."

"Thank you, doctor, thank you," exclaimed Evangeline. "Dr. Floss knows there is no danger, aunty; and you know I am not one bit afraid. How long before the cars leave for Louisville, doctor? will I have time to get ready?"

"Just two hours before the western train will be in," said the old man, taking out his double-cased silver watch, which had measured the time for him the last twenty years of his practice.

"Oh, I could get ready for a trip to Europe in two hours. Aunty, may I go? I know you will not deny me. Doctor, won't you take me to the cars and see my baggage safely on them? I shall have nothing to do but be quiet until I reach home."

The doctor readily assented to acting as her escort. Her aunt protested against the undertaking, but Evangeline had too much at stake to submit to any opposition. Most wonderfully preserving her equanimity, she made all necessary preparations, and when Dr. Floss drove up at the appointed hour, she was ready, bonneted, awaiting him.

Bidding her aunt an affectionate farewell, and enjoining her to come home as soon as possible, she seated herself beside the doctor, who drove her to the depot and placed her on the cars, attending to every minutiæ that would enhance her comfort.

In the excitement of achieving her purpose, Evangeline had had no time for reflection or reason. She could entertain but the one thought, that of reaching Louisville in time to set out with Mary Lawrence for Lexington. When alone, as she was, left to her own reflections, the momentousness of the step she was taking rushed in upon her mind with overwhelming power, and she shrunk as the picture in all its grand and fearful proportions rose up before her. Tremblingly she contemplated it, and as she examined it in all its shades and colorings, she stood back aghast at the magnitude of its gigantic dimensions. Should she succeed? this was the momentous question. Once the wife of Harry Roberts, she defied the sneers and jests of the unappreciative public. She could look down from the heights of her security and laugh at those who would endeavor to assail her. But, then, the fearful opposite! Should she fail in her attempt, and her plans and futile endeavors be exposed to the cold, heartless world! How could she live beneath its power? how submit to its coarse remarks and unfeeling opinions? She felt that her proud, independent spirit could never brook this deep trial—this sad, enduring mortification, which must ever haunt her life. Poor, tried Evangeline! Thou art, indeed, entering in upon a path beset with trial and danger!

CHAPTER LV.

IS THERE NO LIGHT?

The morning after Evangeline reached Louisville, she drove out to Mr. R.'s, to ascertain when Mary Lawrence would leave for Lexington. She found her young friend in the midst of preparation, but foiled in the plan which she had hoped to consummate on the following day. She was now uncertain *when* she should leave. This gave Evangeline more time to perfect her arrangements, and although it but prolonged the suspense which she felt almost unendurable, yet, for some reasons, she was glad of the delay. Applying herself with the utmost assiduity to the task before her, unadvised and unassisted, she succeeded, in a few days, in completing all arrangements deemed by her necessary for the proposed trip. Her trunk was conveyed to Mr. R.'s, to await the day of departure. Her uncle, all unsuspecting, furnished her with what funds she desired, and with miser's care she hoarded them, that she might be ready to meet future exigencies. Meanwhile she received no intelligence from young Lasley. She had expected to be annoyed by the reception of letters, or perhaps the intrusion of his presence. Why he was thus silent she was at a loss to divine, but, amid her wonder, she was grateful to be relieved of this feature of her perplexity. Ah, could she have known what that silence portended—could she have read the secret workings of that heart, bent on its ever fiendish purposes—have understood its act of cruel revenge—how would her soul have sunk within her! how would she have fainted beneath the torturing burden! Anguish, deep, dark, unutterable, would have seized the very lifesprings of her being, and she would have sought death rather than life! Robbed of joy—her every hope perished—the light of the future changed to rayless darkness—what would there have been upon which the weary soul could have leaned for support? what to which the poor broken heart could have looked for consolation? Well it was for her, surrounded as she was by uncertainty, her bosom each moment the prey of doubt and anxiety, that the sad intelligence could not reach her. Well, that while the cloud gathered over her pathway, she saw not its black folds—heard not its fearful thunders!

Incarcerated in the prison at Bardstown, shut out from the light of day, surrounded by a Federal guard, with the penalty of death overshadowing his soul, lay Harry **Roberts**, hopeless, sad, despairing. It was the 8th of October, the day of the sanguinary battle of **Perryville**. He knew not of the conflict that was then raging, **all he knew was the wretchedness** of his condition—the utter hopelessness of his future. And for the first time amid the varied fortunes that **had beset his path for the last** twelvemonth, did he despair. He thought of Evangeline, of his request, with which he felt confident she would endeavor to comply; of her endeavors to join him, her hopes, her fears, the risks she would run, and then of her overwhelming grief when she should learn his dark fate; of the bitterness of her disappointment, the awkwardness of her position, when she should find herself a stranger in a strange land, away from home and friends, alone, unprotected, exposed to the vicissitudes of war, with the deep mortification of failure to encounter, the reproach of Union friends, who would rejoice at her **sorrow** and taunt her with her want of success; of the entire helplessness of her Southern friends to extricate her from the tortures of her position;—all this, like a living panorama, passed before him to heighten his distress and increase the horrors of his imprisonment. Death, he felt, would be a sweet relief, were it not that the happiness of another was involved in his fate. But in his darkest moments the thought of Evangeline would **nerve** him, and he resolved that whatever fate awaited him he would live for her sake.

Gloating with delight over his successful revenge, feasting with a fiendish joy at the contemplation of the picture of the distress he had wrought, Lasley delighted to recount to his friends in vice and dissipation the achievement of his desires. He had vanquished his hated rival, humiliated the heart of her whom he had professed to love, foiling all their plans, darkening their every joy

Young Roberts, believing it more practicable to join the Confederate army at Bardstown than at Lexington, had attempted to reach that point. At every step he encountered the danger of **discovery.** His progress was retarded by the movement of the **Federal troops, who now** thronged every road from Louisville **that led out in the direction of Bardstown.** As he made his way cautiously from house **to house** along the route, he heard that General Bragg had left Bardstown, and was falling back upon

Camp Dick Robinson. The rumors of his movements were conflicting and unreliable, and Roberts determined to prosecute his first intention. Accordingly, he pursued his way to Bardstown. Reaching that place, he found it in the possession of Federal troops. Being known to no one save young Lasley, of whose implacable hatred towards him he knew nothing, and being dressed in citizens' clothing, he felt no fear of recognition, and ventured to walk the streets in open day, to see if he could ascertain the true position of General Bragg, and his safest route to join him. He was walking leisurely along towards the hotel when he met Lasley walking between two young men. The two immediately recognized each other. Roberts, smiling, bowed; Lasley bowed coldly. The two passed on. After proceeding a few steps, Harry turned to look after Lasley. He discovered one of the men he had seen with him following on his steps, while Lasley and the other were hastily crossing the street towards a group of soldiers. Fearing that some evil threatened him, Harry made his way as fast as he could to the hotel. As he entered the door of the bar-room, he observed the individual that had been following him pass by the door and cross the street to the right. Harry stood a few minutes as if uncertain how to proceed. Then walking to the door, he looked cautiously out. There was no appearance of danger—no blue-coats were to be seen in the street. He breathed more freely. Believing that his fears were wholly unfounded, he returned and quietly seated himself in one corner, where he would be free from observation. There were three other men in the room besides the bar-keeper, who were all rejoicing together over the certain retreat of the rebels from the State. Harry listened attentively to all they said, endeavoring to gather from their loud and confused statements any information that would serve him in the future. The bar-keeper joined the trio in their tirade of invective against the rebels, and the four were most unsparing in their wild denunciation of every thing Confederate. Harry felt the blood rush to his face, and the words to his lips, but prudence dictated silence, and he choked down his swelling indignation as best he could, and assumed an air of indifference. Looking out of the window into the cross-street, he was not aware of the approach of any one, until he heard a heavy footfall at the door. He suddenly turned his head in that direction. His gaze encountered three Yankee soldiers approaching him. One stepped forward, and laying his hand on his shoulder said, in a harsh tone, "You are my prisoner—follow me!"

"How dare you arrest me!" said Harry, gazing sternly into the face of his captor, determined to try the force of bravado. It was his only weapon. "How dare you arrest me, I ask, a peaceable citizen! Show me your authority."

The soldier was a man of nerve, and returning Harry's look with one equally as firm and unyielding, he very quickly and without the least perturbation responded:

"You need not try to deceive me. You are one of Morgan's men, who has escaped from prison. Come with me—no words, I have no time for discussion."

Harry saw that he must yield. It was useless to resist. Calmly he arose from his chair and walked out between the soldiers. As he passed along the street that led to the prison, he saw on the opposite side Lasley and his two companions, who were laughing and talking together. He knew that he was the subject of their remarks, the cause of their merriment, and with the ferocity of a demon he scowled upon them. It was all he could do. He dared not speak. He knew the heartlessness of his enemies.

The prison-door was closed, he was left alone with his thoughts. Silent and morose he sat, dwelling on the hopelessness of his fate. The hope that had cheered him during his previous imprisonment was now gone. He could see no way of escape. He knew now that he should be watched with the greatest vigilance, from the fact that he had once evaded them. As he sat, sad and desponding, his head bowed, and his whole attitude expressive of the despair that filled his soul, he heard one of the guard outside say to another:

"We have whipped the rebels all to pieces at Perryville. A man has just reached here, and says they have been fighting there since yesterday morning, and are now fighting, and the rebels are being slaughtered like sheep."

Harry started, and applying his ear to the key-hole listened attentively.

The two continued their conversation only a few minutes. He gathered from what he heard that the Confederates were sadly whipped. Were this the case, he knew they would have to retreat from the State as best they could. It would be impossible for them to remain, if the first engagement should terminate so disastrously.

"What will become of Evangeline?" he said to himself, bitterly, as he resumed his seat on the old stool, and buried his face in his hands, while the great drops that he could not force back streamed through his fingers. "If I knew she was safe, I should ask no more. Oh, God, take care of her, and shield her from all danger!" he exclaimed, vehemently, as he sprang from his seat and paced his narrow room.

Haunted by his fears for her whom he loved, oppressed under a sense of his utter inability to aid her in any way, bereft of all hope in his own case, he was as one bereft of reason. Frenzied, he walked to and fro, until, exhausted from the severe exertion, he sank again on the hard stool.

Could his heartless persecutor have seen him as he sat there, ready to sink under the weight of his fearful doom, surely he would have felt that he was fully avenged. This unfeeling creature was revelling in dissipation and vice, while his victim was writhing in anguish. Why, oh, why is it that the base and grovelling are often so prosperous, are permitted to sit in high places and grind beneath their crushing injustice the proud and noble soul, who finds no means of defence, no power of redress?

When these anomalous aspects of human society present themselves, we are led to ask, is there a hand of inflexible justice dealing out to all, impartially, the reward of their deeds? If so, why do the wicked and debased prosper, and why are the true and elevated dashed to the earth beneath their infamous power? Philosophy cannot solve the question. Enigmatical it must ever remain to that man who seeks not its solution in the words of heavenly wisdom, which tells us, "When the wicked spring as the grass, and when all the workers of iniquity do flourish, it is *that they shall be destroyed forever.* For yet a little while, and the wicked shall not be; yea, thou shalt diligently consider his place, and it shall not be."

Harry Roberts sat in his dark, noisome prison, filled with the most despondent thoughts. He could see no gleam of light, look which way he might. His future was without promise. He saw nothing before him but captivity, ending in death. He felt that having once escaped, he would hereafter be the object of increased vigilance and of additional insult. And when he looked away to the object of his soul's adoration, the gloom deepened, until all was cheerless night. Could he shield her from suffering, chagrin, disappointment, he would not murmur at his own fate. It was for Evangeline far more than himself that he sorrowed. But how unavailing all this grief! He could give her no assistance, no protection. To a proud, self-reliant spirit this sense of utter inability to shield or defend a loved one is maddening. Robbed of the power to exercise the right of protecting the weak and dependent, a noble man sinks in his own estimation into nothingness. How many a brave, defiant Southern heart has had to endure this unspeakable humiliation since the **war** began!

While Harry was thus groping his way amid the darkness of the present and future, Evangeline and her friend, Mary, were pursuing their way towards Bardstown. Having obtained a permit, they entertained but little apprehension of annoyance or delay from the Federal pickets that guarded the road over which they had to pass. They were accompanied by Willie R., the younger brother of Charley, who was to escort them to Bardstown, at which **point** they **were to place themselves** under the charge of Mary's cousin, who would give them safe conduct to Lexington, if it were possible to reach that point; if not, they were to be taken within Confederate lines, and there remain until Mr. Lawrence, or his son, or young Roberts could be heard from.

On the two girls travelled, the subjects of alternate hope and fear. At one moment the prospect before them appeared cheering—the plan agreed upon so feasible, success so certain; and then again all was doubt, difficulty, failure. To Evangeline, who was leaving behind her all the friends and associations of her girlhood, bidding them adieu forever, to go forth into a strange land, where there would be but one heart to appreciate her sacrifices—many to turn with coldness away, some to censure—to her young ardent soul the journey before them was one of the most momentous bearing. Vain were it to attempt a description of her varied and conflicting thoughts and emotions. Sometimes she would weep sadly, **as** the probabilities of disappointment and consequent mortification rose up vividly before her excited imagination; then again she was wild with blissful anticipations at the glad future that opened up before her, when, all her trials past, she would safely repose on the bosom of him for whom she had yielded up every promise which had so brightly beamed over her pathway—should listen to his burning words of love—receive the full and tender sympathy of his **pure affectionate** soul—rest on his strong arm for protection, and claim him her own for life. It was a strange, a novel undertaking for one so young, one reared in the indulgence of every desire, however wild or capricious; but Evangeline possessed, all unknown to herself and her friends, the characteristics of a heroine. Independence of thought and feeling, determination to brave difficulties and endure hardships, a commendable freedom from the trammels of public opinion, will to accomplish undertakings although fraught with danger—all these were traits of character which a close observer would have marked as possessed by her. And now the incentive of love—of deep, deathless affection for him to whom she had given her heart, called into exercise and prompted to unwonted energy these elements of character, which, for want of opportunity to make themselves manifest, had been hitherto comparatively dormant.

Mary shared her young friend's alternate gloom and joy. There was even a darker cloud in her horizon, one that overshadowed all the brightness of her future landscape. It was the uncertainty with regard to Charley's fate, which hourly haunted her thoughts.

"Is he dead?" was the question that constantly recurred to her mind; and the possibility that this might be so, took away the light that would otherwise have gilded the eventful life she was now entering upon. That she should meet her father and brother she did not for a moment doubt. She had set out to do this, and she calculated upon no failure. She might encounter many difficulties, but it was practical and must be achieved.

It was late at night when they reached Bardstown, they having been delayed on the way by the breaking of one of the axletrees to the carriage. Most persons had retired at the hotel at which they rested for the night, so that they had no opportunity of learning any thing respecting the relative position of the two armies. Weary and worn they sought their room, after having partaken of a cup of tea and some cold bread which the landlord had hastily prepared for them.

Morning came, and found them sleeping after the fatigue of their journey. The sun was shining fully when Mary awoke. It had been their plan to drive out to her aunt's before breakfast, that they might proceed several miles on their way during the day.

Awakening Evangeline, the two made a hasty toilet and descended to the breakfast-room. They were but just seated at the table when three young gentlemen entered and placed themselves near the foot of the table, on the same side with themselves. Neither of the young girls looked towards them. They were scarcely in their places before a middle-aged man, who was enjoying his coffee and hot roll on the opposite side, called out in rather a loud tone of voice:

"What news this morning, Lasley? I hear a courier is in."

At the mention of this name Evangeline started, looked suddenly around, and turned deadly pale. The young man who sat next her observed the movement, and fixed his eyes upon her in curious wonder. She was aware of his fixed gaze, and she strove to calm herself. His companions reading his surprise in the expression of his face, followed his example, and directed their look towards the head of the table where the two girls sat. Evangeline was trembling with emotion, vainly endeavoring to preserve an unmoved exterior. Mary saw her agitation, and measurably partook of it, as she realized that the attention of all at table was directed to them. Despite herself, the blood would mount to her face, and her hand perceptibly quivered as she conveyed the cup of coffee to her lips.

Across young Lasley's face there shot a look of triumph, and in his eye there gleamed an expression of revengeful satisfaction, as he became assured of the presence of his helpless victim.

Elevating his voice above its natural tone, so that his words might reach the ear of Evangeline, he replied to the interrogatory of the gentleman:

"The news is most gratifying, indeed. A courier just in from Perryville, brings the reliable intelligence that we whipped the rebels all to pieces on yesterday, and they are now flying, routed and panic-stricken, in the direction of Lancaster, making their way out of the State as fast as they can. Buell is sure to overtake them before they can reach Stanford, and the great probability is that the whole army will be captured."

"Is it possible!" exclaimed the first speaker. "I fear this is too good to be believed. Is the man to be relied on?"

"Most assuredly. This is the news that is to be sent to Louisville. It is official."

"And did we suffer much loss?"

"Pretty heavy, but by no means sufficient to delay an immediate pursuit. General Buell will move on this morning after the scattered and flying troops of Bragg. The Confederate campaign in Kentucky is at an end, sir. The army is literally destroyed, not one in twenty will ever get back to tell the story of their disastrous defeat."

Mary and Evangeline sat like statues, pale and immovable. Riveted to their seats by the very horror of the intelligence they heard, they felt as if they should faint under its crushing weight. They looked at each other with an expression of fearful wonder, but neither spoke. They essayed to eat, that their agitation might not be observed. But they could not swallow their food, and trembling, hopeless, helpless, they sat listening to the conversation, every word of which fell like a death sentence on their ears.

"Oh, we will make short work of these invaders of our soil," said Lasley, his very tone speaking the gratification of his heart. "We'll teach them a lesson they will not soon forget. Their audacity is unparalleled. Who asked them to come into our State to steal, and thieve, and destroy? What right had they to use Union men as they have done, and to possess themselves of our property, as they have been constantly doing? By the way, we have got one of these patriots, one of Morgan's men, in prison here—a fellow that escaped from Louisville on his way to Camp Chase, and who had succeeded in getting this far on his route to the Confederate army."

At this announcement the knife dropped from Evangeline's hand, her heart stood still, all the color forsook her face, her brain reeled, and she felt as if she would fall from her seat.

"Yes, I heard something of it when I reached town on yesterday. Who is the young fellow? and how did it happen he was recognized?"

Evangeline listened with her soul to catch Lasley's answer.

"His name is Harry Roberts," replied the heartless wretch, slowly and emphatically. "He was sauntering along the street here, in all security, when I recognized him, and knowing that he was a fugitive from justice, I had him arrested and placed in confinement until he can be sent back to Louisville."

Evangeline could hear no more. She arose, left the room, and finding, she knew not how, the chamber where they had slept the night before, she staggered to the bed, on which she threw herself, and lay rigid, immovable, as one bereft of life. Mary followed her quickly. Finding her in this frightful condition, notwithstanding her own heart was breaking, she set about restoring her to consciousness. Bathing her face in cold water, and applying to her nose a small bottle of sal. volatile which she chanced to have in her pocket, and chafing her hands and forehead, she succeeded at last in partially arousing her. The young girl opened her eyes, looked wildly about her, and then, with a shudder, closed them again and moaned. Mary was alarmed at her appearance. Her first impulse was to call for aid, but feeling that their position was one that demanded the greatest caution, she determined to keep the whole matter as secret as possible. Dispatching William R. for a servant to bring fresh water, she locked the door, lowered the blinds, and undoing Evangeline's travelling dress, and removing every thing that might impede circulation, she continued to bathe her temples and rub her hands, at intervals applying the ammonia. After awhile Evangeline opened her eyes a second time, and gazed up imploringly into the face of her young friend, who was bending over her with all the tenderness of a sister.

"He is in prison, Mary," she said, slowly and mournfully. "My life is lost; oh, that I could die!"

"Do not talk so, Evangeline, there is yet hope," replied Mary, feeling that she must maintain all calmness and courage. "Better there than dead. We may yet manage to relieve him. Charley, you know, has been a prisoner three times. There is hope for Harry, certainly."

Evangeline shook her head despairingly. "No, no!" she said, as she closed her eyes, while the great liquid tears rolled down her cheeks.

"Oh, yes! there is hope, great hope, Evangeline. I will send for Lasley and get him to interfere. He can be influenced to exert himself in Harry's behalf. Don't give up; it will all be right. These are times when we must not suffer ourselves to be overcome by difficulties, however insuperable they may appear."

"But what shall I do, Mary?" asked Evangeline, aroused by Mary's words and look of calm determination.

"Send for Lasley, and appeal to him—surely he cannot be heartless; he will interfere for Harry."

"Oh, you do not know Lasley, Mary; he is prompted by no motive but self-interest and gratification. I can appeal to him—but oh, it will be so humiliating! yet for Harry's sake I could prostrate myself before him, and plead as a slave to his master; but it will be in vain—he will not hear me—his heart is hard, selfish, brutal."

"But, Evangeline, it is the only hope I see for Harry's release. It may not succeed, but certainly the object is worth the trial; and what is to be done must be done quickly. You heard what he said about the retreat of the Confederates from the State; it may already be too late for us to overtake them."

"Send for Lasley, Mary; and yet, how can I meet him—how ask a favor at his hands?" she said, a look of disdain overspreading her face; "but it is for Harry—for him I will humble myself even to the dust. Were it for myself I would die —die before I would encounter this heartless, detestable man. Perhaps, Mary, he will not see me," she said, as she stood before the mirror, smoothing her dark hair back from her aching forehead.

"You can but try. Willie has gone to ask him to the parlor to meet you there."

"You must go with me, Mary; I cannot see him alone."

"Yes, Evangie, I will go with you, and give you all the assistance I can."

In the course of fifteen minutes, which appeared hours to the waiting girls, William R. returned and informed them that Lasley was in the parlor awaiting them.

Nerving herself for the task before her, Evangeline, leaning on Mary's arm, descended to the parlor and confronted young Lasley. As she met him, she felt all the spirit of defiance of which her nature was capable swell her bosom. Her face assumed a look of hauteur—her eyes fixed themselves resolutely on his—her proud lips compressed, while her nostrils expanded—that unmistakable evidence of determination and conscious superiority.

He received her with the air of one who, aware of his own personal weakness, yet feels strong in the power of circumstances. Mary left them alone, and walked out on the gallery.

"I come," she said to him as she seated herself, "to ask you if it is in your power to have Harry Roberts released from prison."

"Indeed!" he responded, with bitter scorn. "Do you come to me, Miss Lenoir, to ask a favor? to me, whom you have insulted, taunted, derided? I would scarcely think you would ask of me, whom you have thus treated, to render you assistance—to aid my rival, my foe!"

"Harry has never injured you, Edward Lasley. Nor would he ask this at your hands—he would perish first—die in prison a thousand times rather. It is I—I come to beseech you for my sake, for the sake of humanity, of mercy, to act if you have any influence, any power."

"When I besought you, Miss Lenoir, to have compassion on me, to relieve my feelings, did you do it? How did you act when I supplicated? Did I not tell you then we would meet again? and now my words are fulfilled. The scene is changed; it is you who now sues. Should I heed your plea? Remember your own scorn, your indifference, your neglect! Though late, revenge has come at last; we have met again. You shall never marry Harry Roberts. My words are now made good."

"You knew, Edward Lasley, why I did not marry you. I told you I did not love you, that my heart was another's. Would you have wedded me with this fact staring you in the face? Could you have proved so false to yourself, to every pure and noble sentiment, as to wish me to marry you when my affections clung to another?"

"But I loved you, Evangeline. You promised to be mine; you broke that vow, and refused to see me."

"If I have wronged you, Edward Lasley, I ask your forgiveness. I acted hastily in promising to marry you; I should have considered the subject. Had I done this, I would not have fallen into this fatal error. But was it not best, right, just, when I found that I had acted unwisely—that I did not, could not love you—to tell you so, and thus save us both a life of misery! Surely, Edward Lasley, you cannot upbraid me for this. Why, oh! why do you torture me? Will you endeavor to have Harry released, or shall I plead in vain?"

"There is one condition, Evangeline, and only one, on which I will grant your request."

"And what is this!" the excited girl exclaimed eagerly. "Say, say! I promise any thing. Just release Harry, let him once again be free, and you may demand of me whatever you choose. I will grant any request. Name it, name it!"

"Be careful how you promise," he replied, while his lip curled with irony, "you may have again to repent a rash vow."

"Harry, Harry! if he is free, I ask no more! Any thing, even my life, to save him!"

"The condition is"—and the young man fixed his eye intently on the girl before him as he slowly uttered his horrid stipulation. She trembled under his look and the ominous tone of his voice. "The condition is—and it is the only one—that you will marry me at the time mentioned in your last note."

"Oh! heaven pity me!" ejaculated Evangeline, starting frantically from her seat. "Marry you, Edward Lasley? marry you? oh, how can you ask of me to do this? Any thing, any thing but this. This is not the only condition; it cannot be—you would not be so cruel—you could not make yourself unhappy for life—curse yourself and me. Oh, no! you do not mean this; you are jesting, sporting with my feelings. I beseech you, spare me; oh, spare me!"

Her manner was wildly excited, her face livid and rigid, her lip quivered, her voice was harsh and broken, she trembled in every nerve as she gazed upon him. He met her look coldly, calmly, unfeelingly. Around his mouth there lurked a smile of fiendish enjoyment—in his eye there rested a look of dogged determination. He spoke not; but sat, his eyes riveted on the suffering girl, as if gloating over her anguish. Evangeline **read** his thoughts, and her heart beat **wildly.**

"**You do not ask me to marry you, Edward Lasley ?**" she resumed, after some moments' pause, during which he did **not remove** his steadfast gaze. "**Oh!** you do not require this of **me as the** return for releasing Harry from prison! No, no! **you will not be so cruel!**"

"Nothing more I ask—nothing less will satisfy my demand. I love you, Evangeline, and have determined to make you my wife. **Say you** will marry me, and Harry Roberts shall be free in an hour;—refuse, and the setting sun shall find him in Louisville, **on** his way to a Northern prison—and I suppose to death."

"I do not love you—I tell **you once again, I cannot love you,** Edward **Lasley.** How then could I ever consent to **be your wife?**"

"Marry me, and you will afterwards learn to **love me.** Marry me, I ask **no** more. **I will risk all the** consequences."

She bowed her **head, as if in deep thought.** But how could her poor distracted brain think—reeling as it was with the horrors of the destiny that awaited her—let her choose as she might. Silent **and** bewildered **she sat** there, stupefied with grief.

"You must answer me now, Evangeline. There is no time to lose. In half an hour the stage will leave for Louisville, and unless you consent to my proposal, Roberts shall be sent down."

"Oh! wait—wait—let me have time to think. I cannot decide —the question is too momentous."

"No time **for wasting; you** must conclude speedily. **A few** minutes must decide the question forever. It rests with you."

"Oh! Harry, Harry!" exclaimed Evangeline, as she buried her face in her hands. "Must I make this great sacrifice?—must I marry him, and leave you forever? Oh! how **can I do this!** And yet, if I refuse, your life will pay the forfeit. **We shall never meet again!** Yes, yes," she said to herself, "if he can but be free, I am happy. To spare him, I will die; yes, die. I will give myself for him."

"Do I understand that you consent to be my wife, Evangeline?" said Lasley, as these low-spoken words fell on his ear.

She looked suddenly up at him.

"You will **have** Harry released if I promise you this; you will not deceive me?"

"I will not **deceive** you, Evangeline. Roberts shall be a free man and placed in a position of safety before the sun goes down."

"Then I consent," she said, slowly, in a low, husky voice, as if her soul spoke out its eternal doom in these few words.

"And will marry me at the appointed time?"

She bowed assent.

"Remember, Evangeline, what you promise. Do not deceive yourself—think not to deceive me."

She gazed at him, but replied not.

"And when shall Harry be free?" she asked, as if she had naught else on earth to desire but his release and safety.

"Very soon. I will go now and make the arrangements."

"And may I not see him once—just once—to bid him farewell; to tell him all. Oh! deny me not this request. It is but a poor one—the last one."

"Yes; you may go with me to the prison, Evangeline, but you must remain here until I can see about it. I will call in a few minutes and let you know."

"And do you mean, Evangeline, to marry him?" asked her friend, who entered the room as Lasley left, and heard from the lips of the desponding girl the story of her fearful promise.

"Oh, ask me not, Mary. I am wild, wild!" and Evangeline clasped her friend in the agony of despair. "Great God!" she exclaimed, "what have I done—what shall I do! Oh, Harry, Harry! must I be torn from you forever!"

Young Lasley returned to announce that he was ready to go to the prison to see about the release of Harry.

"Oh, go with me, Mary," besought Evangeline, as they ascended the stairway to their room. "Go with me, Mary; it may be the last favor I shall ever ask of you. Will you go through the lines, Mary? Will you risk yourself in the present wild and confused state of things? Oh, do not leave me! Stay, stay, there may yet come relief."

"I must go, Evangeline. You know all I hold most dear on earth is there. My father, my brother, and—Charley—if he still lives. I grieve to leave you, Evangeline, but you know my heart is with the South. I could no longer live amid the scenes of my once happy, but now desolate home. What awaits me in my attempt to get out, or what is before me in the future, I know not. It is all darkly wild, fearfully strange; but I will brave it all, believing it to be right."

Mary threw on her hat and tied it, and was in the act of putting on her gloves to join Evangeline, who stood awaiting her, when Willie R. rushed up the steps and into the room, exclaiming in broken accents:

"Morgan!—Morgan!—Morgan is coming, Miss Mary! Will be in this town directly with his men!"

The two girls looked at the agitated boy in silent astonishment. Had he lost his senses?

"It's true! it's true, Miss Mary! I heard a man say so, who just now dashed into the town—says he saw them all."

"He is deceiving you, Willie," said Evangeline. "Somebody wants to create an excitement."

Just then a rush was heard below-stairs. The two girls ran down to the parlor to ascertain its cause. They there encountered some ladies and several gentlemen, all in the greatest perturbation."

"Morgan! Morgan!" was on every lip.

"Is Colonel Morgan coming here?" asked Mary, of the gentleman next her.

"Yes, miss; is within a few miles of the place. Will be here directly."

"May there not be some mistake about it?"

"None in the world—it is so. I have seen two men whom I know to be truthful. They saw Morgan at the head of his forces but a few minutes ago, coming right in the direction of the town. The whole place is in confusion. Men are running to and fro, and the soldiers are scared to death."

"Will they offer any resistance, sir?"

"Oh, I suppose not. It would be useless to do so. There is comparatively but a small force here, and they have had so little warning, that they could not prepare to fight. Oh, no, they will all be made prisoners."

Evangeline looked around. Lasley was gone. Her heart throbbed violently as she thought that perhaps he had gone to see that Roberts was conveyed to some point beyond the reach of Morgan. By this time the hitherto quiet streets of the little town were filled with frantic people hurrying to and fro. "Morgan! Morgan!" was on every tongue. Many were the bright faces in these busy throngs, as it became certain that the rumor was true. There were many friends to the Southern cause in Bardstown, ever ready to greet the champions of liberty and right.

A few minutes more of suspense and wild conjecture, and the Confederates, headed by their gallant leader, dashed into the town amid the cheers, and shouts, and loud huzzas of the expectant crowd.

As the deafening acclaim **rang out on the** air, Mary and Evangeline rushed with others to the gallery of the hotel. What a moment of rapture to these two anxious hearts!

"**Free! free! Harry** will now be free!" shouted Evangeline, forgetful of the presence of those around her. "Free! free! and I released from that fearful engagement! Oh, God! I thank thee!" and she clapped her hands in the delirium of joy.

"Be still, Evangie. Watch and see if you can find John, my brother. Oh, **if he is only** with them!"

She had but just finished the words, when her brother came prancing by. He **chanced to be** looking in **the** direction of the hotel. As Mary caught a glimpse of his form, she shouted:

"John, John! my brother, **my brother!**"

The soldier recognized his sister. **A moment more, and she** was clasped in his arms.

In a few words Mary made known to him the story of Harry Roberts's imprisonment. Without delay he hastened to inform **Colonel Morgan, who immediately sent a squad of men to** open **the prison doors,** and set the prisoner free.

"My God, Lawrence! is this you?" exclaimed Harry, as, opening the door of his narrow room, **he met, face** to face, the friend of his childhood, his deliverer. How **came you here? and how** did you know I was in this wretched place?"

While he spoke, he continued to shake **the** hand of his friend warmly, his face speaking out the full gratitude of his soul.

"**We came to deliver you from the** clutches of the Yanks, and **we have accomplished our** purpose, you see," **answered Lawrence.**

"Thanks, thanks, **a thousand thanks for** your opportune presence. I was daily looking to be sent to Camp Chase or the gallows. You know this is my second arrest, and I wasn't sure they wouldn't hang me. But, tell me, are all the boys here?"

"Come out and see. Are you so attached to your headquarters as to be unwilling to leave them? Really it looks like it. You are a free man. **Come,** enjoy your liberty."

Just outside the door stood Brent, Irving, Curd, and other of Harry's friends, awaiting his appearance. When they saw him **they made** the air ring with their shouts of congratulation. Each in turn grasped his hand, and shook it warmly, as they welcomed him back to the privileges of a freeman and a soldier. It was a happy moment for Harry, one he had never expected to realize. There was but one apprehension to mar his joy, that was fear for Evangeline. He longed to ask if any thing had been heard from her, but he deemed it so impossible that he dared not venture the question.

The boys conducted him to the hotel. Following Lawrence, he entered the parlor.

"HARRY!" Evangeline could say no more, as she sprang from her seat towards him.

He clasped her in his arms. Not a word escaped his lips. The tears rushed to his eyes, and fell from his manly cheeks.

"Evangeline! Evangeline! Oh, God! and you are here safe!" he said, as soon as he could find utterance. "How came you here, Evangeline? Do tell me! As soon would I have expected to have met an angel visitant from heaven as you. Did you know I was here? No, no, you could not. I thought you were at Lexington, or perhaps had not yet left Louisville."

The young girl related to her lover the outline of her adventures. When she mentioned Lasley's name, Harry sprang to his feet, and asked where he could be found. She dared not tell him of the insult—the infamous promise extracted from her. She knew that Lasley's life would be the propitiation for his deep, damning wrong.

"Oh, do not trouble yourself about him," interposed Lawrence. "Wickliffe will attend to his case. I expect he is now occupying your room at your late headquarters."

"There he goes now, I suppose," said Brent, looking down from the window. "Wickliffe has some young, black-haired upstart in charge."

There was a general rush to the balcony. Lasley looked up at the sudden movement. His eye rested on Evangeline beside Harry Roberts. The vanquisher was vanquished. His eyes fell to the ground, and he marched on powerless as a child, chagrined, disappointed. A short walk brought him to the jail. Conducting him in, the boys left him alone to his own reflections.

Mary immediately informed John of her intention to accompany him through to Tennessee.

"How can this be done, Mary? It is impossible."

"Not impossible, John. You and Harry must get a carriage, and send us under special escort. You tell me ladies have gone out from Lexington. There is Mrs. John C. Breckinridge and others now under the protection of General Bragg's army finding their way South. You know father expected me through. How dreadful he must have felt when he found I did not come! He thinks I am in Louisville, of course, separated from him—perhaps forever. Oh, I must go through, let it cost what it may. I can take no denial."

A plan was soon devised that promised entire safety. A vehicle was procured, and all arrangements made for the party to set out after dinner. John Lawrence was transformed into a plain, peaceable citizen, by donning the civilian's suit of black cloth that Evangeline had purchased to insure Harry's safety, and which she had taken the precaution to place in her carpet-sack while Harry readily metamorphosed himself into a soldier, by enrobing in John's military garb, and taking possession of his horse and all accoutrements.

It was decided that they should travel as rapidly as possible, keeping under the protection of the cavalry force until beyond danger from the few Federals that were scattered around in the country intervening between Bardstown and Elizabethtown.

Never did a happier party set out on a perilous journey. Apprehension had given place to a feeling of security, agitation had changed to tranquillity, sorrow to joy.

On they travelled as rapidly as it was practicable, meeting with no danger, encountering no cause of alarm—a merry, cheery company, where past trials were all forgotten in the bliss of the present, and the promise of the future.

When between New Haven and Elizabethtown, the Confederates encountered a wagon-train of supplies, guarded by a small Federal force. After a slight resistance on the part of the Yankees, the whole was captured and destroyed. This was the first acquaintance with the "art of war" that Evangeline and Mary had had, and brave as they were, their hearts quailed as they heard the rapid clash, the quick, successive firing of the musketry. After this encounter, Colonel Morgan swept over the country between Elizabethtown and Mumfordsville towards the Ohio river, and formed a junction with Colonel Johnson in the neighborhood of Henderson. His object was to secure recruits, and give opportunity to the guerillas of these counties to get through into Tennessee, and in this he succeeded finely, accomplishing his purpose, besides destroying Federal stores at many points, and interrupting communication with Nashville.

CHAPTER LVI.

THE CONSUMMATION.

The two girls under the care of young Lawrence pursued their journey into Tennessee by the way of Glasgow and Hartsville, and on the evening of the sixth day arrived at Mr. Jamison's, in the vicinity of McMinnville. Through the kind assistance and direction of friends, they had avoided every semblance of danger. The trip had been one of fatigue and anxiety, but all this was forgotten by the happy party, as they sat around the cheerful fire of the hospitable farmer and recounted their adventures.

Mr. Jamison informed them that Charley had recovered, and had passed through his neighborhood a few days before, taking dinner with him. He was on his way into Kentucky to join his command.

Mary's eager heart heard the intelligence of his recovery with a thankful joy which no words could portray, but when she was informed of his mission into Kentucky, fear and despondency seized her soul. She felt that fate was against her. She had risked all to come to Charley, and now he was gone, perhaps to become a prisoner in the hands of the enemy.

Evangeline endeavored to console her, by telling her that Charley would very soon obtain information of the Confederate retreat from Kentucky, and return to McMinnville. But her fears were aroused. She could see nothing but disappointment hovering over her future pathway.

Imagine then her joy when, on the day following, Charley rode up to Mr. Jamison's.

As Evangeline had said, he had learned that Colonel Morgan was coming out of the State, and knowing that he would likely establish his headquarters at McMinnville, he had returned to Mr. Jamison's to await him.

The meeting was as unexpected to Charley as Mary, and their mutual joy at thus again beholding each other, after all the trials, suspense, and anxiety that had tortured their hearts during their separation, was akin to the bliss of Eden,—was as the light from the celestial spheres shining into their souls, chasing therefrom every vestige of darkness and **sadness**.

Two days more, and Colonel Morgan, with his force now largely increased from different parts of Kentucky, arrived in the vicinity of McMinnville, and encamped in the neighborhood of Mr. Jamison. Harry Roberts was safe, and never were there happier hearts than the four that, on the evening of the arrival of Colonel Morgan's forces, assembled around the cheerful board of the kind host, Mr. Jamison.

The evening passed in recitals of adventures and escapes. Each had a thrilling story to relate—a history in itself worthy of record. The rapture of the present was heightened by the remembrance of the trials of the past.

There are times in the life of every individual when the bliss of years concentres in a few fleeting moments. No words can picture the joy of such seasons. They are brief, but in their rapid flight they write remembrances on the soul as with the point of the diamond—remembrances which all the vexation, all the grief of after-life cannot wipe out from the tablet whereon they are engraved. There they remain, unmarred, ineffaceable—a well-spring of rapture to the heart as long as it continues to throb. And in old age we look back from the gathering shades of years upon these green and sunny memories, and linger around their blissful haunts until the heart is young again, and our youth is renewed more potently than if we had drank of the famed Elixir of Life of the Oriental magician.

Such a moment was the present one to the bounding hearts of the lovers. How quickly and effectually, as if under the magic wand of some kind genii, did all past sorrows, all apprehensions, fade out in the sunlight which was now flooding their enraptured bosoms!

We need not dwell in detail on the incidents of the few succeeding days, nor give our readers all the suggestions of the various parties as to the proper course to be pursued by the lovers. Suffice it to say, that after much debate, innumerable propositions and devising, a plan was finally adopted, and all necessary arrangements made for its speedy consummation.

A week passed. Within the respectable home of Mr. Jamison, Colonel Morgan and staff, together with all the particular friends of Charley and Harry, and a few of the especial acquaintances of the family, were assembled to witness the marriage of Mary Lawrence and Evangeline Lenoir to the two gallant soldiers, Charley R. and Harry Roberts.

It was a cool evening in October. That month of mingled sadness and beauty was bidding a last, an eternal farewell to earth. The hand of autumn had dyed, with richest hues, the foliage of the forest, and spread, with lavish beauty, over all nature a garment of gilded splendor. But as the eye rested on this gorgeous vesture, the heart read beneath it all lessons of decay and death. The trappings of the tomb were visible through all the gay paraphernalia, and amid the sweet symphonies could be heard the low wail of the dirge which earth chanted for her bright and beautiful children, so soon to sleep forever in the deep, dark grave which had relentlessly swallowed up, age after age, the offspring of her care and nourishment.

The wind sighed, mournfully, the requiem of the dead. Through the boughs of the tall old trees it crept, waking them to notes of saddest music. In striking, genial contrast to the darkness and gloom without, was the happy, cheerful scene within. There glad faces beamed brightly, and heart went out to heart in kindly sympathy. The bright wood-fire which blazed so determinedly on the hearth, as if resolved to add its quota to the general enjoyment, threw a cheery aspect over the scene; and the glad faces of Mr. and Mrs. Jamison plainly spoke the pleasure it gave them to be active participants on an occasion so happy. It was a unique affair—so every one felt. But around it clustered so much of novelty, that the strangely peculiar features of the occasion were lost beneath the interest that this very novelty excited.

Dressed in deepest mourning, her face flushed into the most transcendent beauty, Mary Lawrence entered the room, leaning on the arm of Charley. He bore himself proudly erect, conscious of the responsibility of his position, and the consequences involved in the sacred relation he was about to assume.

Immediately following them were Evangeline and Harry. In consonance with the circumstances, she wore a silk of dark olive, finished at the neck and wrists by a handsome collar and cuffs of Valenciennes lace. Her rich dark hair was combed back from the full round brow, and rolled into a heavy bandeau behind her ears, covering the back of the well-formed head. Some simple rose-buds were her only ornament. In making her bridal toilet she recalled the conversation that had occurred on the occasion of her friend Lu's marriage, and the handsome breastpin and bracelet were left in the case, and the place of the former supplanted by some fresh rose-buds.

It was a strikingly impressive scene. There stood two manly

forms, animated by as brave and daring hearts as ever throbbed in human bosom—exiles from their homes, defenders of the high and holy cause of liberty and right—the representatives of many a fiercely contested and successful battle-field—the escaped victims of fiendish hate and cruelty; while beside them, leaning confidingly on them for protection and support, stood two beautiful females, who, raised in indulgence and luxury, accustomed to all that can make life pleasant, and throw around it the charms of elegance and refinement, had forsaken all these comforts and joys, had encountered hardship and danger, that they might solace in exile, relieve in distress, and comfort in affliction these brave men, to whom they had given the true, undying affection of their young and trusting hearts. Beautiful picture! Life does not often present its counterpart.

The minister approached and stood before them. Alluding in brief, chaste words to the peculiar position of those who were about to take upon themselves the sacred vow, he proceeded solemnly, yet beautifully, to unite them in the holy ties of marriage. And thus, after trials and sorrows, difficulties and disappointments, that but few so young are called on to endure and overcome, these four tried but heroic hearts found at last the full consummation of their hopes, the fruition of earthly joy.

And here, amid their happiness, we leave them; bid them farewell, while gladness beams around their pathway, and fills their young and bounding hearts with bright visions of that future which beckons them on to fresh delights, and ever-awakening joys. We will not now anticipate and portray the cares, the anxieties, the fearful looking-for of news from the dread battle-field—the sickening, racking disappointment at tidings delayed—the nights of watching, the days of waiting, when the girl-wife, in the bitterness of separation from the young husband—gone forth to fresh deeds of valor and blood—shall wait, and watch, and pray, yea, faint, beneath the weight of disappointed hope and torturing suspense. Ah, no! Let us not lift the veil that would reveal this painful panorama. The contrast would be too striking, too sad.

Victories must yet be won; many an ensanguined plain must yet attest the heroic and successful struggles of Morgan and his men, before a nation can shout, in loud and grateful strains, "Victory! victory!! independence! independence!!"

That day approaches. The clouds begin to lift themselves from the horizon of our national future. Already the faint glimmerings of the day-dawn of peace are beginning to throw their glowing light through the dark shades that have so long enveloped us. Let us hope for this glorious realization of our desires, pray for it, and, above all, let us put forth every energy, strain every nerve, avail ourselves of every resource, endure every hardship, surmount every obstacle, vanquish every difficulty, until this blessed era shall burst upon us, and we, a free and independent people, shall unite as with one voice in pæans of triumph and thanksgiving.

Already, since the happy scene we have just described, have Hartsville, Elizabethtown, Muldrough's Hill, and other points borne witness to the indomitable spirit of Morgan and of Duke—of Hanson and of Hunt—of Harper and Gano—of Charley, Harry, Burt, Curd, Irving, Castleman, Wickliffe, Hawkins, young Morgan, and numbers of unknown heroes, whose endurances and achievements, full of chivalry and romance, will yet be added to the page of history, as deeds worthy the emulation and praise of their grateful and admiring countrymen; and whose names, covered with glory, shall become household words with a free and prosperous posterity.

APPENDIX.

APPENDIX.

GENERAL JOHN H. MORGAN

Is one, and the oldest, **of six brothers**, all of whom, **save one**, have been active and useful in the present struggle of our young Confederacy, devoting their all **to** the great cause. Calvin C. Morgan has acted as an agent at home in Kentucky for **the command** of his brother, and has undoubtedly done as much good in that capacity as he would have done had he been in the field. His third brother, Colonel Richard Morgan, is the adjutant-general of the junior Hill, and has been with that gallant officer through his whole campaign. The fourth brother, Major Charlton H. Morgan, is at present in his brother's command, having **been recently transferred** from **the** army of the **Potomac.** When the **present war** broke out, Charlton Morgan represented the United States government abroad. He immediately resigned his **position** and came home to take his part in **the struggle, and was the first member of** his family to come into the Confederate States. The fifth brother, **Lieutenant Thomas** Morgan, **at present a prisoner** at "Camp Chase," Ohio, was one of the first youths of Lexington to shoulder his musket and **march to the defence of** Kentucky. The sixth brother is yet too young to bear arms.

General Morgan, as were all of his brothers, was born and educated **near** the city of Lexington, in Kentucky, and is a lineal descendant of Morgan of Revolutionary fame.

In 1846, during the Mexican war, when the call came for "*more volunteers,*" John H. Morgan, then scarcely of age, raised **a company, and was** just upon the point of starting when the **news** reached the **States that a** treaty of **Peace** had been **concluded.** Well do the **survivors of** that company remember the **conduct of** their captain upon the disbanding of his **company.** Every man of the company (which was principally composed of young men dependent upon their labor for support) was indemnified for the loss of his time during the period of recruiting. 'Twas at this time that Morgan gained the title of captain. The Kentuckians of his command still refuse to recognize or apply any other title to him than that of "THE CAPTAIN."

General Morgan is not a "West Pointer," but **one** of the few men who was born to *command*, as he has incontestably proven. He believes that it is his destiny to fight against **a** race of men whose every principle is so utterly repulsive **to** his own noble nature. **His contempt for the Yankee character** is great and natural, and his daring deeds in **this war show** how thoroughly he understands it.

Some time after the Mexican war, he purchased an establishment and engaged in the manufacture of jeans, linseys, and bagging for the Southern market. About the same time he married **the accomplished Miss Rebecca Bruce** (whose traitor brothers **are all** against us in this war). After years of suffering from sickness, she died about the commencement of the present troubles. After performing the last sad rites to his departed wife, he immediately and secretly collected a little band of followers, not over twenty-five in number, and left the country, making his way to Green river, **where he** reported himself to the Confederate officer in command "ready for duty." His band was rapidly increased by the arrival of exiles from Kentucky, who knew **well the worth and** valor of the man as a leader.

His command, upon reporting, were placed, with some other cavalry, upon picket duty on the Green river, where he began a series of bold and daring exploits, which are unequalled for their boldness and the manner of their execution.

It was his determination when he left his home in Kentucky, should his command ever become numerous enough, to return and drive out the crop-eared Puritans, who, through Kentucky's generosity, had quite ruined his native State, by overrunning it **and** driving her sons to the States of the Southwest.

A little incident, showing the strategic powers of Morgan, **is** here worthy of mention: An order was issued by the authorities **of** Kentucky, from headquarters at Frankfort, that **all the arms in the** State should be forthwith forwarded to the State armory, there to be inspected and repaired for the use of the "*State Guard*," **who** were to maintain what the Union shriekers termed Kentucky's "**ARMED NEUTRALITY.**" General Morgan, then captain of the "Lexington Rifles," was suspected of having evil intentions against the peace and quiet of "Uncle Sam," or rather that "old Hoosier," King Abraham. It was, however, known to all loyal Kentuckians that he was "a good man and true;" in other words, that he was for his State first, last, and all the time. **Hence the** Lincolnites kept **a** sharp eye on the guns held by Morgan's company. Morgan knew that they had determined to get the arms out of his hands, and issued the order mainly for that purpose. And he, in turn, had determined that they should not have them; so, in the dead of night, they **were** removed some distance from the city, and the boxes, in **which they were to have** been placed, neatly filled with bricks instead, and marked "*Guns from Captain Morgan, State Armory, Frankfort.*" Good care was taken that the boxes should reach the depot at Lexington *just too late*, and there they lay exposed to public view. The Lincolnites received the boxes with unspeakable delight, winking and blinking at one another, supposing that they had fixed Morgan and his Secesh company, and flattering **themselves that they had for once** in their lives defeated a man who had always been as a thorn in their sides. That night Captain Morgan, in command of his brave band, passed through Lawrenceburg, Ky., a distance of twenty-**five miles from Lexington, having in their possession** *eighty fine rifles* belonging to the **Yankee government.**

At the commencement of the present struggle, General **Morgan** was possessed of great wealth, all **of which he left** in the hands **of the** enemy **when he came South.** He has ever been a public spirited gentleman, and dispensed his means with a liberal hand for the public good. There are many **who** can testify to his quiet **manner of doing good. There is no man living** who can say of John H. Morgan, that **he went to him "tired and** hungry, and he fed him not; he came cold and naked, and he clothed him not."

General Morgan is now about thirty-six years of age, and in the full vigor of manhood. He is about six feet in his stockings, as straight as an Indian, and magnificently proportioned; **light curly** hair, small gray eyes, and fair complexion. **His** general appearance is that of a gentleman of leisure—his carriage exceedingly graceful and manly, with rather an inclination to be fastidious in **his dress.** His modest, unassuming style of speech, when addressed, at once assures you **that you are in the** presence of an unpretending, thorough-bred Kentucky gentleman. Unlike many other of the great men of war, though a man who entertains great **respect** for religion, he is not a member of the church. His deeds have been heralded throughout the broad limits of the universe, and his name will be cherished wherever the "Stars and Bars" of his beloved Confederacy wave.

MORGAN'S OPERATIONS IN INDIANA AND OHIO.

RICHMOND, VA., Friday, July 31, **1863**.

MESSRS. EDITORS:—As much interest has been manifested in reference to the recent raid of General Morgan, I have thought it but right to add my "mite" to assist in appeasing the appetite of the public, who are eagerly devouring every morsel or crumb of news coming from General Morgan's command. Sincerely sorry that the Federal gunboats cut off the finishing of the account, I shall at once commence.

The command of **General J. H. Morgan**, consisting of detachments from two brigades, numbering 2,028 effective men, with four pieces of artillery—two Parrots, and two howitzers—left Sparta, Tennessee, on the 27th of June, crossed the Cumberland, near Barkesville, on the 2d of July, finished crossing at daylight on the 3d. Means of transportation—canoes and dug-outs, improvised for the occasion. Were met by Colonel Hobson's cavalry, estimated at 6,000, drove them back to Jamestown, Ky., and our column marched on through Columbia, at which point found the advance of Woolford's celebrated Kentucky Cavalry, numbering 250 men, dispersed it, killing seven and wounding fifteen men. Our loss, two killed and two wounded.

Marched on to Stockade, at Green river, on the 4th. Colonel Johnson, commanding the second brigade, attacking stockade, rifle-pits, and abattis of timber. After heavy slaughter on both sides, our forces withdrew: loss about 60 killed and wounded on each side. Of Morgan's command, the gallant Colonel Chenault fell, pierced through the head with a Minnie ball, as he led his men in a charge upon the rifle-pits. The lion-hearted Major Brent also poured out his life-blood upon the field. Indeed, this was the darkest day that ever shone upon our command—11 commissioned officers were killed and nine wounded. Moving on to Lebanon on the 5th, we attacked the town (fortified), and after five hours' hard fighting, captured the place, with a vast amount of stores, 483 prisoners, one 24-pounder, and many fine horses. The commandant of the post was Colonel Charles Hanson, brother to the lamented Brigadier-general Roger Hanson, who fell at Murfreesboro. His command, raised in the heart of the Blue-

APPENDIX. 393

grass region, contained brothers and other near relatives to our brave boys; notwithstanding which, when the gallant patriot young Lieutenant Tom Morgan, a brother to our general, and idol of the command, fell, loud and deep were the maledictions that ascended against the cowardly cravens for seeking shelter in dwelling-houses, and the question was raised as to their right to receive quarter. The enemy lost nine killed and 15 wounded; our loss, three killed and six wounded.

Rapid marches brought us to Brandensburg on the 7th, where Captain Sam Taylor, of the old Rough and Ready family, had succeeded in capturing two fine steamers. From eight A. M. on the 8th until seven A. M. on the 9th, was consumed in fighting back the Federal gunboats, whipping out 300 Home Guards, with artillery, on the Indiana shore, and crossing the command. The first was accomplished by Captain Byrne, with his battery—two Parrots and two 12-pound howitzers; the second, by an advance regiment, capturing the guards, and securing a splendid Parrot gun, elegantly rigged.

9th.—Marched on to Corydon, fighting near there 4,500 State militia, and capturing 3,400 of them, and dispersing the remainder; then moving without a halt through Salisbury and Palmyra to Salem, at which point, telegraphing with our operator, we first learned the station and numbers of the enemy aroused for the hunt; discovered that Indianapolis was running over with them; that New Albany contained 10,000; that 3,000 had just arrived at Mitchell; and, in fact, 25,000 men were armed and ready to meet the "bloody invader."

Remaining at Salem only long enough to destroy the railroad bridge and track, we sent a scout to the Ohio and Mississippi road, near Seymour, to burn two bridges, a depot, and destroy the track for two miles, which was effected in an incredibly short time. Then taking the road to Lexington, after riding all night, reached that point at daylight, capturing a number of supplies, and destroying, during the night, the depot and track at Vienna, on the Jeffersonville and Indianapolis railroad. Leaving Lexington, passed on north to the Ohio and Mississippi railroad, near Vernon, where, finding General Manson, with a heavy force of infantry, we skirmished with him two hours as a feint, while the main command moved round the town to Dupont, where squads were sent out to cut the roads between Vernon and Seymour on the west, and Madison on the south, and Vernon and Columbus on the north. Not much brighter were the bonfires and illuminations in the celebration of the Vicksburg victory by the Yankees, than our counter-illuminations around Vernon. Many old ladies were aroused from their slumbers to rejoice over the brilliant victories recently achieved. Surmises were various and many. One old lady knew that the city of Richmond was on fire; another that Jeff. Davis had been killed; a third that the army of Virginia was used up. Not one knew that General John H. Morgan was within two hundred miles of them.

Daylight brought the news, and then, for miles, houses were found vacant. Loaves of bread and buckets of pure fresh water, with an occasional sprinkle of wines, liquors, and sweetmeats, were thrust upon us. Terror was depicted on every countenance, until a brief conversation assured them that we were not warring upon women and children. Then their natural effrontery would return, and their vials of uncorked wrath would pour upon us streams as muddy as if emanating from old Abe's brain.

From Vernon we proceeded to Versailles, capturing 500 militia there, and gathering on the road. Near this point, Captain P., a Presbyterian chaplain and former line-officer in one of our regiments, actuated by a laudable desire to change steeds, moved ahead, flanking the advance, and running upon a full company of State militia. Imitating his commander's demeanor, he boldly rode up to the company and inquired for the captain. Being informed that there was a dispute as to who should lead them, he volunteered his services, expatiating largely upon the part he had played as an Indiana captain at Shiloh, and was soon elected to lead the valiant Hoosiers against the "invading rebs." Twenty minutes spent in drilling inspired complete confidence; and when the advance guard of Morgan's band had passed without Captain P. permitting the Hoosiers to fire, he ordered them into the road and surrendered them to our command. Crestfallen, indeed, were the Yanks; but General Morgan treated them kindly, returning to them their guns, advised them to go home and not come hunting such game again, as they had every thing to lose and nothing to gain by it.

From Versailles we moved without interruption across to Harrison, Ohio, destroying the track and burning small bridges on the Lawrenceburg and Indianapolis railroad. At Harrison we burned a fine bridge. Leaving Harrison at dusk, with noiseless tread we moved around Cincinnati, passing between that city and Hamilton, destroying the railroad; and a scout running the Federal pickets into the city, the whole command marched within seven miles of it. Daylight of the 14th found us eighteen miles east of Cincinnati; sunset had left us twenty-two miles west, but the circuitous route we travelled was not less than one hundred miles. During this night's march many of our men, from excessive fatigue, were riding along fast asleep. Indeed, hundreds would have been left asleep on the road had it not been for the untiring vigilance of our gallant general. Up and down the line he rode, laughing **with this** one, joking with that, assuming a fierce demeanor with another, and so on. None were left, and when we reached the railroad near Camp Dennison, few persons would have guessed the fatigue the men had undergone from their fresh and rosy appearance. A fight **was imminent**. Madam Rumor had been whispering that old Granny Burnside would pay us a visit that morning, **but** instead of arriving, he sent us a train of cars with several of his officers, who were kindly received, **and in** honor of their arrival a grand fire was made of the cars, &c.

Nothing of special importance occurred after passing Dennison, except at Camp Shady the destruction of seventy-five army wagons and a vast amount of forage: until the morning of the 19th our command had heavy marches over bad **roads**, making detours, threatening both Chillicothe and Hillsboro on the north, and Gallipolis on the South. Daily were we delayed by the annoying cry of "Axes to the front," **a cry that warned us of buskwhackers**, ambuscades, and blockaded roads. From **the 14th to the 19th** every hillside contained an enemy, and **every ravine a blockade**. Dispirited and worn down, we reached **the river** at three A. M., on the 19th, at a ford above **Pomeroy, I** think, called Portland. At four, two companies were thrown across the river, and were instantly opened upon by the enemy; a scout of **three** hundred men were sent down the river half a mile, who **reported back** that they had found a small force behind rifle-pits, and asked permission of General Morgan to charge. He assented, and by five he was notified that Colonel Smith had successfully charged the pits, capturing 150 prisoners. Another **courier** arriving about the same time, reported that a gunboat **had** approached near our battery, and, on being fired upon, **had** retired precipitately.

General Morgan finding both of these reports correct, and believing that he had sufficient time to cross the command, was using every exertion to accomplish the task, when simultaneously could be heard the discharge of artillery from down the river, a heavy drumming sound of small-arms in the rear and right; from the banks of the river came up three black **columns** of infantry, firing upon our men, who were in close column, preparing to cross. Seeing that the enemy had every advantage of position, and overwhelming force of infantry and cavalry, and that we were becoming completely environed in the meshes of the net set for us, the command was ordered to move up the river, double quick. The gallant field, staff, and line officers acted with decision and promptitude, and the command was moved rapidly off the field, leaving three companies of dismounted men, and perhaps 200 sick and wounded men, in the enemy's possession. Our artillery was doubtless captured at the river, as two horses had been killed in one place, and one in each of two others, and the mountain path, from which we made our exit, was too precipitous to convey them over. Two lieutenants and five privates were known to have been killed on our side.

After leaving the river at Portland, the command was marched to Belleville, some fourteen miles, and commenced fording, or rather swimming, at that point. 330 men had effected a crossing, when again the enemy's gunboats were upon us—the iron-clad and two transports. Again we moved up the river. The second brigade, commanded by Colonel Adam Johnson, was ordered to cross, guides having represented the stream as fordable. In dashed the colonel, closely followed by Lieutenant Woodson, Captain Paine, of Texas, young Rogers, of Texas, Captain McClain, A. C. S., second brigade, and myself. The colonel's noble mare falters, strikes out again, and boldly makes the shore. Woodson follows. My poor mare, being too weak to carry me, turned over and commenced going down; incumbered by clothes, sabre, and pistols, I made but poor progress in the turbid stream, but the recollection of home, of a bright-eyed maiden in the sunny south, the pressing need of soldiers, and an inherent love of life, actuated me to continue swimming. Behind me I heard the piercing call of young Rogers for help; on my right, Captain Helm was appealing to me for aid; and in the rear, my friend, Captain McClain was sinking. Gradually the gunboat was nearing me. Should I be able to hold up until it came; and would I then be saved to again undergo the horrors of a Federal bastile? But I hear something behind me snorting! I feel it passing! Thank God I am saved! A riderless horse dashes by; I grasp his tail! onward he bears me, and the shore is reached. Colonel Johnson, on reaching the shore, seizes upon a ten-inch piece of board, jumps into a leaky skiff, and starts back to aid the drowning. He reaches Captain Helm, but Captain McClain and young

Rogers are gone! Yes, Captain McClain, the true gentleman, faithful soldier, and pleasant companion, has been buried in the depths of the Ohio. We sadly miss him at quarters and in the field. His genial smile and merry laughter will no longer ring upon the ear. But from his manly piety and goodness of heart, the angels of heaven will never mark him as an absentee. May the memory of his many virtues serve as a beacon-light to guide us all to the same heavenly abode where he is now stationed.

Two men were drowned in the crossing. The gunboat and transports cutting us off again, General Morgan fell back again, and just as daylight was disappearing, the rear of his command was leaving the river. Sad and dispirited, we impressed guides, collected together 360 men who had crossed—many without arms, having lost them in the river—and marched out towards Claysville. But before leaving the river, I will briefly recapitulate and sum up in short order the damage to the enemy in this raid, and the sufferings through which General Morgan's men passed. On first crossing the Cumberland, we detached two companies—one to operate on the Louisville and Nashville railroad, the other to operate between Crab Orchard and Somerset, Kentucky. The first captured two trains, and returned to Tennessee. The second captured thirty-five wagons, and also returned. We then detached 100 men at Springfield, who marched to Frankfort and destroyed a train and the railroad near that point. We also captured a train, with a number of officers, on the Louisville and Nashville railroad, near Shepherdsville—sent a detachment around Louisville, who captured a number of army supplies, and effected a crossing by capturing a steamer between Louisville and Cincinnati, and rejoined us in Indiana.

We paroled, up to the 10th, near 6,000 Federals, they obligating themselves not to take up arms during the war. We destroyed thirty-four important bridges, destroying the track in sixty different places. Our loss was by no means light—28 commissioned officers killed, 35 wounded, and 250 men killed, wounded, and captured. By the Federal accounts, we killed more than 200, wounded at least 350, and captured, as above stated, near 6,000.

The damage to railroads, steamboats, and bridges, added to the destruction of public stores and depots, cannot fall far short of $10,000,000. We captured three pieces of artillery, and one 24-pounder at Lebanon, which we destroyed; one, a Parrott 3-inch gun, at Brandenburg, and a 12-pounder at Portland. These guns may have fallen into the enemy's hands again; I do not know if it be so, but fear they have.

After crossing into Indiana, the inhabitants fled in every direction, women and children begging us **to spare their lives, and** amazingly surprised to find we were humans. **The Copperheads** and Butternuts were always in the front opposing us. **Occasionally** we would meet with a pure Southron, generally **persons banished** from the border States. In Indiana one recruit was obtained, a boy fourteen years old, who came as an orderly. Our command was bountifully fed, and I think the people of Indiana and Ohio are anxious for peace; and could the idea of their ability to conquer us once be gotten rid of, they would clamor for an immediate recognition. Every town was illuminated, and the people everywhere rejoicing over the downfall of Vicksburg.

Crops of wheat and oats are very good, but **corn very poor,** indeed.

After leaving the Ohio at Belleville, on the night of the 19th, **we marched** to near Elizabethtown, in Wirt county, from there to Steer creek, and across the mountains to Sutton; from Sutton, **on** the Gauley Bridge road, to Birch creek, crossing Gauley at the mouth of Cranberry, and thence into the Greenbrier Country, crossing Cold mountain, passing a heavy blockaded road; tired steeds prevented rapid marches, and six days were consumed ere we reached Lewisburg, near which we left Colonel Grigsby, with **a detachment,** which then numbered about 475 men. From the crossing of the Ohio until our entrance into Greenbrier, our men **lived on beef** alone, without salt, and no bread. Yet their only wish seemed to be for the safety of General Morgan and the command.

To the kind officers, soldiers, and citizens whom we have met upon our journey, since reaching the Old Dominion, in behalf of our command, we tender them our undying regard, and assure them, if unbounded success has not fallen to our lot this time, that we are more fully determined to strive for our country and cause than **ever.**

I **have** the honor to remain your obedient servant,

S. P. CUNNINGHAM,
A. A. A. G. Morgan's Cavalry Division.

GENERAL MORGAN'S ESCAPE.

General Morgan made his daring escape from the Ohio Penitentiary, generally considered one of the strongest prisons in the country, on the night of November 27th.

The bedsteads of the prisoners were small iron stools, fastened to the wall with hinges. They could be hooked up or allowed to stand on the floor; and to prevent any suspicion, for several days before any work was attempted, they made it a habit to let them down and sit at their doors and read. Captain Hines superintended the work, while General Morgan kept watch to divert the attention of the sentinel, whose duty it was to come round during the day and observe if any thing was going on. One day this fellow came in while Hokersmith was down under the floor boring away, and missing him said, "Where is Hokersmith?" The general replied, "He is in my room, sick," and immediately pulled a document out of his pocket and said to him: "Here is a memorial I have drawn up to forward to the government at Washington; what do you think of it?"

The fellow, who perhaps could not read, being highly flattered at the general's condescension, took it and very gravely looked at it for several moments before he vouchsafed any reply. Then, handing it back, he expressed himself highly pleased with it. In the mean time, Hokersmith had been signalled and came up, professing to feel "very unwell." This sentinel was the most difficult and dangerous obstacle in their progress, because there was no telling at what time he would enter during the day, and at night he came regularly every two hours to each cell, and inserted a light through the bars of their door, to see that they were quietly sleeping; and frequently after he had completed his rounds he would slip back in the dark with a pair of india-rubber shoes on, to listen at their cells if any thing was going on. The general says that he would almost invariably know of his presence by a certain magnetic shudder which it would produce; but for fear that this acute sensibility might sometimes fail him, he broke up small particles of coal every morning, and sprinkled them before the cell door, which would always announce his coming.

Every thing was now ready to begin the work; so about the latter part of October they began to bore. All were busy—one making a rope-ladder by tearing and twisting up strips of bedtick, another making bowie-knives, and another twisting up towels. They labored perseveringly for several days, and after boring through nine inches of cement and nine thicknesses of brick placed edgewise, they began to wonder when they should reach the **soft** earth. Suddenly a brick fell through. What could this mean? What infernal châmber had they reached? It was immediately entered, and, to their astonishment and joy, it proved to be an air-chamber extending the whole length of the row of cells. Here was an unexpected interposition in their favor. Hitherto they had been obliged to conceal their rubbish in their bedticks, each day burning a proportionate quantity of straw; now they had room enough for all they could dig. They at once commenced to **tunnel at right angles with this air-chamber, to get** through the foundation; and day after day they bored, day after day the blocks of granite were removed, and still the work before them seemed interminable.

After **23** days of unremitting labor, and getting through a granite wall of six feet in thickness, they reached the soil. They tunnelled up for some distance, and light began to shine. How glorious was that light! It announced the fulfilment of their labors, and if Providence would only continue its favor, they would soon be free. This was the morning of the 26th day of November, 1863. The next night, at twelve o'clock, was determined on as the hour at which they would attempt their liberty. Each moment that intervened was filled with dreadful anxiety and suspense, and each time the guard entered increased their apprehensions. The general says he had prayed for rain, but the morning of the 27th dawned bright and beautiful. The evening came, and clouds began to gather! How they prayed for them to increase! If rain should only begin, their chances of detection **would be greatly** lessened. While these thoughts were passing through their minds, the keeper entered with a letter for General Morgan. He opened it, and what was his surprise, and I may say wonder, to find it from **a poor Irish** woman of his acquaintance in Kentucky, commencing, "My dear ginral, I feel certain you are going to try to get out of prison, but for your sake don't you try it, my dear ginral. You will only be taken prisoner agin, and made to suffer more than you do now."

The letter then went on to speak of his kindness to the poor when he lived at Lexington, and concluded by again exhorting him to trust in God and wait his time. What could this mean? No human being on the outside had been informed of his intention to escape, and yet, just as all things were ready for him to make the attempt, here comes a letter from Winchester, Ky., advising him not to "try it." This letter had passed through the examining office of General Mason, and then through the hands of the lower officials. What if it should excite their suspicion and cause them to exercise an increased vigilance? The situation, however, was desperate. Their fate could not be much worse, and they resolved to go. Nothing now remained to be done but for the General and Colonel Dick **Morgan to** change cells. The hour approached for them to be locked up. They changed coats, and each stood at the other's cell door with his back exposed, and pretended to be engaged **in** making up **their** beds. As the turnkey entered they "turned in" and pulled their doors shut.

Six, eight, ten o'clock came. How each pulse throbbed as they quietly awaited the approach of twelve! It came—the sentinel passed his round—all well. After waiting a few moments to see if he intended to slip back, the signal was given—all quietly slipped down into the air-chamber, first stuffing their shirts and placing them in bed as they were accustomed to lie. **As they moved** quietly along through the dark recess to the terminus where they were to emerge from the **earth, the** general prepared to light a match. As the lurid glare fell upon their countenances a scene was presented which can never be forgotten. There were crouched seven brave men **who had resolved** to be free. They were armed with bowie-knives made out of case-knives. Life, in their condition, was scarcely to be desired, and the moment for the desperate chance had arrived. Suppose, as they emerged from the ground, the dog should give the alarm—they could but die.

But a few moments were spent in this kind of apprehension. The hour arrived, and yet they came. Fortunately—providentially—the night had suddenly grown dark and rainy; the dogs had retired to their kennels, and the **sentinels had** taken refuge under shelter. The inner wall, by the aid of the rope-ladder, was soon scaled, **and now** the outer one had to be attempted. Captain Taylor (who, by the way, is a nephew of old Zack,) being a very active man, by the assistance of his comrades reached the top of the gate, and was enabled to get the rope over the wall. When the top was gained they found a **rope** extending all around, which the general immediately cut, as he suspected it might lead into the warden's room. This turned out to be correct. They then entered the sentry-box on the wall and changed their clothes, and let themselves down the wall. In sliding down, the general skinned his hand very badly, and all were more or less bruised. Once down, they separated, Taylor and Shelton going one way, Hokersmith, Bennett, and McGee another, and General Morgan and Captain Hines proceeded immediately towards the depot.

The general had, by paying $15 in gold, succeeded in obtaining a paper which informed him of the schedule time of the different roads. The clock struck one, and he knew that by hurrying he could reach the down-train for Cincinnati. He got there just as the train was moving off. He at once looked on to see if there were any soldiers on board, and espying a Union officer, he boldly walked up and took a seat beside him. He remarked to him that as the night was damp and chilly, perhaps he would join him in a drink. He did so, and the party soon became agreeable to each other. The cars, in crossing the Sciota, have to pass within a short distance of the Penitentiary. As they passed, the officer remarked, "There's the hotel at which Morgan and his officers are spending their leisure." "Yes," replied the general, "and I sincerely hope he will make up his mind to board there during **the balance** of the war, for he is a great nuisance." When the train reached **Zenia**, it was detained by some accident more than an hour. Imagine his anxiety as soldier after soldier would pass through the train, for fear that when the sentinel passed his round at 2 o'clock their absence might be discovered.

The train was due in Cincinnati at 6 o'clock. This was the hour in which they were turned out of their cells, and of course their escape would be then discovered. In a few moments after it would be known all over the country. The train, having been detained at Zenia, was running very rapidly to make up the time. It was already past six o'clock. . The general said to Captain Hines, "**It** is after six; if we go to the depot we are dead men. **Now or never.**" They went to the rear and put on the brakes. "Jump, **Hines!**" Off he went, and fell heels over head in the mud. Another severe turn of the brakes, and the general jumped. He was more successful, and lighted on his feet. There were some soldiers **near, who** remarked, "**What in the h—l** do you mean by jumping off the cars here?" The general replied, "What in the h—l is the use of my going into town when I live here; and, besides, what business is it of yours?"

They went immediately to the river. They found a skiff, but

no oars. Soon a little boy came over, and appeared to be waiting. "What are you waiting for?" said the general. "I am waiting for my load." "What is the price of a load?" "Two dollars." "Well, as we are tired and hungry, we'll give you the two dollars, and you can put us over." So over he took them. "Where does Miss ——— live?" "Just a short distance from here." "Will you show me her house?" "Yes, sir." The house was reached, a fine breakfast was soon obtained, money and a horse furnished, a good woman's prayer bestowed, and off he went. From there, forward through Kentucky, everybody vied with each other as to who should show him the most attention—even to the negroes; and **young** ladies of refinement begged the honor to cook his meals.

He remained in Kentucky some days, feeling perfectly safe, and sending into Louisville for many little **things he wanted.** Went to Bardstown, and found a Federal regiment had just arrived there looking for him. Remained here and about for three or four days, and then struck out for Dixie, sometimes disguising himself as a government cattle contractor, and buying a large lot of cattle, at other times a quartermaster, until he got to the Tennessee river. Here he found all means of transportation destroyed, and the bank strongly guarded, but with the assistance of about thirty others, who had recognized him and joined him in spite of his remonstrances, he succeeded in making a raft, and he and Captain Hines crossed over. His escort, with heroic self-sacrifice, refused to cross until he was safely over. He then hired a negro to get his horse over, paying him **$20 for it.** The river was so high that the horse came near drowning, and after more than one hour's struggling with the stream, was pulled out so exhausted as scarcely to be able to stand.

The general threw a blanket on him and commenced to walk him, when suddenly, he says, he was seized with a presentiment that he would be attacked, and remarking to Captain Hines, "We will be attacked in twenty minutes," commenced saddling his horse. He had hardly tied his girth, when "bang, bang," went the Minie balls. He bounced his horse, and the noble animal, appearing **to be inspired** with new vigor, bounded off like a deer up the mountain. **The last he saw** of his poor fellows on the opposite side, they were disappearing up the river-bank, fired upon by a whole regiment of Yankees. **By** this time it was dark, and also raining. He knew that a perfect cordon of pickets would surround the foot of the mountain, and if he remained there until morning, he would be lost. So he determined to run the gauntlet at once, and commenced to descend. As he neared the foot, leading his horse, he came almost in personal contact with a picket. His first impulse was to kill him, but finding him asleep, he determined to let him sleep on. He made his way to the house of a Union man that he knew lived near there, and went up and passed himself off as Captain Quartermaster of Hunt's regiment, who was on his way to Athens, Tenn., to procure supplies of sugar and coffee for the Union people of the country. The lady, who appeared to be asleep while this interview was taking place with her husband, at the mention of sugar and coffee, jumped out of bed in her night clothes, and said, "Thank God for that, for we ain't seen any rale coffee up here for God knows how long!" She was so delighted at the prospect, that she made up a fire and cooked them a supper. Supper being over, the general remarked that he understood some rebels had "tried to cross the river this afternoon." "Yes," said the woman, "but our men killed some un um, and driv the rest back." "Now," says the general, "I know that, but didn't some of them get over?" "Yes," was her reply, "but they are on the mountain, and can't get down without being killed, as every road is stopped up." He then said to her: "It is very important for me to get to Athens by to-morrow night, or I may lose that sugar and coffee, and I am afraid to go down any of these roads, for fear my own men will kill me."

The fear of losing that sugar and coffee brought her again to an accommodating mood, and she replied, "Why, Paul, can't you show the captain through our farm, that road down by the field?" The general says, "Of course, Paul, you can do it, and as the night is very cold, I will give you $10 (in gold) to help you along." The gold, and the prospect of sugar and coffee, were too much for any poor man's nerves, and he yielded, and getting on a horse, he took them seven miles to the big road.

From this time forward he had a series of adventures and escapes, all very wonderful, until he got near another river in Tennessee, when he resolved to go up to a house and find the way. Hines went to the house, while the general stood in the road. Hearing a body of cavalry come dashing up behind him, he quietly slipped to one side of the road and it passed by without observing him. They went travelling after Hines, and, poor fellow, he has not been heard of since. How sad to think he should be either captured or killed, after so many brave efforts, not only in his own behalf, but also in that of the general, for the general says that it is owing chiefly to Hines's enterprise and skill that they made their escape.

When he arrived at the river referred to above, he tried to get over, intending to stop that night with a good Southern man on the other side. He could not get over, and had to stop at the house of a Union man. The next morning he went to the house that he had sought the night previous, and found the track of the Yankees scarcely cold. They had been there all night, expecting that he would come there, and had murdered everybody who had attempted to reach the house without hailing them. In pursuing this brutal course, they had killed three young men, neighbors of this gentleman, and went away, leaving their dead bodies on the ground.

After he had crossed Okey's river, and got down into middle Tennessee, he found it almost impossible to avoid recognition. At one time he passed some poor women, and one of them commenced clapping her hands, and said, "Oh, I know who that is!" but catching herself, she stopped short, and passed on with her companions.

The general says that his escape was made entirely without the assistance from any one on the outside, and, so far as he knows, also without their knowledge of his intention; that the announcement of his arrival at Toronto was one of those fortuitous coincidences that cannot be accounted for; that it assisted him materially, no doubt. In fact, he says that his "wife's prayers" saved him, and, as this is the most agreeable way of explaining it, he is determined to believe it.

The above account may be relied on as correct; and, although much has been left out, yet enough is printed to stamp it as one of the most remarkable escapes in history.

MORGAN'S JOURNEY THROUGH KENTUCKY.

S. C. REID, the correspondent of the Atlanta *Intelligencer*, had an interview with **Captain Henry T. Hines**, at Dalton, Ga., on the 4th inst., and obtained the particulars of his capture, escape from the Ohio Penitentiary, and return to Dixie. As the public are familiar with the circumstances of the capture, &c., we confine our extracts to the thrilling incidents of the return to the Confederacy in company with General Morgan, which will amply **repay** perusal.

It had been previously determined **that, on reaching the outer walls, the parties should separate, Morgan and Hines together, and the others to shape their course for themselves.** Thus they parted. Hines and the general proceeded at once to the depot to purchase **their tickets for Cincinnati.** But, lo! where was the money? The inventive Hines had only to touch the magical wand of his ingenuity, to be supplied. While in prison he had taken the precaution, after planning **his escape, to** write **to a** lady friend in a peculiar cipher, which, when handed fo the authorities to read through openly, contained nothing contraband, but which, **on the young lady receiving, she,** according to instructions, sent him some **books, in the** back of one of which she concealed some "**greenbacks," and across** the inside wrote her name, to indicate the place where the money was deposited! The books came safe to hand, and Hines was flush! Going boldly up to the ticket-office, while Morgan modestly stood back and adjusted a pair of green goggles over **his eyes, which** one of the men having **weak** eyes had worn in **the prison.**

They took their seats in the cars without suspicion. How their hearts beat until the locomotive whistled to start! Slowly the wheels turn, and they are off! The cars were due in Cincinnati at 7 A. M. At Dalton, Ohio, they were detained one hour. What keen **anguish of suspense did they not suffer!** They knew that at 5 o'clock A. M. **the convicts would be called,** and that the escape would then **be discovered, when it would** be telegraphed in every direction; **consequently the** guards would **be** ready to greet them on their arrival. They were rapidly **nearing** the city of Abolition hogdom. It was a cool, rainy morning. Just as the train entered the suburbs, about a half a mile from the depot, the two escaped prisoners went out on the platform and put on the brakes, checking the cars sufficiently to let them jump off. Hines jumped off first, and fell, considerably stunned. Morgan followed unhurt. They immediately made towards the river, striking it at Ludlow's Ferry. Here they found a boy with a skiff, who had just ferried across some ladies from Covington. They dared not turn their heads, for fear of seeing the guards coming. "Hines," whispered the general, "look and see if anybody is coming!" The boy was told that they wanted to cross, but he desired to wait for more passengers. The general told him that he was in a hurry, and promised to pay double fare. The skiff shot out into the stream, they soon reached the Kentucky shore, and breathed free!

The boy had told them the place of residence of a lady friend; thither they bent their steps, and were received with the wildest demonstrations of joy and hospitality. They were afraid to tarry long. Horses were immediately procured for them, and that day, the 28th November, they rode to the town of Union, in Boone county, twenty-eight miles from Covington. There they stayed all night and the next day, leaving on the night of the 29th, with volunteer guides, and travelling by neighborhood and by-roads, passing through Gallatin county to Owen county line, where they stopped with a friend and spent the day of the 30th. They resumed their travels at night, passing through New Liberty, crossed the Kentucky river, and at 2 A. M., on the 1st December, stopped twelve miles the other side of Newcastle. Pushing on that day, they arrived at night eight miles this side of Shelbyville, where they spent the day of the 2d with their friends, meeting with a glorious reception. At night they departed again, passing through Taylorsville, and reached the vicinity of Bardstown on the morning of the 3d. Here they remained over until the night of the 5th, having received a most cordial greeting and unbounded hospitality. Again advancing, they passed through glorious old Nelson county, stopping on Rolling Fork. On the 5th, they laid over, and at night reached the vicinity of Greensburg, passing between the pickets of the enemy and their base. The fugitives had been joined by four others, and the party now consisted of six. They remained concealed inside of the enemy's pickets during the day of the 6th. Their trip through Kentucky had been one grand ovation, the ladies going wild with joy, and the men offering them every thing in their power, showing that the true spirit still breathes in that down-trodden State.

On the night of the 6th they procured guides to proceed to the Cumberland river, the road being thickly lined with Yankees. At ten A. M., on the 7th, they reached the Cumberland, nine miles below Burksville, having travelled **sixty** miles that night, and **crossed the** river **in a canoe, swimming** their **horses and** passing **for Federal** cavalry. **That** night **they** stayed **at the house** of a **good Union** friend, who, supposing them to belong to **Jacobs'** cav**alry,** took the best care of them. On the 8th, they passed into Overton county, Tennessee, following in the rear of a large Yankee scouting party, who, they learned, were in hot chase after Morgan! The general here learning that a number of escaped prisoners of his command were in the vicinity, a portion being under Captain Ray, he determined to wait until they could be collected, and **then** take them out, for which purpose he laid over until the **12th of** December.

The squad **was** now increased **to forty men, under** command of Captain Hines, and crossing **a spur of the Cumberland by** way of Crossville, between Sparta **and Knoxville, they arrived** at Bridge's **ferry, on the Tennessee** river, **at ten o'clock on the** morning of **the 13th.** There being no boat or **skiff to cross,** the party was **compelled** to fell trees to make **a raft. This ferry was** within two **miles** and a half **of a** Yankee **cavalry camp. By two P. M.** they **had succeeded in crossing twenty-five men and six horses.** At **this time a cavalry force of the enemy appeared on the north** side **of the river, and fired upon the party who had been engaged in** making **the raft. The enemy succeeded in capturing three or four men, but the others made their escape back into Tennessee. At** the same moment the enemy also **appeared on the south** side of the river, when General Morgan, Hines, **and four others** mounted their horses to escape. After riding two miles **and a half from** the river, Hines rode up to **a house for** the **purpose of procuring** a guide, leaving **Morgan** and the **other** men **in the road. Hines had ob**tained the guide, when **he** heard Morgan **halloo to him, and soon** after **a** party of cavalry dashed up towards **Hines, which at first** he took for a party of **our men, until** they approached so close **that escape was** impossible. **Hines had on a Yankee gun-cloth** which **covered his clothes, and seeing** that **they took** him for an "**Abolish,**" **he feigned to be a Yankee.** The Abolish captain riding up, asked, "**Who are you?**" "**One of** you," replied Hines. "Where are **the rebels?**" asked the captain. "They have just gone down this **road;** come on, and we will catch them," said Hines, riding **off in the** opposite direction from that taken by

Morgan, who, at the time, was near the foot of the hill, and **was** thus enabled to escape. The party followed Hines, but soon after discovered him to be a true rebel, and taking away his arms they threatened to hang him for misleading them.

Hines was carried across **the river** to their camps, and put under guard. He passed off for a private under the name of Bullitt. That night he ate up several letters and private papers, besides the notes of his trip, which would have condemned him, thus making a paper supper, which probably saved his neck. On the evening of the 14th the captain returned from the scout, and reported that the rebels had escaped. He had learned from a citizen that Morgan was one **of the party,** and suspected Hines of being an escaped prisoner. **He charged** him with being a Confederate officer, and **questioned him very closely.** In order to gain Hines's confidence, **and to pump him,** he treated him very kindly, and asked him to **go to a Union man's** house to take supper.

On leaving the house, about nine P. M., which was half a mile from the camp, after getting off about ten steps, the "Yank" remembered he had left his shawl, and **went back.** The night was dark, and Hines struggled with himself to gain **his** consent to escape, but considering the confidence and kindness of **the officer,** he concluded to wait until he got **out of his hands. Hines remained in** camp under guard during **the night of the 14th,** and the next morning was sent to **Kingston, with an escort of ten men,** where he was placed in **jail, and kept for five days without** fire, and almost without food. Here he found three of his comrades who had been captured on the other side of the river. On the 20th, he and his three companions, William and Robert Church, and Smith, of the third Kentucky Cavalry, were **sent to the** camp **of the** Third Yankee Kentucky Infantry, opposite Loudon, on the Tennessee river, nineteen miles from Kingston. The prisoners **were confined in a small** house in the centre of the camp, the timber being cut down in every direction for **half a mile, and there being but one path** leading to the mountain from the camp, **which was** closely guarded. That night **it was bright** moonlight, **but the moon** went down just before daylight.

Hines and **his** companions, by agreement, under pretence **of** being very cold, dressed themselves at the time, and sat down with the guards round the fire. At a given signal his comrades rose and stood round the fire, while Hines, keeping one of the guards busily engaged talking, quietly approached the door unobserved, raising the latch, giving **the** wink at the same time to his

18

friends. Then turning suddenly, he threw the door wide open, and said, with composure, "Gentlemen, we have remained here long enough; it is time we were going.". The guards were struck dumb with surprise, and thought it a joke. But before they could recover their senses, Hines flew past the guards in front of the house, and ran like a deer for the woods. He heard a struggle for a moment near the house, and then a volley of Minie balls whizzed by him. His three comrades must have been caught. The enemy pursued him to the wood and up the mountain for three-quarters of a mile, when they lost his track. Hines travelled six miles across the mountains that morning, and lay concealed during the day. At night he approached a house in a valley, and finding the occupant a Unionist, he passed himself off as a Yankee government agent. In conversing about the rebels, the Unionist said there were a few still lurking about, but as the river was well guarded, there were but few places they could cross at, and mentioned one place five miles below Loudon, where he said a rebel lived who kept a canoe. Hines made an excuse to go out that night, and proceeded to the ferry indicated, where he found the canoe and crossed the river. He soon found many friends on the south side of the river to aid him, and travelling altogether by night till out of danger, he finally arrived at Dalton, Ga., on the evening of the 29th December, having walked the whole distance from Loudon.

THE CAPTURE OF MORGAN.*

In your paper of the 13th of February, this notice appears: "Brigadier-general Shackelford, who captured Morgan, has resigned." You are **not the** first who has been led to believe General Shackelford deserves **all, or** the greater part, of the praise due in that "affair." That "honor may be given, where honor is due," **and** that **your readers may become acquainted** with the *facts*, **and** judge **for themselves,** I give below a plain statement of the whole matter **as it** came to my knowledge, and for which I can vouch.

Before Morgan crossed the Cumberland river, Brigadier-general Judah, commanding the Second division of Twenty-third army corps, ordered Brigadier-general E. H. Hobson, commanding Second brigade of Second division, to move from Columbia to Glasgow, Kentucky. When he arrived within five miles of Glasgow, he received orders from General Judah to move with the Second brigade to Tompkinsville—that he, Judah, had left for Scottsville, south of Big Barren river, and expected to attack Morgan at Carthage, Tennessee. General Hobson arrived with his command at Ray's Cross Roads, eighteen miles from Glasgow. Leaving his infantry at this place, he proceeded to Tompkinsville, with six hundred cavalry, and occupied the place, until General Judah could cross Barren river and join him at Tompkinsville. When General Judah arrived, General Hobson reported to him that Morgan was moving up the Cumberland, and would cross at Burksville. Hobson *insisted* on General Judah giving him orders to move immediately to Burksville, and prevent Morgan's crossing into Kentucky. Judah gave him orders to move his brigade to Marrow-Bone, ten miles southwest of Burksville, and hold the place at all hazards, until further orders. Hobson arrived at Marrow-Bone on the 1st of July, his advance driving the Rebel pickets from the place. On the 2d of July, at daylight, Hobson's picket line was attacked, and the Rebels repulsed. During the whole of that day Hobson fought Morgan's command. He also

* From the Army and Navy Journal.

ascertained that Morgan was crossing his force at Burksville and Cloyd's Ferry, nine miles below Burksville. Hobson informed Judah of his movements, and of the movements of Morgan, and stated that he had ordered General Shackelford's brigade from Ray's Cross Roads to assist him.

Shackelford arrived at Marrow-Bone at 12 p. m. July 2d. Hobson did not put him on duty, but told him to rest and feed his men, and be ready to move at an early hour next morning; that he would attack Morgan's command next morning at Cloyd's Ferry, and prevent him from uniting his two brigades; this he would do in violation of General Judah's orders, as it was the only way to prevent Morgan from entering and devastating the State. Hobson dispatched General Judah, who was then supposed to be at Ray's Cross Roads, fourteen miles in the rear, his plans, and the disposition he intended to make of his forces, and stated it was in violation of orders "heretofore received." General Judah met the courier six miles from Marrow-Bone, and sent an aide at full speed, with verbal orders to General Hobson, *to suspend all military operations*, and to countermand all orders for the moving of troops. General Hobson reluctantly obeyed, and stated to General Judah that Morgan would unite his forces, and get considerably the start, if he (Judah) did not order the troops to move and attack Morgan. After delaying one brigade twelve, and another twenty-four hours, General Judah adopted Hobson's *second* plan; to cross the country, sending one brigade through Columbia, and one through Greensburgh, to unite at Campbellsville. Judah returned to Glasgow. Hobson and Shackelford united at Campbellsville, and proceeded to Lebanon, Kentucky, leaving Judah south of Green river, he having failed to cross his cavalry before the river became too high. General Burnside telegraphed to General Hobson to assume command of all the cavalry at Lebanon, consisting of his own, Shackelford's, Woolford's, and Kants' commands, and to pursue and capture Morgan; and to impress horses, subsistence, &c., for his command. Upon receiving this order Hobson continued the pursuit, and directed all the movements of the troops under him.

Morgan having stripped the country, through which he passed, of horses, &c., Hobson labored under many disadvantages, but pushed ahead, determined to attack Morgan with fifteen men—if no more than that number could keep up with him. At Buffington Island, on the 19th of July, Hobson attacked, routed, scattered, and whipped Morgan; having followed him for *twenty-one days and nights.* Hobson leading in the front when the attack was made, was convinced that Morgan could not cross the river, and would attempt to get to the rear, and take the back track. To prevent this, Hobson sent orders to General Shackelford and Colonel Woolford to occupy positions four miles from the river, and attack Morgan's force, part of which was moving to that point. Also to pursue in every direction, and lose no time in capturing Morgan's scattered and routed forces. These orders were promptly obeyed, and resulted at this point in the capture of four hundred and seventy-five men. Colonels Kants, Sanders, and Lieutenant-colonel Adams had similar orders to follow up Morgan's scattered force, and drive them in the direction of Shackelford and Woolford, all of whom, in obeying these orders, captured quite a number of prisoners.

It is evident that General Hobson was in command of the expedition from the time he left Lebanon, until its close, as he had been placed in command by Major-general Burnside, and received no countermanding orders; although it is true he did receive instructions or information from time to time from Generals Burnside and Boyle.

Major Rue, of the Ninth Kentucky cavalry, is the officer who captured Morgan in person; Sergeant Drake, of the Eighth Michigan cavalry, and a sergeant of the Ninth Michigan cavalry, captured Colonel Basil Duke, Colonel Howard Smith, and one hundred and sixty line-officers and privates.

General Hobson could not, of course, lead in every direction after he had broken up and routed Morgan at Buffington Island. It was his duty to see to his wounded; give orders to the pursuing parties, and see that the prisoners were properly secured and cared for, as well as other details, that none but a commanding general are likely to be familiar with, or think of.

There are many other interesting incidents concerning the action of Generals Hobson, Shackelford, Manson, and Judah, Colonels Woolford, Kants, and others; but it is not my purpose to go into a detailed history, further than to give—what I have endeavored to give above—a plain and truthful statement of facts connected with the pursuit and capture of the rebel General John H. Morgan.

MORGAN, THE HOPE OF THE WEST.

The war-cloud hung lurid and dark,
   And terror each soul did assail,
When anon with fury it burst,
   Sending forth a heartrending wail.
Mothers to their offspring did cling,
   Fair maidens did beat on their breasts,
For the hordes and freebooting bands
   Of Lincoln did ravage the West.

Hearts in supplication arose,
   That God some deliverance might bring,
When lo! a brave leader appears,
   Whose advent in chorus now sing;
For no common leader is he;
   High towering amongst all the rest,
No brand with such terror does flash,
   As Morgan's, the hope of the West.

His advent the Yankees did scorn,
   And dubbed him with every vile name,
Guerilla, land-pirate, outlaw,
   Whom naught but a halter could tame.
But dearer this leader became
   To every Confederate breast,
And never did star brighter shine
   Than Morgan, the hope of the West.

To Abe, this brave chieftain appeared
   A fiend of ubiquitous dread;
A whole mint he'd most freely give,
   The price of this hobgoblin's head.
For oft while his minions feel safe,
   Far, far from this foe to their rest,
Destruction would leap like a flash,—
   'Tis Morgan, the hope of the West.

Whilst fear, consternation, and dread,
    The freebooting hordes sore oppressed,
Bright Hope, with soft pinions, did fan
    The hearts of fair maidens distressed.
A shout, **now spontaneous arose**
    From every fond Southern breast,
No champion of Freedom's so **bold,**
    As Morgan, the hope of the **West.**

GENERAL MORGAN'S KENTUCKY HOLIDAY RAID.

It's of chivalrous Morgan I propose to sing,
And of the brave heroes that round him do cling,
Whose valor has thrilled the heart of the nation,
Whose prowess astounds this lower creation;
But 'mongst his brave deeds, that most worthy of praise
Was his dash in Kentuck during holidays.
The enemy held this entire neutral soil,
And each true Southron was the victim of spoil.
The heart of brave Morgan beat high in his breast,
As the plume of the tyrant waved in his crest,
He vowed that his State should be happy **and free,**
And his watchword was death to all tyranny.
Many brave hearts had flocked to this hero bold,
From that doomed State that to the despot was sold,
Many others, likewise from States further south,
Whose hands they had torn from the gorilla's mouth.
With this heroic band of brave volunteers,
Whose free hearts were strangers **to unmanly fears,**
He set out for Kentuck with high beating heart,
Determined to baffle the enemy's art;
With speed far surpassing the old warrior's code,
By day **and** by night we vigorously rode,
No halting our horses, so weary, to unsaddle,
That **our** foeman might have no time to skedaddle.
We eagerly attacked each bristling stockade—
For railroad defence these strongholds were made,—

But they all surrendered, even seven or more,
And prisoners very numerous,—yea, many a score.
Thus, by boldly baffling the enemy's wiles,
Their railroad we destroyed for forty long miles;
Far had we entered the terror-stricken State,
Where tyranny guards every iron-barred gate;
But the object achieved of this bold foray,
To the South we'd return without delay.
The enemy's rage now with fury did burn,
That to the South they swore we should never return;
So they fiercely beset us on every hand,
In hopes of destroying our heroic band,
Each highway they guarded with a numerous host,
Each far more numerous than Morgan could boast.
Destruction seemed certain, and conquest most sure,
As we appeared now entrapped by the enemy's lure;
But Morgan was there, whose wits never fail him,
Who's always at home when dangers assail him:
By by-ways he led us that cold, dreary night,
And this snarl we escaped by next morning's light;
Each day and each night it was common to hear,
"The foe are pursuing—are fighting our rear;"
The fire we returned, yet right onward we sped,
Though risks we did run, every danger we fled.
Thus dangers we escaped and conquest we made,
In this brilliant Kentuck, this holiday raid.
Some mishaps we met with, some few men we lost,
But each gallant life cost the foeman a host;
A sad mischance occurred to the heroic Duke,
Who's as bold as a lion, but mild as St. Luke:
This brave hero, who is scarce less than Morgan,
Was severely wounded on the cranial organ,
While repelling an attack made on his rear,
He fell by a shell that exploded too near;
But long may he live, a terror to the foe,
For he will perform all that valor can do.
One incident more I will here barely note,
Like that the old Muses so fondly did quote.
Of brave Captain Treble and another as bold,
Whose deeds are equal to the heroes of old.
They met in combat, three champions to two,
Whom fiercely they fought, and a colonel they slew;

The others surrendered, but almost too late,
For the weapon was poised to seal the sad fate
Of one, the most daring of that vanquished band,
As prostrate he lay under bold Treble's hand.
Colonel Halsey fell by brave Eastin's fire;
The doom of the rest was less fatally dire:
Was that of prisoners who surrender in war
To a foe more generous than tyrants by far.
But now, having returned to true Southern soil,
We are calmly reposing after our toil;
But Morgan, our leader, is still scenting his game,
And soon he will have us pursuing the same.
Long, long may he live, this true son of Mars,
And triumphantly wave the Stars and the Bars,
And each Southern sister in glory arrayed,
Recline most gracefully beneath its wide shade.

www.ingramcontent.com/pod-product-compliance
Lightning Source LLC
Chambersburg PA
CBHW050845300426
44111CB00010B/1137